laptop screen

"blind reviews"
Goldin-Rouse
in Riforgiate;

" Not noticing sexist incidents
Supports sexism p.35
Becker; Swim

• DOUBLE STANDARDS

Gender, Communication, and the Leadership Gap

• Riforgiate; Ruder p.93
What other source said that?

• Wendy Davis.

• Christo-Baker & Wilbur p.118

• Social structure
Christo-Baker & Wilbur
p.114

Gender bias in evals of leadership"
Riforgiate; Ruder p.91
• Cunningham
• Murphy.
• West
• Billing "Alvesson.

• • • Shifting the focus from victim (recipient)
to aggressor — p.30   Mckenzie; Halstead
• Benevolent sexism   — Katz —
↳ x-ref Fitmer-Orais; Wood

Males make up the dominant culture. Male allies
are needed and effective.
• Katz.
• Mckenzie; Halstead p.36

★ MARKING p.97
Riforgiate; Ruder

A volume in
Women and Leadership: Research, Theory, and Practice
Susan R. Madsen, Karen A. Longman,
and Faith Wambura Ngunjiri, *Series Editors*

Gender, Communication, and the Leadership Gap

edited by

Carolyn M. Cunningham
Gonzaga University

Heather M. Crandall
Gonzaga University

Alexa M. Dare
University of Portland

Authenticity
Mckenzie ; Halstead p. 37

INFORMATION AGE PUBLISHING, INC.
Charlotte, NC • www.infoagepub.com

Library of Congress Cataloging-in-Publication Data

A CIP record for this book is available from the Library of Congress
http://www.loc.gov

ISBN: 978-1-68123-994-1 (Paperback)
 978-1-68123-995-8 (Hardcover)
 978-1-68123-996-5 (ebook)

Copyright © 2017 Information Age Publishing Inc.

All rights reserved. No part of this publication may be reproduced, stored in a
retrieval system, or transmitted, in any form or by any means, electronic, mechanical,
photocopying, microfilming, recording or otherwise, without written permission
from the publisher.

Printed in the United States of America

CONTENTS

PART III

AROUND THE GLOBE:
CULTURE, COMMUNICATION, AND LEADERSHIP

PART IV

INTERSECTIONS AND CONUNDRUMS

PART V

IN THE ETHER: DIGITAL LEADERSHIP

FOREWORD

A distressing incident early in my leadership journey came to mind when I was reading an early draft of this book. In 1992, shortly after my first election as state representative in Spokane, Washington, I was introduced to a representative from a neighboring district. I was a relatively young White woman from a working-class background, the single mother of an infant, and an assistant professor of economics. Though I was a feminist and an activist in the community, I was insecure about my qualifications, both as an academic and an elected official. Like the women of color interviewed by Annemarie Vaccaro and Melissa J. Camba-Kelsay in "I *Am* versus I *Will Be* a Great Leader" (see this volume, Chapter 14), I did not identify as a leader yet and reacted sensitively when a friend described me as "ambitious" because I viewed that as a negative trait in a woman. Furthermore, I was unsure as to how I would be able to pull off "work–life balance" as mother–professor–legislator.

The man I was meeting was White, middle-aged, experienced, and known as one of the most conservative legislators in the state. He smiled broadly, shook my hand vigorously, and said, "You're going to have to work on that weak handshake. You shake hands like a Democrat!" Of course, he knew I was a Democrat, one of the few in eastern Washington. I still recall feelings of embarrassment and, later, indignation. It seemed to me to be a sexist remark, though it was couched as a political jab. Had I the benefit of reading Kelly Lynch McKenzie and Tammy J. Halstead's chapter in this book, I might have classified it as a "microaggressive" communication act

Gender, Communication, and the Leadership Gap, pages ix–xi
Copyright © 2017 by Information Age Publishing
All rights of reproduction in any form reserved.

and possibly already learned rhetorical strategies to address it, rather than feeling speechless and smiling nervously.

Or better yet, coached by one of these authors, I might have reframed the remark as an awkward attempt to use humor to defuse the somewhat tense situation of meeting a potential political rival. Rather than letting the remark play on my insecurities, I could have seen it as an indication that he took me seriously enough as a colleague to joke with me, which, as I later learned, was part of his reputation.

Fast forward nearly ten years and I was shaking hands with the same man again. We were both state senators by then. I was chair of the Ways and Means Committee, and he was agreeing to buck his leadership "cross the aisle" and cast a critical vote for the $22.8 billion budget bill I was bringing to the Senate floor. His handshake was a sign that I could count on his vote, that he was "a man of his word." Although we seldom voted the same after that, we shared a teasing comradery until his passing a few years ago. For example, when I was charged with appointing someone to the redistricting commission that would redraw the boundaries of congressional and legislative districts, I told him I had directed my appointment to redistrict him to Idaho!

This book resonates with me because my personal life and my professional life in politics and higher education now seem in retrospect to have been a daily tutorial in the concepts covered in this book. Implicit and benevolent biases, critical race feminism and intersectionality, and authentic and courageous leadership are among phenomena I have repeatedly experienced and observed, even when I did not have a name for them.

The editors of this volume have done a great service by bringing into one volume frameworks, concepts, and practical advice from gender studies, communication studies, and leadership studies. The result is a resounding reinforcement of the significance of creating strategies for women from diverse backgrounds to give birth to their own voices, to hear and learn from each other, and to learn how to be heard by all, including by co-workers to those in the seats of power, who might not be listening.

A second notable contribution of this volume is achieved because of the global diversity of the scholars, and the women leaders and the nascent leaders they studied. In national and cultural differences, paradoxically, we can more clearly see the universality of the gendered leadership gap. Whether it is navigating conversational power dynamics in European conference calls, leading from the foreground and the background in the Liberian peace movement, or running for the presidency of the United States, women commonly experience a double bind that goes by many names and takes many forms.

Rather than fall into another false dualism like the ones that create and re-create the leadership gap itself, in these chapters we learn of barriers *and* levers to rising as a leader, of ways that emerging women leaders both conform to traditional gender norms *and* subvert them. We learn communication strategies for fitting in *and* standing out, or in a contemporary vernacular, for leaning in *and* pushing back.

Finally, it must be underscored that women in the United States are left with a tougher leadership hill to climb due to lack of paid family leave policies common in other countries and low accessibility of affordable quality childcare. One of my biggest disappointments in my legislative service was working with activists and fellow legislators to get a modest paid family leave fund passed twice in the state Senate, but not being able to get it enacted into law.

I have hope that all the barriers to women's leadership discussed here will eventually become as weak as my handshake was said to be in 1992. That hope is grounded in the intellectual clarity, passion, and solidarity of the women represented in this collection as research subjects and authors, as well as by the unprecedented women's marches that occurred around the world just yesterday as I was preparing these words.

—**Lisa J. Brown**
Washington State University
Chancellor of Washington State University, Spokane
Former State Senator

INTRODUCTION

Carolyn M. Cunningham
Gonzaga University

Heather M. Crandall
Gonzaga University

Alexa M. Dare
University of Portland

EDITORS' STORIES

Heather's Story

I am one of six people who gather for a meeting to solve a problem; there are three other women and two men, which should not matter but becomes important. The formal leader begins by explaining the goal of the meeting is to brainstorm solutions. I offer one. It is quiet as people make notes and think. The next person to talk, a man, repeats my solution. Suddenly, people around the table are nodding and endorsing the potential of "his" idea. I feel myself becoming angry. I fumble for a way to re-claim the idea without sounding like a jerk. I ask: "What was his idea?" and a woman restates it for me as his face expresses pity for my inability to follow. The situation is not going well, and I wonder whether the time is right to propose implicit bias training. Then I ask myself why I care. My idea is now free

Gender, Communication, and the Leadership Gap, pages xiii–xxvi
Copyright © 2017 by Information Age Publishing
All rights of reproduction in any form reserved.

as a bird and taking flight. It is catching wind and will perhaps bring about a positive change.

I care because my understanding is that I do not think I can become a leader without being perceived as bringing something to the proverbial table. What leader is not heard? My attention snaps back to the meeting when I hear the same individual volunteering to do the work of implementation; having worked with him for quite some time, I know he will not do the work. I then look back to the woman who spoke up, wondering why she did not hear the idea come from my mouth rather than his. I then glance toward the leader. We were to share ideas, but in our ten minutes we have heard one idea twice, yet we seem to have moved to the implementation stage. This process is not taking advantage of collective wisdom that would allow for quality decision-making. Communication choices have consequences. What are my choices? I can disrupt the meeting and risk seeming hostile or difficult. But is there something to be gained by being liked? Is the willingness not to be "heard" required in order to be perceived as nice? There is a personal toll to taking a stand or pushing back in situations such as this. If my ideas are rarely recognized as mine (or heard), it is likely that my own identity and morale suffer. In meetings with communication climates such as these, it takes strength to communicate intrapersonally about my own potential.

Carolyn's Story

As chair of an academic committee, it was my job to ensure that new curriculum proposals contained proper paperwork and signatures and were vetted through the proper committees. However, during my leadership, I was questioned about my bias of favoring certain proposals over others. This questioning came from a department chair who refused to follow and understand the proper flow of work. Rather than talking directly with me in order to challenge my commitment, the department chair decided to send emails to me with my supervisors cc'd to raise awareness about his concerns. In response to his concerns, I composed long emails, apologizing that the systems were difficult to navigate. I found that these feminine speech patterns, which I thought were intended to build rapport with him, did not work. Instead, I resorted to more direct communication, listing the exact steps he needed to take to have his proposal move through my committee. In the end, this form of communication was more effective. However, hours of work were lost in addressing the situation by trying to explain how the process should work through lengthy emails. Throughout this process, I could not help but wonder how these gendered forms of communication would change in a face-to-face context or how they would change based on my immediately adopting a more masculine form of communication.

Alexa's Story

I was six months pregnant and my male supervisor was escorting me to our male boss's office to have a meeting in which I would be negotiating the terms of my hoped-for maternity leave. Upon opening his door, my boss exclaimed, "I haven't seen you in forever." My first reaction was shame. My thoughts raced, "I haven't been working hard enough. I should have figured out a way to go to the faculty social last week (inconveniently scheduled during my once-a-week class). He thinks I'm lazy." But as I awkwardly sank my oversized body down into the plush couch in his office, I could not ignore the irony of his statement: As a pregnant, untenured faculty member, I felt excessively visible. In addition to my regular teaching and research load, I was also sitting on a hiring committee, mentoring our department's Honor Society, and I had just returned from escorting six students to a professional research conference in Washington State. These are all "voluntary" tasks that I "choose" to do for a variety of reasons related to my own preferences and the kind of work that energizes my soul. But these choices, and my professional leadership, apparently did not look like leadership nearly as much as they looked like appropriately feminine ways of being. I "care" for students. I "help" out my colleagues. I "support" my research assistants. And yet, when the shame lifted, I found myself frustrated that what looked and felt to me like leadership was invisible to those who continued to equate leadership with a particular organizational position, or a particular gender, or a particular kind of body.

I find myself drawn to theories and stories about a kind of leadership that is relational rather than positional. I yearn for a vision of leadership that disrupts those myriad cultural notions of leadership that remain stubbornly masculine and that equate leadership with individuality. One of the most beautiful and unexpected effects of being a pregnant academic (and now an academic parent) is that it is an undeniable reminder of the way that we humans are always growing and changing. We miss important pieces of the leadership story when we forget that we are *dynamic* selves and that we exist and lead and communicate in *dynamic* organizations. How might we better account for the embodied and communicative dimensions of leadership? What strategies can we use to lead collaboratively and to build capacities together?

BACKGROUND

We begin this volume with these stories, individual examples of the everyday confounding entanglements at the intersection of gender, communication, and leadership. To look at numbers broadly is to get a glimpse of how interpersonal and organizational biases add up to larger systemic gender inequality. For example, only 5% of Fortune 500 companies are led by women Corporate Executive Officers (CEOs; Long 2016). Globally, women hold 23% of parliamentary seats (Inter-Parliamentary Union, 2016). Similar levels of inequality extend beyond the corporate and political world into the realm of entertainment, an important outlet for constructing representations of reality. Women make up 9% of filmmakers in Hollywood (Buckley, 2016). Although Geena Davis, in a 2016 letter to Hollywood, has expressed the opinion that "gender inequality in entertainment could be fixed overnight" and that we can easily "create worlds where women are half of the characters and do half of the interesting things" (para. 8), who is motivated to apply this pressure? Who wants to experience something different?

Why is the gendered leadership gap so persistent? Is it that women have to fix themselves in order to climb ladders to economic success and influence? Or are women really making different personal choices about how to spend their lives, choosing instead to opt out of leadership positions? This debate has been renewed with the publication of Sheryl Sandberg's (2013) widely acclaimed book, *Lean In: Women, Work, and the Will to Lead*. As the chief operating officer (COO) at Facebook, Sandberg draws from her experiences at the top to offer career advice for women seeking leadership roles in business. In general, the advice centers on individual solutions to the gender gap in leadership, such as increasing women's confidence, addressing the insecurities that hold them back, and negotiating equality with their partners at home. The popularity of *Lean In* (Sandberg, 2013) is important, but so is broadening these individual solutions to address cultural barriers and structural inequalities. Accordingly, we argue that women can overhaul themselves if they want, but we also need a much larger overhaul of some unexamined problematic practices in workplaces and in systems—as well as in the broader culture.

Much of the gap in leadership is due to a "double bind" in communication differences between men and women (Catalyst, 2007, p. 1). Some of the common gender differences in communication lie in feminine versus masculine speech patterns that are learned through socialization. These gendered socialization processes can be seen on a continuum with masculine at one end and feminine at the other. As Wood (2015) describes, "masculine speech communities tend to regard talk as a way to accomplish concrete goals, exert control, preserve independence, entertain, and enhance status" (p. 131), while feminine speech communities regard talk as a means to gain understanding, to build and maintain relationships with others, to establish equality, and to provide support. Both men and women interrupt each other, yet for different end goals. Whereas men more typically interrupt to gain control and power over the conversation, women more often interrupt to show support for others' ideas (Sandberg & Grant,

2015). Additionally, feminine speech patterns often establish powerlessness through tentative language use such as hedges, intonations, and introducing phrases such as, "This may not be important, but . . . " These differences often limit women's ability to lead groups effectively.

Even as the gender gap in leadership continues, research has repeatedly documented that the most effective leadership includes a blend of both masculine and feminine traits (Eagly & Carli, 2003; Holden & Raffo, 2014). Women in leadership positions are expected to be both feminine and masculine, yet perceptions of their leadership styles show that they cannot achieve either ideal. Although some research findings suggest that women may have an advantage in leadership positions because they tend to use a collaborative leadership style (Paustain-Underdahl, Walker, & Woehr, 2014), a problem referred to by Williams and Dempsy (2014) as the "tightrope" persists. Women who use more "masculine" communication are often respected but not considered to be nice, and women who use more "feminine" communication are considered to be nice but are not respected (Catalyst, 2007). Who wants influence without respect? Who wants to be respected but alone? We are all social creatures who like to be in community.

Beyond language use, perceptions people hold about leadership and gender remain an important consideration. Naschberger, Quental, and Legrand (Chapter 9 of this volume) asked male and female managers in France questions about their career barriers and career levers or advantages. "Being a woman" was ranked first as a career barrier for women aged 36–40, whereas no male claimed that "being a man" was an obstacle for career progress. Christo-Baker and Wilbur (Chapter 7 of this volume) review the theory and literature on authentic leadership and argue that this style, when enacted by female leaders, may not have the same engaging, productive effects due to the perceptions held by followers.

In addition to gender differences in communication, we know that some of the gendered leadership gap is related to unequal access to the more important business functions in organizations. Some of the gap is attributed to differential treatment in mentoring and performance reviews. Some of the gap is explained by work–life balance demands. Perceptions and stereotypes of women that people in society hold are problematic and explain why women do not experience the same considerations for top leadership positions (Hackman & Johnson, 2013). Many of these reasons, when viewed from a communication perspective, are addressed by different authors in this volume.

Eagly's (1987) social role theory is often cited in the leadership and gender literature as a useful lens for understanding gender differences. Social role theory explains that people behave in ways consistent with the gendered expectations society has of them because these behaviors attract more praise than blame. Women leaders, therefore, are more likely to be more nurturing and male leaders more competitive. Social role theory is reminiscent of a theory often used in the communication discipline, Bandura's (1978) social learning theory, which holds that people learn to do what is socially rewarded and avoid what is socially punished. Thus, when women leaders take on more masculine traits, either through verbal or nonverbal communication, they do not achieve success in the same way that men do.

Why is it important to pay attention to these real and perceived gender differences and how they impact leadership? Sally Helgesen (this volume, Chapter 1) observes that leaders who have good communication can articulate a strong vision. Because vision is about storytelling and bringing one's audience into the story to work for needed change, vision is key to effective leadership. Helgesen argues that women may have strong vision yet lack a sense of who is comprehending that vision. Failing to communicate generally, and to communicate vision particularly, can limit women's leadership effectiveness.

When Heather and Carolyn began teaching a graduate-level class on women, communication, and leadership in the MA program in Communication and Leadership Studies at Gonzaga University, another problem became clear. There are hundreds of books on leadership, and many books that have focused on gender differences in communication. Yet more writing and more research on the intersection of these areas is needed. We found the work of Julia Wood, who writes about gender and communication as socially constructed, to be particularly helpful to us. As communication scholars teaching leadership, we struggled to find practical, useful, and insightful readings for our students about the intersections of gender and leadership. Recognizing this gap in the literature was the impetus for gathering authors to prepare *Gender, Communication, and the Leadership Gap.*

From our perspective, we understand leadership to be primarily enacted through communication. However, the leadership literature tends to focus on individual traits and leadership styles, rather than looking closely at how men and women are socialized into masculine and feminine speech and behavior patterns. These speech patterns influence leadership styles and how leaders are perceived. Similarly, research in the field of leadership studies offers preliminary guidance on addressing the problem of gender inequality in leadership. Leadership scholars Jackson and Parry (2008) contend, "there is no consensus in the literature about gender differences in leadership styles" (p. 25). However, behavioral differences that do emerge are likely related to, as Burke and McKeen explain, the different ways women and men see the world (as cited in Jackson & Parry, 2008). Jackson and Parry argue that research on gender and leadership should be cautious of biological perspectives and call for future inquiry to move to a social identity perspective. They believe such a perspective sheds more light on how the experiences of different contexts, different support at home, and the different gender ratios in different industries influence how leadership styles and positions are enacted by gender.

This volume, then, is designed to bridge the gaps between the bodies of literature in communication and leadership and to broaden and update the current academic discussion of gender and leadership. Second, despite the gains women have made in obtaining leadership positions, there continues to be a gendered leadership gap in the workforce. *Gender, Communication, and the Leadership Gap* offers insight into the communication challenges women leaders experience, such as their use of powerless speech patterns and experience of microaggressions, as they navigate their professional lives. This volume helps clarify the contradictory communication dynamics women in leadership positions navigate in organizational contexts. Additionally, this volume offers insight into contemporary issues, such as the role of social media and digital leadership and the intersections of race, class, gender, and sexuality.

These chapters offer practical, useful, and insightful perspectives and practices. *Gender, Communication, and the Leadership Gap* is designed to offer a number of workable solutions—from the perspective of communication and leadership studies—that all genders can employ and endorse in the work toward equality. We argue that the social construction of gender has resulted in different leadership styles ascribed for men and women, which limits everyone. The fact that understandings of leadership have been socially constructed also means we can construct something better.

In the chapters that follow, the authors speak to the many ways that communication influences leadership, and the chapters are designed to offer practical solutions to enduring problems. In our view, increasing diversity is not necessarily about women fitting into masculine organizations, but instead we support the nascent idea that diversity done well through inclusion makes organizations—and the lives of those working within them—better.

PART I: FOUNDATIONS: COMMUNICATION IN PRACTICE

Part I provides perspectives from two well-known authors in the fields of leadership and communication. Sally Helgesen's chapter draws on neuroscience to argue that women and men are different noticers. Helgesen describes women as being "broad-spectrum noticers," (this volume, p. 7) whereas the perspective men typically bring is more laser focused; these differences in vision and leadership can result in miscommunication. Helgesen's chapter concludes by offering several strategies for helping women translate their vision in a way that can be effective in reaching a laser-focused audience. Brenda J. Allen's chapter on intersectional identities and six inclusive leadership practices (commitment, courage, cognizance of bias, curiosity, cultural intelligence, and collaboration) provide practical strategies for conceptualizing and implementing "an intersectional ethic to inclusive leadership" (this volume, p. 17). Because Allen's contribution to the book is so important to our work, it appears near the beginning in order to inform the chapters that follow.

PART II: ON THE GROUND: EVERYDAY COMMUNICATION

Part II focuses on interpersonal challenges women face in different organizational contexts. These challenges include responding to microaggressions effectively, confronting implicit and benevolent biases in teams, identifying the way power is negotiated in workplace conversations, acquiring the power (or not) of communicating through roles, and realizing the importance of workplace cultures to that process; finally, questions of gender are applied to the emerging leadership style known as authentic leadership.

In Chapter 3, "Narrowing the Leadership Gap: Communication Strategies to Combat Microaggressions," Kelly Lynch Mackenzie and Tammy J. Halstead explain what microaggressions are and offer insight into how women can address them in the workplace. Microaggressions are slights and insults targeted at individuals who are not accepted as part of the dominant male group. Among some examples are verbal assaults like telling sexual jokes or nonverbal insults such as ignoring women. The authors' goal is to show how women can constructively respond to microaggressions in the workplace (e.g., being intentional in enacting assertive accommodation, using inclusive communication, and utilizing humor). The chapter also offers insight into communication strategies that can be used to shift the focus away from those who receive microaggressions to those who are the aggressors.

In Chapter 4, "Confronting Implicit and Benevolent Bias in Teams: Concepts and Communication Strategies for Women in Leadership," Steve Mortenson argues that women have to be prepared to confront subtle bias and sexism where it occurs, in everyday interactions. Mortensen's chapter details the problems of gender bias and how an understanding of facework and interpersonal projection can be an effective means for confronting and reducing gender bias. Facework is a process for managing one's self-image during conflict. Interpersonal projection is when personal emotions color perceptions of present interactions. This chapter also provides specific emotional and behavioral strategies for de-escalating both internal and interpersonal tensions when confronting and correcting biased behavior in order to build collaboration.

In Chapter 5, "Talking Power: Women's Experiences of Workplace Conversations," Anne Murphy uses data gathered during a series of short, women-only leadership development programs that addressed the expression of power in corporate settings to examine the relationship between women's leadership and the micro-detail of ways in which power is "talked" into place in everyday interactions. Murphy draws on feminist organizational theory to reveal dialectic tensions in the ways participants interpret and articulate their experiences. The result is a contribution to understanding these women's experience of agency in professional settings and ways in which theoretic insights can translate into leadership development practices.

In Chapter 6, "Embracing and Contesting Gender Roles: Communication Strategies of Women in Engineering Leadership Roles," Sarah E. Riforgiate and Emily M. Ruder examine the verbal and nonverbal communication practices of women in leadership roles in a national engineering professional organization to explore how communication creates both opportunities and challenges for women's participation in STEM fields. This chapter, which presents the findings of an ethnographic study of women's participation in a professional STEM organization, provides close analysis of the ways women navigate the organization and provide support systems for each other.

In Chapter 7, "Gender, Authentic Leadership, and Communication," E. Anne Christo-Baker and Daniel Stuart Wilbur describe the relatively new and celebrated features of authentic leadership. Given the prevalence of gendered expectations of leadership commonly found in organizations, these authors explore the extent to which women can effectively practice authentic leadership. The chapter concludes by providing several organizational and individual-level solutions aimed at reducing the difficulties women encounter when they try to practice authentic leadership in contemporary organizations.

PART III: AROUND THE GLOBE: CULTURE, COMMUNICATION, AND LEADERSHIP

Part III includes cases that highlight specific ways in which different areas of the world face a variety of pressures and leadership contexts. The chapters in this section imagine constructive ways of responding to the need for more women in leadership positions. The authors in this section offer insight into how people outside the United States have developed and implemented strategies for gender equity.

In Chapter 8, "The Efficacy of Strategies to Elevate Gender Equality in Leadership: Assessing the Netherlands," Wilma Henderikse, Annemieke van Meek, and Babette Pouwels offer insights from their detailed, multi-year assessment of a Dutch initiative designed to increase the number of women in corporate leadership roles. Arguing that efforts that focus on leadership development are only part of the solution to bridging the gender-leadership gap, the authors turn their attention to assessing which strategies and programs are most effective in increasing the number of women "at the top." Their findings demonstrate the success of a particular gender equality program, and they identify strategies that organizations worldwide can adopt when there is a commitment to elevate women and encourage diverse leadership.

Chapter 9, "The Leaky Leadership Pipeline in France: A Study of Career Levers and Barriers to Foster Women's Leadership Development," by Christine Naschberger, Camilla Quental, and Céline Legrand, offers a fascinating analysis of the barriers and levers (advantages) of career development perceived and communicated by French female managers in comparison to their male counterparts. This chapter offers a more accurate understanding of where women leaders tend to drop out, or leak, and not pursue top positions in their organizations. The analysis takes into account gender and age in suggesting career policies. The authors offer recommendations concerning managerial implications for human resource professionals and practitioners to boost female managers' careers as well as for women to manage their careers more effectively.

In Chapter 10, "Emergent Yet Contested: Interrogating the Relationship Between Leadership and Gender in Organizing for Peace," Stacey L. Connaughton and Jasmine R. Linabary present an enthralling case of grassroots peacebuilding organizing in Ghana and Liberia. The authors advance a notion of courageous leadership, wherein leadership is neither solitary nor masculine, but is instead a collective co-creation that values interconnectedness and context. From this perspective, one need not wait until reaching a position of power to "do leadership," and, relatedly, the courage needed to make change is not simply a trait, but can be co-constructed and nurtured in collaborative contexts.

Chapter 11, "Transcending Self: An African Girl's Journey," provides a comprehensive look at Rosemary Muriungi's own leadership development. She was influenced by the elder women in her community, as well as her father, who encouraged her to gain an education. Her chapter, an autobiographical account of her own leadership journey, shows that mentoring should occur before girls and women enter the professional world as a way to support their holistic development.

PART IV: INTERSECTIONS AND CONUNDRUMS

Part IV focuses on the different kinds of confusions faced by those who lead from intersectional positions that are raced, classed, and gendered.

This section begins with Diane A. Forbes's chapter, "Intersectionality and Feminist Praxis: An Interdisciplinary Framework to Examine Assets and Advantages in Women's Leadership." In this chapter, Forbes draws from intersectional feminist theory to develop a praxis-fueled approach to leadership. She argues that leadership theories that treat "woman" as a singular and unified category are unable to fully account for the ways in which other identities such as race, class, nationality, disability, and others intersect with gender in organizational contexts. Forbes proposes an intersectional model of leadership that is urgently needed in diverse organizations and societies. Awareness of privilege and oppression as it operates within individuals makes us cognizant of the unexamined challenges of inclusive leadership.

In Chapter 13, "She Just Doesn't Seem Like a Leader: African American Women College Presidents and Rhetorical Leadership," Dorine L. Lawrence-Hughes found that an African American woman leader was not perceived as a leader to her students, who were all women. She conducted a rhetorical analysis of inaugural speeches made by four newly appointed African American women college presidents at predominantly White colleges and universities with the goal of understanding how these women leaders selected language to legitimize their leadership. She approached her study with the idea that these strategies could be of use to other leaders who want to increase their leadership credibility in certain contexts. The study reveals conventional and unconventional rhetorical choices in the inaugural addresses of these presidents that were used to communicate vision, employ metaphor, claim leadership identity, and frame diversity goals. With its focus on underrepresented leaders, her study contributes to the scholarship about African American women leaders.

In the fourteenth chapter, "*I Am* versus *I Will Be* a Great Leader: Using Critical Race Feminism to Explore Gender Differences Among College Students of Color," Annemarie Vaccaro and Melissa J. Camba-Kelsay provide an overview of their Sister Stories leadership course and use critical race theory and feminist theory to analyze the differing ways that male and female students understood leadership during and after taking the course. Focusing on questions of voice, silence, power, and confidence, Vaccaro and Camba-Kelsay examine leadership narratives from men and women of color, highlighting both the successes and the challenges of the course. The chapter concludes with suggestions for ways to work with college student leaders.

In Chapter 15, "Mexican American Women Leaders: Filling a Gap in the Study of Gender, Communication, and Leadership," Yolanda Chávez Leyva and Patricia Dennis Witherspoon report on the findings of a study involving interviews with 10 Mexican American women leaders. This chapter contributes to the literature about Mexican American women's leadership in presenting major themes that emerged from the analysis of data. These

Mexican-American women leaders were from different leadership contexts. Some lead in communities, some lead in organizations, some lead locally, and some lead nationally, yet they reported similar communication behaviors as being central to enacting leadership from their own perspectives. These behaviors include serving others first, recognizing the importance of family and community, listening, and using narrative strategies. The authors discuss how their findings inform the field of women and leadership by focusing specifically on Mexican American women and offer suggested future research.

PART V: IN THE ETHER: DIGITAL LEADERSHIP

Part V focuses on gender dynamics and communication strategies available on the digital platforms on which we conduct more and more of our organizational and personal lives. These chapters offer strategies for navigating online environments for more effective leadership.

In her chapter, "Theorizing and Researching Gender and Digital Leadership in 'Tech Cities,'" Mariann Hardey analyzes the experiences of women working in three tech cities and areas, including London, Silicon Valley (San Francisco, California, and surrounding towns), and New York City. Her chapter is part of a larger project on women working in technology fields. Using narrative research, Hardey interviewed three women working in high tech to understand how they navigated workplace experiences such as toxic masculinity, sexism, and trolling behaviors. In addition to noting these challenges, Hardey also highlights the positive aspects of working in tech fields, such as networking opportunities and work environments that encourage flexibility and sociality. These dynamics lead to a different dilemma for women working in tech companies, which typically have a pervasive culture of masculinity with men in the majority of leadership positions combined with male-dominated control of investment. In the end, Hardey argues that tech cities, such as London, can be venues for looking constructively at new structures of work and organizational communication.

In Chapter 17, "The Links of LinkedIn: Impression Management of Professional Social Media," Evelyn H. Thrasher reports on research involving LinkedIn, a social media site that provides online professional portfolios. Thrasher highlights the nuances of impression management related to the performance of gender using LinkedIn. LinkedIn, which also has the capability of sharing of business and industry news, can offer women opportunities to build their professional presence, yet only when they do so effectively. The chapter offers practical suggestions for an effective LinkedIn profile that can assist in reducing gender bias and support positive impression management.

In Chapter 18, Newly Paul and Gregory Perreault in "Leader or Lady? The Visual Rhetoric of Hillary Clinton's Twitter Images" use the lens of symbolic convergence theory and fantasy theme analysis to evaluate the most popular images from the 2016 presidential campaign. While situating their study within the larger research related to gender and political campaigns, the authors identified fantasy themes from the most retweeted images on Clinton's Twitter account. Their findings provide helpful insights for understanding how visual rhetoric employs images for emotional appeals. Twitter images reportedly become effective as they are spread through being retweeted.

Finally, in Chapter 19, "Her Gospel Truth: Bloggers Rewriting Grand Narratives of Women of Faith in Church Leadership," Karen Sorensen-Lang describes and analyzes the movement of women Christian egalitarian and intersectionality bloggers who are addressing gendered church leadership norms and male-authority narratives through online, digital leadership. She found that women bloggers were able to circumvent patriarchal church leadership through their blogs. However, she cautions against being too celebratory of this medium, since intersectionality bloggers, who are more critical of sexism, racism, and classism in churches, offer a different perspective on how women can participate in church leadership.

CONCLUSION

Taken together, these chapters offer insight and perspective on the intersectionality of gender, communication, and leadership. Many examples illustrate why and how women's communication styles are critiqued as not measuring up to men's and how these styles prevent women from obtaining leadership positions. Each chapter includes practical solutions from a communication and leadership perspective that all genders can employ to advance the work of equality. Some solutions will be of use in organizational contexts, such as leadership development and training initiatives. Some solutions will be of use to individuals, such as the guidance provided regarding how to identify and respond productively to micro-aggressions or how to be cautious rather than optimistic about practicing authentic leadership. Implementing organizational and individual solutions may help us narrow gender-based leadership gaps and have more fulfilling, empowered lives.

REFERENCES

Bandura, A. (1978). Social learning theory of aggression. *Journal of Communication,* *28*(3), 12–29.

Buckley, C. (2016, January 12). Number of female directors of top films ticks up, study says. *The New York Times.* Retrieved from paragraph 1 https://www.nytimes.com/2016/01/13/movies/number-of-female-directors-of-top-films-ticks-up-study-says.html?mcubz=0&_r=0

Catalyst. (2007). The double-bind leadership dilemma for women in leadership: Damned if you do, doomed if you don't. Retrieved from http://www.catalyst.org/system/files/The_Double_Bind_Dilemma_for_Women_in_Leadership_Damned_if_You_Do_Doomed_if_You_Dont.pdf

Davis, G. (2016, December 7). Geena Davis' letter to Hollywood: Want a female president? Put them onscreen first. *The Hollywood Reporter.* Retrieved from http://www.hollywoodreporter.com/news/geena-davis-roles-women-hollywood-how-shatter-glass-ceiling-952466

Eagly, A. H. (1987). *Sex differences in social behavior: A social-role interpretation.* Hillsdale, NJ: Lawrence Erlbaum Associates.

Eagly, A., & Carli, L. L. (2003). The female leadership advantage: An evaluation of the evidence. *The Leadership Quarterly, 14*(6), 807–834. doi:10.1016/j.leaqua.2003.09.004

Hackman, M. Z., & Johnson, C. E. (2013). *Leadership: A communication perspective* (6th ed.). Long Grove, IL: Waveland Press.

Holden, K. E., & Raffo, D. M. (2014). A potential generation gap: Perspectives on female leadership. *Gender in Management: An International Journal, 29*(7), 419–431. doi:10.1108/GM-11-2013-0132

Inter-Parliamentary Union. (2016). *Women in national parliaments.* Retrieved from http://www.ipu.org/wmn-e/world.htm

Jackson, B., & Parry, K. (2008). *A very short, fairly interesting and reasonably cheap book about studying leadership.* Thousand Oaks, CA: SAGE.

Long, H. (2016, September 29). Female CEOs are at record level in 2016, but it's still only 5%. *CNN Money.* Retrieved from http://money.cnn.com/2016/09/29/investing/female-ceos-record-high/index.html

Paustian-Underdahl, S. C., Walker, L. S., & Woehr, D. J. (2014). Gender and perceptions of leadership effectiveness: A meta-analysis of contextual moderators. *Journal of Applied Psychology, 99*(6), 1129–1145. http://dx.doi.org/10.1037/a0036751

Sandberg, S. (2013). *Lean in: Women, work, and the will to lead.* New York, NY: Alfred A. Knopf.

Sandberg, S., & Grant A. (2015, January 12). Speaking while female. *The New York Times.* Retrieved from https://www.nytimes.com/2015/01/11/opinion/sunday/speaking-while-female.html?_r=0

Wood, J. T. (2015). *Gendered lives* (11th ed.). Stanford, CT: Cengage Learning.

Williams, J. C., & Dempsey, R. (2014). *What works for women at work: Four patterns working women need to know.* New York, NY: New York University Press.

PART I

FOUNDATIONS: COMMUNICATION IN PRACTICE

CHAPTER 1

GENDER, COMMUNICATION, AND THE LEADERSHIP GAP

Sally Helgesen
Independent Scholar, Consultant, and Author

Aspiring women leaders, and even those who hold positions of substantial authority, often feel caught in a communication bind. The two main strategies they select to navigate the bind are either focusing their efforts on being forceful and direct or adopting a more invitational style in hopes of engaging listeners and diffusing potential resistance. If women take the first approach, they risk being perceived as aggressive, arrogant, abrasive, or hectoring. If they hold back, they are often tagged as weak, lacking the courage of their convictions, sorely in need of the confidence and verve that effective and persuasive leaders display.

Sheryl Sandberg and Adam Grant (2015), writing in *The New York Times*, noted that men and women tend to be judged by different standards when they make presentations, lead meetings, or offer ideas to colleagues in a team setting. Women are more likely to be interrupted, questioned, and criticized; they are more apt to be ignored, or simply not heard. In 27 years of working with women in organizations around the world, I have met very few who have not had the experience of raising a point in a meeting only

Gender, Communication, and the Leadership Gap, pages 3–11
Copyright © 2017 by Information Age Publishing
All rights of reproduction in any form reserved.

to be met with silence. This silence is often broken when a male colleague echoes what the woman just said and is met with encouragement: "Great idea, Bob!"

Such scenarios occur not only with relatively mid- or entry-status women, but also with exceptional women leaders who hold positional power. For example, Christina Romer, who *chaired* the Council of Economic Advisors in the first Obama administration, reported that colleagues routinely ignored what she said in meetings or talked over her. But they listened attentively when her ideas were repeated by male Council members (Suskind, 2012).

While there are ways both to reframe and handle such experiences (which I will address later on), the general impatience with and disregard for women as communicators, both documented and anecdotal, is so deeply rooted that it is popularly referred to as "speaking while female." Although disappointing, this should not be especially surprising given that most women rarely spoke in mixed public settings until 40 or 50 years ago and almost never as leaders except in all-female venues. When women were present in public settings, they were expected to be supportive of men and the ideas they put forth. If women had an active role, it was often in executing men's ideas rather than proposing ideas themselves.

I want to stress here that women's challenges with communication are two-fold. While women do at times struggle to present their ideas, thoughts, and findings in mixed venues confidently and clearly, they also often speak before audiences pre-disposed to skepticism, or simply not willing or able to listen. In other words, they stir resistance that may have nothing to do with how they articulate their perspective, although the repeated experience of not being heard may over time erode the capacity to express their ideas persuasively and with power.

In part, as a result of this inhibitory environment, women often struggle, particularly in the formative years of their careers, to find and use their voices. This lack of presence can manifest itself as a tentativeness that sets women up to be overlooked or to invite pushback. The foundational and brilliant work on voice, *Women's Ways of Knowing: The Development of Self, Voice, and Mind,* set the stage for numerous subsequent studies that have explored how this struggle manifests (Belenky, Clinchy, Goldberger, & Tarule, 1997). I have witnessed vivid examples in many venues and at every level: Women using phrases such as, "I'm not sure if this is right" or "you might not agree," to introduce a thought; sprinkling their remarks with qualifiers ("only," "just") that signal the speaker's desire to claim less space in the listener's mind; or habitually employing a rising intonation at the close of their sentences in a manner that seems to question the validity of their own observations.

These verbal tics, and the body language that accompanies them, have been documented in much of the recent literature about women and

Tentativeness (Fixmer-Oraiz ; Wood)

communication (Cuddy, 2015). Because research spurs awareness, most women who have achieved positions of authority have worked to correct these habits, either through their own efforts or with the aid of coaching. I therefore want to focus my observations in this chapter on an aspect of female communication behaviors, and male receptivity, that has received far less attention in both academic and popular literature, but which my decades of experience suggest is not only widespread but may be an underlying factor in gender miscommunication. I do so in the hope that bringing it to awareness may help aspiring women leaders become more effective communicators in challenging environments.

VOICE AND VISION

Because voice is most powerful when translating vision, in 2008 I became intrigued by the subject of women's vision. This interest had initially been spurred by work I had done in 2004 with the Washington Quality Group (WQG), a coaching consortium based in Madrid, Spain. WQG had recently run a substantive but unpublished survey of client companies that gauged male executives' perceptions of women's strengths and weaknesses. As it turned out, the executives surveyed rated the women in their organizations highly in almost every category except "vision." Although women were perceived as strong negotiators, relationship builders, communicators, and motivators, they were seen to be deficient when it came to vision. This was viewed as a key impediment to their reaching high positions.

My interest in perceptions of women's vision was further engaged in 2009, when the *Harvard Business Review* published "Women and the Vision Thing" by Herminia Ibarra and Otilia Obodaru, which also found male leaders skeptical of women's capacity to be visionary, even when rating women high on other leadership qualities. Ibarra offered some reasons for her finding, yet I had some questions about how perceptions might be addressed. I decided to investigate further and so joined forces with Julie Johnson, one of America's top executive coaches, to try to understand *why* women were viewed, at least by many senior organizational leaders, as lacking in vision. The result was *The Female Vision: Women's Real Power at Work*, published in 2010 (Helgesen & Johnson, 2010)

What exactly do we mean when we talk about vision? Our work suggests that vision is comprised of three elements: what we notice, what we value, and how we connect the dots or tell a story about why what we notice is important. Vision is conveyed by voice, but it begins with perception. *Notice* is the building block upon which any authentic vision rests.

An individual's style of noticing is therefore important. And what my co-author and I found is that women tend to have a different noticing style

Multidirectional noticing = female

than men. This finding has been verified by research using functional MRIs that show the brain in operation. These studies demonstrate that multiple regions of women's brains tend to be activated when their attention is engaged, which results in their noticing a lot of different things at once. By contrast, men's brain activity is more focused, demonstrating that their attention is engaged sequentially. Women's attention may thus be said to operate like a radar, scanning the environment and picking up clues, whereas men's attention operates more like a laser, focusing deeply on the matter at hand (Helgesen & Johnson, 2010). As always, it is important to note that we are all individuals, and accordingly we fall at different places on the spectrum: some women have more laser-like notice and some men have more active radar. It is also important to notice that, thanks to neuroplasticity, our brains tend to develop new capacities in response to our experience, so as women's and men's experience grows more similar, our noticing capacities will probably shift in response, with each of us developing more flexible styles of notice. However, given men and women's contrasting evolutionary histories—men charged with hunting and warfare and women charged with gathering and child care—it is hardly surprising that our neural pathway capacity would be affected.

Still, given that notice is essentially the building block of vision—shaping both how we value what we see and how we tell a story about why it matters—it is not surprising that the ways in which women articulate their vision would be slightly different than the ways men speak about what they see. Nor is it surprising that men's tendency to favor a laser-focused style of notice should be privileged in mainstream organizations and viewed as a leadership behavior, given that men until very recently shaped the culture and expectations of virtually every mainstream organization.

What does this have to do with gender and communication? Quite a bit, as it turns out. In particular, it explains some of the common interactions women experience in the workplace, such as having observations they believe are relevant and even vital dismissed as "beside the point."

In *The Female Vision* (Helgesen & Johnson, 2010), we cite an example typical of our experience. Jim and Jill are walking out of a presentation in which their regional manager has outlined the sales targets he expects the team to meet in the next quarter. Jim is scribbling down numbers he believes will enable the team to meet the projection, when Jill observes that Ron, a member of the team who typically assumes an enthusiastic leadership role, appeared almost entirely disengaged. As we note in the book:

> Jim doesn't respond. He's wondering why Jill is making an irrelevant comment. She needs to be thinking about how they can make their numbers, not worrying about what someone else is feeling. Besides, Jim wasn't looking at Ron. For one thing, he doesn't have eyes in the back of his head. Plus, he

was focused on the presentation, which is exactly what the regional manager would expect.

Jill, was paying attention too, but not in a single-minded way. For example, she was aware that some of the attendees couldn't hear what the presenter was saying—not surprising since he has a habit of speaking too fast and then getting testy when someone asks him to repeat his remarks. But it was Ron's disinterest that most caught her attention. He's key to the team's effort, and it's going to be a rough road for everyone if he's struggling. (Helgesen & Johnson, 2010, p. 5)

The exchange in the book ends with Jill sensing Jim's irritation and even incomprehension. Wanting to signal that she is on board with the larger team effort, she tells him she thinks his numbers are on target and leaves it at that. Their exchange typifies a classic interaction my co-author and I have each observed in the organizations we have worked with over many decades. Both Jim and Jill are bringing useful information to their encounter, Jim by being focused and Jill by employing her highly active radar. Yet because only Jim's point of view reflects the organization's vernacular, Jill loses confidence in the value of her insights and backs off as soon as she senses Jim's lack of interest.

One explanation for such interactions is that the broad-spectrum noticing practiced by many women is not as valued as focused notice, nor is its potential value recognized. Because broad-spectrum notice can seem diffuse and, by its very nature, *un*focused, it often gets ignored by those who place a premium on focused notice. As a result, women who share their perspective in a broad-spectrum frame may be ignored.

When *The Female Vision* (Helgesen & Johnson, 2010) was published, I believed the main value of this research would be helping women recognize the validity of their distinctive yet often misunderstood style of notice. And this did indeed happen. Over the years, thousands of women in organizations where I have spoken or presented workshops have told me that the book had helped them understand that what they noticed had value and deserved to be shared. "I thought it was just how *I* saw things, but now I see it's a whole noticing style," said one, a sentiment I have heard echoed many times.

But within a year of publication, as a result of working with women in a wide range of venues, I began to realize that how we interpret "women and the vision thing" could also be helpful to women seeking to communicate more effectively. The countercultural nature of broad-spectrum vision could indeed explain the response women frequently encounter in the workplace when they attempt to convey their ideas: criticism that they are "all over the map," have gotten bogged down in irrelevant or purely narrative details, and give too much weight to pointless tangents—even tangents that could be vital to the organization's success.

Empowering women to affirm their noticing style as a legitimate style could therefore go only so far in helping them position themselves as visionaries in organizations. They needed to bring this awareness to crafting the presentation of their ideas in a way that could be understood in cultures in which highly focused notice is the accepted norm.

TRANSLATING VISION

Helping women communicate the fruits of broad-spectrum notice *in a way that those who place a premium upon focused notice can hear and understand* is therefore essential if we want to help women position themselves as visionaries. In order to be recognized for their strategic thinking as well as their specific and concrete skills, women who identify themselves as broad-spectrum noticers would be well advised to anticipate and prepare for ways their ideas might be misheard.

I remember the moment this insight became clear to me. I was working with a group of women in the biotech sector in San Diego. A participant in our session was telling the assembled group about a meeting in Switzerland in which she had presented the findings of her research project the previous month. She had been excited because she felt it was the most important research she had ever done and believed it could help the company achieve a stronger position in a market where it had been lagging. She prepared thoroughly and felt confident that she had made a strong start, but about ten minutes into her presentation she became aware that her listeners—fellow researchers, all male—seemed to have lost interest. She tried to speed up her presentation so as not to lose them (a classic mistake), but when at the end of her presentation no one asked a single question, she knew she had not achieved her desired effect.

She felt humiliated throughout the rest of conference. Seeing a male researcher from Egypt at the airport, she worked up the courage to ask him what had gone wrong. He told her the male researchers in the room could not follow her conclusions. "You didn't connect the dots for them. You never told them *why* what you were saying was important or what you expected them to do with the information."

Reflecting back on this experience, she said, "It didn't occur to me that the dots needed to be connected. I thought they would see why the results of my study were important and how they could be applied." She now wondered if the difference between broad-spectrum and focused notice might have been at the root of the miscommunication. She observed that, in the future, taking this perceptual difference into account could help her communicate in a way that focused noticers would find more relevant to their concerns.

(Why you should care — What you should do)

Include in talks

In the years since that encounter, I have worked on communication challenges with women at every level, in sectors ranging from law to pharmaceuticals, energy to finance, technology to education. I have seen them struggle to share what they notice, value, and believe to be true and have come to appreciate the difficulties inherent in communicating a broad vision to those accustomed to focusing on one thing in sequence. But I have also seen the potential power of taking these differences into account when preparing to offer ideas in workplace settings.

I find six practices to be particularly useful for women struggling to be heard.

Recommendation 1: Start with the numbers. Many women find narratives persuasive, but highly focused noticers are more likely to want to "get to the bottom line." Women can therefore benefit from quantifying their observations, even when making contextual points. For example, Jill in the story recounted above might have said to Jim, "Ron's team is responsible for 60% of our sales so we need him 100% engaged to hit our $10K target. I estimate he could have a 30% falloff in results if he is distracted, and I believe he may be. I can share the reasons, but more important is having a plan to get him engaged."

Recommendation 2: Do not offer a backstory. Women often enjoy sharing how they came up with an idea—the logic path, the conversations that spurred the insight. Laser noticers rarely care about this kind of background; again, they are looking for the bottom line. Women can benefit by top-lining their best idea in a single sentence, using numbers as required. They can then add, "If you are interested in how I came up with this idea, I'm glad to share that later." This often ends up eliciting interest because it enables the listener to take the initiative to ask.

Recommendation 3: Be concise. Banishing prolixity is perhaps the most important practice for women who seek to communicate effectively with senior leaders. Many such leaders have notoriously short attention spans and may be chronically impatient; this is certainly also true of female leaders who have become acculturated to the normative communication style in their organization. Given this reality, women who know they have a tendency to be verbose or want to provide a lot of information can benefit by working ahead of time to cut out as many words as possible from a presentation, keeping only the essentials, and in particular editing out introductory material. Similarly, vigilantly rooting out stalling or apologetic language ("Sorry, but I was wondering if you") will aid women seeking to be more concise.

(handwritten margin note: keep audience curious)

Recommendation 4: Anticipate objections. The biotech researcher cited above could have avoided the disappointing reception she received if she had run her remarks by a skeptical colleague in advance and asked for honest feedback. Doing so could have enabled her to frame her presentation in a way that someone with a different perspective could better understand.

Recommendation 5: Seed the room with allies. Similarly, women can increase their chances of successfully presenting an idea in a meeting by asking a colleague to observe what happens when they speak and offer support if they think it is appropriate. This approach has the effect of engaging that colleague as an ally. It can be particularly effective in venues in which women have experienced their ideas being ignored or claimed by colleagues, for the allies may decide to speak up on their behalf.

Recommendation 6: If someone repeats an idea, thank him or her for agreeing with what you said. Women are often confused about how to handle a colleague who echoes an idea they have proposed. When this happens, women often respond by passively waiting for someone to speak up on their behalf: When this does not happen, they may feel hurt and disrespected. Recognizing that objecting—"Hey, that was my idea!"—does not work well; it is often better to handle the situation with humor. "Jake, I am so glad you agree with me!" is a more successful response than taking umbrage or suffering in silence.

CONCLUSION

My work in organizations has convinced me that broad-spectrum and laser notice deeply affect our communication styles in ways that can penalize women and prevent their best insights from being heard and fully valued. It is not simply that men can be impatient listening to women, it is that the content and style of what women present may strike men (and more acculturated women) accustomed to operating in a bottom-line environment as unfocused, long-winded, or beside the point. Being aware of differences in how laser and radar noticers operate, and taking these into account in advance of presenting an idea, can enable women to share their vision more effectively.

REFERENCES

Belenky, M. F., Clinchy, B. M., Goldberger, N. R., & Tarule, J. M. (1997). *Women's ways of knowing: The development of self, voice, and mind.* New York, NY: Basic Books.

Cuddy, A. (2015). *Presence: Bringing your boldest self to your biggest challenges.* New York, NY: Little Brown & Company.

Helgesen, S., & Johnson, J. (2010). *The female vision: Women's real power at work.* San Francisco, CA: Berrett-Koehler.

Ibarra, H., & Obodaru, O. (2009). Women and the vision thing. *Harvard Business Review, 87*(1), 62–70.

Sandberg, S., & Grant, A. (2015, January 12). Speaking while female. *The New York Times.* Retrieved from http://www.nytimes.com/2015/01/11/opinion/sunday/speaking-while-female.html?_r=0

Suskind, R. (2012). *Confidence men: Wall Street, Washington, and the education of a president.* New York, NY: Harper Perennial.

CHAPTER 2

WOMEN AS INCLUSIVE LEADERS

Intersectionality Matters

Brenda J. Allen
University of Colorado Denver

While writing this essay at the end of 2016 and the beginning of 2017, I followed discussions about the Women's March on Washington, scheduled for the day after the presidential inauguration on January 20. More than 600 "sister marches" were planned for the same day in the United States and around the world. When I learned that one was scheduled to be held in Denver, I debated whether or not to attend. My reticence was based on my experiences that initiatives about women often assume a pre-existing "unity" among women that neglects to acknowledge differential power relations and systems of oppression that women from varying backgrounds can experience (Butler, 1990). I also had read reports that because the original national march organizers were White women, some prospective attendees were concerned that the march would fail to address concerns of marginalized women, especially women of color. The leaders responded by inviting three young women of color who are experienced activists and

Gender, Communication, and the Leadership Gap, pages 13–23
Copyright © 2017 by Information Age Publishing
All rights of reproduction in any form reserved.

organizers to become national co-chairs of the event. They also created a diverse national committee, and they appointed a group of honorary co-chairs who are civil rights icons. In addition, the leaders invited presenters and performers who represent a wide variety of human rights issues.

The organizers decided to focus on the premise that "women have intersecting identities and are therefore impacted by a multitude of social justice and human rights issues" (Women's March, 2016b, para. 2). Their comprehensive policy statement highlights diverse gender categories: "We must create a society in which all women—including Black women, Native women, poor women, immigrant women, Muslim women, lesbian, queer, and trans women—are free and able to care for and nurture their families, however they are formed, in safe and healthy environments free from structural impediments" (Women's March, 2016a, para. 1).

Media coverage described varying responses up to and after the marches. Although many people applauded the comprehensive focus on diverse issues, others did not. Racial tensions persisted related to the march itself and to the feminist movement. Some White women who reported feeling uneasy, excluded, or attacked by calls to acknowledge race and privilege opted out of the march. Some women of color declined to participate because they were offended at the omission of their voices at the outset, as well as frustrated that many White women had not previously seemed to care about their plight. Unfortunately, these conflicts and challenges are not new. They reflect enduring critiques about feminists and feminisms that trace back to the origins of demands for gender equality.

When a Muslim student leader-activist from my campus told me that she was a speaker for the Denver march, I was impressed that the organizers had invited her. The event program listed a wide variety of speakers who represented diverse perspectives on women's issues (e.g., Native American, African American, transgender, and the deaf community). Heartened by this information, I attended the march. I am grateful that I did because the experience exceeded my expectations. As a result of participating in the march, I feel more optimistic about the future of fighting for gender equity, and I have more clarity about what I can do as a woman leader. I appreciate the opportunity to share my ideas as they relate to the goal of this volume to address the under-representation of women in leadership. To achieve that goal, we should promote leadership practices that encourage, edify, and empower *all* women to enact formal roles where they have primary responsibility for guiding others to achieve organizational, institutional, or group goals. I stressed *all* in the preceding sentence because we must acknowledge a need to focus on women from non-dominant social identity categories (examples include but are not limited to race, ethnicity, sexuality, gender identity, ability status, and nationality). We also should be mindful of how these and other aspects of identity intersect with one another.

Despite an increasing emphasis on intersectionality in work about gender equity, as well as repeated calls and demands to consider diverse women in feminist-focused endeavors, a need persists to become more committed and intentional. As I discuss below, those of us in leadership positions can create and optimize opportunities to enhance inclusion and attend to intersectionality within a variety of contexts.

INCLUSION AND INTERSECTIONALITY

The everyday definition of inclusion refers to the act of making something part of a whole or a set. In groups, organizations, or institutions, inclusion refers more specifically to creating environments where everyone feels respected and valued for their role in achieving the goals of the group, institution, or organization. Inclusion also can refer to explicitly acknowledging and involving individuals who might be excluded or marginalized due to their social identity. To ensure that efforts to be inclusive encompass women from traditionally marginalized groups, leaders should focus on intersectionality. Anticipating that the primary audience of this volume will be women, this essay speaks to women leaders; however, the ideas presented are relevant to all leaders.

The concept of intersectionality is based on the idea that, in addition to belonging to a marginalized gender category (i.e., woman), many women are also members of other marginalized groups. Proponents of intersectionality contend that we cannot effectively address gender equity without considering other identity categories that inform gender constructions and meanings. Legal scholar Kimberlé Crenshaw (1991) is credited with coining the term "intersectionality," although she has noted that the concept existed long before she named it. Her early work critiqued how mainstream theories on feminism and anti-racism excluded Black women because they focused separately on sexism and racism. Thus, those theories neglected to allow for how the two types of oppression can intersect to create something qualitatively distinct from either sexism or racism.

Roots of interesectionality reside in the early 1970s during the era of feminism known as the second wave, which was when scholars of color discerned that feminist scholarship tended to concentrate on middle-class, educated, White women. They advocated a more inclusive view of women that acknowledged how social positions can overlap and therefore have varying consequences for women. Womanist and feminist scholars and others have integrated ideas of intersectionality into research and practice. They also have expanded from centering on gender and women to encompass other aspects of identity. As Risman (2004) observed, "[T]here is now considerable consensus growing that one must always take into consideration multiple axes of oppression; to do otherwise presumes the Whiteness of women, the maleness of people of color, and the heterosexuality of everyone" (p. 442). For purposes of this volume on women, communication, and leadership, intersectionality invites us to recognize the complexities of women's identities because women usually embody dominant and non-dominant social identity categories. That is, a woman may be likely to enjoy privilege or experience discrimination as a result of her gender identity, race, ethnicity, sexuality, social class, ability status, nationality, age, citizenship, religion, and their intersections. For example, I might experience privilege because I am a straight, cisgender, middle-class, able-bodied, U.S. citizen. Simultaneously, I might experience or perceive discrimination due to being a Black, female baby boomer, with multiplicative implications of intersections of those marginalized identities.

INCLUSIVE LEADERSHIP

An emerging area of leadership studies stems from the idea that leaders need to understand and be skilled at inclusion if they want to succeed in increasingly diverse environments. This body of work summons leaders to learn how to engage with persons from diverse backgrounds based on the multiple ways that individuals define themselves. To explore how inclusive leadership matters to women, I highlight a research report from Deloitte University Press, which heralds inclusive leadership as "a new capability that is vital to the way leadership is executed" (Dillan & Bourke, 2016, p. 3). Based on a comprehensive review of literature and experiences with more than 1,000 global leaders across Australia, Canada, Hong Kong, New Zealand, Singapore, and the United States; in-depth interviews with leaders and subject matter experts; and surveys of more than 1,500 employees on their perceptions of inclusion interviews; the researchers concluded that inclusive leadership is about

1. treating people and groups fairly—that is, based on their unique characteristics, rather than on stereotypes;
2. personalizing individuals—that is, understanding and valuing the uniqueness of diverse others while also accepting them as members of the group; and
3. leveraging the thinking of diverse groups for smarter ideation and decision making that reduces the risk of being [caught off guard] (para. 32).

Dillon and Bourke (2016) also delineate six interrelated signature traits (commitment, courage, cognizance of bias, curiosity, cultural intelligence, and collaboration) of what highly inclusive leaders think about and do in order to achieve those goals. As I illustrate later, these traits refer explicitly or implicitly to various formal and informal communication behaviors. Embodying and enacting these traits can help leaders achieve organizational, institutional, or group goals, while those leaders also enable individuals from diverse groups to reach their full potential.

While reviewing explanations of these six traits, I discerned implications for how women can apply an intersectional ethic to inclusive leadership. An intersectional ethic provides a lens to perceive how multiple aspects of identity "compound and complicate oppressions and marginalizations" (Uwujaren & Utt, 2015, para. 15). As Uwujaren and Utt explain, "Intersectionality must be about more than intellectualizing the work. It must be grounded in an ethic of feminist praxis that blends critical theory, like that of Kimberlé Crenshaw, with self-work and activism" (para. 34).

In the section that follows, I share ideas about how to apply an intersectional ethic (along with some personal examples) within brief descriptions of each trait. In addition, I refer to communication practices, and I offer some personal examples.

Commitment

Highly inclusive leaders are dedicated to inclusion and diversity because these principles align with their personal values and because they believe that being inclusive helps them achieve their goals (Dillon & Bourke, 2016). Being committed to effecting change and to being fair, highly inclusive leaders perform elements of inclusion cited earlier, and they help individuals feel connected to the group, institution, or organization. Inclusive leaders also monitor and adapt their practices to meet others' needs. As diversity champions, inclusive leaders exhibit their commitment by frequently and consistently articulating how and why diversity and inclusion matter. Moreover, they routinely allocate resources to develop and advance diversity and inclusion.

To employ an intersectional ethic, women leaders should analyze their commitment to categories of social identity to which they do and do not belong, with an emphasis on marginalized groups. For example, thanks in large part to my friend and former colleague, Anna Spradlin, I became aware of how I had been enacting heteronormativity, despite my commitment to diversity and inclusion. After Anna came out to me as a lesbian, she and I discussed our experiences with discrimination. I talked with her about being Black (she is White), and she shared experiences and challenges of being lesbian (I am straight). Her stories prompted me to comprehend my heterosexual privilege at the same time I was trying to help White students understand their racial privilege.

I acted upon my newfound knowledge in a few ways. For instance, as director of graduate students who taught an introductory course in organizational communication, I required those students to assign readings about sexual orientation. I also asked Anna and a female graduate student to present our experiences as women from different backgrounds at a national convention, and I encouraged Anna to submit her presentation for publication (Spradlin, 1998). In addition, I wrote about our experiences in an essay entitled "Sapphire and Sappho: Allies in Authenticity" (Allen, 2004).

Courage

Highly inclusive leaders confront difficult situations by challenging the status quo with others, with systems, and with themselves (Dillon & Bourke, 2016). They respectfully require those whom they lead to monitor their behaviors and consider their impacts. They challenge deep-seated organizational practices and perspectives that promote homogeneity. In addition, they hold themselves and others accountable for non-inclusive behaviors. One of the leaders the researchers interviewed reported "gently challenging followers to see their behaviors and the impact they have on others" (Dillon & Bourke, p. 10) and also regularly giving them feedback on such behaviors. Inclusive leaders also are willing to detect and acknowledge their own limitations, to admit mistakes, and to learn from criticism.

An intersectional ethic of courage prompts women leaders to question individual and systemic dynamics related to social identity categories, starting with themselves. For example, after Anna helped me recognize my heterosexual privilege, I sought and shared knowledge about LGBTQ history and challenges. I continue to seek information and insights related to privileged facets of my identity, and I try to alter my attitudes and actions according to what I learn.

Women who embody other marginalized identities should resist internalizing negative stereotypes about themselves. When I was introduced to feminist studies, challenges that confront Black women and other women of color were described as "double jeopardy." Although I agreed with the premise, I did not want to embrace a victim mentality. To share an alternative perspective, I wrote and presented a paper entitled "Twice Blessed, Doubly Oppressed" (Allen, 1995) that delineates and celebrates ways that I have been socialized as a Black woman. I often encourage persons whom I mentor or supervise to heighten their awareness of valuable attributes of

Intersectional ethic of courage

aspects of their identity that society marginalizes or devalues, and I give them feedback about those attributes.

An intersectional ethic of courage guides women to contest entrenched attitudes and practices that promote homogeneity. To illustrate, here is an example of what this kind of courage looks like in an ordinary organizational interaction. When I was invited to be on the selection committee for a leadership program for women in academia, I asked for the selection criteria and learned that there were none. I also inquired about how the leader of the program solicited nominations and whether the committee sought a diverse pool of nominees, given the institution's stated commitment to diversity. One of my colleagues had told me that the previous group of nominees had included a Black female who had worked at the sponsoring organization for many years and was disappointed that she had not been chosen. Instead, the committee had selected a White woman who was brand new to the organization. When I asked how the committee had chosen that employee, the chair said that the committee believed that the program would help the newcomer develop a professional network. While that was an admirable goal, it was not a stated criterion. Inquiring further, I also found out that the committee had never considered diversity nor tracked demographics of program participants.

The chair graciously accepted my offer to review the selection processes, and she convened a small group that discerned a need to strive for more diversity in participants' racial-ethnic identities as well as their organizational roles (i.e., staff and faculty in mid to high level positions). We developed explicit selection criteria, and we added a statement to the call for nominations that we sought a diverse pool of nominees. In this example, my colleague and I both performed behaviors that Dillon and Bourke (2016) cite in their overview of courage.

Cognizance of Bias

Highly inclusive leaders understand that organizations and institutions, despite good intentions, have implicit preferences and institutionalized -isms built into policies, processes, and practices that tend to favor members of some identity categories more than others (Dillon & Bourke, 2016). In addition to being alert to institutional biases, inclusive leaders self-regulate for personal biases.

To apply an intersectional ethic to cognizance of bias, inclusive women leaders should accept that we all have been socialized to harbor implicit biases for or against individuals (including ourselves) based on social identity. They should try to identify and mitigate their biases, solicit feedback from peers and those whom they lead, and cultivate receptive cultures where members feel empowered to offer feedback about perceived biased behavior. They also should identify and address organizational processes that are likely to embed bias. In addition, as my example about the leadership program exemplifies, they should employ transparent, inclusive, and consistent decision-making processes.

During a meeting with a group of staff who report to me, a female employee stated that I had paid more attention to males than females during a previous meeting of all the offices that I oversee. I thanked her for expressing her observations. I promised to pay closer attention to my behaviors and be more inclusive of all staff. Ironically, I had recently given similar feedback to a male colleague who was the chair of a search committee on which I served, after noticing that he tended to solicit input from the men much more frequently than from the women. After a few meetings, I privately described the pattern to him. He was taken aback but receptive and apologetic.

Curiosity

Highly inclusive leaders have an open-minded, genuine desire to understand other persons' viewpoints and experiences, especially those who have viewpoints different from them (Dillon & Bourke, 2016). They seek opportunities to interact with a diverse range of people. They welcome and value insights, they respectfully ask questions to deepen their understanding, and they listen actively and empathically. They also model and promote divergent thinking.

To apply an intersectionality ethic to curiosity, inclusive leaders should connect and dialogue with members of non-dominant groups. I recently hired a transgender employee who frequently experiences interactions where others refer to him using inaccurate pronouns. Another employee (who is acutely aware of these dynamics because she is a queer Latina and a strong advocate for marginalized groups) observed some of these interactions and recommended that I offer LGBTQ safe zone training for staff. I readily agreed. I knew that many persons introduce themselves by stating their pronouns, and I somewhat understood why that was important. However, after the staff member expressed his frustration, I delved more deeply into the topic. I found a few online resources that augmented my awareness and strengthened my commitment to educating others. I asked him to review those resources and to provide others if he had any. He shared a few very helpful resources that were quite illuminating for me (see, for example, Reis, 2016).

Culturally Intelligent

Highly inclusive leaders understand that cultural differences and similarities exist and they realize that their own culture impacts their personal worldview (Dillon & Bourke, 2016). They also know that cultural stereotypes can influence their expectations of others. Therefore, they value cultural differences, and they work to expand their knowledge about them. They also try to be aware of ethnocentric tendencies that might affect their attitudes and actions. Note that Dillon and Bourke's description of this trait refers mainly to national cultures.

An intersectional ethic of being culturally intelligent can illuminate differences in women's behaviors based on their nationality. Inclusive leaders should observe and respect varying communication styles, language, and other ways of expression based on differing cultural norms and socialization. For example, an employee from outside the United States who was seeking guidance about a conflict on her job brought her husband to a meeting with me, and he did most of the talking for her. Although I do not believe my frustration showed, I struggled with accepting this cultural difference. I wanted to meet with the woman alone and to encourage her to speak for herself. However, I did try to understand the situation, to temper my judgment, and to not let it influence how I assisted her. In addition to national cultures, an intersectionality ethic of cultural intelligence also should incorporate perspectives on intercultural interactions from the field of communication that expand beyond nationality to encompass cultural concepts about social identities such as gender, race, ethnicity, and sexuality (Nakayama & Martin, 2012).

Collaborative

Highly inclusive leaders foster creativity and cooperation among diverse individuals by empowering them to contribute their unique perspectives to team or group efforts (Dillon & Bourke, 2016). They understand that collaborating across difference can be challenging due to power dynamics, varying communication styles, and a lack of trust. Recognizing that individuals must feel safe and respected before they engage fully, inclusive leaders create environments and endorse processes that ensure everyone feels welcomed and valued.

An intersectional ethic of collaboration directs inclusive leaders to pay special attention to social identity power dynamics that can permeate group interactions. If leaders are not familiar with these dynamics, they should learn about them, and they should educate those whom they lead. For example, standpoint theory explains that members of marginalized groups often can offer valuable insights because they understand reality both from dominant perspectives and their own (Collins, 1986). In addition, inclusive leaders can optimize teamwork by offering and engaging in implicit bias training to help individuals understand how their biases related to marginalized groups might hamper collaboration, and to acquire strategies and techniques to mitigate bias.

In conclusion, this overview of signature traits and ideas for an intersectional ethic to enact them offers explicit and implicit communication guidelines for inclusive leadership. To contribute to the goal of this volume, I concentrated on how women's gender intersects with other aspects of identity. However, because intersectionality refers to other social identity categories, leaders also should consider them as they strive to be inclusive. I encourage women who want to develop inclusive capabilities to learn more about intersectionality and to be self reflexive.

As Uwujaren and Utt (2015) caution, applying an intersectional ethic will not be easy. However, they assert that "We must take upon ourselves the desire to learn about issues and identities that do not impact us personally" (para. 36). We should analyze how our social identity composite matters to why, how, and whom we lead. We should conscientiously apply the lessons we learn in order to realize the potential of inclusive leadership traits. I have begun to identify resources (e.g., KCL Intersectional, n.d.; Paul, 2016) to enlighten me about categories of identity about which I have limited knowledge (e.g., transgender and Muslim). If women leaders work diligently to become more inclusive while also attending to implications of intersectionality, we will help increase the number and the diversity of women leaders. As a result, our organizations, institutions, and groups will reap rich rewards.

REFERENCES

Allen, B. J. (1995). Twice blessed, doubly oppressed: Women of color in academe. ERIC, EBSCOhost (accessed June 16, 2017).

Allen, B. J. (2004). Sapphire and Sappho: Allies in authenticity. In A. Gonzales, M. Houston, & V. Chen (Eds.), *Our voices: Essays in culture, ethnicity, and communication* (4th ed., pp. 198–202). Los Angeles, CA: Roxbury.

Butler, J. (1990). *Gender trouble: Feminism and the subversion of identity.* New York, NY: Routledge.

Collins, P. H. (1986). Learning from the outsider within: The sociological significance of Black feminist thought. *Social Problems, 33*(6), S14–S32.

Crenshaw, K. (1991). Mapping the margins: Intersectionality, identity politics, and violence against women of color. *Stanford Law Review, 43*(6), 1241–1299.

Dillon, B., & Bourke, J. (2016, April 14). The six signature traits of inclusive leadership: Thriving in a diverse new world. In *Global human capital trends,* Deloitte University Press. Retrieved from https://dupress.deloitte.com/dup-us-en/topics/talent/six-signature-traits-of-inclusive-leadership.html

KCL Intersectional Feminist Society. (n.d.) Reading list. Retrieved from https://kclintfemsoc.wordpress.com/reading-list/

Nakayama, T. K. & Martin, J. N. (2012). *Intercultural communication in contexts* (6th ed.). New York, NY: McGraw-Hill.

Paul, C. (2016, March 10). 12 books to keep your feminism intersectional. *Bustle*. Retrieved from https://www.bustle.com/articles/143803-12-books-to-keep-your-feminism-intersectional

Reis, E. (2016, September 25). Pronoun privilege. *New York Times*. Retrieved from https://www.nytimes.com/2016/09/26/opinion/pronoun-privilege.html

Risman, B. J. (2004). Gender as a social structure: Theory wrestling with activism. *Gender & Society, 18*(4), 429–450.

Spradlin, A. L. (1998). The price of "passing: A lesbian perspective on authenticity in organizations. *Management Communication Quarterly, 11*(4), 598–605.

Uwujaren, J., & Utt, J. (2015, January 11). Why our feminism must be intersectional (and 3 ways to practice it). *Everyday feminism*. Retrieved from http://everyday-feminism.com/2015/01/why-our-feminism-must-be-intersectional/

Women's March. (2016a). Unity principles. Retrieved from https://www.womensmarch.com/principles/

Women's March.(2016b). Guiding vision and definition of principles. Retrieved from https://static1.squarespace.com/static/584086c7be6594762f5ec56e/t/587ffb20579fb3554668c111/1484782369253/WMW+Guiding+Vision+%26+Definition+of+Principles.pdf

PART II

ON THE GROUND:
EVERYDAY COMMUNICATION

Individuals who study and teach interpersonal communication typically emphasize the point that conversations are critical to creating and maintaining our social realities. For example, both Scott (2004) and Stewart (2011) observed that it is in conversation that we "do things" like form relationships, make decisions, hatch ideas, (dis)agree on meaning, and manage our conflicts. Organizational contexts add important dimensions to conversations and interactions. Conversations within the context of organizations are also complicated. Organizational members strive to accomplish goals, enact roles, live up to mission statements, and align with organizational values, all while also forming and navigating relationships. Communication in relationships and in organizations is much more than simple information transfer. Instead, communicative practices both produce and offer possibilities for resisting organizational structures.

Similarly, what we think of as "gender" and "leadership" are constructed (and resisted) in everyday relational and organizational communication. For example, interviews conducted by Buzzanell and Liu (2005) with pregnant women in organizations revealed that although the women did not feel different than others, they perceived that people treated them differently and that bosses treated them negatively. Negotiating maternity leave became a reason for bosses "to blame them, demote them, or deny raises or promotions that were promised previously—all of which negatively impacted these women's incomes, work life quality, or career development" (p. 12). According to the authors, this treatment could be

Gender, Communication, and the Leadership Gap, pages 25–27
Copyright © 2017 by Information Age Publishing
All rights of reproduction in any form reserved.

attributed to masculine workplace norms. In their words, the women are stuck "between their lives and ideal worker images with masculine performance evaluation systems. A 'good' or ideal worker is not someone who chooses pregnancy, who exhibits feminine and sexual qualities, who prioritizes personal needs such as childbearing over corporate needs" (Buzzanell & Liu, 2005, p. 12). Another example of how we construct "gender" and "leadership" in relational and organizational communication would be an unofficial "women leaders" mentorship/support group that emerges in a masculine work space and which may offer support for individual women leaders and may ultimately shift the organizational culture toward more collaborative norms and practices.

As the stories in the Introduction to this volume reflect, attention to our ordinary conversations and group dynamics in organizations—what is said, what is not said, who listens, who is listened to, who gains power, and who does not—often uncovers insights about gender dynamics and cultural forces in action. Thirty years ago, West and Zimmerman (1987) argued that through our everyday interactions with each other, we perform or "do gender" and this gender performance is assessed against cultural norms of masculine and feminine ideals. So, for instance, when women defer to men, and when men dominate conversation, as gender socialization subtly teaches, women are (re)created as dependent and men as capable. These conversational turns, or verbal communication, construct our social realities. Non-verbal communication matters, too, of course. As Tannen (1993) described, women at work are "marked," so that regardless of appearances related to hair, make-up, or personal style or wardrobe, they are evaluated into categories that signal women as "not quite serious, often sexual (para, 11). Men have fewer choices and traditionally have enjoyed more power, so their fashion choices are unnoticed or "unmarked," according to Tannen. By way of contemporary examples, is there a male equivalent of "resting bitch face" (Gibson, 2016, para. 2)? Is there a female equivalent of "mansplaining," "manterrupting," or "manspreading"? Paying attention to the communication patterns and practices in conversations can help women in leadership positions choose effective strategies and responses and begin to change these frustrating conversational dynamics. Attention to these everyday interactions will help men who want to share leadership roles and who want to work with a diverse set of people. Attention to the dynamics of communication, the power of gendered discourses and assumptions, and the ways our own perceptions color our interactions can lead to new ways of thinking, talking, and leading. The following set of chapters highlight how scholars are conducting inquiry in conversational and interpersonal contexts to ameliorate some of the problems faced by women in leadership positions, or even women trying to rise to positions of influence.

REFERENCES

Buzzanell, P. M., & Liu, M. (2005). Struggling with maternity leave policies and practices: A poststructural feminist analysis of gendered organizing. *Journal of Applied Communication Research, 33*(1), 1–25. 10.1080/0090988042000318495

Gibson, C. (2016, February 2). Scientists have discovered what causes Resting Bitch Face. *Washington Post.* Retrieved from https://www.washingtonpost.com/news/arts-and-entertainment/wp/2016/02/02/scientists-have-discovered-the-source-of-your-resting-bitch-face/?utm_term=.0641d6829347

Scott, S. (2004). *Fierce conversations: Achieving success at work and in life, one conversation at a time.* New York, NY: Berkley Publishing Group.

Stewart, J. (2011). *Bridges not walls* (11th ed.). New York, NY: McGraw-Hill Education.

Tannen, D. (1993, June 20). Marked women, unmarked men. *The New York Times Magazine, 18,* 52, 54. http://www.deborahtannen.com/s/marked-woman.pdf

West, C., & Zimmerman, D. H. (1987). Doing gender. *Gender & Society, 1*(2), 125–151.

forms of microaggressions

∘ Assertive accommodation
  authentic confrontation
∘ Assertive communication
  more direct than accom.

CHAPTER 3

Bystander (collab w/someone else) comm.

NARROWING THE LEADERSHIP GAP

∘ collab comm
- women tog confront the sit
∘ inclusive comm
- use male allies

Communication Strategies to Combat Microaggressions

Subtle & discrete forms of sexist behavior

Kelly Lynch McKenzie
East Stroudsburg University of Pennsylvania

Tammy J. Halstead
Franklin and Marshall College

Laws regulating overt sex discrimination in the workplace in the United States have changed social norms related to explicit sexist behavior. However, gender and sex discrimination still persist (Hong, 2013; Nadal, Meterko, Vargas, & Wideman, 2016; Roos, 2008). Because explicit sexual behavior is no longer tolerated in the workplace, there has been an increase in more subtle and discrete forms of sexist behavior, referred to as gender microaggressions (Cortina, 2008; Nier & Gaertner, 2012). Gender microaggressions are brief and commonplace instances of verbal and nonverbal communication—intentional or not—that are slights and insults targeted

Gender, Communication, and the Leadership Gap, pages 29–45
Copyright © 2017 by Information Age Publishing
All rights of reproduction in any form reserved.

at individuals who are not accepted as part of the dominant male gender group (modified from Capodilupo et al., 2010; Sue, Capodilupo, Nadal, & Torino, 2008).

Due to the subtle nature of microaggressions, today's discriminatory communication behaviors are more challenging to identify and easier to deny than in the past (Basford, Offermann, & Behrend, 2014). In fact, an individual who engages in microaggressive behavior—hereafter referred to as an *aggressor*—may be unaware that he or she has engaged in communication that is demeaning or sexist (Sue, 2010). Similarly, someone who is the recipient of the microaggressive behavior—hereafter referred to as a *receiver*—may be uncertain as to whether the aggressor intended the communication to be discriminatory (Sue, 2010).

Despite their subtle nature, microaggressions have a substantial negative impact on the self-esteem, self-regulation, and task performance of receivers (Cortina, 2008; Jones, Peddie, Gilrane, King, & Gray, 2016; Nier & Gaertner, 2012). In fact, microaggressions can be more harmful than overt behaviors because of the cognitive and emotional energy required to recognize, decipher, and deal with ambiguous forms of sex discrimination (Jones et al., 2016). The common result is that women lower their expectations for success. For instance, women who earn lower incomes than men still consider themselves to be as successful as their male counterparts (Deaux, 1995; Hogue, Yoder, & Singleton, 2007), which conveys that women are satisfied with less than men. Further, women may be held back because they tend to internalize negative communication experiences, believing that the discriminatory behavior is their fault rather than the fault of the aggressor (Jones et al., 2016). In addition, women who experience discrimination report decreased organizational commitment, diminished well-being and self-worth, and lower confidence in their ability to achieve goals (Basford et al., 2014; Gifford, 2009; Jones et al., 2016).

Although it is common for women to be thought of as failing to reach top leadership positions due to not being aggressive enough or lacking commitment to their jobs, in reality subtle bias is partially responsible for blocking women from obtaining top leadership positions (Ibarra, Ely, & Kolb, 2013). In fact, women who actively aspire to leadership roles are the most at risk of being receivers of microaggressions because they tend to be perceived as threatening to the dominant majority (Cortina, 2008). Given the pervasive negative effects of microaggressions on individuals and their career success, identifying ways to mitigate and ultimately eliminate microaggressions is vital to ending gender inequality in the workplace and beyond.

The purpose of this chapter is to provide specific communication strategies that can be used by women as a catalyst to shift focus away from women being the recipients of microaggressions toward focusing on aggressors. This important work begins by becoming more aware of how aggressors and receivers commonly and unintentionally approach communication in the workplace. The chapter then continues by discussing the specific communication strategies that can be used to mitigate microaggressions and concludes with a section that explains how communication can be used to shift the focus away from the receiver to the agressor.

THE AGGRESSOR'S COMMUNICATION APPROACH AND MINDSET

Specific types of discriminatory communication approaches that are damaging to women—microassaults, microinsults, and microinvalidations—are used by aggressors to maintain power differentials and to perpetuate inequality in the workplace. The terms *microassaults, microinsults,* and *microinvalidations* have been used in literature to refer to discrimination by race, gender, and sex. However, in this chapter the terms are specifically applied to gender discrimination enacted against women.

Microassaults are intentional or unintentional nonverbal and verbal messages communicating that women are inferior or that they do not belong (Nadal, Hamit, Lyons, Weinberg, & Corman, 2013). Microassaults include verbal insults, such as using derogatory names and telling sexual jokes, as well as nonverbal insults such as laughing at, ignoring, or avoiding women (Nadal et al., 2013). An example cited by McKenzie and Halstead (2014) in the academic workplace is when men refer to one another as *Doctor* but refer to a woman with the same credentials as *Ms.*, essentially communicating that she does not belong to a particular group of professionals and is inferior to men.

By contrast, microinsults are unintentional verbal or nonverbal negative messages about women (Nadal et al., 2013). If witnessed by the receiver or a bystander, these behaviors may go unnoticed. While microinsults may be considered rude, insensitive, and demeaning (Sue, 2010), they may not be recognized as discriminatory. Benevolent sexism is an example of a microinsult that begins with the "women are wonderful" notion (Glick & Fiske, 2001, p. 110), in which women are communicatively attributed the characteristic of "wonderful" based on specific, stereotypically gendered traits (e.g., nurturing, care-taking, warm). Benevolent sexism is discriminatory because it communicates that women are less capable than men of physical labor or that women are intellectually challenged and that they need to be protected because they are the "fairer sex." While aggressors may think they are showing appreciation for women, the resulting message is that women are inferior.

Microinvalidations, another type of microaggression, are messages that negate the realities, feelings, and experiences of women (Nadal et al., 2013;

Sue, 2010). With this type of microaggression, women's worldviews and perspectives remain unconsidered (Nadal et al., 2013). Examples of this dynamic are situations in which a female leader discusses her experiences of microaggressions with a dominant group member and is told that she is being too sensitive, or is taking words and actions out of context, or is seeing discrimination where none exists. While it is understandable that he or others may have difficulty understanding her perceptions because they themselves do not recognize microaggressions or have little to no experience being the receiver of microaggressive acts, when the male communicates that his perceptions and experiences must also be hers, a microinvalidation occurs.

Embedded in acts of microaggression are mindsets that reflect sexist biases. Examining these mindsets provides a better understanding of the underlying beliefs that are expressed in everyday communicative acts and that are necessary for microaggressions to occur and to continue in the workplace. The mindsets, the underlying beliefs that correspond with these mindsets, and examples of how they are expressed in the workplace are illustrated in Table 3.1.

THE RECEIVER'S COMMUNICATION APPROACH

When faced with a microaggression, a receiver may not communicate in a way that serves to recognize and to halt the discrimination as it occurs. This may be due to the receiver unintentionally approaching interactions as a member of a muted group and a co-cultural group in the male dominated workplace. Additionally, the receiver may not address microaggressions if she does not recognize them as a violation until well after the discriminatory act has taken place. Muted group theory, co-cultural communication theory, and expectancy violation theory are theoretical frameworks that illuminate the unintentional and common communication approaches used by women when they are encountering microaggressions.

Muted Group Theory

According to muted group theory, those who do not participate equally in the generation of ideas and the subsequent encoding into communication are silenced, leaving the group who holds power to control the nonparticipants' expression of ideas (Ardener, 2005). Because women leaders historically have been underrepresented in leadership roles in the United States, they were effectively absent from the formation of communication norms within organizations. As a result, the language practices developed

TABLE 3.1 Underlying Mindsets Imbedded in Microaggressions		
Mindset	**Underlying Belief**	**Example**
Women as Objects	Women's bodies are not their own; women are reduced to their physical appearance.	Employees gossip that a female leader has been given her position because she is having an affair with the boss.
Stereotyped Gender Roles	Women should be caretakers and homemakers; women should be in supportive roles at home and work.	A woman leader is told by her supervisor that her task is to support him and his efforts by answering phones and writing reports.
Second-Class Citizen	Women are inferior to men; women cannot handle difficult or physical tasks; women should be paid less than men and not hold high status roles.	A woman leader is not given a task that requires analyzing quantitative data, because men are better with numbers.
Denial of Existence of Sexism	Women see discrimination when it is not there or are hyper-sensitive to communication from men.	A woman expresses to co-workers that the boss's comments about her appearance are inappropriate; her co-workers laugh and suggest that she should be appreciative of the compliment.
Ignoring Gender	Men and women are the same and experience the world in the same ways; men deny that women may have a unique world experience.	Concerned that a male coworker is not responding to her requests because she is a woman, the female leader tells her supervisor; he denies it is sexism and suggests it is a personality issue.

Source: Adapted from Nadal et al., 2013; Sue, 2010

primarily by male leaders are the only ones available to women leaders to express their experiences (Henley & Kramarae, 2001). Women, therefore, tend to be "more constrained than are men in what they can say, when and with what results" (Kramarae, 2005, p. 55). This lack of representation and subsequent silencing leads women to operate as what Orbe (1998) referred to as a co-cultural group, or a group that is outside of the dominant male culture.

Co-Cultural Theory

yes·?

When experiencing a microaggression that is not immediately recognized as a violation, women may inadvertently enact a reactionary communication approach rather than a strategic communication approach to cope with the discriminatory act. According to co-cultural theory, women may unintentionally use the co-cultural communication approaches of *non-assertive assimilation, nonassertive separation,* or *assertive accommodation* (Camara & Orbe, 2010).

When using nonassertive assimilation, women remain silent and mute themselves to assimilate into the dominant culture (Camara & Orbe, 2010). Women may silence themselves due to a concern for being penalized, labeled a complainer, accused of playing "gender politics," or not being taken seriously (Acker, 2006; Basford et al., 2014; Cortina, 2008; Ryan & Haslam, 2007). When women talk about discriminatory acts, they may emphasize commonalities and traits they share with the dominant culture (Camara & Orbe, 2010).

Nonassertive separation takes place when women communicate in ways that distance them from the dominant culture. They may disengage at meetings, attending only if required to do so, and not participate or make eye contact. They may also avoid aggressors. For example, women may close their office door to avoid contact, they may ask to be transferred to another area, or they may resign from their position.

Another common response to a microaggression is *assertive accommodation.* This occurs when individuals modify their verbal communication style as well as their appearance and take on actions more aligned with commonly valued leadership traits such as being direct and using aggressive language (Baker, 1991; McKenzie & Halstead, 2014; Piderit & Ashford, 2003), or they downplay gender in order to attain individual success (Ryan & Haslam, 2007). For instance, a female leader might "try on" a communication style that she perceives to be in alignment with the communication style of dominant group members. If this is a successful imitation of the dominant group's communication style, she may receive acceptance and approval from the dominant group members. These types of responses often occur when a female engages in interactions that should be considered violations of expected communication practices but are not recognized as violations.

Expectancy Violation Theory

Microaggressions in a co-cultural environment are communication expectancy violations, which can perpetuate discrimination in the workplace. As Burgoon (1993) explained, "Expectancy in the communication sense denotes an enduring pattern of anticipated behavior" (p. 31). A communication expectancy violation occurs when communication deviates from anticipated communication behaviors (Burgoon & Hale, 1988). When an individual uses communication that is outside the social norms of the workplace, the receiver of the message as well as any bystanders will likely recognize the communication as inappropriate and feel uncomfortable with the interaction. When a recipient recognizes that an aggressor is violating the expectations within the organizational culture, the receiver shifts her focus from the topic at hand toward the violator and the violation to try to figure out the meaning of the violation (Burgoon & Hale, 1988). At the same time, the receiver evaluates the extent to which the transgression has a positive or a negative valence (Burgoon & Hale, 1988).

Positive and Negative Valence

Expectancy violation theory predicts that violations with a positive valence (i.e., perceived as pleasant) lead receivers to be moderately or highly satisfied with the interaction. Conversely, a violation that has a negative valence (i.e., perceived as averse) leads to dissatisfaction with the interaction. It is the valence of the violation that predicts whether it is better to do what is expected or to deviate from the norm. For example, an unexpected hug between coworkers when a coworker expresses sadness may be seen as a positive violation. However, "catcalling" in the workplace, because it goes beyond socially recognized appropriate behavior, has a negative valence.

When a violation's meaning is unclear, the receiver is apt to consider the reward valence of the violation based on the reward valence of the aggressor, meaning that the message is interpreted based on what the aggressor can do for the receiver and what the aggressor can do to the receiver. If the relationship is one that the receiver values and that may further the receiver's goals, it is predicted that she is less likely to perceive the microaggression as a violation (Burgoon & Hale, 1988). If the aggressor is admired, is higher in the social hierarchy, or is thought of as a friend, the violation may be perplexing but may not be interpreted as a slight and is therefore not recognized as a microaggression. For example, if the aggressor is a leader who behaves amicably, but who communicates in a way that is outside social norms and rules—perhaps telling lewd sexual jokes to the receiver over a period of time—the communication may still not be recognized as a violation of communication expectancy even though it makes the receiver feel uncomfortable. Because microaggressions should be perceived by men and women alike as violations but often are not, microaggressions continue to be problematic in the workplace. Therefore, recognizing microaggressions as an expectancy violation of accepted communication behavior no matter the positive or negative reward valence is important to promoting equality in the workplace.

Recognizing a Microaggression as a Violation

Recognition of a microaggression as an expectancy violation is essential because "not noticing sexist incidents supports sexism" (Becker & Swim, 2011, p. 227). Not recognizing a microaggressive behavior as a violation

of expected communication means an effective response is impossible because the phenomenon is not noticed; therefore, it is not open to negotiation through discussion. Thus, even in instances in which the aggressor may
not be conscious of the effect he or she has on maintaining inequality in
the workplace, it may be important to engage in an ongoing dialogue about
how and why others perceive of the behavior as an expectancy violation,
and how the behavior mutes and silences individuals. This is important because when a violation occurs and is recognized as such, attention tends to
move away from the topic under discussion and towards the aggressor and
the violation (Burgoon & Hale, 1988). In essence, aggressors are more likely to recognize microaggressive acts as discriminatory and be less accepting
of those acts when communication in the work place includes both raising
awareness of discrimination and developing empathy by taking a woman's
perspective into consideration (Becker & Swim, 2011).

COMMUNICATION STRATEGIES

How can communication strategies be used to help end microaggressions
and promote equality in the workplace? As a catalyst for shifting attention
away from receivers being the recipients of microaggressions and shifting
attention to aggressors, specific communication strategies can be used as a
means to narrow the leadership gap. This section explores these communication strategies and demonstrates ways in which they can be enacted in the
workplace. The strategies shared here can be enacted by anyone, regardless of gender. Enacted by males, these interventions may be particularly
powerful because males make up the dominant culture and therefore tend
to control the expression of ideas in the workplace (Ardener, 2005). However, because women are more apt to notice microaggressions (Bassford
et al., 2014), the majority of these strategies would be enacted by women
until awareness is raised such that males become more apt to take notice
of microaggressions. Further, because research shows that women can communicate intentionally in environments where microaggressions exist, the
strategies below focus on women themselves taking action.

These communication strategies go beyond the automatic, unintentional styles identified previously in co-cultural theory, focusing instead on
strategies that help women become more adept at recognizing microaggressions and equipping them with techniques to mitigate workplace discrimination. It is important to note that any response to a discriminatory
behavior is risky. Because responses are risky, it is unlikely that all individuals who experience microaggressions will have the capacity or the necessary
safety net to speak out against discrimination, making it vital for those who
are able to speak out to respond in ways that are likely to have the greatest

level of success. Certainly, the entire population of women cannot act for the greater good. Some may not have the luxury of disrupting the status quo because they cannot risk having their livelihood on the line.

To begin this important and purposeful effort, individuals can follow these strategies: (a) intentionally enact *assertive accommodation*, (b) purposefully employ *assertive* communication, (c) deliberately utilize humor, (d) engage in bystander interpersonal communication, (e) become actively involved in collaborative communication, and (f) use *inclusive* communication. These strategies have been shown to be effective by various studies and data gathered through observation and introspection (Basford et al., 2014; Becker & Swim, 2011; Camara and Orbe, 2010; Jones et al., 2016; McKenzie & Halstead, 2014; Orbe & Roberts, 2012; Piderit & Ashford, 2003). Although these strategies are not exhaustive, they can be used to disrupt gender-oppressive acts.

Communication Strategy 1: Assertive Accommodation

One communication strategy that women can use in a purposeful way to disrupt microaggressive behaviors is *assertive accommodation.* When using this approach, receivers communicate a strong self-concept, they name the discriminatory act, and they express their unwillingness to tolerate the behavior while also sharing how the act made them feel (Camara & Orbe, 2010). Women enact assertive accommodation when they use their own authentic voices and express confidence in their right to express ideas and to not feel silenced by others (McKenzie & Halstead, 2014; Orbe & Roberts, 2012). When women stand up for themselves, they are better able to understand, analyze, and respond to discriminatory behaviors (Camara & Orbe, 2010).

For instance, a woman leader who feels devalued because she is ignored and dismissed at meetings by her male co-leaders could use assertive accommodation as a strategy to confidently and respectfully address the situation. With one or more of her male coworkers, she can genuinely and openly discuss what she has experienced by talking about how being ignored as a woman in a meeting that mostly consists of men is a discriminatory act and should not be tolerated. She may also seek their guidance about how to ensure that she is included in discussions and she may ask for suggestions about how to remedy communication problems. She can explain that she is genuinely concerned that the shared goal of allowing all voices to be heard is not being actualized and let them know that communication will need to change so that she is included in the discussion of ideas. In this case, her response to the microaggressive experience is to openly and honestly discuss the discrimination while remaining authentic to her own voice.

This strategy encourages the aggressors to understand the receivers' perspectives and encourages empathy while also clearly communicating that sexist beliefs will not be tolerated (Becker & Swim, 2011). In utilizing assertive accommodation, receivers should also inquire about the aggressors' intentions and engage them in clarifying the purpose of their statements and their nonverbal behavior. In the case mentioned previously, the woman leader may ask her coworkers to consider why the only female in the group is often ignored or dismissed, and then make a statement about the underlying beliefs that are being intentionally or unintentionally expressed through their nonverbal communication. It is also important that dominant male group members create an equal communication space so that all voices are heard because they are central to constructing inclusive work environments (Anicha, Burnett, & Bilen-Green, 2015; Prime, Foust-Cummings, Salib, & Moss-Racusin, 2012). Dominant members can create an environment of gender equality by actively including women's voices and redirecting conversation to those members of the organization whose voices are frequently silenced (Anicha et al., 2015; Ashcraft, DuBow, Eger, Blithe, & Sevier, 2013).

Communication Strategy 2: Assertive Communication

Assertive communication is a different type of communication strategy that can be used to combat and end microaggressions while they are occurring. When using assertive communication, receivers say what is reasonably necessary to stop the discriminatory behavior and use succinct communication to convey confidence and authority. This strategy provides a quick and direct way to draw attention to the behavior and halt the discriminatory action (McKenzie & Halstead, 2014). Although direct confrontation carries risks, including the possibility of ill feelings or prompting a counterattack, remaining silent or diverting communication to a different topic can imply that the receiver is accepting of the overtly sexist act.

The following is an example of how an individual can use assertive communication to halt a discriminatory act. A female has noticed over the course of the last several months that ideas presented by her male colleagues are more valued than hers. In a meeting earlier in the day she had raised an idea and it was ignored. About ten minutes after she mentioned the idea, a male colleague raised the same idea and it was quickly accepted by the group. After the meeting, the woman approached one of her male leadership counterparts to discuss her perceptions of the meeting. He responded by grabbing her around the waist, bringing her close to him and saying in a jovial tone, "Don't be so sensitive." She recognized this as overt discrimination in which she is being seen as inferior and as a sexual object. She decided to halt the discrimination by immediately and confidently drawing attention to it stating, "Your language and tone suggest that you don't think my concerns are valid or legitimate, and your grabbing me around the waist implies that you think you can physically control me. Both are discriminatory and inappropriate. Do not do it again." Use of this strategy can be effective in ending the immediate, overt, discrimination. After she has halted the discrimination, she can employ assertive accommodation to identify a longer-term resolution of the issue.

Communication Strategy 3: Humor

Utilizing *humor* is a communication strategy that can lessen the impact of discriminatory behaviors while also being a safer or less risky pathway to diffusing microaggressions (McKenzie & Halstead, 2014). Choosing humor to disrupt microaggressions sends a message that the receiver is aware of the discriminatory act but at the same time does not want to increase the level of tension between communicators (McKenzie & Halstead, 2014). Because it is an indirect approach, using humor may lessen the likelihood of aggressors immediately engaging in defensive communication and may help them to more openly consider their discriminatory behaviors since they are not being directly indicted. Just as the benefit of humor is its subtlety, the risk is that the rebuke may go unnoticed. Paying close attention to the nonverbal and verbal responses of both the aggressor and bystanders can help the receiver of the discriminatory act determine whether the message was received as intended.

For instance, if a woman is in a meeting where a male colleague's idea is accepted, although the idea was rejected when she proposed it, she may make a light-hearted joke about the incident by saying in a teasing tone, "This idea is great and for some reason sounds a whole lot better the second time it's talked about, because when I suggested it just a few minutes ago no one said a word. What's up with that?" When the woman jokes about the incident, she communicates that she is aware that a microaggression has occurred but also provides an opening for the group to respond without being humiliated. For example, a person in the group might then appropriately respond, "I totally forgot that you had just mentioned it. Thanks for the reminder that the idea originated with you."

Communication Strategy 4: Bystander Interpersonal Communication

Bystander interpersonal communication is a strategy that can assist individuals who do not feel empowered to stop microaggressions themselves. Bystanders are those individuals, regardless of gender, who witness microaggressions and assist receivers by speaking with them in one-on-one conversations about the incident and discussing how microaggressive acts devalue a woman's worth in the workplace (Piderit & Ashford, 2003). Interpersonal communication in this context occurs when the bystander and the receiver engage in dialogue where they self-disclose information about their experiences related to microaggressions. A bystander and a receiver communicating interpersonally lessens the threat that the receiver may feel (Piderit & Ashford, 2003), helps her begin to understand that silence will not change discriminatory behaviors, and helps her learn effective communication strategies to use to stop microaggressions.

For instance, the female leader whose idea was not recognized in a meeting may feel uncomfortable addressing the microaggression herself. However, a bystander who recognizes the nonverbal behavior as a communication expectancy violation and who is comfortable addressing discriminatory behaviors may speak to the woman privately about the witnessed microaggression. By opening up dialogue with the female leader and inviting her to share her feelings, the bystander creates an opportunity to teach the female leader certain strategies to communicatively combat microaggressions. The bystander can then encourage and help the female leader take action and serve in a support role as the female leader tries out new strategies.

Bystanders can also act as communication mentors who can help other women recognize and address microaggressive behaviors as they occur (McKenzie & Halstead, 2014). Women who aspire to leadership roles tend to informally seek out other women to mentor and teach, sharing their first-hand experiences of the practices they have used to be recognized as equals in the workplace (McKenzie & Halstead, 2014). In fact, when women leaders advise women about how to handle gender-equity issues, they often suggest finding an ally who is in a position of authority or a peer within the organization with whom to discuss the situation and determine the best way to proceed (Piderit & Ashford, 2003). Communication mentoring requires that individuals who are comfortable speaking up and using communication to disrupt microaggressions reach out in order to transfer their own knowledge about how to successfully disrupt microaggressive acts to other women who are then encouraged and motivated to do the same.

Communication Strategy 5: Collaborative Communication

Collaborative communication is another strategy individuals can use to combat microaggressions. By joining together, women can freely express themselves in a safe setting without fearing backlash. Women who feel comfortable speaking out can establish an intragroup communication network to support each other. Following this approach may entail convening a group of individuals to openly discuss equality in the workplace. Individuals who are comfortable sharing and implementing communication strategies to stop microaggressions can educate others through role play and discussion, helping receivers to practice communication behaviors and to envision how they will feel and think when they experience microaggressions or when they witness microaggressive behaviors aimed at others.

For example, an individual who feels devalued because her ideas are not recognized can convene a group of other women who work in different units in the organization to discuss communication strategies that can be used to stop these types of microaggressive behaviors. The group can work within the organization to encourage everyone to be accountable for watching and correcting microaggressions. Additionally, conversations during meetings can also include the mindsets and corresponding beliefs that lead to microaggressive environments so that underlying stereotypes and prejudices can be acknowledged and weakened. This group can also engage in dialogue with dominant group members in order to share their goals and philosophies, identify dominant group members who will provide support and guidance, and engage dominant group members in discussions about co-cultural norms and values (Orbe & Roberts, 2012).

Communication Strategy 6: Inclusive Communication

Inclusive communication can be used so that women are not perceived to be a separate co-cultural group. Through developing a dominant culture of communication that recognizes "all employees of our organization," community-building (e.g., creating common traditions and practices to bring the groups together) is possible, which can broaden peoples' conceptions of who belongs to the dominant group (Cortina, 2008). To end the actions of the aggressors, all members in the workplace should be educated about how to use communication to foster perceptions of women as equals. When women establish themselves as leaders by taking purposeful action (Ibarra et al., 2013), others can either facilitate acceptance of womens' leadership or deny it (Baker, 1991; Ibarra et al., 2013). By communicatively accepting or deferring to women or other non-dominant group members who are leaders, men can help build a culture where microaggressions and the mindsets from which microaggressions emerge are diminished.

For instance, a female leader could identify dominant group members who understand microaggressions and the need to stop them. Together they can nonverbally communicate in meetings that the ideas of non-dominant group members have equal merit. To communicate that the ideas of women leaders are valued, the dominant group members could yield the floor when the female begins to speak, lean in, nod and make eye contact, as well as state that the point she is making has worth. Over time, as it normalizes for the dominant group members to communicate nonverbally and verbally their acceptance of the non-dominant group members, leadership expands, easing the way for women to effectively engage in leadership.

SHIFTING THE CULTURE: PRACTICAL IMPLICATIONS

Strategic communication can help with recognizing microaggressive acts and can take the place of reactionary, automatic responses to microaggressions. It can also effectively disrupt the cycle of microaggressions and send clear consistent messages that microaggressive acts are not tolerated. Yet, even this is not enough. Attention must shift away from women responding to and coping with discrimination towards aggressors and the cessation of microaggressions when those acts are happening. Following is an explanation of ways in which communication strategies may be helpful in creating this shift as a means of narrowing the leadership gap.

When individuals learn effective communication strategies for halting microaggressions, they may feel more comfortable taking action when microaggressions occur. As other women witness a woman taking a stand against microaggressions in an effective and respectful way, they may be more inclined to take action when they experience discrimination in the workplace. As this cycle of using purposeful communication to take effective action against microaggressions continues, more and more women will speak out. Further, as these instances of discrimination are acknowledged, more and more people will begin seeing these subtle acts of microaggression as violations of communication norms. Once microaggressions are consistently recognized as violations, and communication strategies are actively enacted to halt them, a shift in the prevailing culture can occur.

Much of the conversation about microaggressions focuses on how women can address and manage microaggressive acts. To change the culture and narrow the leadership gap, communication strategies must be used to shift focus from women's responses to microaggressions, and to the aggressor and the communicative behaviors used in performing microaggressions (Cortina, 2008; Mahapatro, 2014). As individuals utilize these intentional strategies, taking action against microaggressions will become normalized and the focus will be on the behaviors of the aggressor rather than on the ways women cope with and react to microaggressive acts. When this shift happens, microaggressions will lose their influence and power. Shifting the focus toward aggressors' behaviors, therefore, is a means of permanently halting microaggressions and changing organizational culture. Free from the impact of microaggressive acts and the mindsets from which they develop, women may be considered for and move into leadership positions more freely.

Closing the leadership gap is essential because achieving complete equality in leadership roles has the potential to improve the leadership experience for both individuals and organizations. When a woman who holds a top decision-making position no longer wastes valuable time and energy coping with microaggressive acts that diminish her self-worth and her self-esteem, she can focus her leadership efforts on the important tasks at hand. When women leaders are no longer perceived as unequal in number or status, they will have an opportunity to participate as equals in addressing and solving the most perplexing societal and human problems, and, in turn, women will be given a greater chance to participate in creating societal change for the betterment of all.

REFERENCES

Acker, J. (2006). Inequality regimes: Gender, class, and race in organizations. *Gender & Society, 20*(4), 441–464. doi:10.1177/0891243206289499

Anicha, C. L., Burnett, A., & Bilen-Green, C. (2015). Men faculty gender-equity advocates: A qualitative analysis of theory and praxis. *Journal of Men's Studies, 23*(1), 21–43. doi:10.1177/1060826514561974

Ardener, S. (2005). Ardener's "Muted Groups": The genesis of an idea and its praxis. *Women and Language, 28*(2), 50–54.

Ashcraft, C., DuBow, W., Eger, E., Blithe, S., & Sevier, B. (2013). Male advocates and allies: Promoting gender diversity in technology workplaces. National Center for Women & Information Technology. Retrieved from https://www.ncwit. org/sites/default/files/resources/menasadvocatesallies_web.pdf

Baker, M. A. (1991). Reciprocal accommodation: A model for reducing gender bias in managerial communication. *The Journal of Business Communication, 28*(2), 113–130.

Basford, T. E., Offermann, L. R., & Behrend, T. S. (2014). Do you see what I see? Perceptions of gender microaggressions in the workplace. *Psychology of Women Quarterly, 38*(3), 340–349. doi:10.1177/0361684313511420

Becker, J. C., & Swim, J. K. (2011). Seeing the unseen: Attention to daily encounters with sexism as a way to reduce sexist beliefs. *Psychology of Women Quarterly, 35*(2), 227–242. doi:10.1177/0361684310397509

Burgoon, J. K. (1993). Interpersonal Expectations, Expectancy Violations, and Emotional Communication. *Journal of Language and Social Psychology, 12*(1–2), 30–48. doi:10.1177/0261927X93121003

Burgoon, J. K., & Hale, J. L. (1988). Nonverbal expectancy violations: Model elaboration and application to immediacy behaviors. *Communications Monographs, 55*(1), 58–79.

Camara, S. K., & Orbe, M. P. (2010). Analyzing strategic responses to discriminatory acts: A co-cultural communicative investigation. *Journal of International and Intercultural Communication, 3*(2), 83–113.

Capodilupo, C. M., Nadal, K. L., Corman, L., Hamit, S., Lyons, O. B., & Weinberg, A. (2010). The manifestation of gender microaggressions. In D. W. Sue (Ed.), *Microaggressions and marginality: Manifestation, dynamics, and impact* (pp. 193–216). Hoboken, NJ: Wiley & Sons.

Cortina, L. M. (2008). Unseen injustice: Incivility as modern discrimination in organizations. *Academy of Management Review, 33*(1), 55–75.

Deaux, K. (1995). How basic can you be? The evolution of research on gender stereotypes. *Journal of Social Issues, 51*(1), 11–20. doi:10.1111/j.1540-4560.1995.tb01305.x

Gifford, G. T. (2009). *Stigma in the workplace: Testing a framework for the effects of demographic and perceived differences in organizations* (Unpublished doctoral dissertation). University of Nebraska, Lincoln.

Glick, P., & Fiske, S. T. (2001). An ambivalent alliance: Hostile and benevolent sexism as complementary justifications for gender inequality. *American Psychologist, 56*(2), 109–118. doi:10.1037//O003-066X.56.2.1O9

Henley, N. M., & Kramarae, C. (2001). Gender, power and miscommunication. In D. M. Juschka (Ed.), *Feminism in the study of religion: A reader* (pp. 34–60). New York, NY: Continuum.

Hogue, M., Yoder, J. D., & Singleton, S. B. (2007). The gender wage gap: An explanation of men's elevated wage entitlement. *Sex Roles, 56*(9/10), 573–579. doi:10.1007/s11199-007-9199-z

Hong, G. S. (2013). The main obstacle to female leadership at the executive level and in traditionally masculine fields: How we can erase implicit discrimination through the law. Law School Student Scholarship Paper 239, eRepository@Seton Hall, Seton Hall. Retrieved from http://scholarship.shu.edu/student_scholarship/239/

Ibarra, H., Ely, R., & Kolb, D. (2013). Women rising: The unseen barriers. *Harvard Business Review, 91*(9), 60–66.

Jones, K. P., Peddie, C. I., Gilrane, V. L., King, E. B., & Gray, A. L. (2016). Not so subtle: A meta-analytic investigation of the correlates of subtle and overt discrimination. *Journal of Management, 42*(6), 1588–1613. doi:10.1177/0149206313506466

Kramarae, C. (2005). Muted group theory and communication: Asking dangerous questions. *Women and Language, 28*(2), 55–61.

Mahapatro, M. (2014). Mainstreaming gender: Shift from advocacy to policy. *Vision 18*(4), 309–315. doi:10.1177/0972262914551663

McKenzie, K. L., & Halstead, T. J. (2014). Women leaders in higher education: Constructing an active voice. *Pennsylvania Communication Annual, 70*(1), 41–69.

Nadal, K. L., Hamit, S., Lyons, O., Weinberg, A., & Corman, L. (2013). Gender microaggressions: Perceptions, processes, and coping mechanisms of women. In M. A. Paludi (Ed.), *Psychology for business success, volume 1: Juggling, balancing, and integrating work and family role and responsibilities* (pp. 193–220). Santa Barbara, CA: Praeger.

Nadal, K. L., Meterko, V., Vargas, V. M., & Wideman, M. (2016). Empowering women leaders to rise above microaggressions. In M.A. Paludi (Ed.), *Why Congress needs women: Bringing sanity to the House and Senate* (pp. 121–136). Santa Barbara, CA: Praeger.

Nier, J. A., & Gaertner, S. L. (2012). The challenge of detecting contemporary forms of discrimination. *Journal of Social Issues, 68*(2), 207–220.

Orbe, M. P. (1998). An outsider within perspective to organizational communication: Explicating the communicative practices of co-cultural group members. *Management Communication Quarterly, 12*(2), 230–279.

Orbe, M. P., & Roberts, T. L. (2012). Co-cultural theorizing: Foundations, applications & extensions. *The Howard Journal of Communications, 23*(4), 293–311. doi:10.1080/10646175.2012.722838

Piderit, S. K., & Ashford, S. J. (2003). Breaking silence: Tactical choices women managers make in speaking up about gender-equity issues. *Journal of Management Studies, 40*(6), 1477–1502.

Prime, J., Foust-Cummings, H., Salib, E. R., & Moss-Racusin, C. A. (2012). Calling all White men!: Can training help create inclusive workplaces? Retrieved from http://www.catalyst.org/system/files/calling_all_white_men_can_training_help_create_inclusive_workplaces_0.pdf

Roos, P. A. (2008). Together but unequal: Combating gender inequity in the academy. *Journal of Workplace Rights, 13*(2), 185–199.

Ryan, M. K., & Haslam, S. A. (2007). The glass cliff: Exploring the dynamics surrounding the appointment of women to precarious leadership positions. *Academy of Management Review, 33*(2), 549–572.

Sue, D. W. (2010). *Microaggressions in everyday life: Race, gender, and sexual orientation.* Hoboken, NJ: John Wiley & Sons.

Sue, D. W., Capodilupo, C. M., Nadal, K. L., & Torino, G. C. (2008). Racial microaggressions and the power to define reality. *American Psychologist, 63*(4), 277–279.

Take a sec to calm down
Sep from the past
Establish safety - facework
    ↳ *no shame*
Contrast when confronting
    ↳ *Antic. erroneous offense*
    ↳ *Descr offense, reassure good intent*
    ↳ *Descr intent (shared goals)* " *covert bias* "

CHAPTER 4   *p. 51*

CONFRONTING IMPLICIT AND BENEVOLENT BIAS IN TEAMS

Concepts and Communication Strategies for Women in Leadership

Steve Mortenson
University of Delaware

Within American corporations and legislative bodies, multiple sources indicate a persistent leadership gap between men and women (Parker, Menasce Horowitz, Wang, & Brown, 2015). Theorists and policy makers increasingly present evidence of systemic sexism in our culture and organizations (Case, Iuzzini, & Hopkins, 2012; McIntosh, 2012). Research further suggests that subtler forms of bias, such as implicit bias (which occurs outside of conscious awareness) and benevolent bias (which is often confused with well-intentioned but awkward behavior), can be just as damaging to women but are more difficult to identify and correct (Barreto, Ellemers, Piebinga, & Moya, 2010). In response to this problem, some educators have developed

Gender, Communication, and the Leadership Gap, pages 47–68
Copyright © 2017 by Information Age Publishing
All rights of reproduction in any form reserved.

forms of intervention designed to raise awareness of implicit and benevolent bias (Case, Hensley, & Anderson, 2014). Such programs have helped people understand how the accumulation of apparently minor or benevolent biases not only wounds and burdens women emotionally; the accumulation also hinders women's advancement into leadership (Becker & Swim, 2012; Shields, Zawadzki, & Johnson, 2011).

While leadership scholars acknowledge the value of educational programs, many recognize that substantial numbers of women leaders work without the benefit of such resources. Due to such constraints, the most accessible form of intervention emerges as interpersonal confrontation, one of the strengths of which is that it relies on the power of the individual rather than on systematic interventions or programs (Czopp & Ashburn-Nardo, 2012).

As recipients of discrimination, women leaders confronting sexism face the added challenge of managing feelings regarding their own past experiences of discrimination. Women experiencing sexist behavior report intense feelings of anger and depression-related emotions that can last for weeks after the initial event (Bosson, Pinel, & Vandello, 2010). This is particularly evident in cases of benevolent sexism in which women are assumed to be emotionally *warm* but *incompetent* (Glick & Fiske, 1996, 2001). Compared to overt and hostile sexism, benevolent sexism typically leaves women with fewer resources or strategies for coping and responding to discrimination (Good & Rudman, 2010). When individuals are unable to discuss, cope, or otherwise express emotional pain, they hold onto their painful feelings and develop an *emotional charge* around the suppressed pain (Richo, 2008). The emotional charge can be triggered by events or people that recall the original suppressed pain, and it adds to the cognitive and emotional effort needed to deal with feelings in the present moment (Hollis, 2008).

When women do confront sexism, research suggests there are both positive and negative consequences: Women who confront sexism and gender inequity at work can be viewed unfavorably and regarded as over-reactors, complainers, impolite, and aggressive; they may be at risk of being perceived to be self-interested and egoistic (Czopp, Monteith, & Mark, 2006; Hyers, 2007; Kaiser & Miller, 2004; Swim & Hyers, 1999). However, targets who confront prejudice also report an increased sense of competence, self-esteem and empowerment, and satisfaction (Gervais, Hillard, & Vescio, 2010; Hyers, 2007; Swim & Thomas, 2006). In addition, confronting prejudice can reduce stereotype use in perpetrators and observers (Czopp, Monteith, & Mark, 2006; Rasinski & Czopp, 2010). When women in leadership confront sexist behavior and provide effective advice and correctives to subordinates, the women face the additional tasks of managing their own feelings and working to identify these subtler and more corrosive forms of sexism.

This chapter is designed to provide women in leadership with practical concepts and strategies for engaging in interpersonal conversations about biased behavior. In addition to offering specific communication strategies, this chapter discusses emotional strategies for managing painful emotions around past experiences of sexual discrimination. With this in mind, this chapter first discusses the problem of gender bias and highlights the role that both implicit and benevolent bias play to further gender inequality and render bias more difficult to identify and prevent. Next, this chapter describes how an understanding of facework (i.e., behaviors intended to help others avoid embarrassment) and interpersonal projection can transform interpersonal communication into an effective means for confronting and reducing gender bias in addition to offering effective strategies for giving advice and corrections. This chapter also details specific emotional and behavioral strategies for de-escalating and reducing both internal and interpersonal tensions when confronting and correcting biased behavior in order to build collaboration. Finally, this chapter presents message strategies designed to confront gender bias and facilitate greater awareness and cooperation in reducing bias. The next section begins with a scenario that illustrates both an ineffective and an effective example of intervention using the tactics described in the rest of the chapter.

Tiny-Toaney?

A TALE OF TWO INTERVENTIONS

Consider the following scenarios for an interpersonal intervention: Pat has just finished giving an excellent presentation to her team when Cal approaches her.

> **Cal:** That was really good, Pat. It's great to see a young gal show that kind of poise up there.
>
> [Pat gives a strained smile and nods. Janet, the team leader, also heard Cal's remarks. She has been told the same thing countless times and she's had enough. After the meeting, Janet visits Cal in his office.]
>
> **Janet:** Cal, do you have any idea how sexist it was to say that to Pat after her presentation?
>
> **Cal:** (visibly taken aback) What? Sexist? I just told her she did a great job! How's that sexist? I was complimenting her on her work!
>
> **Janet:** You called her a young gal—that's demeaning—and you complimented her poise, not the quality of her work.

Cal: She is a young gal. She's just out of college! Look, Janet, I'll tell you what's demeaning—supporting a colleague and then being labeled sexist.

This is an ineffective intervention that makes conscious the dynamics of gender bias. Consider an alternative:

After Pat's presentation, Janet can feel her anger over Cal's remarks. In her office, she realizes that her anger in the moment is driven by pain from her own past experiences of gender discrimination. She takes a few minutes to reflect and to separate her feelings about the past from the needs of the present situation. When she feels clearer and less angry, she decides on her communication goals for confronting Cal about his behavior. When she's clear on that, she calls him in to have a private conversation with her.

Janet: Hi, Cal. I wanted to talk with you about something—and let me say up front that I know you value the women you work with, and I know that when you compliment Pat on her presentation in the meeting, you're sincere in what you say—you'd never say anything to demean her. But, when we attach someone's youth or gender to her accomplishments, it does diminish her accomplishments. It sets her apart from the standard instead of holding her up as the standard. It might be a surprise to us that a young woman like Pat can present her ideas with such authority, but surprise at her skill doesn't help her, and it can cause divisions within the team. I know you don't want that either, so may I show you this video on implicit bias and benevolent bias? I think it will make clear what I mean, and I think you'll be glad you saw it—I know I was. Our culture makes it really easy to fall into bias and hurt someone else without even realizing it. This video really made these subtle forms of bias more understandable for me—would you like to watch it?

thank you.

[Cal is a little surprised—but doesn't feel attacked or demeaned. He's willing to learn, and he watches the video with Janet. Afterward they have a civil and productive discussion and understand each other better.]

What makes for an effective interpersonal intervention against unconscious or well- meaning, but ultimately corrosive and patronizing forms of bias? Before addressing this question, it is important to identify subtler forms and sources of gender bias in implicit and benevolent biases.

GENDER AND GENDER BIAS

Gender can be described at once as a complex phenomenon, a field of study, and an ongoing debate. The World Health Organization (2016) offers a succinct definition of gender that aligns with this chapter's use:

> Gender refers to the socially constructed characteristics of women and men—such as norms, roles, and relationships of and between groups of women and men. It varies from society to society and can be changed. While most people are born either male or female, they are taught appropriate norms and behaviours—including how they should interact with others of the same or opposite sex within households, communities, and work places. When individuals or groups do not "fit" established gender norms they often face stigma, discriminatory practices or social exclusion—all of which adversely affect health. It is important to be sensitive to different identities that do not necessarily fit into binary male or female sex categories. (para. 1)

What's more, gender discrimination takes many forms, from overt acts of hostility that openly demean and injure, to socially embedded cultural norms and subtle acts that patronize while still wounding and impairing women. In many ways, overt prejudice and bias have been driven underground and camouflaged behind concerns for social desirability and the impression management tactics people use to mask bias (Dasgupta, 2013; Greenwald et al., 2002). Because many people hide their conscious sexism behind propriety, they fall into sexist behaviors and attitudes unknowingly (Kang, 2012; Nosek, Greenwald, & Banaji, 2007). As such, leaders have to address subtler forms of sexism that often function outside the awareness of individual perpetrators. Covert bias calls for more nuanced ways for leaders to effectively advise and guide subordinates, and it can be more complicated for women leaders interpersonally. To be clear, conscious sexism and overt discrimination remain strong and pervasive in American society (Kang, 2012). Research into the mechanisms behind implicit gender bias does not question the existence of overt sexism in America; instead, research provides ways to help people who consciously endorse gender equity to avoid implicit bias and better embody and enact their ideals.

Implicit Bias: Sexism as Cognitive Process

To clarify, explicit bias reflects the attitudes or beliefs that one knowingly endorses on a conscious level. In contrast, implicit bias is the bias in judgment and/or behavior that stems from cognitive processes operating on a level below conscious awareness and without intentional control (Staats, 2014). Implicit bias arises out of the human tendency for snap judgment.

Attribution theory

Everyone is a "cognitive miser"; people want to avoid thinking any more than necessary when making quick decisions (Fiske & Taylor, 1991). In doing so, people avoid "fact-checking" the "evidence" that supports their judgment or decision. So for example, instead of having a *conscious reason* for an assessment (I promote one person over another based on data from an objective performance metric), an *implicit association* is made (I unknowingly promote one person over another because one candidate shares a more similar, sex, race, or cultural identity with me).

Everyone is susceptible to implicit biases (Rutland, Cameron, Milne, & McGeorge, 2005), and from a young age, children develop biased associations directly from authority figures and indirectly through observation (Castelli, Zogmaister, & Tomelleri, 2009; Kang, 2012) and media exposure (Dasgupta, 2013). As adults, implicit biases, which encompass both benevolent and unfavorable assessments, are activated involuntarily and without an individual's awareness or intentional control (Blair, 2002; Rudman, 2004). Because implicit associations arise outside of conscious awareness, they do not necessarily align with an individual's declared beliefs or even the stances they would explicitly endorse (Graham & Lowery, 2004; Greenwald & Krieger, 2006; Reskin, 2005). Emotionally, people generally associate bias or prejudice with hostility or antipathy towards an out-group member. However, research suggests that episodes of implicit bias are accompanied by feelings of fear, anxiety, a sense of being startled, and discomfort, rather than emotions such as anger, hostility, or a sense of disapproval (Dovidio et al., 1997; Dunton & Fazio, 1997).

The good news is that while implicit biases are deeply rooted and largely unconscious, they are nonetheless malleable and manageable when brought to awareness. Through counter-bias training, the implicit associations people form can be gradually unlearned and replaced with new mental associations (Blair, 2002; Blair, Ma, & Lenton, 2001; Dasgupta, 2013; Kang & Lane, 2010; Roos, Lebrecht, Tanaka, & Tarr, 2013). Research also suggests that making sense of personal accountability conscious (i.e., to imagine being called upon to justify one's attitude or actions) can decrease the influence of bias (Reskin, 2000, 2005). Similarly, taking the perspective of others and considering contrasting viewpoints have shown promise in reducing automatic biases (Benforado & Hanson, 2008).

Benevolent Bias: Kindly and Corrosive Traditions

The concept of benevolent sexism describes the implicit view that women are emotionally warm but incompetent. In contrast to the open hostility of most overt sexism, benevolent sexism appears positive on the surface but still furthers patronizing beliefs about women (Barreto et al., 2010). Glick and Fiske (1996, 2001) identify three components of benevolent sexism:

protective paternalism (i.e., the belief that women should be protected by men), complementary gender differentiation (i.e., the belief that women have typically social and domestic qualities that few men possess), and heterosexual intimacy (i.e., the belief that women fulfill men's romantic needs).

Like hostile sexism, benevolent sexism relies on gender stereotypes but differs in the way the stereotypes are communicated (Glick & Fiske, 2001). Benevolent sexism often takes the form of well-intentioned, paternalistic concern or awkward compliments that exaggerate the warmth or relational skills of women while devaluing their competence and leadership potential (Bosson et al., 2010). Cal's backhanded compliment to Pat in the previous scenario is a good example.

Bosson and her colleagues (2010) found that acts of benevolent sexism are just as emotionally corrosive to women as acts of hostile sexism. Female participants recalling personal incidents of hostile or benevolent sexism reported experiencing similar levels of anger, sadness, and fear in response to the sexist act, and a similar length of time to recover emotionally from the incident. Despite this, women reporting experiences of benevolent sexism were more likely to refrain from discussing their experiences out of a belief that others might not understand their distress. Tellingly, both men and women rated hostile sexism as more damaging and longer lasting than benevolent sexism. Additional research has suggested that exposure to benevolent sexism leads women to unwittingly confirm gender stereotypes to a greater extent than exposure to hostile sexism (Jost & Kay, 2005) and alters their self-perception in ways that impair their leadership and career-related aspirations (Dardenne, Dumont, & Bollier, 2007).

TWO STRATEGIES FOR RESPONDING TO IMPLICIT AND BENEVOLENT BIAS

Confronting a team member's biased behavior can easily escalate into a dysfunctional conflict when defenses arise and lead a person to feel personally attacked or critiqued. It is crucial for leaders to mentally and conversationally frame bias in a way that allows them to critique the behavior while still supporting the person. Research on implicit bias and benevolent sexism suggests important mental strategies for doing this: (a) detach the bias and the behavior from the actor and avoid attributing conscious motives to their actions; and (b) when discussing the bias with a team member, treat implicit or benevolent bias as the social product or cognitive error that it is rather than as a personality trait or character flaw.

The difficulty of identifying and describing implicit bias and benevolent sexism requires savvy communication skills. The next section discusses interpersonal communication as a means of confronting biased behavior, focusing on two useful concepts. The first, facework theory, describes the universal rules for managing self-image (both our own and others') during tense situations. The second, interpersonal projection, identifies the process in which difficult emotions from the past exacerbate and escalate conflicts in the present.

Interpersonal Communication

This section focuses on interpersonal communication as a context for interventions to correct biased behavior within organizations. Fundamentally, interpersonal communication involves a verbal and nonverbal interaction between two or more people who share a sense of connection or interdependence, and an ongoing relationship (Adler, Rosenfeld, & Proctor, 2012). Important aspects of interpersonal communication are the content and relational dimensions of messages that people communicate (Fisher, 1979). While the content dimension of a conversation between friends may involve talking about what was on TV last night, the relational dimension of their messages may involve emotional support, a bid for closeness, or a chance to laugh together. In other words, the content of an interpersonal message only represents the surface communication, and the relational messages create, manage, and maintain the relationship.

The cultural and gender-based norms that structure interpersonal communication for men and women often lead to gender inequity regarding communication styles. Stereotypical expectations tend to restrict women's interactional behaviors in leadership positions and to allow men a wider variety of styles. For example, while men are allowed a more explicitly powerful style of communication, women are expected to use more tentative language (i.e., hedges, softeners, and tag questions) and a more accommodating and less powerful style of communication (Carli, 1990; Hannah & Murachver, 1999). Such cultural sanctions against women present a further challenge for women leaders confronting male and female team members about often-unacknowledged sexist communication. These kinds of interactions require a greater level of emotional awareness and skill. This next section discusses the concept of facework as both a foundation of face-to-face interpersonal communication and a sophisticated system of interpersonal skills that are crucial for giving advice and corrections effectively.

Facework and Interpersonal Communication

A central force in any face-to-face interaction is the need to maintain and defend a positive social-image, or sense of face (Goffman, 1967). Cupach and Metts (1994) define face as:

the conception of self that each person displays in particular interactions with others. . . . When a person interacts with another, he or she tacitly presents a conception of who he or she is in that encounter and seeks confirmation for that conception. . . . The individual offers an identity that he or she wants to assume and wants others to accept. (p. 3)

Everyone performs these social identities, and successfully upholding face for oneself and others requires skillful communication (Goldsmith, 1999, 2000; Metts, 2000; Zhang, Cao, & Grigoriou, 2011). Across cultures, effective facework for oneself and others is necessary if people are to successfully cooperate, demonstrate respect, appear likeable and competent, and engage others who are emotionally distraught (Baumeister, 1998; Oetzel et al., 2003; Oetzel, Meares, Myers, & Lara, 2003; Oetzel & Ting-Toomey, 2003; Ting-Toomey, 2004, 2005).

Researchers generally identify two universal face needs that are met in different ways across cultures: *autonomy*, the desire to have one's rights respected, unimpeded, or uninvaded (Zhang & Stafford, 2008), and *validation*, the sense that one is understood and appreciated by others (Lim & Bowers, 1991). Together, these desires motivate all face needs. When a listener evaluates a message as face threatening, that listener believes that the speaker has failed to satisfy the listener's needs for autonomy, validation, or both (Cupach & Metts, 1994).

Advice and Face

Whenever leaders feel it important to correct a team member's biased behavior, they present a face threat to the offending person's sense of autonomy and potentially to their need for validation. While the offending party's conduct may merit their face loss, face threats still undermine a leader's advice and ability to offer correctives (Goldsmith, 2000). When leaders include face-saving messages in their efforts to correct biased behavior and hold team members accountable, their messages are more likely to be interpreted successfully.

Face theory argues that needing and receiving advice is inherently face threatening: Advice calls into questions the recipient's sense of value and competence, and it limits the autonomy and range of their future behavior (Feng, 2014). Giving advice threatens face when recipients perceive advice as "butting in" and constraining autonomy, and when people interpret advice as implying ignorance or incompetence (Goldsmith, 1999, 2000; Goldsmith & MacGeorge, 2000).

In contrast, effective communication functions to mitigate threats posed to recipients' face. A body of research in face-saving advising provides a useful blueprint for giving advice effectively. Foremost is the distinction that advice designed to support the recipient's face and assess specific problems and behaviors is perceived as more effective than blunt advice without any face support. Likewise, the least effective advice is language that further threatens the target person's face in ways that are actively challenging and demeaning through insults or hostility (Feng, 2015; MacGeorge, Lichtman, & Pressey, 2002; MacGeorge, Feng, & Thompson, 2008).

Face-Saving Strategies for Advice

Further unpacking the relevant research reveals several important strategies for giving advice:

1. Include choices with your advice; recipients strongly prefer advice with multiple options for response and multiple outcomes that signify success (MacGeorge et al., 2008). Such messages re-inscribe personal control and efficacy into a recipient's responses (Albrecht & Goldsmith, 2003).

2. Make sure to support the receiver's self-image and sense of face. Effective advice includes messages supporting the recipient's identity and an understanding of the challenges or struggles that a recipient may be facing (Goldsmith, 2004; MacGeorge et al., 2016).

3. Use personal narratives and accounts of success as evidence to take your advice; Personalized narratives increase perceptions of an advisors' credibility and similarity with the recipient (Wang, Walther, Pingree, & Hakwins, 2008).

4. Recipients value the explanations behind successful advice and prefer hearing about the positive consequences of taking it. Advice should include reasons why a solution will work and why the advisor thinks the recipient can carry it out. Advisors need to visualize how the recipient can accomplish a change and what the outcome may look like (MacGeorge et al., 2016).

5. Finally, recipients prefer advice that features normative adaptiveness, the sense that the advice is specific and tailored to meet their problem (MacGeorge, Feng, & Thompson, 2008).

Face threats stem from the fear of being shamed (Goffman, 1967). In a similar sense, interpersonal projections, which often stem from childhood shaming, are also activated in the face of real and perceived threats to one's face (Mortenson, 2009). Hence, confronting a team member over biased communicative behavior creates a tense situation at best and an openly hostile one at worst. Whenever possible, it is important to emotionally prepare for a confrontation by separating feelings of past anger or shame from the needs of the present moment (Mortenson, 2013; Mortenson, Luchey, & Creasy, 2015).

Interpersonal Projection and Destructive Confrontation

Research identifies those communication strategies that are productive and destructive and shows how a person's psychological attributions of the situation and of the other person influence their choice of communication during interpersonal confrontations (Fincham & Bradbury, 1993; Gurman, 2002; Sillars, 1981, 1998; Sillars, Roberts, Leonard, & Dun, 2000). Sillars (1981) first showed that attributing blame to the other person and perceiving the confrontation as more stable (and unchangeable) rather than situational (and evolving) results in emotional arousal, destructive communication, unresolved issues, and lower relationship satisfaction. However, when individuals strategically use communication to defuse negative emotions and attributions, they are more likely to share responsibility for the situation with their partners, to listen and share information, and to develop compromises that move from confrontation to cooperation (Sillars et al., 2000; Sillars & Wilmot, 1994).

Further, research in psychiatry reveals that the destructive attributions in conflict actually function as primitive emotional-defense mechanisms that are activated when an individual becomes emotionally overwhelmed (Conte & Plutchik, 1993; Cramer, 2006; Plutchik, 1995). Emotional arousal is a key factor of behavioral mistakes in confrontation, and even skilled communicators can have their defenses triggered or "set off" and fall into defensive and dysfunctional attributions and behaviors (Cramer, 2006; Geyer, 2012; Hollis, 2008; Mortenson, 2013).

Interpersonal Projection

One particular defense mechanism, interpersonal projection (IP), plays a decisive role in exacerbating confrontations (Geyer, 2012; Mortenson, 2007). IP is a mental safeguard that protects self-esteem against threatening thoughts and feelings that generate excessive anxiety (Conte, Plutchik, & Draguns, 2004; Cramer 2006). IP operates by unconsciously disavowing negative thoughts, feelings, or beliefs about the self that cause high levels of anxiety and then attributing them to another person (Conte & Apter, 1995; Plutchik, 1995). The person doing the projecting is unaware of the shift that has taken place and thus experiences an external threat, unaware of its internal origin. Projection can be seen as the externalization of a negative trait onto another person in order to defend one's self-esteem (Cramer, 1998).

IP originates in childhood as part of early cognitive development and functions as a defense against overwhelming experiences. A good example of interpersonal projection is the cycle of the victim and the bully: Children who are bullied at home by parents or older siblings often deny their own powerlessness and victimhood by projecting it onto other more vulnerable children and then bullying them. When bullies see a weak or vulnerable child, it triggers their own feelings of fear and powerlessness and activates the defense. They project their own weakness onto a target child. Having transformed their fear into aggression, bullies aggress on weaker children and further disavow their own feelings of powerlessness.

The victims of childhood bullying may not turn into childhood bullies themselves, but as adults, they are more likely to be triggered by adult acts of bullying, even when they are only bystanders or observers. In the same manner, the triggered victim transforms old fear into new aggression and "bullies" the bully with the same lack of skill or consciousness (Hollis, 2008; Mortenson, 2007; Patterson, 1976). Given the hostility and bullying style of overt sexism, it is reasonable to assume that girls who have suffered the demeaning shame of sexism in their past are also likely to be triggered into unskillful aggression by incidents of bias during adulthood.

Defusing Defenses: Strategies for Identifying Projections

When people become cognizant of the triggers and "contents" of their projections, they are able to defuse their defensive attributions and feelings and enact more mindful and skillful responses (Hollis, 2008; Richo, 2008, 2011). It is a relatively straightforward process of reflection, of identifying one's projections and the types of people one targets for projection. With that in mind, this next section summarizes three strategies developed as part of an award-winning, co-curricular leadership program[1] for catching and defusing one's interpersonal projections (Mortenson, 2013; Mortenson et al., 2015).

Identifying Projections of Self-Judgment

One way to raise awareness of projection is to realize that we project self-judgment onto others and then falsely accuse them of critiquing us. We often attribute personal motive and judgment to the unskilled behavior of others toward us; we decide people are dismissive with us *because* they think we are flakey or incompetent instead of simply being busy or overwhelmed themselves (Hollis, 2008; Richo, 2011). We decide people are short with us *because* they look down on us, not because they are having a bad day. Catching self-judgment reigns in unnecessary anger and shows us glimpses of what we fear in ourselves and project onto others. Catching self-judgment may involve asking yourself: Where is the evidence that he or she feels this way?

ot feared? ↑

Identifying Projections of Critique

A useful strategy for understanding how we project our own flaws onto others is to identify people who bother or irritate us but never actually cross a line with us; they just "get under our skin." Often such people mirror some denied aspect of our own personality, such as arrogance, greed, incompetence, or laziness (Cramer, 2006). For example, we may see a colleague display a moment of bias or prejudice in a meeting; their display activates the anxiety (and potential shame) we have around our own biases. We then dispel these unpleasant self-feelings by turning them into anger and aggressive judgment towards our target person. By projecting our "bigot" onto a colleague, we make our target person doubly biased: now that individual possesses both his/her bias and ours. Further, in the future, we feel greater license to treat that individual poorly. Projection obscures our ability to relate to people objectively because we always see them as worse than they actually are (Cramer, 1998; Hollis, 2008).

In contrast, if we can recognize and "own" our personal capacity for bias instead of denying and projecting it onto others, we may realize, "My colleague is acting like a total bigot right now, and sometimes I have prejudiced thoughts and moments as well." Taking this strategy further entails first listing to all the "jerks" we put up with in life and all their negative traits, then assessing our own capacity for such traits, as well as the moments we have embodied the same negative traits. In short, owning what set us off helps us control our reactions. TRUE

Separating the Past From the Present

A projection occurs when pain from the past is triggered and erupts into the present situation, whether it is warranted or not (Richo, 2008). If confronting biased behavior triggers strong feelings of anxiety or aggression, leaders should remember that such feelings are part of the past and try to separate them from the present. One method a leader can use to defuse anxiety/aggression around personal experiences with discrimination is to "name and claim" the emotion (i.e., when, where, and from whom did the anxiety or aggression originate?) and put it into a proper historical context rather than let past emotions project onto and influence the present moment. It is also useful to remind one's self that unlike in the past, one presently has the resources and ability to deal with biased behavior with skill and confidence.

ENGAGING STRATEGIC COMMUNICATION WITHIN CONFRONTATION: BUILDING COLLABORATION

Effective leaders of all genders should recognize the value of confrontation as an opportunity to build collaboration with another person. Importantly,

① Antic offense (erroneous offense)
② Descr poss. offense + reassure good intent
③ Descr intent.
↳ establish mutual goals

60 ▪ S. MORTENSON

collaboration involves both people pooling individual needs and goals toward a common goal. It requires assertive communication and cooperation to achieve a better solution than either individual could have achieved alone. This next section summarizes work from Patterson, Grenny, McMillan, and Switzler's (2005) compelling work on building collaboration and confrontation with safety.

Briefly, *confronting with safety* begins by defusing the other person's fears and establishing mutual respect. Next, leaders speak toward mutual purpose and tell their story and what they want while emphasizing the mutual goals they share with the other person. Finally, the leader should ask the other person a question that invites collaborative action (Patterson et al., 2005). These next sections further describe the process of confronting with safety.

Contrasting

Leaders should initiate confrontation with a strategy called *contrasting*. This is an effective way of defusing another person's defensiveness (and projections) when a leader has to confront or correct a subordinate over sexist behaviors. First, anticipate how the other might erroneously take offense when presented with advice that is contrary to their beliefs or self-image. Second, describe this possible offense and assure the target person this is not what is intended. Third, explain exactly what is intended by initiating the confrontation (Patterson et al., 2005).

Share Your Story

Next, leaders need to share their story. Tell the target person what leaders want and how it will meet a common purpose that they share with that person. It is important to tell the story without inducing blame or fear: Respectfully state the problem and how it is related to a specific mutual purpose (Senge, 1990).

Ask a Question

Finally, leaders should try to finish with a question: As leaders finish their description of the problem, they should invite their subordinate to participate in the solution. Doing so injects a sense of choice into the intervention and invites further collaboration.

Strategies such as contrasting, working toward mutual purpose, and asking questions that invite collaboration, function to defuse defenses and produce a psychologically safer space to address a team member's biased behavior. When Janet skillfully confronted Cal for attaching gender and age to Pat's accomplishments, she first assured Cal that she knew he valued women and was not a bigot. Then she shared her concerns for Pat and her understanding of implicit bias. She told her story and connected her concerns to mutually shared values and purpose. Janet also supported Cal's sense of face by avoiding "you" statements (which can sound accusing) in favor of "we" statements (which assume shared responsibility). She infused both a sense of choice and collaboration by asking a question at the end. Here is another scenario in which Janet uses facework and confronting with safety to help identify and correct Cal's biased behaviors:

> **Janet:** Hi, Cal, I wanted to talk to you about who you're sending to do the presentation for the East Office.
>
> **Cal:** I was going to send Blake and Dan.
>
> **Janet:** But not Pat? She did the lion's share of the analysis....
>
> **Cal:** I know, and she did a great job, it's just—well, you know—the East Office has some pretty rough characters; I didn't want to put her through all that.
>
> **Janet:** I see. You know, I can tell you have good intentions here; you're trying to shield Pat from some of the harsher personnel. I understand that, and I know you'd never consciously pass her over or shut her out of anything important, but—at the same time, if Pat is going to grow professionally and take on more leadership responsibilities, she needs to show that she can handle situations like this. If we take her out of those situations, we could rob her of an opportunity to show what she is made of. So—your concern might help her avoid something unpleasant in the short term, but it may end up impairing her professional growth in the long run. I know you respect and appreciate her and that you don't want that.
>
> **Cal:** No, I really don't. I guess I thought I was doing her a favor.
>
> **Janet:** I can see that—and that's sort of the issue. We don't really feel the need to step in and protect Blake or Dan because they're both guys, but because Pat is a young woman, we assume she needs protection. It's an unconscious, cultural thing, but we still have to catch ourselves or it will end up hurting Pat's career. The problem is if my biases are well intended, I don't see how I am impairing a person's professional growth. We have to assume Pat's as tough as the guys here and can handle the same challenges, or she won't live up to her career potential. So can I take moment here and tell you a bit more about benevolent forms of bias?

CONCLUSION

Closing the leadership gap requires that leaders exercise the communication skills that describe implicit or benevolently biased behaviors when they occur among team members. When women effectively confront bias, they not only feel an increase in competency, self-esteem, and empowerment, they also discourage biased behaviors in individuals and bystanders.

This chapter presents a series of cognitive and communicative strategies to help women in leadership effectively confront implicit or benevolently biased behaviors in teammates. This chapter suggested the following cognitive strategies:

1. Mentally separate the act from the actor. Implicit and benevolently biased behaviors are often unconscious and/or well-meaning. They are errors in cognition or social norms, but not character flaws or reasons to punish or embarrass a team member.
2. Separate one's own anger and pain regarding past discriminatory experiences from the present situation. Understand and identify one's emotional triggers and interpersonal projections around biased behaviors and defuse them before confronting a team member on their biased behavior.

This chapter also suggested a number of interpersonal communication strategies:

1. Discuss implicit and benevolent bias as flaws in human cognition or cultural norms rather than as conscious acts of aggression or injustice.
2. Protect the "social face" of the perpetrator; use "I" or "we" statements instead of "you," show understanding of their good intentions and the challenge they face, and put choices into any advice given.
3. Confront a team member with safety; use contrasting to defuse any defensive reactions they may have, tell your story of mutual purpose without blaming or indicting the perpetrator, and finish your story with a question that invites collaboration.

When their self-awareness is coupled with strategic communication, leaders have the means to manage both their own feelings and to defuse another's defensive behaviors when identifying, advising, and correcting biased behavior and conduct.

NOTE

1. The Blue Hen Leadership Program at the University of Delaware

REFERENCES

Adler, R. B., Rosenfeld, L. B., & Proctor II, R. F. (2012). *Interplay: The process of interpersonal communication* (12th ed.). New York, NY: Oxford University Press.

Barreto, M., Ellemers, N., Piebinga, L., & Moya, M. (2010). How nice of us and how dumb of me: The effect of exposure to benevolent sexism on women's task and relational self-descriptions. *Sex Roles, 62*(7), 532–544. doi:10.1007/s11199-009-9699-0

Baumeister, R. F. (1998). The self. In D. T. Gilbert, S. T. Fiske, G. Lindzey (Eds.), *The handbook of social psychology* (4th ed., Vol. 1, pp. 680–740). New York, NY: McGraw-Hill.

Becker, J. C., & Swim, J. K. (2012). Reducing endorsement of benevolent and modern sexist beliefs: Differential effects of addressing harm versus pervasiveness of benevolent sexism. *Social Psychology, 43*(3), 127–137. doi:10.1027/1864-9335/a000091

Benforado, A., & Hanson, J. (2008). The great attributional divide: How divergent views of human behavior are shaping legal policy. *Emory Law Journal, 57*(2), 311–408.

Blair, I. V. (2002). The malleability of automatic stereotypes and prejudice. *Personality and Social Psychology Review, 6*(3), 242–261.

Blair, I. V., Ma, J. E., & Lenton, A. P. (2001). Imaging stereotypes away: The moderation of implicit stereotypes through mental imagery. *Journal of Personality and Social Psychology, 81*(5), 828–841.

Bosson, J. K., Pinel, E. C., & Vandello, J. A. (2010). The emotional impact of ambivalent sexism: Forecasts versus real experiences. *Sex Roles, 62*(7), 520–531. doi:10.1007/s11199-009-9664-y

Carli, L. L. (1990). Gender, language, and influence. *Journal of Personality and Social Psychology, 59*(5), 41–951. doi:10.1037/0022-3514.59.5.941

Case, K. A., Iuzzini, J., & Hopkins, M. (2012). Systems of privilege: Intersections awareness, and applications. *Journal of Social Issues, 68*(1), 1–10. doi:10.1111/j.1540-4560.2011.01732.x

Case, K. A., Hensley, R., & Anderson, A. (2014). Reflecting on heterosexual and male privilege: Interventions to raise awareness. *Journal of Social Issues, 70*(4), 722–740. doi:10.1111/josi.12088

Castelli, L., Zogmaister, C., & Tomelleri, S. (2009). The transmission of racial attitudes within the family. *Developmental Psychology, 45*(2), 86–591. doi:0.1037/a0014619

Conte, H. R., & Apter, A. (1995). The life style index: A self-report measure of ego defenses. In H. R. Conte, & R. Plutchik (Eds.), *Ego defenses: Theory and measurement.* Einstein Psychiatry Publication (pp. 179–201). Oxford, England: John Wiley & Sons.

Conte, H. R., & Plutchik, R. (1993). The measurement of ego defenses in clinical research. In U. Hentschel, G. Smith, W. Ehlers, & J. G. Draguns (Eds.), *The concept of defense mechanisms in contemporary psychology: Theoretical, research, and clinical perspectives* (pp. 275–289). New York, NY: Springer-Verlag.

Conte, H. R., Plutchik, R., & Draguns, J. G. (2004). The measurement of ego defenses in clinical research. In U. Hentschel, G. Smith, J. G. Draguns, & W.

Ehlers (Eds.), *Defense mechanisms: Theoretical, research, and clinical perspectives* (pp. 393–414). Amsterdam: Elsevier.

Cramer, P. (1998). Coping and defense mechanisms: What's the difference? *Journal of Personality, 66*(6), 19–946. doi:10.1111/1467-6494.00037

Cramer, P. (2006). *Protecting the self: Defense mechanisms in action.* New York, NY: Guilford Press.

Cupach, W. R., & Metts, S. (1994). *Facework.* SAGE series on close relationships. Thousand Oaks, CA: SAGE.

Czopp, A. M., & Ashburn-Nardo, L. (2012). Interpersonal confrontations of prejudice. In D. W. Russell & C. A. Russell (Eds.), *The psychology of prejudice: Interdisciplinary perspectives on contemporary issues* (pp. 175–202). Psychology Research Press, Hauppauge, NY: Nova Science.

Czopp, A. M., Monteith, M. J., & Mark, A. Y. (2006). Standing up for a change: Reducing bias through interpersonal confrontation. *Journal of Personality and Social Psychology, 90*(5), 784–803. doi:10.1037/0022-3514.90.5.784

Dardenne, B., Dumont, M., & Bollier, T. (2007). Insidious dangers of benevolent sexism: Consequences for women's performance. *Journal of Personality and Social Psychology, 93*(5), 64–779. doi:10.1037/0022-3514.93.5.764

Dasgupta, N. (2013). Implicit attitudes and beliefs adapt to situations: A decade of research on the malleability of implicit prejudice, stereotypes, and the self-concept. *Advances in Experimental Social Psychology, 47*(7), 33–279. doi:10.1016/B978-0-12-407236-7.00005-X

Dovidio, J. F., Kawakami, K., Johnson, C., Johnson, B., & Howard, A. (1997). On the nature of prejudice: Automatic and controlled processes. *Journal of Experimental Social Psychology, 33*(5), 510–540.

Dunton, B. C., & Fazio, R. H. (1997). An individual difference measure of motivation to control prejudiced reactions. *Personality and Social Psychology Bulletin, 23*(3), 316–326. doi:10.1177/0146167297233009

Feng, B. (2014). When should advice be given? Assessing the role of sequential placement of advice in supportive interactions in two cultures. *Communication Research, 41*(7), 913–934. doi:10.1177/0093650212456203

Feng, H. (2015). Understanding cultural variations in giving advice among Americans and Chinese. *Communication Research, 42*(8), 143–1167. doi:10.1177/0093650213486668

Fincham, F. D., & Bradbury, T. N. (1993). Marital satisfaction, depression, and attributions: A longitudinal analysis. *Journal of Personality and Social Psychology, 64*, 442–452.

Fisher, B. A. (1979). Content and relationship dimensions of communication in decision-making groups. *Communication Quarterly, 27*(4), 3–11. doi:10.1080/01463377909369345

Fiske, S. T., & Taylor, S. E. (1991). *Social cognition* (2nd ed.). New York, NY: McGraw Hill.

Gervais, S. J., Hillard, A. L., & Vescio, T. K. (2010). Confronting sexism: The role of relationship orientation and gender. *Sex Roles, 63*, 463–474. doi:10.1007/s11199-010-9838-7

Geyer, C. D. (2012). *Understanding destructive conflict: The role of projection in attribution bias and selection of conflict strategies in a study of college roommates.* (Unpublished master's thesis). University of Delaware, Newark, DE. Retrieved from University of Delaware Online library, http://udspace.udel.edu/handle/19716/12884

Glick, P., & Fiske, S. T. (1996). The ambivalent sexism inventory: Differentiating hostile and benevolent sexism. *Journal of Personality and Social Psychology, 70*(3), 491–512. doi:10.1037/0022-3514.70.3.491

Glick, P., & Fiske, S. T. (2001). An ambivalent alliance: Hostile and benevolent sexism as complementary justifications for gender inequality. *American Psychologist, 56*(2), 109–118. doi:10.1037/0003-066X.56.2.109

Goffman E. (1967). *Interaction ritual: Essays on face-to-face behavior.* New York, NY: Anchor Books.

Goldsmith, D. J. (1999). Content-based resources for giving face sensitive advice in troubles talk episodes. *Research on Language and Social Interaction, 32*(3) 303–336. doi:10.1207/S15327973rls3204_1

Goldsmith, D. J. (2000). Soliciting advice: The role of sequential placement in mitigating face threat. *Communication Monographs, 67*(1), 1–19.

Goldsmith, D. J., & MacGeorge, E. L. (2000). The impact of politeness and relationship on perceived quality of advice about a problem. *Human Communication Research, 26*(2), 234–263. doi:10.1111/j.1468-2958.2000.tb00757.x

Good, J. J., & Rudman, L. A. (2010). When female applicants meet sexist interviewers: The costs of being a target of benevolent sexism. *Sex Roles, 62*(7–8), 481–493. doi:10.1007/s11199-009-9685-6

Graham, S., & Lowery, B. S. (2004). Priming unconscious racial stereotypes about adolescent offenders. *Law and Human Behavior, 28*(5), 483–504. doi:0147-7307/04/1000-0483/1

Greenwald, A. G., & Krieger, L. H. (2006). Implicit bias: Scientific foundations. *California Law Review, 94*(4), 945–967.

Greenwald, A. G., Banaji, M. R., Rudman, L. A., Farnham, S. D., Nosek, B. A., & Mellott, D. S. (2002). A unified theory of implicit attitudes, stereotypes, self-esteem, and self-concept. *Psychological Review, 109*, 3–25. doi:10.1037//0033-295X.109.1.3

Gurman, A. S. (2002). Brief integrative marital therapy: A depth-behavioral approach. In A. S. Gurman, & N. S. Jacobson (Eds.), *Clinical handbook of couple therapy* (pp. 180–220). New York, NY: The Guilford Pres.

Hannah, A., & Murachver, T. (1999). Gender and conversational style as predictors of conversational behavior. *Journal of Language and Social Psychology, 18*(2), 153–174. doi:10.1177/0261927X99018002002

Hollis, J. (2008). *Why good people do bad things: Understanding our darker selves.* New York, NY: Gotham Books.

Hyers, L. L. (2007). Resisting prejudice every day: Exploring women's assertive responses to anti-Black racism, anti-Semitism, heterosexism, and sexism. *Sex Roles, 56*(1), 1–12. doi:10.1007/s11199- 006-9142-8

Jost, J. T., & Kay, A. C. (2005). Exposure to benevolent sexism and complementary gender stereotypes: consequences for specific and diffuse forms of system justification. *Journal of Personality and Social Psychology, 88*(3), 498–509. doi:10.1037/0022-3514.88.3.498

Kaiser, C. R., & Miller, C. T. (2004). A stress and coping perspective on confronting sexism. *Psychology of Women Quarterly, 2*(1), 168–178. doi:10.1111/j.1471 -6402.2004.00133.x

Kang, J. (2012). Communications law: Bits of bias. In J. D. Levinson & R. J. Smith (Eds.), *Implicit racial bias across the law* (pp. 132–145). Cambridge, MA: Cambridge University Press.

Kang, J., & Lane, K. (2010). Seeing through colorblindness: Implicit bias and the law. *UCLA Law Review, 58*(2), 465–520.

Lim, T. S., & Bowers, J. W., (1991). Facework, solidarity, approbation, and tact. *Human Communication Research, 17*(3), 415–450. doi:10.1111/j.1468-2958.1991. tb00239.x

MacGeorge, E. L., Feng, B., & Thompson, E. R. (2008). "Good" and "bad" advice: How to advise more effectively. In M. T. Motley (Ed.), *Studies in applied interpersonal communication* (pp. 145–164). Thousand Oaks, CA: SAGE.

MacGeorge, E. L., Guntzviller, L. M., Bailey, L., Brisini, K., Salmon, S., Severen, K., Cummings, R. (2016). The influence of emotional support quality on advice evaluation and outcomes. *Communication Quarterly, 62*(1), 1–17. doi:10.1080/ 01463373.2016.1176945

MacGeorge, E. L., Lichtman, R. M., & Pressey, L. C. (2002). The evaluation of advice in supportive interactions: Facework and contextual factors. *Human Communication Research, 28,* 451–463. doi:10.1111/j.1468-2958.2002.tb00815.x

McIntosh, P. (2012). Reflections and future directions for privilege studies. *Journal of Social Issues, 68*(1), 194–206. doi:10.1111/j.1540-4560.2011.01744.x

Metts, S. (2000). Face and facework: Implications for the study of personal relationships. In K. Dindia & S. Duck (Eds.), *Communication and personal relationships* (pp. 77–93). Chichester, England: John Wiley & Sons.

Mortenson, S. T. (2007). Raising the question #7: Should we teach personal transformation as a part of interpersonal communication? If so, how is it done? *Communication Education, 56*(3) 401–409. doi:10.1080/03634520701349198

Mortenson, S. T. (2009). Interpersonal trust and social skill in seeking social support among Chinese and Americans. *Communication Research, 36*(1), 32–53. doi:10.1177/0093650208326460

Mortenson, S. (2013, November). *Transformative education in the interpersonal classroom.* Paper presented at the National Communication Associations Conference, Washington D.C.

Mortenson, S., Luchey S., & Creasy M. (2015, July). *When the rubber hits the road: Tools and challenges for student leaders.* Invited Presentation at the Association of Leadership Educators Conference, Washington D.C.

Nosek, B. A., Greenwald, A. G., & Banaji, M. R. (2007). The implicit association test at age 7: A methodological and conceptual review. In J. A. Bargh (Ed.), *Social psychology and the unconscious: The automaticity of higher mental processes* (pp. 265–292). New York, NY: Psychology Press.

Oetzel, J., Meares, M., Myers, K., & Lara, E. (2003). Interpersonal conflict in organizations: Explaining conflict styles via race-negotiation theory. *Communication Research Reports, 20*(1), 106–115. doi:10.1080/08824090309388806

Oetzel, J., & Ting-Toomey, S. (2003). Face concerns in interpersonal conflict: A cross-cultural empirical test of the face negotiation theory. *Communication Research, 30*(6), 599–624. doi:10.1177/0093650203257841

Oetzel, J., Ting-Toomey, S., Chew-Sanchez, M., I., Harris, R., Wilcox, R., & Stumpf, S. (2003). Face and facework in conflicts with parents and siblings: A cross-cultural comparison of Germans, Japanese, Mexicans, and U.S. Americans. *Journal of Family Communication, 32*(1), 67–93. doi:10.1207/S15327698JFC0302_01

Parker, K., Menasce Horowitz, J., Wang, W., & Brown, A. (2015, January 14). Women and leadership: Public says women equally qualified but barriers persist. *Pew Research Center.* Retrieved from http://www.pewsocialtrends.org/2015/01/14/women-and-leadership/

Patterson, G. R. (1976). The aggressive child: Victim and architect of a coercive system. In E. J. Mash, L. A. Hamerlynck, & L. C. Handy (Eds.), *Behavior modification and families: Theory and research* (Vol. 1, pp. 267–316). New York, NY: Brunner/Mazel.

Patterson, K., Grenny, K., McMillan, J., Switzler, R. (2005). *Crucial confrontations: Tools for resolving broken promises, violated expectations, and bad behavior.* New York, NY: McGraw-Hill.

Plutchik, R. (1995). A theory of ego defenses. In H. R. Conte, & R. Plutchik (Eds.), *Ego defenses: Theory and measurement. Einstein psychiatry series.* (pp. 13–37). New York, NY: John Wiley & Sons.

Rasinski, H. M., & Czopp, A. M. (2010). The effect of target status on witnesses' reactions to confrontations of bias. *Basic and Applied Social Psychology, 32,* 8–16. doi: 10.1080/01973530903539754.

Reskin, B. F. (2000). The proximate causes of employment discrimination. *Contemporary Sociology, 29*(2), 319–328.

Reskin, B. (2005). Unconsciousness raising. *Regional Review, 14*(3), 32–37.

Richo, D. (2008) *When the past is present: Healing the emotional wounds that sabotage our relationships.* Boston, MA: Shambala.

Richo, D. (2011) *Daring to trust: Opening ourselves to real love and intimacy.* Boston, MA: Shambala.

Roos, L. E., Lebrecht, S., Tanaka, J. W., & Tarr, M. J. (2013). Can singular examples change implicit attitudes in the real-world? *Frontiers in Psychology, 4*(2). Retrieved from http://journal.frontiersin.org/article/10.3389/fpsyg.2013.00594/full. doi:10.3389/fpsyg.2013.00594

Rudman, L. A. (2004). Sources of implicit attitudes. *Current Directions in Psychological Science, 13*(1), 79–82. doi:10.1111/j.0963-7214.2004.00279.x

Rutland, A., Cameron, L., Milne, A., & McGeorge, P. (2005). Social norms and self-presentation: Children's implicit and explicit intergroup attitudes. *Child Development, 76*(5), 451–466. doi:10.1111/j.1467-8624.2005.00856.x

Senge, P. M. (1990). *The fifth discipline: The art and practice of the learning organization.* New York, NY: Doubleday/Currency.

Shields, S. A., Zawadzki, M. J., & Johnson, R. N. (2011). The impact of the workshop activity for gender equity simulation in the academy (WAGES–Academic) in demonstrating cumulative effects of gender bias. *Journal of Diversity in Higher Education, 4*(2), 120–129. doi:10.1037/a0022953

Sillars, A. L. (1981). Attributions and interpersonal conflict resolution. In J. H. Harvey, W. Ickes, & R. F. Kidd (Eds.), *New directions in attribution research* (Vol. 3, pp. 279–305). Hillsdale, NJ: Lawrence Erlbaum.

Sillars, A. L. (1998). (Mis)understanding. In B. H. Spitzberg & W. R. Cupach (Eds.), *The dark side of close relationships* (pp. 73–102). Mahwah, NJ: Lawrence Erlbaum.

Sillars, A. L., Roberts, L. J., Leonard, K. E., & Dun, T. (2000). Cognition during marital conflict: The relationship of thought and talk. *Journal of Social and Personal Relationships, 17,* 479–502. doi:10.1177/0265407500174002

Sillars, A. L., & Wilmot, W. W. (1994). Communication strategies in conflict and mediation. In J. A. Daly & J. M. Wiemann (Eds.), *Strategic interpersonal communication* (pp. 163–190). Hillsdale, NJ: Lawrence Erlbaum.

Staats, C. (2014). State of the science: Implicit bias review 2014, Kirwan Institute for the Study of Race and Ethnicity, The Ohio State University. Retrieved from http://www.kirwaninstitute.osu.edu/wp-content/uploads/2014/03/2014-implicit-bias.pdf

Swim, J. K., & Hyers, L. L. (1999). Excuse me—What did you just say?! Women's public and private responses to sexist remarks. *Journal of Experimental Social Psychology, 35*(1), 68–88. doi:10.1006/jesp.1998.1370

Swim, J. K., & Thomas, M. A. (2006). Responding to everyday discrimination: A synthesis of research on goal directed, self-regulatory coping behaviors. In S. Lavin & C. Van Laar (Ed.), *The Claremont Symposium on applied social psychology* (pp. 105–126). Mahwah, New Jersey: Erlbaum.

Ting-Toomey, S. (2004). Translating conflict face-negotiation theory into practice. In D. R. Landis, J. M. Bennett, & M. J. Bennett, *Handbook of intercultural training* (pp. 217–248). Thousand Oaks, CA: SAGE.

Ting-Toomey, S. (2005) The matrix of face: An updated face-negotiation theory. In W.B. Gudykunst (Ed.), *Theorizing about intercultural communication* (pp. 71–92). Thousand Oaks, CA: SAGE.

Wang, Z., Walther, J. B., Pingree, S., & Hawkins, R. P. (2008). Health information, credibility, homophily, and influence via the internet: Web sites versus discussion groups. *Health Communication, 23*(4), 358–368. doi:10.1080/10410230802229738

World Health Organization. (2016). Gender. Retrieved from http://www.who.int/gender-equity-rights/understanding/gender-definition/en/

Zhang, X., Cao, Q., & Grigoriou, N. (2011). Consciousness of social face: The development and validation of a scale measuring desire to gain face versus fear of losing face. *The Journal of Social Psychology, 151*(2), 129–141. doi:10.1080/00224540903366669

Zhang, S., & Stafford, L. (2008). Perceived face threat of honest but hurtful evaluative messages in romantic relationships. *Western Journal of Communication, 72*(1), 9–39. doi:10.1080/10570310701828628

[Handwritten margin notes:]

CEO women in the EU discussing English and power

—the struggle to be heard

AGENCY

—Suggestion: use bricks or counters to show who in meetings have power over turn, topic, and directness (pp 84-85)

CHAPTER 5

TALKING POWER

Women's Experiences of Workplace Conversations

Anne Murphy
Leiden University
Lancaster University, UK

This chapter explores women's experiences of power and influence in workplace conversation. Gendered norms are woven into the patterns of mundane everyday workplace interaction; they shape people's choices about what is appropriate, and they influence the ways in which power and authority are expressed. Therefore, to explore the connections between gender, communication, and the leadership gap, the chapter examines the relationship between women's leadership and the conversational detail of how power is "talked" into place in everyday interactions. Working with data gathered during a series of short, women-only development programs dealing explicitly with the expression of power in corporate settings, the chapter's aim is to contribute to understandings of women's experience of agency in professional settings and to explore ways in which theoretical insights can be translated into leadership development practices. This

Gender, Communication, and the Leadership Gap, pages 69–88
Copyright © 2017 by Information Age Publishing
All rights of reproduction in any form reserved.

chapter combines organization studies and discourse studies perspectives to reveal how patterns of spoken interaction in the workplace produce and reproduce gendered-power relations. This dual perspective frames two interconnected research questions:

1. How do women experience power, influence, and inclusion in workplace conversations?
2. Which discourse features shape the dynamics of power in spoken interaction in these settings?

The chapter focuses on the meanings women give to these concerns in their professional worlds and the ways in which they are expressed in terms of the dynamics of power in workplace conversations. I draw on feminist organizational theory to reveal dialectic tensions in the ways participants interpret and articulate their experiences, and on discourse analysis to examine some example features of spoken interaction, which mediate their experiences of power, inclusion, and agency.

GENDER, LEADERSHIP, LANGUAGE, AND POWER

A growing number of multi-national corporations have introduced learning and development initiatives aimed at increasing the numbers of female managers in their executive teams. Under the banner of "diversity and inclusion," or "gender balance," these initiatives aim to bring about a significant increase in the numbers of women in senior roles (see, for example, Mercer, 2016). However, despite a more relational discourse of leadership (Fairhurst & Uhl-Bien, 2012) that potentially allows women to express authority in ways beyond those traditionally associated with leadership (Cameron, 2000), very significant challenges continue to face women in positions of authority. This constraint on women's behavior highlights a conflict between the attributes stereotypically associated with femininity and those traditionally associated with leadership (Baxter, 2010; Litosseliti, 2006). This classic "double bind" for women in positions of authority is widely recognized by gender and organizational scholars (Lewis & Simpson, 2012; Mavin & Grandy, 2012; Stead & Elliott, 2009) as well as by scholars working in the field of language, gender, and workplace discourse (Angouri & Marra, 2011; Cameron, 2003; Eckert & McConnell-Ginet, 2003; Holmes 2006; Litosseliti, 2013.)

Scholars with their homes in different disciplinary traditions examine different constellations of gender, leadership, language, and power. Before applying them together, it is useful to examine them separately.

→ Externalize bias ⇒ defuse it Mortenson ✱

Externalize/ biased structures ⇒ change ✱Murphy
illumine   them

Gender and Leadership

In mainstream management literature as in organizational life, women's lives and experiences are largely invisible. Leadership theory has been "developed for men on male samples based on men's experience of leadership" (S. Madsen, personal communication, May 25, 2016). Feminist scholars whose work is informed by post-structuralism focus on the hidden processes that (re)produce the underlying structures of power, keeping this privileged norm hidden from view (Simpson & Lewis, 2005, 2007). These processes are not held in place by particular people in certain positions of power, but are diffuse and hidden. One hidden area is the way language is used in interaction. Workplace conversations often follow predictable and stable patterns, which conceal the norms and values within them. Such norms can override our surface awareness of fairness and inclusivity precisely because we take such conversational patterns for granted, and because of this, the exclusionary processes and effects remain invisible.

In discussing this phenomenon in relation to visibility, invisibility, and power in organizations, Lewis and Simpson (2012) have noted that while "judgments about normality are based on visibility and surveillance, the power of normalization lies in its *invisibility*" (p. 146, emphasis in original). Drawing on Lewis and Simpson's (2010) concept of the "(In)visibility Vortex" (p. 9) which represents processes of revealing, exposure, and disappearance around the strong pull of an invisible norm, these authors theorize that standing out on the periphery brings the threat of exposure and erasure, a backdrop against which some women sometimes "seek to enter" what Lewis and Simpson (2010) call "the invisible norm" (p. 5) to avoid being marked as women. For example, some female business leaders choose to distance themselves from stereotypically feminine behaviors and enact a version of leadership that draws principally on the stereotypically masculine. Gendered advantage and disadvantage thus remain hidden in normative, gendered expectations to which both men and women hold women accountable (Mavin & Grandy, 2012). Language is one such expectation. Women who express their power in traditional masculine ways—in fact, women who want power at all—violate social norms by disrupting the gender and structural hierarchies that protect the invisible norm (Mavin, Gandy, & Williams, 2014). Thus, gender conformity and structural invisibility combine to naturalize the rules of who gets to gain and use power. To resist these rules, women have to be the same and different—to fit in and stand out. To theorize how this might work, feminist organizational scholars explore ways of going beyond limiting oppositional binaries by questioning the over-simplified dualisms of mainstream management and leadership literature and by examining mutually (and simultaneously) reproductive dialects such as control/resistance, dissent/consent, and men/women (Collinson, 2005; Fairhurst, 2001; Mumby,

SANDBERG

2005; Mumby & Stohl, 1991; Putnam, 2015). Dialectics of (in)visibility, [not] speaking, and powerful[less]ness shape women's experiences of leadership.

Gender and Language

A close study of situated language use can provide a window into the way such experiences are shaped. Feminist linguistics is interested in "identifying, demystifying, and resisting the ways in which language is used to create and sustain gender inequalities" (Litosseliti, 2013, p. 24). In what ways, for example, do people draw on discourses of gender difference, and what are the consequences of these differences; what linguistic practices are seen as appropriate for particular workplace interactions, and what is the social meaning of these on a large scale; how do specific linguistic choices made by women and men in everyday interactions shape views about gender differences that ultimately serve to reinforce female disadvantage (Litosseliti, 2013). Although some feminist language scholars have commented that expectations of leaders have been influenced by a relational discourse of leadership that holds the potential to license women to express authority in ways that are not limited to acceptable feminine (motherly) leadership models (Baxter, 2008; Cameron, 2000), expectations of appropriate behavior for women in the workplace continue to be associated with normatively consistent ways of doing femininity (Baxter, 2010; Holmes, 2006; Litosseliti, 2006). In fact, despite growing evidence that challenges stereotypical expectations about the conversational behavior of women and men at work, traditional expectations endure and lead to the negative evaluation of anyone who does not conform (Litosseliti, 2013). Constraints such as this shape and are shaped in discourse (Eckert & McConnell-Ginet, 2003; Litosseliti & Sunderland, 2002; Mullany, 2007; Sunderland, 2004). Such gendered discourses offer common-sense knowledge about the ways in which women and men "should" behave at work, including the way they behave, or are perceived to behave, in conversation. To consider this further is to examine language and power.

Language and Power

Discourse, language, and power are inextricably linked. Discourses, or ways of understanding and experiencing the world, reflect and constitute a web of explanations that create practical knowledge about the world that shape and are shaped by social processes. The role of discourse in creating

Situ?

and maintaining such power relations has long been the focus of study for critical linguists (Fairclough, 1989, 1992, 2003).

This chapter draws on two separate but connected conceptualizations of power because power is at the core of approaches to analyzing talk in institutional settings. The first conceptualization of power comes from linguistically informed approaches to studying the detail of situated talk that assume power is made visible, and thus can be analyzed, in conversational moves (Thornborrow, 2002). Power, from this perspective, is a shared conversational resource that is dynamically and collaboratively constructed (Holmes & Stubbe, 2003). In this approach, the direction of analyses mostly moves from the detail of talk in situ, to its socially constituting effects. For example, the specific linguistic feature of interruption, when analyzed in the context of a culturally diverse business meeting, may reveal not only different social and cultural assumptions and expectations about when one is able to speak, but also the asymmetrical patterns of legitimate access to power which then reinforce social and cultural inequalities.

The second understanding of power, favored by feminist organizational studies and organizational communication researchers—which is connected but stands on different theoretical ground—is influenced by Foucauldian notions of power. A constantly shifting set of relations emerges from social interaction, which is "everywhere, not because it embraces everything, but because it comes from everywhere" (Foucault, 1990, p. 93). In this approach, the direction of analyses mostly moves from social practices toward their manifestation in the Foucauldian sense of discourse as historically and culturally specific sets of ideas and their expression in social interaction through language. For example, who gets to speak in an ordinary management meeting is largely shaped not by particular ways of using language, but by deeper, structural inequalities. By combining the two perspectives, my research aims to understand the dynamics of power from the participants' point of view, and at the same time I bring the magnifying glass closer to the linguistic activity, allowing the hidden to come into view.

THE RESEARCH PROJECT

The analysis was carried out on excerpts drawn from a larger project aimed at understanding the meanings professional women attach to transacting power in workplace conversations. Methodologically, the project was informed by linguistic ethnography (Blommaert & Rampton, 2016; Rampton, 2007; Rampton, Maybin, & Roberts, 2015), which combines an ethnographically informed, field-based approach to investigating and comprehending understandings of participants' perspectives and activities, with linguistic and discourse analytical tools and empirical procedures. The research was situated in sites of leadership learning and development directed at professional women. In order to engage with research participants in reflective conversations about experiences of power in corporate settings, a community of interest was built so as to afford opportunities for inquiry and for gathering data relevant to answering the research questions. The project researches and, at the same time, builds a community of professional women with management and leadership roles, sympathetic to the research, and prepared to engage in sharing and reflecting on their experiences of power. This "English and Power" project was a short (stand-alone) individual and small-group learning event aimed at raising awareness of the relationship between conversational behavior and power in workplace conversations in corporate settings. The event, which was repeated on several occasions in five different European cities during 2014 and 2015, was held jointly with members of the European Professional Women's Network (PWN), an international network of professional women that offers opportunities for training, mentoring, and networking. The learning event, which comprised guided reflection, one-to-one coaching, and a group workshop, was designed to serve both as a method of data collection and as a learning intervention in its own right. The participants, all PWN members or their guests, represented a range of levels of seniority, professional roles, nationalities, native languages, businesses, and sectors.

The data set comprises 60 individual written reflections about power and influence completed as pre-work, field notes taken during preparatory telephone coaching conversations with each participant, and 14 total recorded hours of the same women talking in their (geographically) different small groups about their experiences of influence and power in corporate conversations. In their written accounts and in the workshops, participants described their experience of the conversational balance of power and drew attention to features of spoken interaction such as interruption, politeness, turn taking, and topic management. Thus, these data offer access to first-hand accounts of the stories, meanings, and linguistic or pragmatic features that were important to the women themselves.

The data were analyzed inductively by adopting a grounded approach, identifying unresolved tensions and their potential meanings within the specific encounters the women describe (Charmaz, 2006). After close reading and comparative analysis of codes, emerging categories of the experience of power and influence were identified. Informed by feminist post-structural discourse analysis (Baxter, 2003), the next step was a more detailed analysis of the texts, focusing on specific features of spoken interaction, which, according to the women's accounts, played an important role in shaping their experiences. By articulating conversational dynamics, the women's accounts offer a metalinguistic commentary on their experiences of influence.

Aspects of power and powerlessness interact in complex ways in the women's accounts, shaping and shaped by their experiences of inclusion and exclusion. Oppositional binaries and dialectic tensions evident in their reflections—being present (or not), heard (or not), powerful (or not)—revealed an opaque and uneasy relationship with power. It was clear from the accounts that for these (women) leaders and managers, specific conversations, and specific conversational behaviors, constitute important sites for the experience of power asymmetries. These experiences were described by the participants in terms of their distinctive linguistic features. Three related areas of interest were identified from the data, discussed in relation to theory, and analyzed from a discourse perspective: First, *what* are the women saying about their experience of power, and how this is reflected in conversational behavior? Second, *where* does this take place? Where do they experience this absence and presence most keenly? What are these sites of inclusion and exclusion? And third, *how* does this happen? What are some of the specific discourse features through which these elements of experience are realized?

EXPERIENCES OF POWER

I draw attention to two main categories to discuss what the women said about their experiences of power in everyday, mundane workplace conversations. The first category is the tension in the women's descriptions of how power is exercised and experienced. The second category is how this experience is framed by the sense of being either present or absent in a conversational space. In both categories, the women described their experiences in binary terms—for example, being seen (and/or overlooked), being heard (and/or ignored or silenced), being powerful (and/or powerless). The categories intersect with each other and also with meanings the women assigned to being included or excluded in interactions where power is was exercised, brokered, and/or withheld. The names used are not the women's real names.

A Sense of Powerful(less)ness

Given that the group is comprised of successful, professional (and relatively powerful) managers, powerlessness is omnipresent. Ana, a senior human resource (HR) director in a global manufacturing company, said,

It is difficult to be seen as senior as I am. How do I get the attention of others without having to show my business card with "director" on it? Are there clues to status and presence in the tone of voice or the words you use? I want to know how to feel more powerful, and more comfortable with that feeling.

Ana's reflections on her experience of power are a testament to an important unresolved tension. She holds a senior-level role but does not feel powerful, or at least she does not feel comfortable with her authority. She wants her authority to be heard and interpreted differently. She went on to say: "I feel judged. Men are always judging what women say. They just give their opinions; they are not afraid to fail and be judged while we women, (or at least me), are." Women fear being judged

Being unmarked and unseen can indeed be a powerless position to occupy, or it can be part of a strategy to take up power, as Yolanda explained: "I want to possess and convey power (a new thing for me), so I need to strengthen my message and learn how to translate it into this entrepreneurial tough business talk—a language they will understand." Gendered power is often assumed, and "fitting in" presents itself as the best strategy to avoid the discomfort (and powerlessness) of standing out from the norm. Powerlessness, however, is always present in that it is part of judging the experience of being powerful. The (In)visibility Vortex (Lewis & Simpson, 2012) manifests in spoken interaction as a powerful pull towards a conversational norm.

Being There (Or Not)

Being present and being absent are central to the experience of power, which is mainly about being seen and being heard and is often expressed through dualistic interpretations of conversational behavior. For example, some cast blame upon themselves for what they experience as unwanted behaviors (aspects such as not speaking in meetings), while at the same time they aspire to occupy more of the conversational floor. However, the women were very clear about *wanting* to be seen and heard, and they provided rich detail of the conversational constraints, which account for their "failure" to speak out. Juana, manager of a 70-strong international customer experience team in financial services, reflected on her experience of influence:

When there is a meeting or conference call where I am not leading the meeting but would like to give my opinion to add value to the conversation, I normally struggle to be heard as I am not sure when I can start talking, and I often lose the moment to talk, so then it is too late and the topic has already been discussed.

Unexamined dualisms —
assertive + masculine + ~~bad~~ good
passive + feminine + ~~good~~ .
Talking Power ▪ **77**

This is not about shyness. Francesca, a senior partner in a professional services firm, the only woman at her level in her country, explained what prevents her from being fully present:

> My lack of a strong command of English stops me from more proactive participation. My colleagues are much more proud of their capability in general and take a much more proactive word-turn in the discussion. This lack of confidence in my English prevents me from taking advantage from the conversation with top managers when they visit my country. This is a mix between the opportunity for certain comments and the way to express them in English. Due to this under-confident feeling, I usually prefer to shut up and pass to a second line.

In terms of linguistic disadvantage, Francesca is not alone in making sense of her experience of the tension between standing out or standing back. For older (now senior) women whose first language is not English, there was a particularly strong sense of frustration at being somehow prevented, or preventing themselves, from "being there."

Unexamined dualisms were evident in many of the women's accounts and present "good" conversational behavior (assertive, powerful, masculine) against "bad" (passive, powerless, feminine). Donna, a brilliant young engineer, began her career with confidence and assertiveness but was warned by her line manager that her colleagues felt threatened, that she should hold back. Now she's gone too far the other way: "My fear is that because I speak less now, they might think I am not so aggressive as the others and therefore not so good at my job."

Frequent comparisons were made to the behavior of other people the women perceive as powerful (e.g., senior men, native speakers of English, northwestern Europeans), which they contrasted with their own experience of feeling unseen and powerless. For example, one participant reflected, "I can't process my thoughts quickly enough. It makes me withdraw, choose to stay silent—and be unhappy." The problem of simply *being there* presented itself in personal terms. Power was experienced as personal, finite, and something to be gained or lost. It is difficult to see—or people are unaccustomed to looking for (or it is simply hidden from view) —how one "side" of the experience of power simultaneously serves to construct the other. When personalized in this way, dichotomous values may reinforce passivity because assuming personal responsibility for this "failure" could also lead to self-exclusion. Becoming more comfortable with visibility and power promised a different experience as Cristina, a senior consultant in an international professional services firm explained: "I want to come out of the place of hiding (behind the numbers); come out and be seen. I know if you're not seen, you're not promoted, and I want to get some space for myself."

CONVERSATIONAL SITES

Where does the negotiation of power take place, and where did these women experience absence and presence most keenly? What were their sites of inclusion and exclusion? I distinguish here between internal and external conversations in order to explore two related sites where a sense of inclusion and exclusion seemed to play an important role. These are a reflective site, which is mainly focused on "being me," and an interactive site where the women explore "being different."

The Reflective Site

The first site is reflective. These were inward-looking places where the participants pondered about power in their accounts of themselves in flux. Moments of individual and organizational transition heightened the experiences of power as well as many cases of powerlessness and exclusion. Individual transitions (taking up a new position, returning from maternity leave, being promoted, and so on) brought with them what seemed like a perpetual need to position and present oneself in an unfamiliar and often hostile conversational setting. For Monica for example, promotion brought a new and difficult boss. She reflected:

> I am feeling completely powerless—judged and undermined and criticized— feeling under attack. I am 48, but in this situation I'm like a baby. . . . The thing is we keep going, keep trying to solve the problem because we think if we ask for help we will show ourselves to be weak, and we know can't do that.

For Emilia, who has a senior role in a technology consulting firm recently taken over by another "foreign" firm, proving herself was becoming exhausting:

> My new interlocutors don't know me personally, and most of our interactions take place on the phone. I have to demonstrate my professional value in this diverse environment, fully populated by men, without being myself. I'm just fighting, trying to demonstrate my worth again and again.

Accounts like this are a testament to the women's consideration of the importance of their own conversational performances, trying as they present themselves as professionals who matter, to make sense of themselves as people. The reflections were infused with a strong sense of the importance of "being me," of designing themselves, celebrating who they are, defining what they will and will not tolerate as part of their professional identities. Melody, a foreigner in a northern European country explained:

I need to make my presence here felt but not in the local, overbearing way. I can't fake it. I want to be genuine. I want to make things work better but without being very uncomfortable and not being myself.

The participants reflected on how they used language to achieve their goals: which words to choose, when to speak and when to stay quiet, and how to defend their sense of self-worth. The reflective space was where the participants reflected out loud about the ways language is used both in snippets of remembered conversation and in imagined talk, but where no *actual* interaction takes place.

The Interactive Site

This site involves interactive contexts, such as formal meetings in both face-to-face and virtual settings. Of these, virtual settings stand out as being particularly problematic. In their accounts, the women repeatedly cited conference calls as a primary site of exclusion, raising concerns about the effect of imbalanced participation, ineffective chairing practices, and reified, exclusionary patterns of talk (Murphy, 2015). Participants talk about their frustration with the apparent lack of awareness of their interlocutors. For many, the conversations were unproductive, unstructured, and alienating. Frequently, the participants with the most organizational power would take control. Susana, a communications manager in the banking sector explained:

> There is a weekly conference call with all the Comm & Marketing Heads in EMEA. Normally the Heads of the "strongest" countries lead the conversation (Netherlands, Germany, and Nordics), so there are not many opportunities to make comments or to interrupt. They talk a lot, no matter if they are monopolizing the conversation.

It was so difficult to be part of the discussion that some of the women opted out altogether. Belinda, marketing manager in the automobile industry remarked:

> On international conference calls, I often want to make a comment but cannot because either suddenly everyone is talking at the same time or I am not able at all, no chance. Therefore, in the last meetings I tend not to talk unless being asked. I don't think is the best behavior but it is very tiring to try to speak without success.

In this virtual context, the most openly (and viscerally) cited mechanism of exclusion is what the participants call "native speaker power" (i.e., the power native speakers hold because they are native speakers of English). Again and again the women pointed out that their most keenly felt daily disadvantage is being one step behind the native speakers who, even if they are less expert, are able to influence more because they control the language better. Disadvantage here came from *being different* from what is accepted in many corporate contexts as the linguistic norm. Experiences of power for these women were across and between a complex discriminatory intersectionality of gender, culture, and native language. Georgina, HR manager in a global professional services firm, explained:

> Non-native speakers have less credibility than they deserve. Because we are sometimes uncertain about our language, they perceive us as insecure. They just take up all the space. And because you can't compete in the conversation, you lose ground and power with native speakers; you feel you are being put on a different level.

She concluded:

> The best English speakers get their action plans approved. It takes my energy away and makes me feel like not trying. It's not just that the native speakers take over. We give up. We sit back and think—so let them get on with it.

Contexts, places, and occasions like these, where the negotiation of power in conversation is particularly salient, point to specific discourse features, and can benefit from closer examination.

DISCOURSE FEATURES

Finally, how does all this happen? What are some of the specific discourse features through which these elements of experience are realized? Here I examine two broad areas related to dynamics of power in workplace conversations. These are as follows:

1. Opportunities to access the conversational floor (Thornborrow, 2002).
2. Politeness and power, and how the former is often in tension with people's perception of the latter (Angouri & Marra, 2011; Holmes & Stubbe, 2003).

The Conversational Floor

The accounts disclose internal commentaries that associate (dis)engagement with the negotiation and control of turns and topics, a perspective that equates influence with domination of the conversational floor. Thornborrow (2002) explains:

> This type of approach is based on what I can best describe as a "territorial" model of power in interaction, where the more turns you can take (or stop other people from taking) and the greater your occupation of the floor, the more power you have as a participant in the talk. (p. 27)

The participants appeared to prefer this conceptualization of power in interaction. Being unable to hold on to one's turn, find the right time to interject, or simply speak out, were the most cited features of spoken interaction in the women's accounts.

While this understanding reveals significant patterns on the surface of the interaction, it also conceals the ways in which this finite manifestation of power in conversation is normalized and reproduced. By drawing attention only to conversational power as a finite resource that can be shared either equally or unequally, this interpretation does not account for possible alternative meanings and positions. Establishing and defending speaking rights, reducing or maintaining social distance, and building solidarity are equally important discursive strategies to assert or subvert power relationships (Holmes & Stubbe, 2003). We can get a glimpse of this in Amelia's analysis of the reified nature of turn-taking patterns:

> If the situation is with a well-established team, they have established patterns of interaction. They know each other well, and they interact in a way that doesn't invite participation. They are mostly men, and they have certain patterns of talk. It seems as if they have an informal agreement on how to proceed—they know the rules. If you raise your hand to speak everyone looks at you as if to say, it's not your place to speak.

This, and accounts like it, bring the relational nature of doing power (Grint, 2005) into much sharper focus. To reveal more of how inclusion and exclusion are collaboratively produced (or not), it is helpful to look beyond trading power in interaction as a finite resource and pay attention to the ways speakers, discourse, and contexts interact, a perspective explored in the section that follows.

Politeness and Power

Influenced by unfounded but persistent popular accounts of "women's language," the participants described an uneasy relationship with power in which confusion over speaking styles, deference and powerlessness, directness and appropriateness, and politeness and weakness combined to keep them silent. They did not want to be "too strong or too direct," or to be seen to be either rude or weak. This was not courtesy; it was the process of delicately negotiating power. They do not know how to take up the power their position *should* hold for fear of causing offence or of appearing incompetent in a language which is not their own.

Monica, regional HR manager in a global construction firm, explained: "You don't want to use words that may sound impolite or too strong, but you don't want to be too soft either. Between one and the other, I would chose being soft, and that's what makes me fail." Directness was experienced as gendered. It was not that women or men were more or less direct in their interaction because they are women or men, or have been socialized this way or that—there is ample linguistic evidence to the contrary (Cameron, 2007)—rather, the persistence of gendered stereotypes of feminine and masculine behavior provides scripts for ways of speaking, as Monica pointed out: "Maybe I speak too directly and could be softer and more smiley. If I smile, the president likes it. He likes women to be more girly."

The main issue, though, is accomplishing appropriateness: how to interrupt or change the subject, clarify a point, or introduce a different perspective without sounding rude, and this is highly contextual. Contextual variables include considerations of who else is in the conversation, how much power each person has, the nature of the joint task. The variables combine to constrain what is and is not appropriate. Power and politeness are both important here. Angelina, whose international risk and quality role brings her into frequent contact with people of different cultures, reflected:

> When there's a big power distance you daren't ask—you don't want to be rude or threaten face. So in order not to be impolite, you let it slide. It's like walking a tightrope.... How do I interrupt without sounding too abrupt, and yet I don't want to sound too informal. My main problem is how to communicate and sound more senior.

This analysis has drawn upon two conceptualizations of power to illustrate, by means of examples of situated conversations, how these perspectives intertwine to frame experiences of power for this group of professional women. First, using categories and ideas drawn from discourse studies, specifically interactional sociolinguistics and conversation analysis, the chapter has examined conversational behavior that is visible on the surface of the talk. Here power, which is a collaboratively constructed resource, is quite literally talked into place in and through interaction (Holmes, 2006). This surface expression of power dynamics is visible and felt in experience. Threaded through every conversation, and deeply constitutive of the experience of power, are practices, norms, and values that are hidden from view. Informed by post-structuralist understandings of (in)visibility (Lewis & Simpson, 2010; Simpson & Lewis 2005, 2007), this perspective, rooted in Foucauldian understandings of power, offers an analytical means of revealing deeper social and political asymmetries that are shaped and reinforced in everyday workplace interaction. These perspectives, combined with accounts of experience, reveal tensions and contradictions in everyday conversational practices that open potential new ground for women's leadership and leadership development.

WOMEN'S LEADERSHIP AND LEADERSHIP DEVELOPMENT

How can the insights from the "English and Power" project be translated into leadership development practice? Normative advice about how to behave or speak differently is superficial and short lived, yet it all too easily fits the dominant discourse of corporate learning and development programs. The sort of programs that are based on binary differences perpetuate gender stereotypes and conceal the power relations that protect the norm (Lewis & Simpson, 2012; Mavin & Grandy, 2012). To engage with critical feminist debates while also working effectively in multiple contexts is an important aspect of feminist praxis. This may involve making what is hidden more visible and, thus, available for shared reflection and discussion. Anchoring the debate in the realm of practice, Stead (2013) used the theoretical lens of (in)visibility to interpret how the lived experience of women leaders provides a context for learning that both reveals and conceals power relations. Similarly, awareness of interactional processes that shape the experience of power can also contribute to learning, which reveals such hidden dynamics and mechanisms (Murphy & Parkinson, 2016). To that end, it is important to create learning spaces where women can explore together some of the constraints and possibilities of their power and agency while, at the same time, developing insights into the relationship between language use and the sites of experience.

In the final section of the chapter, three examples of linguistically informed approaches to leadership development are described. These approaches, which developed out of the research insights and with the research participants, function by changing conversational behavior on the visible surface of the interaction. These subtle shifts in power dynamics, connected as they are to the invisible values and norms that usually remain hidden, offer a developmental space where experiences of power can be reflected upon and shared, and where, returning once more to the surface, discursive changes that disturb the conversational and political norm—but also get the job done—can be realized.

Collaborative communication

Changing Conversations

This section describes three of the conversation tools that have been tested with the research community. By tools I mean physical artifacts that externalize aspects or patterns of conversations in order to render the relationship between interaction and power more visible, and, therefore, more readily available for scrutiny and discussion. The principle learning objective for the women participating in the research was to improve their understanding of and skill in navigating the conversational power dynamics of their everyday interactions. All had significant managerial responsibilities (with differing degrees of positional power) and all wanted to be able to change their conversations in some way. Irrespective of their formal power, the majority of participants expressed frustration and confusion about how to break through or challenge established communication patterns. Externalizing the normally hidden patterns of power in interaction furnished the participants with choices about their conversational behavior. Choosing to be hyper-polite, for example, was thus no longer only associated with normatively defined "feminine" and powerless conversational behavior (Lakoff, 2004), but also with flexible and powerful discursive strategies that could be calibrated according to the context, the task, the power others bring, the power each participant wants to exercise in that moment, and so on. Small and seemingly inconsequential conversational moves (whose turn it is to speak, or who can, and who cannot ask questions) are thus recast as opportunities for change.

Three key discourse features identified through the research and described in this chapter are turn, topic, and directness. To conclude the chapter, I briefly describe the three "conversation tools" with which research participants worked and which can be easily replicated in discussions and meetings.

By using markers such as counters, coins, or children's building bricks to visualize the interaction process, it becomes possible to see how different choices are available to change the course of a conversation. For example, to visualize the power asymmetries of imbalanced turn-taking and to enable participants to recalibrate their contributions, put a pile of counters or small bricks in the center of the table and ask everyone, every time they speak, to take one and leave it in front of them on the table. Some people may have a great many, where others have none. By seeing this power dynamic unfold, and perhaps even noticing their own role in enacting it, participants can choose to change their behavior by staying quiet, by inviting an opinion, or by asking a question of someone who has not found the space to speak out.

The bricks can also be a useful tool to make visible the subtle moves around the topic of conversation. The individual who defines the agenda topic

often gets to define the action, so maneuverings around topic are an important conversational power dynamic. To visualize this, have each person take two bricks that, this time, represent a new topic. Whenever someone changes the subject or introduces a new theme, a brick should be played. But there are only two chances. Once an individual has played both, he or she can participate in the conversation, but he or she cannot change the subject or introduce any new ideas—*unless* one of the other participants freely chooses to give them one of their bricks—for which *in return* he or she is allowed to take two from the pile in the center. This exercise reverses the usual dynamic of excluding a colleague or her ideas in order to win more conversational power and topic territory.

Finally, confusion and doubt about how to be direct enough—but not be impolite—can, as we have seen, put severe limitations on a person's ability to grasp leadership opportunities. In this exercise, everyone has three bricks, which represent legitimate turns at speaking out to raise important issues. When a person chooses to speak out to say, "I have a question," "I'd like to challenge that," or "I have some thoughts about that" in the right time, everyone else stops to listen so that appropriateness can be seen and collaboratively achieved. Speakers must play a brick when they speak out so that everyone can see this legitimacy and give way. Speakers must use all three of their bricks during the course of the meeting. This constrains some and challenges others in the name of re-balancing the micro-dynamics of power.

By providing a visual means of illustrating some of the dynamics of difference that conceal the conversational norm, the tools create a more nuanced awareness of the way certain patterns of interaction produce and reproduce gendered power relations. The tools enhance linguistic awareness and illustrate the discursive choices about changing power dynamics in practice.

CONCLUSION

The research reported here reveals how patterns of spoken interaction in the workplace produce and reproduce gendered power relations. Overall, the analysis adds linguistic detail to understandings of power dynamics in workplace conversations and the ways in which these contribute to women's experiences of agency in professional settings. There is evidence in the accounts of the ways women police their own conversation styles and habits in line with traditionally masculine norms of leadership behavior. At the same time, the analysis revealed parallel inner commentaries that referred superficially to a sense of passivity but which, by examining the dialectic tension of experiences of power in conversation, were also testament to a powerful sense of agency.

The ultimate aim in praxis of the research program is to illuminate the way patterns of spoken interaction constrain (and enable) getting work done and how they shape (gendered) asymmetries of power. These are important issues for scholars and practitioners who share a commitment to creating discursive spaces in which women are able to formulate oppositional interpretations of their experiences in corporate life.

REFERENCES

Angouri, J., & Marra, M. (Eds.). (2011). *Constructing identities at work.* Basingstoke, England: Palgrave Macmillan.

Baxter, J. (2003). *Positioning gender in discourse: A feminist methodology.* Basingstoke, England: Palgrave Macmillan.

Baxter, J. (2008). Is it all tough talking at the top? A post-structuralist analysis of the construction of gendered speaker identities of British business leaders within interview narratives. *Gender and Language, 2*(2), 197–222.

Baxter, J. (2010). *The language of female leadership.* Basingstoke, England: Palgrave Macmillan.

Blommaert, J., & Rampton, B. (2016). Language and superdiversity. In K. Arnaut, J. Blommaert, B. Rampton, & M. Spotti (Eds.), *Language and superdiversity* (pp. 21–48). New York, NY: Routledge.

Cameron, D. (2000). *Good to talk? Living and working in a communication culture.* London, England: SAGE.

Cameron, D. (2003). *Gender and language ideologies.* In J. Holmes, & M. Mayerhoff, (Eds.), *The handbook of language and gender* (pp. 447–467). Malden, MA: Blackwell.

Cameron, D. (2007). *The myth of Mars and Venus: Do men and women really speak different languages?* Oxford, England: Oxford University Press.

Charmaz, K. (2006). *Constructing grounded theory: A practical guide through qualitative analysis.* Thousand Oaks, CA: SAGE.

Collinson, D. (2005). Dialectics of leadership. *Human Relations, 58*(11), 1419–1442. doi:10.1177/0018726705060902

Eckert, P., & McConnell-Ginet, S. (2003). *Language and gender.* Cambridge, England: Cambridge University Press.

Fairclough, N. (1989). *Language and power.* New York, NY: Longman.

Fairclough, N. (1992). *Discourse and social change.* Cambridge, England: Polity.

Fairclough, N. (2003). *Analysing discourse: Textual analysis for social research.* London, England: Routledge.

Fairhurst, G. T. (2001). Dualisms in leadership research. In F. M. Jablin & L. L. Putnam (Eds.), *The new handbook of organization communication: Advances in theory, research, and methods* (pp. 379–439). Thousand Oaks, CA: SAGE.

Fairhurst, G. T., & Uhl-Bien, M. (2012). Organization discourse analysis (ODA): Examining leadership as a relational process. *The Leadership Quarterly, 23*(6), 1043–1062.

Foucault, M. (1990). *The history of sexuality, volume I: An introduction* (R. Hurley, Trans.). New York, NY: Vintage.

Grint, K. (2005). Problems, problems, problems: The social construction of "leadership." *Human Relations, 58*(11), 1467–1494. doi:10.1177/0018726705061314

Holmes, J. (2006). *Gendered talk at work: Constructing gender identity through workplace discourse.* Malden, MA: Blackwell.

Holmes, J., & Stubbe, M. (2003). *Power and politeness in the workplace: A sociolinguistic analysis of talk at work.* London, England: Longman.

Lakoff R. T. (2004). *Language and woman's place: Text and commentaries.* New York, NY: Oxford University Press. [Ed. Bucholtz M. Rev. and expanded edn.]

Lewis, P., & Simpson, R. (2010). Introduction: Theoretical insights into the practices of revealing and concealing gender within organizations. In P. Lewis & R. Simpson (Eds.), *Revealing and concealing gender: Issues of visibility in organizations* (pp. 1–22). Basingstoke, England: Palgrave Macmillan.

Lewis, P., & Simpson, R. (2012). Kanter revisited: Gender, power, and (in)visibility. *International Journal of Management Reviews, 14*(2), 141–158. doi:10.111/j.1468-2370.2011.00327.x

Litosseliti, L ([2006] 2013). *Gender and language: Theory and practice.* New York, NY: Routledge.

Litosseliti, L., & Sunderland, J. (Eds.) (2002). *Gender identity and discourse analysis.* Philadelphia, PA: John Benjamins.

Mavin, S., & Grandy, G. (2012). Doing gender well and differently in management. *Gender in Management, 27*(4), 218–231.

Mavin, S., Grandy, G., & Williams, J. (2014). Experiences of women elite leaders doing gender: Intra-gender micro-violence between women. *British Journal of Management, 25*(3), 439–455.doi:10.1111/1467-8551.12057

Mercer. (2016). When women thrive, businesses thrive. Retrieved from http://www.mercer.com/our-thinking/when-women-thrive.html

Mullany, L. (2007). *Gendered discourse in the professional workplace.* Basingstoke, England: Palgrave Macmillan.

Mumby, D. K. (2005). Theorizing resistance in organization studies: A dialectical approach. *Management Communication Quarterly, 19*(1), 19–44.

Mumby, D. K., & Stohl, C. (1991). Power and discourse in organizational studies: Absence and the dialectic of control. *Discourse and Society, 2*(3), 313–332.

Murphy, A. (2015, October). So have we heard from everybody? A pragmatic analysis of exclusion and inclusion in international conference calls. Paper presented at the International Communication Association regional conference, Copenhagen, Denmark.

Murphy, A., & Parkinson, C. (2016, December). Women's experiences of power in everyday workplace conversations: Discourse features of power-in-interaction. Paper presented at the International Studying Leadership Conference, Edinburgh, Scotland.

Putnam, L. L. (2015). Unpacking the dialectic: Alternative views on the discourse–materiality relationship. *Journal of Management Studies, 52*(5), 706–716. doi:10.1111/joms.12115

Rampton, B. (2007). Neo-Hymesian linguistic ethnography in the United Kingdom. *Journal of Sociolinguistics, 11*(5), 584–607.

Rampton, B., Maybin, J., & Roberts, C. (2015). Theory and method in linguistic ethnography. In J. Snell, S. Shaw, & F. Copland (Eds.), *Linguistic ethnography: Interdisciplinary explorations.* Palgrave Advances Series (pp. 14–50). Basingstoke, England: Palgrave MacMillan.

Simpson, R., & Lewis, P. (2005). An investigation of silence and a scrutiny of transparency: Re-examining gender in organization literature through the concepts of voice and visibility. *Human Relations, 58*(10), 1253–1275. doi:10.1177/0018726705059840

Simpson, R., & Lewis, P. (2007). *Voice, visibility and the gendering of organizations.* Basingstoke, England: Palgrave Macmillan.

Stead, V. (2013). Learning to deploy (in)visibility: An examination of women leaders' lived experiences. M*anagement Learning, 44*(1), 63–79.

Stead, V., & Elliott, C. (2009). *Women's leadership.* Basingstoke, England: Palgrave Macmillan.

Sunderland, J. (2004). *Gendered discourses.* London, England: Palgrave Macmillan.

Thornborrow, J. (2002). *Power talk: Language and interaction in institutional discourse.* Harlow, England: Pearson.

How women volunteers rise to leadership roles.
↓
and stay
How women manage leadership roles in STEM orgs
- *Careful balance of feminine expression. (MARKING)*
- *relational capital*
- *"let me socialize that idea" p.99*

CHAPTER 6

EMBRACING AND CONTESTING GENDER ROLES

Communication Strategies of Women in Engineering Leadership Roles

Sarah E. Riforgiate
Kansas State University

Emily M. Ruder
Kansas State University

The female president of an international professional engineering association stands on the stage facing a sea of approximately 2,000 men to share annual information and to welcome them to the conference. In this organization, of the 29,000-plus members, women represent approximately 6% of the membership, according to an internal report in 2013. Defying the odds, the volunteer leadership executive board, including the president on the stage, has strong female representation (5 of 22 board positions or 23%). Like many professional organizations, individuals pay dues to become members, and the association is run by elected volunteers. To better

Gender, Communication, and the Leadership Gap, pages 89–109
Copyright © 2017 by Information Age Publishing
All rights of reproduction in any form reserved.

illuminate how women volunteers rise to leadership roles against the statistical odds, this chapter explores the connections between gender, leadership, and communication. First, we discuss women in engineering and leadership to provide a context for the analysis, then we use four gendered frames to analyze two years of qualitative field observations, focus groups, and interviews pertaining to how these women leaders communicate gender as leaders, and finally we conclude with practical gendered communication implications for women in leadership.

WHERE ARE THE WOMEN?

To better understand women's leadership communication behaviors in this association, first it is necessary to describe the context of science, technology, engineering, and math (STEM) fields and women in leadership. Similar to the makeup of the volunteer professional association studied, in a majority of countries men occupy the lion's share of STEM positions (Bystydzienski, 2009) and leadership roles (Furst & Reeves, 2008). Further, women across industries experience difficulty making their way to senior leadership positions (Beeson & Valerio, 2012; Eagly & Carli, 2007; Furst & Reeves, 2008).

Because women are as capable as men and contribute important benefits to organizations, industry and grant agencies are focusing on ways to encourage female participation in STEM careers (Jahn & Myers, 2015). Increasing female participation is important because "data suggests that women will be more fairly evaluated if they are at least 25 percent of a group" (Valian, 1999, p. 309). Myriad programs across the United States are designed to accelerate inclusion and socialize girls/young women to embrace STEM majors and careers (AAUW, n.d.; NGCProject, n.d.)

Although there are challenges, progress has been made; women excel in STEM fields and climb the leadership ladder. An analysis of test scores of 7 million United States second- through twelfth-grade students shows no significant sex differences between girls and boys in mathematical ability (Hyde, Lindberg, Linn, Ellis, & Williams, 2008). Further, female leaders contribute positively to organizations and "the inclusion of larger numbers of women leaders correlates with improved corporate performance" (Beeson & Valerio, 2012, p. 418).

Although programs encourage female participation in STEM majors, there is disproportionate enrollment in higher education. According to the National Center for Education Statistics (n.d.), in 2012 female students made up 56.8% of college enrollment figures across majors and are projected to make up 58.1% of the students enrolled in 2018. However, only 13% of women are in STEM majors, compared to 34% of men (Griffith, 2010).

There is also high attrition: Only 37% of women STEM majors persist to graduation (Griffith, 2010). Women entering STEM fields professionally remain in the minority of membership and leadership. However, the presence of female faculty and graduate students positively influences retention of women in STEM majors (Griffith, 2010), and the presence of female work colleagues enhances career persistence (Drury, Siy, & Cheryan, 2011).

Researchers are also examining why women do not enter or persist in STEM and rise to leadership positions. At the heart of this research, communication functions to create perceptions of possibility and/or barriers for entry and success (Buzzanell, Long, Anderson, Kokini, & Batra, 2015). Communication research spans pre-entry in STEM to studies of how women navigate STEM workplaces. Myers, Jahn, Gailliard, and Stoltzfus (2011) report that enthusiastic teachers and encouraging parents expose children and young adults to favorable conceptualizations or, conversely, discourage involvement in STEM classes and experiences. Messages need not be direct; messages may occur in simple conversations when a father comments that he enjoyed high school chemistry, and his daughter realizes they share similar interests and that she might be good at science. In the workplace, Buzzanell and colleagues (2015) examine persistence in STEM, explaining that not all mentoring and communication are equally weighted or helpful, with women of color needing different types of mentoring based on individual situations. Allen, 2017. Intersectionality.

Equally important are studies exploring why there are so few women leaders (Eagly, 2015) when women occupy almost half the workforce (Dworkin, Maurer, & Schipani, 2012). Studying effective language in business settings, Baxter (2012) reports that women are stuck in stereotypical supportive roles and ultimately are limited in obtaining leader positions because of language use. Especially in male-dominated settings, constraints on the way women are expected to speak and act become impediments for women to obtain leadership positions (Baxter, 2012). "Research on the leadership styles of men and women has revealed relatively small sex differences, albeit ones that show women as more collaborative, democratic, and relational than men" (Eagly, 2015, p. xii). However, a gender bias in evaluations of leadership behaviors exists, with male leaders being rewarded and female leaders going unrecognized for displaying desirable relational behaviors (Eagly & Carli, 2007; Loughlin, Arnold, & Bell Crawford, 2011). Language influences gender hierarchies; it thereby affects how and whether women assert themselves by speaking up within organizations (Babcock & Laschever, 2003; Ridgeway, 2001), thus excluding women from conversations and leadership roles.

Both women and men leaders can also make it difficult for women to advance in organizations. While women in power may be expected to pave a path for and support other women as allies, Queen Bee syndrome can

Sandberg

occur when women who have risen to positions of power deny that systematic discrimination of women is an issue, contending that there is no need to help other women (Mavin, 2006). Derks, Ellemers, van Laar, and de Groot (2011) explain that the women who are most likely to enact Queen Bee syndrome "(i.e., increased masculine self-description, increased gender stereotyping and distancing from other women) were women who reported being low gender identified when they entered the workforce and who experienced a high degree of gender discrimination on their way up" (p. 530). These findings highlight the need to better understand intersections of gender, leadership, and communication in order to level the playing field for women.

Unfortunately, low percentages of women in STEM and leadership roles, as well as potential issues with leaders within organizations, may force women to seek support outside their workplace. Volunteer professional associations provide one context in which women can potentially support each other, find role models or mentors, and give women an opportunity to serve as leaders. While programs and incentives for women to enter STEM fields are valuable, it is fruitful to consider women who currently occupy leadership positions (Furst & Reeves, 2008). Female leaders represent an anomaly to the predominantly white, middle- to senior-aged male cohorts of leaders across STEM fields and serve as powerful examples and mentors for other women, enhancing retention (Drury et al., 2011).

Therefore, it is necessary to explore the intersections between leadership, gender, and the communication practices of women who have risen to leadership positions to better understand effective practices. Focusing on the verbal and nonverbal behaviors of women leaders allows for closer examination of the ways communication creates opportunities and challenges for women's participation in STEM fields and leadership. By identifying communication behaviors intersecting with leadership and gender using qualitative data collected in an international professional engineering association, we hope to create discussion and increase awareness of communication choices women can use to leverage additional agency and create change.

THEORIZING GENDER COMMUNICATION

Communication is a complex process that occurs verbally and nonverbally, consciously and unconsciously, on many levels and reflects multiple facets to shape identities over time (Tracy & Trethewey, 2005). Importantly, communication is central to identity and organizational culture because it constitutes understanding of who we are, how we are supposed to act, and how we make meaning (Trethewey, 2000). Women face challenges in navigating identity in formal organizations because, as Trethewey (1999) explains, "historically, discourses of professionalism have privileged formal terms such as male, public, mind, and rational over their informal opposites—female, private, body, and emotional. [...] Women's professional selves or gendered identities, then, are always already positioned by organizational discourses" as secondary (p. 426).

Unfortunately, female leaders face double standards for their communication, with the potential to be criticized for being "too masculine" while subscribing to traditional expectations of leadership or "too feminine" for enacting gender roles in line with their biological sex (Beeson & Valerio, 2012). This tension is exacerbated in STEM fields, where women are in the minority and risk being labeled "honorary men" or "flawed women" (Powell, Bagilhole, & Dainty, 2009, p. 412).

It is necessary to enhance understanding of the ways female leaders navigate masculine spaces as "the other" to negotiate gendered identity and performance. Communication conforming to gendered expectations is often assumed or taken for granted, making it appear natural and invisible; therefore, to better identify gendered communication behaviors of women leaders, we use Ashcraft's (2004) gender frame theory, which posits four levels of gender performance: (a) gender as a fixed identity, (b) gender as an ongoing performance, (c) organizational narratives of gender and power, and (d) cultural expectations of gender performance. Each of the four frames may overlap, working in concert or contradiction in communicating identity.

The first frame, *gender as a fixed identity*, begins at the micro level and asserts that our discourse reflects "predispositions towards ways of talking, using language and orienting to human relationships," reflecting biological influences (Ashcraft, 2004, p. 276). The second frame, *gender as an ongoing performance*, views gender as discursively enacted through everyday actions and interactions as we perform gendered scripts. The third frame, *organizational narratives of gender and power*, expands to the meso level, where organizational patterns of discourse across members operate to coordinate meanings of gender. This frame positions the organization as both the product and producer of gender discourses and takes into account how power is understood and organized, recognizing some gendered behaviors over others. The fourth and final frame, *cultural expectations of gender performance*, occurs at a macro level in which the societal discourses influence expectations about gender in organizational contexts. The comprehensive nature, spanning from micro to macro-level discourses, provides important insight to examining how women leaders resist and conform to gender expectations.

SPENDING TIME WITH WOMEN LEADERS

Taking advantage of a unique opportunity to observe and analyze female leadership, this study extends understanding of how women persist in engineering fields and move to successful leadership roles. The data pertaining to women and leadership in this study is truly emergent; the original focus of the data collection was to examine communication technology use and to study ways to improve member recruitment and retention. However, the data generated from qualitative field observations, focus groups, and interviews conducted for this study of one organization also pertains to women and leadership in STEM fields.

Using ethnographic field methodology, the first author followed the executive committee of a professional, volunteer-run, international engineering association with over 29,000 members for more than two years, collecting approximately 240 hours of ethnographic field observations of executive board meetings, conferences, and social events (196 pages of typed, single-spaced data). In this organization, the percentage of women holding formal leadership positions is significantly higher (23%) than overall female membership (6%). Ethnographic observations of this organization worked well to explore "the nature of a particular social phenomenon" (Atkinson & Hammersley, 1994, p. 248) and understand the ways individuals and groups work to create identity (Geertz, 1973).

Additionally, the first author spoke formally with 91 participants, from past presidents and board members, to industry and academic groups, to different age ranges, to male and female groups using qualitative interviews and focus groups (403 pages of typed, single-spaced transcripts). Although the conversations focused on communication technology use, gender performance was observed, and intersections of communication, gender, and leadership emerged naturally in the organizations' efforts to recruit and retain more women. Informal conversations were ongoing throughout the two years with executive board members (included in the field observation notes), and informal correspondence has continued with several of the female leaders three years after the completion of formal data collection.

Analysis began with a close reading of the field notes and transcripts for segments pertinent to female leadership and/or gender performance, followed by open coding (Charmaz, 2006; Saldaña, 2016). Then, using Ashcraft's (2004) four frames of identity as a theoretical guide to heighten awareness of gendered communication practices, we noted when the data fit one or more of the four gender frames, including: (a) gender as a fixed identity, (b) gender as an ongoing performance, (c) organizational narratives of gender and power, and (d) cultural expectations of gender performance. Throughout our analysis, we used an iterative and immersive process, moving back and forth between the data and theory to categorize and re-categorize, allowing meaning to emerge throughout the process (Braun & Clarke, 2006; Tracy, 2012). Preliminary results were shared and confirmed with some of the female leaders to ensure accuracy of the findings.

• HIRING
comm. ;
procedures

• ALGORITHMS • JOB DESCR that
employs both masculine ; fem.
characteristics.
(stereotypically)

Embracing and Contesting Gender Roles ▪ **95**

FRAMING GENDER IN STEM

Frame One: Gender as a Fixed Identity

Starting at the individual, or micro level, Ashcraft's (2004) first frame considers gender as a fixed identity based on biological predispositions. Although research indicates that there are minor differences in the ways that men and women communicate, stereotypes regarding masculine and feminine communication patterns abound (Canary & Mattrey, 2002; Dindia, 2006). According to this frame, individuals display their gender identity aligned with stereotypical expectations based on predispositions to use certain types of language and relationship orientations. Specifically, women are expected to be nurturing, relationship oriented, and cooperative, while men are expected to be assertive, agenda driven, and competitive (Eagly, 2015).

Women in leadership roles in this professional engineering association actively resisted the stereotypical expectations of the fixed identity frame, particularly in terms of biological predispositions toward abilities. For example, several of the women rejected the idea that becoming an engineer was more difficult for women than for men. This was surprising at face value given that women are not well represented in STEM fields and so many programs exist to encourage women to enter STEM; however, in probing the women in both informal discussions and recorded interviews, these women actively resisted the idea that women were any less capable than their male counterparts.

Women admitted there were social barriers; there were few (if any) female mentors. For example, one leader and professor explained in an informal conversation there were "no female professors in my department" when she attended college. These women also recognized they were a minority in the classroom, with a female graduate student noting in a personal interview there are "about 10 [males] to two [females]" in her classes. But women, from graduate students to executive board members, were adamant that there was not a magical engineering gene that only males had; women were just as capable and could certainly excel. Yet another female graduate student explained in an interview, "I never thought I would face any challenges being an engineer." Additionally, a female executive in an informal conversation shared that she did not see herself as "different" because "engineering is just what I wanted to do." She never "felt self-conscious or limited" by her sex. These women were able to enter and succeed in engineering, which represented resistance to stereotypical gender norms through physical presence, while voicing outright rejection of narratives that "girls" could not grow up to be in STEM fields. Additionally, they did not see themselves as special or having unusual abilities, making them more suitable to engineering compared to other women. Ultimately, they wanted to be evaluated as an "engineer," not as a "female," compared to their male colleagues.

The rejection of a biological predisposition of women for particular industries, in this case engineering, provided active resistance of dominant gender narratives. Both leader and non-leader women resisted characterizations that they might be less genetically predisposed for this male-dominated field, rejecting unfavorable and inaccurate feminine stereotypes that women have less ability to succeed in STEM.

Frame Two: Gender as an Ongoing Performance

Gender as an ongoing performance moves away from individual identity predispositions, to consider how men and women perform gender through communication (Ashcraft, 2004). Essentially, individuals enact social scripts through nonverbal and verbal communication to "do gender" based on societal expectations (West & Zimmerman, 1987). In contrast to the first frame, the second frame asserts that gendered behaviors are learned, not inherent, and can be adjusted. These discursive communication practices may be conscious or unconscious and are often performed through small everyday practices.

Professional women are often cognizant of presentation choices to craft a work identity that causes others to take them seriously, while not casting them as threatening (Trethewey, 1999). "Women who exhibit too many masculine traits are often ridiculed and lose trust" (Carlin & Winfrey, 2009, p. 328). As such, women must be selective in using masculine communication behaviors to align with professional expectations for leadership, while also communicating femininity to match the expected gendered performance of their biological sex (Valian, 1999).

Considering nonverbal communication, the women leaders in this association navigated the competent, but nonthreatening line by adopting some masculine professional norms like wearing pant suits, keeping short but stylish haircuts or hair pulled back away from the face, and minimizing makeup use. However, they simultaneously, consciously or unconsciously, "appeared" feminine by wearing more colorful clothing, accessorizing using scarves and jewelry, and wearing subtle makeup. At one point, one of the female leaders recorded a video for the members that sparked a discussion of whether she had enough and the right color lipstick on to look feminine, yet still professional. When asked for feedback on the video, she was told, "If you re-tape any of your introduction, just wear a touch of lipstick." To which the female leader responded, "Unfortunately, I did have lipstick on, but it was too light compared to the dark clothes. If we re-shoot, [...] I will make sure it is darker."

Women leaders certainly could have attempted to blend with the majority of their male colleagues; however, the leaders often dressed in ways that did not. One leader always wore bright-colored jackets in shades of magenta and woven warm colors with her black business slacks. Another bundled her long dark wavy hair loosely on her head with tendrils hanging down, while wearing navy pant suits. Still several others wore silk scarves with formal suits for a pop of color and a feminine touch.

Appearing feminine but not *too* feminine is a practice of conforming and contesting gender in this male-dominated space. Based on field observations, the women always looked professional by adhering to business dress expectations. However, rather than looking like men or asexual, they added feminine touches which conformed to feminine nonverbal gender expectations, yet also challenged dominant masculine dress expectations. Further, feminine nonverbal gendered communication, whether conscious or unconscious, drew attention to the presence of female leaders in a male-dominated field.

Importantly, feminine ongoing performances occurred more frequently at executive levels of leadership compared to the membership at large. Women in their 20s and early 30s who were not in leadership positions, particularly graduate student members, did not draw attention to their femininity. Their behavior mirrored the strategy of "acting like one of the boys" identified by Powell, Bagilhole, and Dainty's (2009) research that showed how female engineers attempted to blend in.

Younger female members outside of leadership wore dark-colored suits, less makeup, and kept their hair tightly tied back to not call attention to themselves. An example of this occurred at an industry sponsored event: two male industry representatives took one female and seven male graduate students to dinner for recruiting. The first author observed the female student doing her best not to draw attention to herself—this was surprising since she was supposed to stand out as a job candidate and her research presentations had gone well. She seldom talked and only when directly spoken to, fashioned her shoulder-length silky dark hair tightly pulled back, wore black slacks with a nondescript loose white button-down top, and did not wear any makeup or jewelry. This behavior was in stark contrast to the male students who wore dark suits, but took off their jackets and rolled up their sleeves during dinner, joked loudly about how hungry they were and how much they could eat, teased each other about where to go for some evening fun, and were boisterous and jovial. In this case, being "one of the boys" was about blending in unnoticed, becoming invisible, and not calling attention to the fact that she is a woman. Interestingly, this was one of the women interviewed earlier for this study who insisted vocally that she felt no pressure being a female in a male-dominated class, sharing that her professors "treat us equally; they expect the same amount of work from all of us." The extent to which she was conscious of her communication decisions is difficult to determine, but she likely gave some thought to her dress.

The contrast between the women leaders and the younger female members was salient. While women leaders pushed boundaries and appeared more feminine, younger members did not model that behavior. This may be because the women leaders had been in the association for a longer period of time, allowing them to feel more secure or because they were in positions of power, allowing them increased agency. Ultimately, the women leaders nonverbally communicated femininity that allowed them to stand out as women in a predominately male field, while not being too extreme by still subscribing to some masculine expectations of professional appearance.

Frame Three: Organizational Narratives of Gender and Power

At the meso level of the third frame, organizational narratives of gender and power, individuals do not simply perform gender, but respond to, resist, and reinforce communication systems that organize larger understandings of gender and power (Ashcraft, 2004). Organizational narratives predominantly privilege masculine-agenda-driven and direct-communication behaviors (Valian, 1999). However, these behaviors do not match expectations for feminine communication, putting women at a disadvantage. "It is appropriate for men to use their power directly but less acceptable for women to do so" (Babcock & Laschever, 2003, p. 153). A departure from task-driven masculine leadership behaviors has been highlighted in recent research on leadership, including transformational leadership, in which leaders are expected to perform relational behaviors to motivate and empower followers to exceed expectations (Bass & Riggio, 2006). Interestingly, transformational leadership research indicates that male leaders are rewarded for relational communication that counter the expected masculine task-focused behavior, while women leaders are not rewarded because relational communication is expected (Loughlin et al., 2011). Ultimately, when women communicate in masculine ways, they are criticized, and when they communicate in feminine ways, their actions are unrecognized or dismissed.

Applying the organizational narrative frame to understand communication, women leaders in this association used collaboration and relationally oriented communication that matched feminine gender role expectations. Women leaders were more likely to use communication to build off others' ideas and to acknowledge contributions of other members, reflecting greater relational attentiveness conforming to expectations for female leadership (Loughlin et al., 2011). For example, during field observations of a particularly heated meeting, a female executive board member recognized and summarized the positions of three men who were arguing in order to facilitate more collaborative behavior rather than proposing her own alternative solution. Although listening and attending to others' ideas may be considered professional politeness behavior, the women leaders throughout this study went to greater lengths than their male counterparts to listen attentively and to use collaborative communication strategies.

Then, by leveraging relationships, women leaders were strategically able to accomplish masculine task-focused actions, such as being ambitious and directive. These women leaders were cognizant of organizational decision-making patterns and actively worked with and around power structures to make decisions and support other women. In order to change "rules," they first had to master them; these women leaders knew the rules and could easily articulate how decision-making would take place prior to board meetings and elections. For example, in one observation over an informal lunch, two women board members discussed who would propose an idea, who would second that idea, and who they could get to support the idea to make sure it moved forward.

Women leaders were aware of time constraints, how to frame issues, and how to collect support by working through relationships before bringing issues to executive meetings. One woman leader explained that another male consistently waited until something was an "emergency" and required action without a vote. To circumvent this process, she began to schedule pre-emptive calls with other board members and ask about issues well before a decision was needed so this individual could not make "executive decisions" independent of the group. She gathered support for opening up communication by talking about the collective good of the organization and the importance of including everyone in decision making. Throughout field observations, women leaders would say, "Let me socialize that idea," which involved talking with many individuals and fully understanding concerns prior to meeting so they could most effectively address the issues and move forward to take action.

Consistently using behind-the-scenes collaborative communication, the women leaders developed strong relational networks, adhering to gender stereotypical expectations for feminine behavior. At the same time, they demonstrated that they understood the power dynamics involved to resist opposition and rise to positions of power in the organization. Women used the power they gained in leadership roles to promote other women who were equally qualified as men. They modeled behaviors that Valian (1999) notes can level the playing field for women: "Leaders [. . .] can play two roles in equitable treatment of men and women. First, they can establish and publicize policies designed to create fairness; second, they can legitimize and support the leadership of both women and men" (p. 316).

From a policy standpoint, women leaders supported initiatives for formal and informal subgroups of women engineers to encourage women to participate nationally and internationally and create support networks. Men already had ready-made networks as majority members. At each conference, women leaders made sure the executive board sponsored receptions with appetizers for women and those who supported women in engineering. Both women and men attended the receptions, but unlike walking through the conference hallways and seeing an occasional woman, the receptions were approximately 50% women. At receptions there was always a female speaker who shared what it was like to be a woman in a male-dominated field and ideas to encourage women in engineering such as "women should be mentors, which doesn't mean you need to be perfect" and "people should be more tolerant."

Women leaders also arranged informal dinners for women members to socialize, network, and seek advice from each other. At one of these dinners with about eight women, the women went around the table to talk about their "successes" that year and encourage each other. At another, the conversations around the elongated table with about 25 members drifted from challenges at work, to advice for women on the job market, to family and children. Introductions were made, but many of the women had been informally gathering for years, enjoying the familiarity while welcoming other women into the group.

When volunteer leadership positions opened, several of the women leaders sought out and talked with each other about which women they could mentor, recommend, and jointly support for positions in addition to the qualified male candidates. During lunch, a woman leader squatted down next to another who was sitting at the table to discuss who they could nominate that had enough experience, presentation skills, and social capital in the organization to have a chance at winning the election. They explored several possibilities and shared what they knew about the potential nominees' background (i.e., what committees they had served on, where they were in their careers) and networks (i.e., who they knew in the association that would support them) to decide who would be the best candidate. Women leaders kept an eye out for potential leadership traits and invited members into small roles to vet individuals and groom them for future positions. Communication strategies were not only about filling positions with women but also creating pathways for women to gain experience and articulate how they were equally or more qualified compared to male candidates. This strategy is important because research indicates that men are provided with opportunities to prove themselves and develop skills more frequently than women (Babcock & Laschever, 2003; Furst & Reeves, 2008; Valian, 1999). In essence, the women leaders found ways to create equal opportunities among members.

Women leaders also leveraged communication in ways that allowed them to appear feminine while enacting masculine direct communication. An example of this occurred at one of the opening receptions over food and beverages; a male leader from another association sought out a woman leader to talk informally about developing a partnership to support his initiative. He indicated that she had the authority to make the decision to approve his request, and his boldness indicated he expected her to oblige. She welcomed the conversation, but shared that she wanted to speak with other executive members before giving him a decision, allowing her use of relationally oriented communication to reinforce feminine expectations. However, she also exercised power to tell him "no" as he pressed for an answer, reflecting direct masculine behavior.

Perhaps most interesting is that women leaders circumvented rules in ways that "appeared" feminine, such as building relationships, hearing the concerns of others, and caring about other members' opinions. Yet the focus to increase equitable female membership, representation, and support was agenda driven—a characteristic associated with male leadership (Eagly & Karau, 1991). Therefore, in understanding the rules, women leaders worked within the organizational structure and power dynamics to level the playing field, make space to contest issues that were important to them, and mentor and promote other women.

Frame Four: Cultural Expectations of Gender Performance

The fourth frame, cultural expectations of gender performance, occurs at the macro level, as individuals are constantly bombarded with messages about gender expectations (Ashcraft, 2004). Media is one important source to consider in this frame, where men on prime time television predominantly are shown as focused on work-related tasks, and women are shown as focused on relationships (Lauzen, Dozier, & Horan, 2008). Website content and other mediated representations of men and women are another frequent source of information. Considering STEM initiatives, drawing attention to the scarcity of women simultaneously highlights women's absence as a concern while confirming the overwhelming presence of males in the field.

Both male and female leaders in this association actively worked to counter gendered expectations and create change by including photos of women on website pages and promotional materials. For example, during field observations, ten male students and one female student were presenting posters, but the photographer took a photo of the female student with her poster to include in marketing materials. There were also conversations during executive meetings about creating more press on women engineers.

One discussion revolved around contacting companies to interview female employees; companies would benefit from free advertising while the association could promote women in engineering by publishing the interviews in the association magazine.

Further, association leaders actively worked to recruit women into the association and engineering worldwide. A female leader presenting at an executive board meeting shared photos of women participating in workshops in Saudi Arabia, commenting she has never "seen so many women participating; it was amazing." Then she showed photos from Dubai, explaining how the association waived registration fees for 150 women and worked with the local media to cover the conference attended by 173 participants, most of whom were female. The photos of women and the international press heightened the visibility of women in engineering and women in leadership. While the women leaders did not share whether they were influenced by images of women in engineering, female graduate students noted that perceptions of women in engineering had changed, with one sharing that "in the last ten years I think there has been an incredible increase in women in the industry."

Part of women's rise to leadership positions occurred because men recognized the need to have women participate, then supported and encouraged them to do so. While members actively work to change the "face" of engineering (one photo at a time), female leadership in this association also resists and conforms to some cultural narratives. The presence of women in leadership contests cultural expectations, with 23% holding executive leadership positions to provide a visual representation of women in leadership in STEM. Yet, these women leaders are still clearly in the minority of both membership and leadership positions, outnumbered by more than four to one.

A potential explanation for the acceptance of women leadership in this association may come from alignment of cultural expectations of women as service oriented (Furst & Reeves, 2008) and because this is a volunteer run organization. In the United States, women volunteer more frequently (31.1%) compared to men (23.8%; Boraas, 2003), which makes women in voluntary leadership positions seem more natural or acceptable. Several women leaders were also leaders in their professional organizations, reflecting research indicating that as individuals "progress up the career ladder, their likelihood of volunteering for their professional association or a professional organization in the community increased" (Nesbit & Gazley, 2012, p. 574). Generally, women working full time are less likely to volunteer (Osborne, Ziersch, & Baum, 2008), yet these women leaders go against that trend. This may be because the volunteer work aligns with their professional roles while bringing prestige to their workplaces.

Volunteers can benefit from involvement by developing leadership skills to enhance their careers (Willems et al., 2012) and social capital through formal and informal networks in professional associations (Osborne et al., 2008). However, volunteers also freely dedicate time, energy, expertise, and financial resources to serve the association that otherwise could be invested in careers. Women leaders in this study indicated that their professional institutions encouraged their involvement in volunteer leadership positions, while noting that time spent volunteering took away from time to dedicate to their career. Women volunteers are more susceptible to time-related stress than men (MacDonald, Phipps, & Lethbridge, 2005). Thus participating in voluntary service offers greater exposure and leadership opportunities for these women, but it also comes at some sacrifice.

ADJUSTING THE FRAME FOR WOMEN'S LEADERSHIP

This study provided an opportunity to examine how women leaders in an engineering professional association use four gender frames: (a) gender as a fixed identity, (b) gender as an ongoing performance, (c) organizational narratives of gender and power, and (d) cultural expectations of gender performance (Ashcraft, 2004). Examples illustrate how gender was negotiated and enacted through communication. Following are practical implications of this study.

First, considering *gender as a fixed identity*, women in this study rejected the idea that biological differences are a barrier in STEM fields and for leadership roles because men and women are equally capable; this assertion is further supported by research (Beeson & Valerio, 2012; Hyde et al., 2008). Therefore, one powerful strategy is being aware of and sharing research that highlights equal abilities, thereby calling into question stereotypical biased perceptions and to create more accurate views. Additionally, it is necessary to evaluate individuals based on qualifications to minimize implicit gender biases. For example, removing names and pronouns that indicate biological sex from written evaluation documents prior to reviews (Loughlin et al., 2011) or completing "blind reviews," where individuals are shielded from visibility and only their work is evaluated, can move the needle toward fairness and allow individuals to be hired or promoted based on their merits (Goldin & Rouse, 2000). Further, revisiting evaluation criteria to account for both masculine and feminine gendered skills is necessary. As will be discussed below in the third frame, relational skills that are largely cast as feminine are enacted by both male and female high-quality leaders and benefit organizations.

Second, *gender as ongoing performance* was enacted by women leaders in this study to fulfill stereotypical expectations, while the women function as leaders. Women leaders struck a careful balance when making decisions on how to display or not display femininity. Positive benefits can occur when women display femininity to help soften the image of a task-focused woman to appear more relationally focused. Women leaders can take the lead on gently adjusting nonverbal masculine norms of professional appearance in the workplace, accentuating the presence of women in this space. For example, in 2008 both Sarah Palin and Hillary Clinton used a mothering frame to help balance being framed as an overly masculine "iron maiden" typology (Carlin & Winfrey, 2009). Similarly, the women leaders in this association displayed femininity using nonverbal appearance cues while maintaining their focus on a clear agenda.

Interestingly, *ongoing performance* may be a skill that is learned over time once women become confident in their positions in male-dominated fields. Females in their 20s and 30s did not attempt to display femininity or draw attention to themselves. As Powell, Bagilhole, and Dainty (2009) explain, these attempts to "blend in" might actually harm women in the long run by maintaining the status quo and not questioning the masculine engineering culture. To create cultural changes of women in engineering and leadership, it is important that the physical presence of women is noticeable. Successful women leaders modeling how to balance appearing both feminine *and* professional serve as important role models. Finally, the physical presence of women in engineering and leadership shows that women are capable in these positions and encourages other women that they can also be members of these groups.

Third, considering *organizational narratives of gender and power*, being relationship oriented is an expected feminine quality for women, but it is also a desirable quality for leaders generally (Loughlin et al., 2011). Relational leaders have greater influence (Avolio & Bass, 1995) and promote information-sharing behaviors while increasing perceptions of satisfaction and commitment (de Vries, Bakker-Pieper, & Oostenveld, 2010). As demonstrated by the women leaders in this study, relational skills encouraged collaboration, brought different perspectives into meetings, and helped members understand and support issues. Identifying and recognizing women's relational aptitude as something desirable and including it among other evaluation criteria allows for fairer evaluations of women.

Furthermore, a relational orientation improves networking to establish connections with others and open new doors. While men benefit from numerous weak network ties, women benefit more from strong network ties (Babcock & Laschever, 2003). If organizations are serious about increasing women's participation in leadership, it is necessary to find ways to encourage them to develop strong network ties. These women leaders did so by creating spaces where women could develop deep relationships and support each other.

Gathering regularly to create strong networks allowed women leaders to work together to make sure younger women were given developmental experiences, nurtured professionally, and put on a level playing field with comparably skilled men. These actions mirror the popular culture campaign "lean in together" initiated by Sheryl Sandberg to encourage women helping other women at work (McDermott, 2016); these behaviors work and are necessary to create progress for women in professional settings. It is far more effective for women to work together, supporting each other, to change the representation of women in leadership rather than to compete for one position. Further, mentoring women increases retention (Drury et al., 2011).

Fourth, both in STEM fields and in leadership, *cultural expectations of gender performance* highlight the prevalence and stereotypical preferences for men. Women leaders occupying 23% of the association's executive positions reshapes organizational expectations to be more accepting of women in STEM and leadership. Multiple women need to occupy a team or level in order to be taken seriously, so ensuring competent representation is highly important (Valian, 1999). Association members in this organization—both men and women—worked together to encourage women's participation and to make sure women were represented to provide a solid foundation on which to build.

This association recognized that this is not a "women's issue" but an organizational issue to address, and male leaders supported women in STEM and as leaders. The support of male group members highlights the importance of dominant group members' work in promoting women as leaders in addition to women supporting other women. While women can rise to leadership independently, identifying allies and supporters can expedite the process. As is noted in the findings, the support of women leaders is likely not typical of all organizations; as a volunteer-run organization, women may appear more acceptable in voluntary leadership roles. However, even though volunteering may take time away from professional career development, these women leaders were supported by their formal employers and gained important leadership experience through this work.

Communication is an important means to resist dominant stereotypes and to create space for women in predominately male STEM fields and leadership roles. Throughout this chapter we explored how gender, leadership, and communication intersect in important ways. At individual, performative, organizational, and cultural levels, women leaders challenge gender norms through verbal and nonverbal communication. Recognizing that women leaders still must negotiate their position, we are encouraged that they are finding ways to form paths for themselves and others.

REFERENCES

AAUW. (n.d.). American Association of University Women: STEM education. Retrieved from https://www.aauw.org/what-we-do/stem-education

Ashcraft, K. L. (2004). Gender, discourse, and organization: Framing a shifting relationship. In D. Grant, C. Hardy, C. Oswick, & L. Putnam (Eds.), *The Sage handbook of organizational discourse* (pp. 275–298). Thousand Oaks, CA: SAGE.

Atkinson, P., & Hammersley, M. (1994). Ethnography and participant observation. In N. K. Denzin & Y. S. Lincoln (Eds.), *Handbook of qualitative research* (pp. 248–261). Thousand Oaks, CA: SAGE.

Avolio, B. J., & Bass, B. M. (1995). Individual consideration viewed at multiple levels of analysis: A multi-level framework for examining the diffusion of transformational leadership. *The Leadership Quarterly, 6*(2), 199–218. doi:10.1016/1048-9843(95)90035-7

Babcock, L., & Laschever, S. (2003). *Women don't ask: Negotiation and the gender divide.* Princeton, NJ: Princeton University Press.

Bass, B. M., & Riggio, R. E. (2006). *Transformational leadership* (2nd ed.). Mahwah, NJ: Lawrence Erlbaum Associates.

Baxter, J. (2012). Women of the corporation: A sociolinguistic perspective of senior women's leadership language in the U.K. *Journal of Sociolinguistics, 16*(1), 81–107. doi:10.1111/j.1467-9841.2011.00520.x

Beeson, J., & Valerio, A. M. (2012). The executive leadership imperative: A new perspective on how companies and executives can accelerate the development of women leaders. *Business Horizons, 55*(5), 417–425. doi:10.1016/j. bushor.212.05.002

Boraas, S. (2003). Volunteerism in the United States. *Monthly Labor Review, 126*(8), 3–11.

Braun, V., & Clarke, V. (2006). Using thematic analysis in psychology. *Qualitative Research in Psychology, 3*(2), 77–101. doi:10.1191/1478088706qp063oa

Buzzanell, P. M., Long, Z., Anderson, L. B., Kokini, K., & Batra, J. C. (2015). Mentoring in academe: A feminist poststructural lens on stories of women engineering faculty of color. *Management Communication Quarterly, 29*(3), 440–457. doi:10.1177/0893318915574311

Bystydzienski, J. M. (2009). Why so few women? Explaining gendered occupational outcomes in science, technology, engineering and mathematics fields. *Sex Roles, 60*(9), 751–753. doi: 10.1007/s11199-008-9548-6

Canary, D. J., & Mattrey, M. J. (2002). How does meta-analysis represent our knowledge of interpersonal communication? In M. Allen, R. W. Preiss, B. M. Gayle, & N. Burrell (Eds.), *Interpersonal communication research: Advances through meta-analysis* (pp. 389–406). Mahwah, NJ: Erlbaum.

Carlin, D. B., & Winfrey, K. L. (2009). Have you come a long way, baby? Hillary Clinton, Sarah Palin, and sexism in 2008 campaign coverage. *Communication Studies, 60*(4), 326–343. doi:10.1080/10510970903109904

Charmaz, K. (2006). *Constructing grounded theory: A practical guide through qualitative analysis.* Thousand Oaks, CA: SAGE.

Derks, B., Ellemers, N., van Laar, C., & de Groot, K. (2011). Do sexist organizational cultures create the Queen Bee? *British Journal of Social Psychology, 50*(3), 519–535. doi:10.1348/014466610X525280

de Vries, R. E., Bakker-Pieper, A., & Oostenveld, W. (2010). Leadership = communication? The relations of leaders' communication styles with leadership styles, knowledge sharing and leadership outcomes. *Journal of Business Psychology, 25*(3), 367–380. doi:10.1007/s10869-009-9140-2

Dindia, K. (2006). Men are from North Dakota, women are from South Dakota. In K. Dindia & D. J. Canary (Eds.), *Sex differences and similarities in communication,* (2nd ed., pp. 3–20). Mahwah, NJ: Lawrence Erlbaum and Associates.

Drury, B. J., Siy, J. O., & Cheryan, S. (2011). When do female role models benefit women? The importance of differentiating recruitment from retention in STEM. *Psychological Inquiry, 22*(4), 265–269. doi:10.1080/104784 0X.2011.620935

Dworkin, T. M., Maurer, V., & Schipani, C. A. (2012). Career mentoring for women: New horizons/Expanded methods. *Business Horizons, 55*(4), 363–372. doi:10.1016/j.bushor. 212.03.001

Eagly, A. H. (2015). Foreword. In S. R. Madsen, F. W. Ngunjiri, K. A. Longman, & C. Cherrey (Eds.), *Women and leadership around the world* (pp. ix–xiv). Charlotte, NC: Information Age.

Eagly, A. H., & Carli, L. L. (2007). Women and the labyrinth of leadership. *Harvard Business Review, 85*(9), 1–12. Retrieved from http://www.diversityresources. stlrbc.org/wp-content/uploads/2013/10/Women-and-the-Labyrinth-of-Leadership.pdf

Eagly, A. H., & Karau, S. J. (1991). Gender and the emergence of leaders: A meta-analysis. *Journal of Personality and Social Psychology, 60*(5), 685–710. doi:10.1037/0022-3514.60.5.685

Furst, S. A., & Reeves, M. (2008). Queens of the hill: Creative destruction and the emergence of executive leadership of women. *The Leadership Quarterly, 19*(3), 372–384. doi:10.1016/j.leaqua.2008.03.001

Geertz, C. (1973). *The interpretation of culture.* New York, NY: Basic Books.

Goldin, C., & Rouse, C. (2000). Orchestrating impartiality: The impact of "blind" auditions on female musicians. *The American Economic Review, 90*(4), 715–741. doi:10.3386/w5903

Griffith, A. L. (2010). Persistence of women and minorities in STEM field majors: Is it the school that matters? *Economics of Education Review, 29*(6), 911–922. doi:10.1016/j.econedurev.2010.06/010

Hyde, J. S., Lindberg, S. M., Linn, M. C., Ellis, A. B., & Williams, C. C. (2008). Gender similarities characterize math performance. *Science, 321*(5888), 494–495. doi:10.1126/science.1160364

Jahn, J. L. S., & Myers, K. K. (2015). "When will I use this?" How math and science classes communicate impressions of STEM careers: Implications for vocational anticipatory socialization. *Communication Studies, 66*(2), 218–237. doi:10.10 80/10510974.2014.990047

Lauzen, M. M., Dozier, D. M., & Horan, N. (2008). Constructing gender stereotypes through social roles in prime-time television. *Journal of Broadcasting and Electronic Media, 52*(2), 200–214. doi:10.1080/08838150801991971

Loughlin, C., Arnold, K., & Bell Crawford, J. (2011). Lost opportunity: Is transformational leadership accurately recognized and rewarded in all managers? *Equality, Diversity and Inclusion, 31*(1), 43–64. doi:10.1108/02610151211199218

MacDonald, M., Phipps, S., & Lethbridge, L. (2005). Taking its toll: The influence of paid and unpaid work on women's well-being. *Feminist Economics, 11*(1), 63–94. doi:10.1080/1354570042000332597

Mavin, S. (2006). Venus envy: Problematizing solidarity behaviour and queen bees. *Women in Management Review, 21*(4), 264–276. doi:10.1108/09642061066657979

McDermott, M. (2016, June 23). Sheryl Sandberg's new message to women: "Lean in together." *USA Today.* Retrieved from https://www.usatoday.com/story/life/entertainthis/2016/06/23/sheryl-sandberg-together-woman-can-lean-in-together/86292106/

Myers, K. K., Jahn, J. L. S., Gailliard, B. M., & Stoltzfus, K. (2011). Vocational anticipatory socialization (VAS): A communicative model of adolescents' interests in STEM. *Management Communication Quarterly, 25*(1), 87–120. doi:10.1177/0893318910377068

National Center for Education Statistics. (n.d). Digest of Education Statistics. Retrieved from https://nces.ed.gov/programs/digest/d13/tables/dt13_303.10.asp

Nesbit, R., & Gazley, B. (2012). Patterns of volunteer activity in professional associations and societies. *Voluntas, 23*(3), 558–583. doi:10.1007/s11266-011-9218-0

NGCProject. (n.d.). National Girls Collaborative Project Website. Retrieved from http://www.ngcproject.org/

Osborne, K., Ziersch, A., & Baum, F. (2008). Who participates? Socioeconomic factors associated with women's participation in voluntary groups. *Australian Journal of Social Issues, 43*(1), 103–122. Retrieved from http://search.proquest.com/openview/6f52be7ec491f8690eaaaf6e9b43ad40/1?pq-origsite=gscholar

Powell, A., Bagilhole, B., & Dainty, A. (2009). How women engineers do and undo gender: Consequences for gender equality. *Gender, Work and Organization, 16*(4), 411–428. doi:10.1111/j.1468-0432.2008.00406.x

Ridgeway, C. L. (2001). Gender, status, and leadership. *Journal of Social Issues, 57*(4), 637–655. doi:10.1111/0022-4537.00233

Saldaña, J. (2016). *The coding manual for qualitative research* (2nd ed.). Thousand Oaks, CA: SAGE.

Tracy, S. J. (2012). *Qualitative research methods: Collecting evidence, crafting analysis, communicating impact.* Hoboken, NJ: John Wiley & Sons.

Tracy, S. J., & Trethewey, A. (2005). Fracturing the real-self↔fake-self dichotomy: Moving toward "crystallized" organizational discourses and identities. *Communication Theory, 15*(2), 168–195. doi:10.1111/j.1468-2885.2005.tb00331.x

Trethewey, A. (1999). Disciplined bodies: Women's embodied identities at work. *Organizational Studies, 20*(3), 423–450. doi:10.1177/0170840699203003

Trethewey, A. (2000). Cultured bodies: Communication as constitutive of culture and embodied identity. *The Electronic Journal of Communication, 10*(1–2). Retrieved from: http://www.cios.org/EJCPUBLIC/010/1/01016.html

Valian, V. (1999). *Why so slow? The advancement of women.* Cambridge, MA: MIT Press.

West, C., & Zimmerman, D. H. (1987). Doing gender. *Gender and Society, 1*(2), 125–151. Retrieved from http://www.jstor.org/stable/189945

Willems, J., Huybrechts, G., Jegers, M., Vantilborgh, T., Bidee, J., & Pepermans, R. (2012). Volunteer decisions (not) to leave: Reasons to quit versus functional motives to stay. *Human Relations, 65*(7), 883–900. doi:10.1177/0018726712442554

CHAPTER 7

GENDER, AUTHENTIC LEADERSHIP, AND COMMUNICATION

E. Anne Christo-Baker
Purdue University Northwest

Daniel Stuart Wilbur
Purdue University Northwest

This chapter focuses on challenges women may face in maintaining personal authenticity in organizational communication while also feeling the responsibility of projecting a powerful leader identity, as examined through the theoretical perspectives of authentic leadership and communication theory. Previous research demonstrated linkages between authentic leadership, communication, employee engagement, and attendant positive organizational outcomes (Jiang & Men, 2015). Thus, the degree to which leaders can enact authenticity in communication may impact their effectiveness. An interdisciplinary exploration of the extant body of literature on authentic leadership, gender communication, and leadership development may reveal patterns and consequences of authentic communication and may provide more informed strategies for improving organizational communication

Gender, Communication, and the Leadership Gap, pages 111–122
Copyright © 2017 by Information Age Publishing
All rights of reproduction in any form reserved.

while enacting authentic leadership. Toward this end, the key questions to be explored are as follows: (a) Can women enacting leadership maintain the integrity and authenticity of their communication style and persona in male-normed organizations?; (b) What barriers, if any, prevent women from enacting relational authentic leadership in communication?; and (c) What strategies are effective for addressing or removing these barriers?

AUTHENTIC LEADERSHIP

The study of authentic leadership (AL) is relatively new, emerging in the early 2000s and steadily gaining prominence among both researchers and practitioners. A 2015 article in *Harvard Business Review* characterizes authentic leadership as the "gold standard for leadership" (Ibarra, p. 54). As a conceptual construct, AL has not been defined in a consistent manner in the literature.

Components that have been common across various definitions describe AL as "a pattern of leader behavior that includes self-awareness, balanced processing of information, relational transparency with followers, and an internalized moral perspective" (Gardner & Carlson, 2015, p. 245). Similarly, Northouse (2015) expressed the view the behavior of authentic leaders toward others is based on their understanding of their personal values. Northouse further suggested that AL was characterized through internal processes of self-awareness and personal development, and enacted in relational contexts. Ilies, Morgeson, and Nahrgang (2005) described authentic leaders as not only engaged in self-development but also the development of followers. Given that women in leadership positions face a specific set of challenges bound up in perceptions of followers, it is important to examine how gender may affect those who exhibit AL in male-normed organizational cultures.

Despite observing any significant gender differences in the findings of AL studies, Jiang and Men (2015) noted that male participants appeared to generate significantly higher levels of employee engagement than did female participants. These results suggested that gender might affect the outcomes of enacted authentic leadership.

Scholars across several disciplines are increasingly recognizing the fundamental role of communication in shaping organizations. Communication is not simply something an organization "has" to be used as a tool to accomplish tasks, to inform, and at times control members; additionally, an "organization" is the ongoing communicative accomplishment of all the members. In other words, organizational reality is continuously produced and reproduced through interaction and communication practices of its members. Thus, the conception of the term "organization" as a static noun is replaced by the verb, "organizing" (see Weick, 1979). By recognizing that an organization is a site of ongoing processes with its members producing and reproducing meaning, norms, rules, humor, judgments, authenticity, and so on, we are able to unmask opportunities for effecting change, including creating a climate that fosters the ability of all organizational members to practice AL. An interdisciplinary exploration of the relevant literature on AL, gender communication, and leadership development may reveal patterns and consequences of authentic communication and may provide more informed strategies for improving organizational communication while enacting authentic leadership. Toward this end, we explore the role of gender and authentic communication in organizational contexts and the role of communication in constituting those contexts (i.e., the Communicative Constitution of Organization [CCO]; see Craig, 1999). In addition, we provide strategies for helping women who are interested in exhibiting authentic leadership to develop authentic communication practices.

GENDER, RELATIONAL TRANSPARENCY, AND AUTHENTIC LEADERSHIP

Relational transparency, a component of authentic leadership, is manifested through openness and honesty in self-presentation when interacting with others (Northouse, 2015). Eagly (2005) noted that the onus for successful relational authenticity cannot be solely the responsibility of leaders; it requires agreement, cooperation, and involvement of leaders and followers. In other words, the leader's authenticity derives its legitimacy from others. This granting of legitimacy may be influenced by gender. According to Eagly and Karau's (2002) role incongruity theory, women's styles of leadership, communication, and interpersonal relations are generally not regarded as being synonymous with accepted characteristics of leaders. Followers, therefore, may not be supportive of women leaders exhibiting AL in male-normed cultures. Consequently, inclusivity may be more difficult for female leaders to attain than it is for male leaders (Eagly, 2005). Moreover, Liu, Cutcher, and Grant (2015) noted that "women as 'outsiders' are less likely to be accepted by their followers as authentic leaders" (p. 237), which raises the question: do women have to be less than authentic than men do in their communication in order to be included in the leadership equation?

GENDER AND COMMUNICATION

In addition to the previously identified features of authentic leadership, a linguistic turn in social theory has increasingly recognized the constitutive

role of language, discourse, and communication in society and its institutions (Mumby, 2007). There has also been a shift in the view of the traditional bureaucratic structure of organizations that value rationality as the
norm to organizational structures that embrace the complexity, irrational-
ity, and continuous change inherent in human communication (Trethewey
& Ashcraft, 2004). Consequently, a more communication-centered focus
on leadership is required. In addition to being a gendered phenomenon,
leadership communication is transmissional and meaning centered; relational; inherently power based; diverse and global; and alive with the potential for reflexivity, moral accountability and change (Fairhurst & Connaughton, 2014). Thus, our discussion of authentic leadership and gender
warrants a consideration of the constitutive role of communication, given
the need for awareness of the communication behaviors that constitute AL.
Furthermore, if such communication behaviors are enacted by leaders who
are women, what is the likelihood that followers will perceive those behaviors as they were intended?

The communicative process of gendering tends to create a system in
which the interests of one group are being better served by the labeling
process than those of another, and the masculine gender typically ends
up having the most power.[1] According to West and Zimmerman (1987),
gender is a "routine accomplishment embedded in everyday interaction"
(p. 125). Although gender is accomplished by individual social actors, communication is essential to that accomplishment, which is influenced by
dominant meanings present in the larger organizational and social structures in which those individuals are acting. Local production of culture is
constrained or informed by broad forces, such as gender ideologies and
affiliations that put their imprints on organizational life (Alvesson & Due
Biling, 1997). In this sense, gender "is a mechanism whereby situated social
action contributes to the reproduction of social structure" (West & Fenstermaker, 1995, p. 21). Accordingly, if such a social structure is obscuring its
own inherent contradictions, we can better understand how gender can be
willingly produced, reproduced, and legitimated by the same people that it
subordinates. Therefore, we should also look deeper into how gender is accomplished in order to "reveal the mechanisms by which power is exercised
and inequality is produced" (West & Fenstermaker, 1995, p. 9). Doing so
will help us better understand the interactions between gender, communication, and leadership.

The contributions that organizational communication scholars offer to
discussions of strategy stems from a rising area of study called the *Communicative Constitution of Organization* (see Bencherki & Snack, 2016; Brummans,
Cooren, Robichaud, & Taylor, 2014; Craig, 1999, 2015; Kuhn, 2012; Putnam & Nicotera, 2009). Although viewing communication as being foundational to organizations seems obvious on the surface, communication

scholars strive to understand exactly how that process works, as Mumby and Ashcraft (2006) said: "Indeed, the default condition of our field [organizational communication] means that we claim to problematize processes often assumed by scholars in other fields and that we take these processes as fundamental to the very constitution of organizing" (p. 72). Marchiori and Bulgacov (2012) similarly observed: "[T]he relatively young phenomenon of communication and strategy process and the growing complexity of organization processes offer a context in which to examine a central question in the study of organizations—how communicational practices contribute to the construction of strategic practices" (p. 199).

STRATEGIES FOR DEVELOPMENT OF AUTHENTIC COMMUNICATION IN WOMEN LEADERS

As Ely, Ibarra, and Kolb (2011) noted, traditional modes of developing women as leaders often focus on one-size-fit-all strategies that suggest women merely need to learn the rules of organizations and adjust their behavior accordingly. In the realm of communication, this implies learning to communicate like men, who are the majority of organizational leaders. Hence, "the prevailing [organizational] context within which women and men communicate is dominated by male values and forms" (Marshall, 1993, p. 126). Fitzsimmons, Callan, and Paulsen (2014) noted that the process of leadership development begins much earlier than in the workplace, given that different processes and outcomes based on gender are evident even in childhood. Accordingly, organizations require different foci for the leadership development of men and women, in relation to communication content and style. The process of such development for women faces the additional challenge that women who communicate in more masculine ways may be perceived as violating gender norms (Eagly, 2005) and consequently may not be perceived as being authentic. Moreover, women attempting to fit into male-normed organizational environments may question their enactment of authenticity (Hopkins & O'Neil, 2015).

May, Chan, Hodges, and Avolio (2003) proposed that the responsibility for authentic leadership developments should rest primarily at the organizational level. Accordingly, their suggestions include selection, support for leadership development efforts, and performance metrics. Regarding the actual process of leadership development, these scholars recommended discussions, self-reflection, fostering self-efficacy of moral intentions through role-plays, case studies, coaching, and creating organizational climates that are supportive of ethical behaviors. The methods suggested by May et al. (2003) are frequently employed in leadership (and employee) development programs and may prove effective in instances where the organizational climate supports authentic communication. Problematic, however, is the fact that "the prevailing [organizational] context within which women and men communicate is dominated by male values and forms" (Marshall, 1993, p. 126). The challenge therefore is whether and how women can develop authenticity and authentic communication in the absence of the requisite climate and organizational structure. In fact, Walker and Aritz (2015) assert that "teaching women to enact masculine leadership behaviors will likely not aid in improving their numbers in management. Instead, business schools need to focus on the value of changing organizational cultures to become more supportive and inclusive and to understand the value of talk in creating those realities" (p. 474).

The individual leader also plays a key role in his/her own development of authentic leadership. Northouse (2015), for example, observed that self-knowledge, awareness, and understanding of self-other interactions are an integral part of the authentic leadership development process. If one accepts Northouse's premise that the construct of authentic leadership is primarily individual rather than organizational, authentic leadership development can take place outside the confines of the organization. Baron and Parent (2015), in a study of middle managers from several different organizations who participated participants in a three-year leadership training program, found that AL could be developed within the context of a training program; thus, even when existing organizational climates were unsupportive, the development of AL in individuals could occur. Specifically, these researchers found that self-awareness, relational transparency were crucial; further, in regards to communication skills, they found that balanced information processing that increased the propensity to listen and analyze others' communication could be developed through a training program. The findings of the study also suggested that such training would require a significant investment of time rather than being captured in a quick-fix, one-time workshop. Similarly, Shapira-Lishchinsky (2014) in a study using education leaders demonstrated that team-based simulations, outside of the organizational context, could be used effectively for authentic leadership development and could then be transferrable to other situations. Of particular significance to our current discussion is relational transparency, which is one of the dimensions of AL developed in the study. Relational transparency was defined as "openly sharing information through honest communication with others while trying to minimize displays of inappropriate emotions" (p. 982), which implies that simulations may be utilized in authentic communication training.

The use of small groups in leadership development is not an entirely novel concept. An alternative use of small groups in AL development is that of "True North Groups." George (2011, 2012) characterizes these groups as safe fora that afford individuals the opportunity for open self-expression and dialogue with peers; they have been proven to be effective in develop- [*small groups*] ing authentic leaders. Giving and receiving feedback are among the (communication) skills that can be developed through such groups (George, 2012).

Our discourse thus far has focused on very general strategies for developing authentic leaders, especially those who can communicate authentically, and the strategies could be used by all genders. However, individuals responsible for designing leadership development programs should be cognizant of gender differences if they are to develop programs that effectively address the need of all leaders. Specifically, because organizations are not gender neutral, perceptions of authenticity are not as much a function of specific actions/behaviors as they are the function of gender (Hopkins & O'Neil, 2015; Liu, 2010).

It is important to consider the role of communication in creating and reinforcing gender roles. According to Clair (1994), "there exist numerous choices with regard to how we talk, act, and react to our everyday experiences. How we choose to format our discourse reflects and creates social reality" (p. 237). Thus, rooted at the intersection of leadership, gender, and organization is the process of human communication. Similarly, as Mumby and Ashcraft (2006) have noted, "Communication can literally invent—not merely reframe or reproduce—material conditions, as when an occupational group invokes discourses of professionalism to vie for higher salaries and political influence" (p. 80). One way such invention can occur is through negotiation. Communication skills are crucial in organizational negotiations ranging from procuring office space to enacting office policies. Indeed, all leaders engage in negotiations of some form. If women are to communicate authentically in organizational negotiations, they must frame the negotiations such that congruence exists between their internal self and the external interactions with others. On the other hand, in negotiating in male-normed organizational cultures, their modes of communication may be discredited. Anecdotal evidence suggests that women are not skilled negotiators because they fail to ask or advocate for themselves. Ely et al. (2011) disagreed with the notion that women do not ask; their position is that women more typically ask and negotiate on behalf of others rather than on behalf of themselves. Because women often take stands against inequity and injustice, Ely et al. (2011) suggested that it might be productive for women who are leaders to think of negotiation in terms of agency rather than self-promotion. Doing so can be a strategy for increasing their comfort with negotiation and enhancing their authentic communication during the negotiation process.

Likewise, communicating a compelling vision is a requirement for leadership (Ibarra & Obodaru, 2009). Confidence, clarity, and directness are requisites for effectively articulating a vision and thereby inspiring and motivating

"Women cannot lead authentically while trying to fit into male-normed patterns."

others. Yet the research by Ibarra and Obodaru found that women were perceived to be less adept at communicating their vision than men (2009), bringing into question their leadership abilities. Consequently, Ibarra and Obodaru described this deficit: "One of the biggest developmental hurdles that aspiring leaders, male and female alike, must clear is learning to sell their ideas—their vision of the future—to numerous stakeholders" (2009, p. 64). This lack may be due to women's linguistic styles and apparent lack of confidence or assertiveness in communicating. For example, Grant and Taylor (2014) found significant variance in the manner in which men and women articulated their accomplishments and projected confidence, with women appearing less assertive, having more vocal and fidgeting pauses (e.g., "um" and "ah") and being less succinct. To address this apparent communication deficit (by women), Grant and Taylor recommended that "mentally structuring responses like a bulleted list underneath a main point or headline provides the confidence to eliminate hesitancies and fillers" (p. 76).

outline to eliminate hesitance or fillers.

Although women are viewed anecdotally as being more talkative than men are, a meta-analysis of the literature on authentic leadership by Tibbs, Green, Gergen, and Montoya (2016) found that males were rated as being more talkative than females. In their meta-analysis, Tibbs et al. (2016) found that the degree of disclosure and affiliative speech was generally higher for females, which may be the reason for these perceptions. Moreover, Tibbs et al. found that the degree of self-disclosure and perceptions of self-disclosure or relational transparency differed between male and female followers, with females being more likely to associate higher levels of disclosure of female leaders with authenticity, while male followers perceived this behavior as blurring the leader/follower roles. These finding suggests that female leaders may have to alter their communication styles when communicating across gender in order to be perceived as being authentic, and it illustrates the conundrum women face in that they cannot lead authentically while trying to fit into male-normed patterns.

○ Females expect higher levels of self-disclosure from female leaders

● Men see more self-disclosure as blurring leader/follower roles

SUMMARY

The development of gendered communication styles is a socialization process, which starts early in life and translates into organizational contexts. Societal and organizational norms dictate the acceptable forms and styles of communication by gender. Within traditional organizations, women's communication styles are generally not perceived as being indicative of leader or leadership effectiveness. The double-bind—that neither using so-called feminine styles of communication nor adopting male styles of communication—results in the acceptance or legitimization of the communication styles of women. As such, women leaders are less likely to be perceived as being authentic in their communication within organizations. We, however, propose that the barriers are not insurmountable.

We have identified some challenges and possible opportunities for women leaders in developing and fostering authentic communication. The onus for developing authentic communication cannot rest solely on the individual woman leader; it is imperative that the entire organization recognize the value and be involved in the process. At the organizational level, authentic leadership and transparent communication positively impact both internal communication and employees' relationship with the organization (Men, 2014; Men & Stacks, 2014). Thus, a multi-pronged approach that includes all organizational stakeholders must be adopted in the construction and implementation of any authentic leadership development program. Previous research appears to indicate that authentic leadership can be developed and augmented through the creation of organizational climates that foster self-awareness, authenticity, and ethics. For example, Buzzanell and Wilbur (2013) conceptualize a feminist organizational culture that "entails ethical considerations, or discourses of advocacy—monitoring, challenging, and transforming the presumptions of ordinary operating processes by (re)creating cultures that empower stakeholders, embrace inclusion, and constantly think ahead to responsibilities in and consequences of organizing" (p. 106).

Even in the absence of the requisite organizational structures and climates, education and training of women to be authentic leaders can be effective. Both women and men must be educated in the variances and the legitimacy of gender difference in communication, which requires openness to a shift in paradigms. By problematizing the structure of male-normed organizations, we illustrate opportunities to effect such change. As with most change processes, a significant investment in time is required to alter attitudes and perceptions. Approaches to addressing issues related to authentic communication must take into account the individual leader's gender, the gender of followers, and the organizational climate. Previous studies have identified solutions that have proven to be effective in developing leaders who communicate effectively. However, caution must be exercised in adopting any of the strategies proposed in the literature. Such strategies must be tailored to individual needs, and needs assessment should be an integral part of the process. If the benefits of authentic communication are to be more fully realized, researchers, and practitioners must work together to develop comprehensive, multi-pronged strategies for developing authentic communication that address the needs of all leaders, regardless of gender. This would encompass individual self-reflection; small-group work that promotes such reflections (e.g., True North Groups); work in single-gender groups, which are more likely perceived to be safe places; and organizational training programs. Furthermore, followers need to be aware that communication differences, and potentially inaccurate perceptions of communication, may disadvantage some leaders.

NOTE

1. There are important distinctions in how we define such dichotomies as feminine/masculine and female/male. Following West and Zimmerman (1987, 2009), we want to analytically distinguish between sex, sex categorization, and gender. Gender is defined in many ways. The World Health Organization (2016) defines gender as "the socially constructed characteristics of women and men—such as norms, roles and relationships of and between groups of women and men" (para. 1). In discussing gender, however, we also understand that people identify with, and are identified by, their position on a continuum from extremely feminine to extremely masculine. Thus, men (biological males) may rest more on the feminine side of the scale, and vice versa for women (biological females). We are conscious of our choices when we use the terms "female" and "feminine" and do not intend to dichotomize or essentialize female leaders; rather, we are accounting for organizational actors' perceptions of a "female leader" or a "male leader." For the purpose of this discussion, we believe it is important to distinguish between female and feminine leaders.

REFERENCES

Alvesson, M., & Due Biling, Y. (1997). *Understanding gender and organizations.* Thousand Oaks, CA: SAGE.

Baron, L., & Parent, E. (2015). Developing authentic leadership within a training context:

Three phenomena supporting the individual development process. *Journal of Leadership & Organizational Studies, 22*(1), 37–53.

Bencherki, N., & Snack, J. P. (2016). Contributorship and partial inclusion: A communicative perspective. *Management Communication Quarterly, 30*(3), 279–304. doi:10.1177/0893318915624163

Brummans, B. H. J. M., Cooren, F., Robichaud, D., & Taylor, J. R. (2014). Approaches to the communicative constitution of organizations. In L. L. Putnam & D. K. Mumby (Eds.), *The SAGE handbook of organizational communication: Advances in theory, research, and methods* (3rd ed., pp. 173–194). Thousand Oaks, CA: SAGE.

Buzzanell, P. M., & Wilbur, D. S. (2013). Uma visño feminista para cultura organizacional [Taking a feminist lens to organizational culture]. In M. Marchiori (Ed.), *Faces of organizational culture and communication* (Vol. 3, pp. 105–124). São Paulo, Brazil: Difusao.

Clair, R. P. (1994). Resistance and oppression as a self-contained opposite: An organizational communication analysis of one man's story of sexual harassment. *Western Journal of Communication, 58*(4), 235–262.

Craig, R. T. (1999). Communication theory as a field. *Communication Theory, 9*(2), 119–161.

Eagly, A. H. (2005). Achieving relational authenticity in leadership: Does gender matter? *The Leadership Quarterly, 16*(3), 459–474. doi:10.1016/j.leaqua.2005.03.007

Eagly, A. H., & Karau, S. J. (2002). Role congruity theory of prejudice toward female leaders. *Psychological Review, 109*(3), 573–598. doi:10.1037//0033-295X.109.3.573

Ely, R. J., Ibarra, H., & Kolb, D. M. (2011). Taking gender into account: Theory and design for women's leadership development programs. *Academy of Management Learning & Education, 10*(3), 474–493.

Fairhurst, G. T., & Connaughton, S. L. (2014). Leadership: A communicative perspective. *Leadership, 10*(1), 7–35.

Fitzsimmons, T. W., Callan, V. J., & Paulsen, N. (2014). Gender disparity in the C-suite: Do male and female CEOs differ in how they reached the top? *The Leadership Quarterly, 25*(2), 245–266. doi:10.1016/j.leaqua.2013.08.005

Gardner, W. L., & Carlson, J. D. (2015). Authentic leadership. In J. D. Wright (Ed.), *International Encyclopedia of the Social & Behavioral Sciences* (2nd ed., pp. 245–250). Amsterdam, the Netherlands: Elsevier Science Direct.

George, B. (2011). True North Groups: Leadership development for the 21st century. *Public Management, 93*(11), 20–23.

George, B. (2012). True North Groups: A big idea for developing leaders. *Leader to Leader, 2012*(63), 32–37. doi:10.1002/ltl.20007

Grant, A. D., & Taylor, A. (2014). Communication essentials for female executives to develop leadership presence: Getting beyond the barriers of understating accomplishment. *Business Horizons, 57*(1), 73–83.

Hopkins, M. M., & O'Neil, D. A. (2015). Authentic leadership: application to women leaders. *Frontiers in Psychology, 6* (959), 1–5. doi:10.3389/fpsyg.2015.00959

Ibarra, H. (2015). The authenticity paradox. *Harvard Business Review, 93*(1/2), 52–59.

Ibarra, H., & Obodaru, O. (2009). Women and the vision thing. *Harvard Business Review, 87*(1), 62–70.

Ilies, R., Morgeson, F. P., & Nahrgang, J. D. (2005). Authentic leadership and eudaemonic well-being: Understanding leader–follower outcomes. *The Leadership Quarterly, 16*(3), 373–394. doi:10.1016/j.leaqua.2005.03.002

Jiang, H., & Men, R. L. (2015). Creating an engaged workforce: The impact of authentic leadership, transparent organizational communication, and work-life enrichment. *Communication Research, 44*(2), 225–243. doi:10.1177/0093650215613137

Kuhn, T. (2012). Negotiating the micro-macro divide thought leadership from organizational communication for theorizing organization. *Management Communication Quarterly, 26*(4), 543–584. doi:10.1177/0893318912462004

Liu, H. (2010). When leaders fail: A typology of failures and framing strategies. *Management Communication Quarterly, 24*(2), 232–259.

Liu, H., Cutcher, L., & Grant, D. (2015). Doing authenticity: The gendered construction of authentic leadership. *Gender, Work & Organization, 22*(3), 237–255. doi:10.1111/gwao.12073

Marchiori, M., & Bulgacov, S. (2012). Strategy as communicational practice in organizations. *International Journal of Strategic Communication, 6*(3), 199–211. doi:1 0.1080/1553118X.2012.654550

Marshall, J. (1993). Viewing organizational communication from a feminist perspective: A critique and some offerings. *Annals of the International Communication Association, 16*(1), 122–143. doi:10.1080/23808985.1993.11678848

May, D. R., Chan, A. Y. L., Hodges, T. D., & Avolio, B. J. (2003). Developing the moral component of authentic leadership. *Organizational Dynamics, 32*(3), 247–260. doi:10.1016/S0090-2616(03)00032-9

Men, L. R. (2014). Internal reputation management: The impact of authentic leadership and transparent communication. *Corporate Reputation Review, 17*(4), 254–272.

Men, L. R., & Stacks, D. (2014). The effects of authentic leadership on strategic internal communication and employee-organization relationships. *Journal of Public Relations Research, 26*(4) 301–324. doi:10.1080/1062726X.2014.908720

Mumby D. K. (2007). Organizational communication. In Ritzer G. (Ed.), *The encyclopedia of sociology*, (pp. 3290–3299). London, United Kingdom: Blackwell.

Mumby, D. K., & Ashcraft, K. L. (2006). Organizational communication studies and gendered organization: A response to Martin and Collinson. *Gender, Work, & Organization, 13*(1), 68–90.

Northouse, P. G. (2015). *Leadership: Theory and practice* (7th ed.). Los Angeles, CA: SAGE.

Putnam, L. L., & Nicotera, A. M. (Eds.). (2009). *Building theories of organization: The constitutive role of communication*. New York, NY: Routledge.

Shapira-Lishchinsky, O. (2014). Toward developing authentic leadership: Team-based simulations. *Journal of School Leadership, 24*(5), 979–1013.

Tibbs, S., Green, M. T., Gergen, E., & Montoya, J. A. (2016). If you are like me, I think you are more authentic: An analysis of the interaction of follower and leader gender. *Administrative Issues Journal, 6*(1), 118–133. doi:10.5929/2016.6.1.8

Trethewey, A., & Ashcraft, K. L. (2004). Practicing disorganization: The development of applied perspectives on living with tension. *Journal of Applied Communication Research, 32*(2), 81–88.

Walker, R. C., & Aritz, J. (2015). Women doing leadership: Leadership styles and organizational culture. *International Journal of Business Communication, 52*(4), 452–478. doi:10.1177/2329488415598429

Weick, K. E. (1979). *The social psychology of organizing* (2nd ed.). Reading, MA: Addison-Wesley.

West, C., & Fenstermaker, S. (1995). Doing difference. *Gender & Society, 9*(1), 8–37.

West, C., & Zimmerman, D. H. (1987). Doing gender. *Gender & Society, 1*(2), 125–151.

World Health Organization. (2016). Gender, equity and human rights. *World Health Organization*. Retrieved from http://www.who.int/gender-equity-rights/understanding/gender-definition/en

PART III

AROUND THE GLOBE:
CULTURE, COMMUNICATION, AND LEADERSHIP

Leadership is fundamentally positional. Traditional perspectives on leadership (over)emphasized the connection between leadership behaviors and organizational position. In other words, being identified as a leader was equated to holding a leadership position. More recent scholarship, particularly communication scholarship, recognizes that leadership practices are and can be emergent and dynamic. Rather than being a trait that one has or strives for, an emergent view of leadership notes that different contexts and different groups of people provide conditions for one or more leaders to emerge. Leadership is also culturally contextual, and fascinating insights can be gained by looking at leadership practices and policies around the globe. To take a global approach to understanding leadership involves, in part, thinking about how leadership is shaped by culture: How is leadership effectiveness and even legitimacy assessed differently within different cultures? What perspectives are made possible by examining and comparing leadership practices in different locations around the world?

This book aims to bridge the gendered leadership gap by paying attention to those communication practices that are at the heart of most leadership experiences. Transnational feminist theory adds a useful layer to the understanding of how gender, leadership, and communication are impacted by global forces This theory suggests that thinking globally about a subject (e.g., gender, communication, leadership) reveals *both* points of similarity across borders *and* instances in which power is deployed and enacted in uneven ways (Hegde, 1998). In other words, looking at global examples

Gender, Communication, and the Leadership Gap, pages 123–125
Copyright © 2017 by Information Age Publishing
All rights of reproduction in any form reserved.

123

of leadership may offer insight into some of the taken-for-granted assumptions that underlie some contemporary leadership theories.

The chapters in this section offer a view of leadership practice and policy in the Netherlands, France, Ghana, and Liberia, along with a personal reflection about leadership and mentorship in Kenya. Although each chapter offers a culturally unique perspective on leadership, the thread that ties the cases together is that many existing theories of leadership do not adequately account for gender, nor for the impact of culture on leadership. As Connaughton and Linabary (this volume, Chapter 10) argue, most leadership scholarship is "shaped by cultural expectations about what leadership in those settings looks like and whose leadership is privileged" (p. 172). The four chapters that follow provide a careful corrective to this kind of scholarship and offer important insights about shared challenges that women leaders face, even as they also show the unique elements specific to each country. Women leaders in France and the Netherlands are supported by robust national policies that encourage gender parity, and insights from Chapters 8 (Henderikse, van Beek, & Pouwels) and 9 (Naschberger, Quental & LeGrand) help to show both the advantages and the limits of these policies. Both Connaughton and Linabary and Muriungi (this volume, Chapters 10 & 11) focus their research on Africa, and show how gendered leadership practices exist within broader power structures that impact whose voices get heard, who has access to resources, and who can be considered a legitimate leader.

One of the most clear insights produced when taking a global perspective on leadership is that the challenges that face women leaders are both universal, at one level, while also being profoundly shaped by the local cultural context. Gender is not only intersected with other social categories such as race and nationality, but is also profoundly shaped by spatial and cultural forces. Accordingly, researchers have shown that cultural preferences for individualism or collectivism color and guide attendant assumptions about the kinds of communication behaviors that are appropriate for leaders (Javidan, Dorfman, Howell, & Hanges, 2010). Beyond an awareness of cultural preferences, it is also necessary for researchers to move beyond simple comparison of different cultural approaches. This is where transnational feminist theory can be especially useful, given that it focuses on "purposive attempts by people from different backgrounds and social locations to work together around common goals while attending to their differences" (Dempsey, 2011, p. 62). How might leadership be enhanced by focusing on "the between" of leader relationships and practices? Taking this perspective offers insights into the fundamental role that communication plays in developing and negotiating leadership among diverse groups of people and, more broadly, leadership in a diverse world.

The four chapters in this section together offer a transnational view of gender and leadership. These chapters illustrate that there are many different ways to bridge the gender gap rather than assuming the existence of a unified vision of global communication practices. Together, these chapters serve as a reminder that leadership is not only a collaborative achievement, but also that such collaboration must balance the tensions between sameness and difference.

REFERENCES

Dempsey, S. E. (2011). Theorizing difference from transnational feminisms. In D. K. Mumby (Ed.), *Reframing difference in organizational communication studies: Research, pedagogy, practice* (pp. 55–75). Thousand Oaks, CA: SAGE.

Hegde, R. S. (1998). The view from elsewhere: Locating difference and the politics of representation from a transnational feminist perspective. *Communication Theory, 8*(3), 271–297.

Javidan, M., Dorfman, P. W., Howell, J. P., & Hanges, P. J. (2010). Leadership and cultural context: A theoretical and empirical examination based on Project GLOBE. In N. Nohria & R. Khurana (Eds.), *Handbook of leadership theory and practice: An HBS centennial colloquium on advancing leadership* (pp. 335–376). Boston, MA: Harvard Business Press.

CHAPTER 8

THE EFFICACY OF STRATEGIES TO ELEVATE GENDER EQUALITY IN LEADERSHIP

Assessing the Netherlands' "Charter Talent to the Top" Initiative

Wilma Henderikse, Annemieke van Beek, and Babette Pouwels
VanDoorneHuiskes en Partners

This chapter addresses workplace policies as solutions to elevate gender equality in leadership by raising the number of women in high-visibility roles such as top management. Increasing the visibility of women in leadership communicates a positive image of women working in male-dominated ranks and provides role models for aspiring female managers (Elmuti, Jia, & Davis, 2009; Schwanke, 2013). Women's relative presence or absence in powerful organizational positions also underscores the value of women to the organization. For example, stereotypical gender roles are more problematic when the share of senior women is low, and women are less likely

Gender, Communication, and the Leadership Gap, pages 127–149
Copyright © 2017 by Information Age Publishing
All rights of reproduction in any form reserved.

to experience their shared gender as a positive basis for identification with each other. Furthermore, senior women are less likely to be perceived as role models (Ely & Rhode, 2010).

This chapter is not about how women become leaders and who they are as leaders. Taking a leader role involves internalizing a leadership identity and developing a sense of purpose. However, integrating leadership into one's core identity is particularly challenging for women, who must establish credibility in a culture that is deeply conflicted about whether, when, and how they should exercise authority (Ibarra, Ely, & Kolb, 2013). These kinds of questions call for research on the interplay between organizational features and individual-level processes (Ely & Rhode, 2010). Two relevant questions addressed in this chapter are what are the organizational conditions under which differences between men and women in communication styles and influence tactics can flourish and what helps to encourage women to take on leadership roles?

Before we can focus on women's leadership development, we first need women in leadership positions. The underrepresentation of women in top leadership positions is a worldwide phenomenon, and only modest progress has been made. The question of how organizations can increase the number of women in the top of their organizations and improve gender balance deserves more attention. What strategies and programs are used, and what has proved most effective in increasing the number of women at the top?

Using a longitudinal research approach, we reviewed the efficacy of strategies of more than 200 organizations in the Netherlands used to address the persistent problem of the underrepresentation of women in top management positions. The organizations studied are a special group in that all are dedicated to realizing gender diversity in the top of their organization and therefore all have signed up for the Dutch initiative Charter "Talent to the Top." Organizations that sign up for the Charter commit themselves to a target and strategy to raise the representation of women in senior management and at the board level. They form a tight community of organizations with the common goals of creating gender diversity and exchanging experiences with other organizations on the lessons learned. The majority of the Charter organizations operate in the private sector. Charter organizations in the public sector are mainly universities, medical centers, and public authorities.

By sharing our findings, our goal is to provide future, emerging, and current leaders with practical strategies and tools that will help them to elevate gender equality in leadership by raising the number of women in high visibility roles. Our aim is to help close the gap between research and practice by addressing the implications for practice of our research findings. We will do so by illustrating our research findings, describing best practices of organizations using effective strategies, and addressing the implications for practice of interventions in the way of lessons learned.

A LOT OF WORK REMAINS TO BE DONE

"My concern is building a vital, creative, sustainable and strong organization. It just works better with a diverse workforce. We live in a network society. And women are networkers par excellence. This is their moment" (Henderikse & Pouwels, 2015, p. 5). The CEO who spoke these words did so honestly and consciously. If this is the moment for women, however, there is still a lot of work to be done. Even though European women have made a breakthrough in labor market participation, they still have not succeeded in breaking the glass ceiling that prevents them from getting to the top of organizations and politics (European Commission, 2012a, 2015). Specifically, men in boardrooms continue to vastly outnumber women. Although the proportion of women is gradually increasing by around 1.5% per year, in 2014 women occupied on average only 13% of the executive board seats of the largest publicly listed companies in EU member States. In 2014, the share of women on supervisory boards averaged 20% (European Institute for Gender Equality, n.d.)

The persistence of the glass ceiling has resulted in discussions on the need and desirability of quotas for women in leading positions in Europe (Seierstad, 2011). With its Strategy for Equality between Women and Men (2011), the European Commission put the issue of women on boards on the political agenda in 2010. In 2011 it called for credible self-regulation by companies to ensure better gender balance on the board (European Commission, 2011). Since as of yet there is no joint European framework on how to address gender balance in leadership positions, several countries have undertaken initiatives to improve the percentage of women on boards. Initiatives can be divided into legislative measures and voluntary initiatives. So far, the data collected indicate that legislative measures result in the greatest amount of progress. Legislative measures can be divided among binding quotas with sanctions, quotas without sanctions, and rules concerning state-owned companies (European Commission, 2012b). In 2003, Norway introduced a binding quota for listed companies to have at least 40% women on the board (Marinova, Plantenga, & Remery, 2010; Seierstad, 2013). France, Italy, and Belgium have followed the example of Norway and introduced binding quota legislation for company boards that include sanctions. Voluntary initiatives have been developed by many European countries, covering a wide range of programs and tools.

In contrast, the Netherlands has developed an approach that focuses primarily on voluntary commitment and the responsibility for companies to create their own path to gender diversity in their leadership. Although a legislative target was introduced in 2013 that aimed for a minimum of 30% women (and a minimum of 30% men) in executive and supervisory boards, there are no penalties envisaged for non-compliance. Companies that do not meet the target have to provide an explanation for not doing so in their annual report and articulate a plan for addressing the non-compliance (Pouwels & Henderikse 2015; 2016a).

THE BLACK BOX OF ELEVATING GENDER EQUALITY

Although the under-representation of women in senior positions has been abundantly problematized, identifying effective corrective measures remains overdue (Merens, Henderikse, & Pouwels, 2015). Many companies have implemented diversity policies. In the Netherlands, these policies were originally aimed at increasing the labor-market participation of women (Merens et al., 2015). Later, the focus was placed on the representation of women in senior positions. But if and how diversity policies help to reach this aim has hardly been studied. Insight into what organizations can do to elevate gender equality in leadership remains sorely lacking. After reviewing managing diversity literature, Foster Curtis and Dreachslin (2008) concluded that the current evidence base provides limited guidance to human resource professionals. Despite increased investment in diversity management practices, there has been little systematic effort to investigate what practices are more likely to yield results (Richard, Roh, & Pieper, 2013). Specifically, Olsen and Martins (2012) identified diversity management as an area of research in considerable need of theory development and testing; accordingly, he developed a framework. Kulik (2014) also argued that research is needed about which diversity management activities should be adopted, and when.

The problem is not that there is a shortage of academic research on diversity management, but that there is a gap between research findings and managerial practice, to use Kulik's (2014) wording. Reflecting on conversations with Human Resources (HR) professionals about diversity management, Kulik elaborates on the kind of research that is needed to answer HR professionals' questions about the effectiveness of various diversity management activities. Her conclusion is that research so far has focused too much on organizational practices as experienced by employees—"below-the-line research"—while more "above-the-line research" (p. 129) is needed into the effects of programs. Only a limited number of studies have explicitly focused on the effectiveness of diversity management programs that impact gender diversity at the top of organizations (Groeneveld & Verbeek, 2012; Kalev, Dobbin, & Kelly, 2006; Kulik & Roberson, 2008; Merens et al., 2015).

One particular exception is Kalev et al.'s (2006) research, which examined the effects of common diversity programs on the representation of men and women in the management ranks of 700 large companies. Kulik (2014) calls for more diversity management research that investigates cross-organization program effects such as research that asks HR professionals what their organization is doing to promote diversity, that examines the full range of diversity management activities, that focuses on finding where diversity management programs are more and less effective, and that incorporates a longitudinal focus.

As reported in this chapter, we are taking up the task to provide leaders with insights that will help them to elevate gender equality in leadership. The Dutch initiative Charter "Talent to the Top" enables us to follow the progress made by organizations that are dedicated to increasing the number of women in top-level leadership and, therefore, have signed the Charter. The Charter's database represents more than 200 organizations, providing information about their diversity programs over a range of years and enabling us to analyze the efficacy of these programs in promoting gender equality in top management positions. Furthermore, monitoring these organizations and interviewing individuals to learn more about best practices allows us to tackle the practical aspects of what organizations are doing and what proves to be effective. The information gathered from this network of change makers provides insight into the black box of elevating gender equality in organizations.

CHARTER "TALENT TO THE TOP"

The Charter "Talent to the Top" was started in 2008 by two female promoters and was financially supported by the Dutch government's Ministry of Education and the Ministry of Economic Affairs, with the aim of bringing about real and structural improvements in gender equality in organizations. The purpose of the Charter is to achieve higher inflow, promotion, and retention of women in top-level leadership. In the Charter, the top is defined as women in senior managerial ranks, which includes the board and the two levels directly below the board. Signing the Charter is voluntary, but doing so entails obligations: signatories commit themselves to measurable targets for the representation of women in senior management positions and to a timetable and strategy for implementation. These organizations agree to develop policies and measures to achieve their goals and to report and be monitored on their achievements annually by the Charter's Monitoring Committee, an independent group of representatives from science and industry. Since 2008, 257 organizations have signed the Charter (Pouwels & Henderikse, 2016a). Organizations represent both the private and the public sectors and represent a variety of sectors including trade, culture, media and communication, housing associations, health care, education, business services, industry, transport, technology, and consultancy.

On an annual basis, the Monitoring Committee provides individual feedback to each signatory organization and presents a report on overall progress. As independent researchers, we perform the monitoring research among Charter organizations on behalf of the Monitoring Committee. Based on the gathered data, we identify organizations that have performed well so that the Committee can identify and publicize best practices to serve as examples to other organizations.

METHOD

Our dataset draws from the Charter "Talent to the Top" database compiled from 2008–2015. The data are produced through an online questionnaire that organizations complete annually. The questionnaire gathers information about the numbers of men and women in the different levels of the organization, inflows and outflows, and it asks detailed questions about the characteristics of the diversity management program of the organization. In 2015, the 205 organizations that had signed the Charter were asked to complete the questionnaire with a net response of 86%. Together, these organizations employ 15,868 men and women in top management positions. For the effectiveness analysis, we gathered data from multiple measuring points, selecting only organizations that signed the Charter in 2008 or 2009 and were still members in 2015. This resulted in a sample of 159 organizations for which all relevant information was available.

Diversity Programs

The term "effectiveness" in this research was operationalized as the change in the share of women at the top, defined as the board and two levels beneath. The dependent variable is the share of women at the top. Diversity management programs are the independent variables. Six dimensions are used to operationalize the diversity management activities of the organizations in this research; these dimensions are described below. For each dimension, four levels are used to score the efforts and performance of organizations.

Six Dimensions of Diversity Management

In 2013 the questionnaire of the "Talent to the Top" Monitor was revised, particularly the "quality" part and questions about strategy and policies. Revision of the monitoring questionnaire (the monitoring tool) was conducted in the following steps: first, the relevant key areas for achieving diversity in organizations were identified based on the monitoring findings to date, and on insights drawn from the research literature and the experience of working on diversity within organizations, including company visits (Pouwels & Henderikse, 2014a); second, two management models were used to integrate the results of the first step into an assessment model: the INK-management model (INK, 2008) and the Diversity Driver (Farrer, 2004). The third step determined the appropriate indicators identified in the key issues and described the characteristics of organizations that excel in these areas. The fourth step created new questions for the questionnaire in the monitoring tool based on insights drawn from questionnaires from relevant, comparable research. The fifth step checked whether the questionnaire was consistent with the way that the monitoring commitments of signatories are defined in the Charter. Finally, a sample of 20 Charter organizations tested the new monitoring tool and provided feedback, which was used to further refine the tool.

Six important dimensions of diversity management were identified: Leadership, Strategy and Management, HR Management, Knowledge and Skills, Communication, and Climate. Pouwels and Henderikse (2014a) define the six dimensions as described in the following sections.

Leadership: The way in which leaders lead the organization and inspire the organization to set ambitions and reach a target. To what extent is "gender diversity" taken seriously by those at the top? Are leaders involved in actively propagating, promoting, and encouraging gender diversity management?

Strategy and Management: The extent to which vision and ambition are translated into concrete targets, measures, policies, and organizational goals and objectives. And the extent to which these are implemented by lower-level management/line management.

HR Management: The extent to which organizations use HR management and HR instruments and activities to realize gender diversity goals and objectives. Focusing on reconciliation of work and private life balance at the top, career development programs, and recruitment and selection.

Knowledge and Skills: The extent to which organizations, managers, and staff know which mechanisms promote and constrain gender diversity at the top.

Communication: The extent to which an organization actively, clearly, and repeatedly communicates its vision, sense of urgency, goals and objectives, and measures.

Climate: The extent to which an organization values gender diversity. The extent to which gender diversity is alive within an organization, a positive diversity climate.

As mentioned above, to assess the way in which gender diversity management is carried out in practice, we score the level of development of diversity management activities within the six dimensions focusing on the *effort* and *performance* of organizations. Each dimension can be scored on four levels of development as defined by Pouwels and Henderikse (2014a).

The first level is the lowest level and relates to the phase of *orientation, exploring opportunities for policy development*. On this level, the organization is exploring possible ways to realize equal representation of women at the top. Both current and future situations are analyzed and possible solutions are examined. The second level refers to the phase of *development of policies and getting started*. It focuses on the development of strategy and activities and plans of actions. Organizations are writing goals and setting targets. Arrangements are being made about how gender diversity is going to be managed. Programs are being launched. The third level relates to the phase of *realization: the organization is well under way*. In this stage, strategies are being pursued in order to realize gender diversity. Agreements are being kept. Strategy and policies are, however, not perfect, and there is room for improvement. The fourth and last level can be indicated by the key words *control* and *mastery*. In this stage, the organization focuses on the completion of tasks and accomplishment of goals and objectives. The organization has expertise in achieving gender diversity goals and knows what works. Evaluation for strategic learning is an integral part of business strategy in this stage. The organization strives for continuous improvement.

Analytical Approach

We analyzed the performance of Charter organizations using the six dimensions of diversity management, then examined how the six dimensions affected the increase in the proportion of women at the top. To measure the effect of each dimension, we used ordinary least square (OLS) regression with a lagged dependent variable/conditional change models (Pouwels & Henderikse, 2016a). We used the six dimensions, the percentage of women at the top in the year the organization signed the Charter (=lagged variable), and size, sector, and starting year as controls. The results of our analysis can be interpreted as the change in the percentage of women in top-level leadership of these organizations.

RESULTS

More Women at the Top

The latest results of the yearly monitoring of Charter organizations indicate that between 2014 and 2015 the percentage of women at the top increased from 20.9% to 21.5% (Pouwels & Henderikse, 2016a). Furthermore, the proportion of women at the subtop (i.e., management from the third level below the board of management/executive board) increased

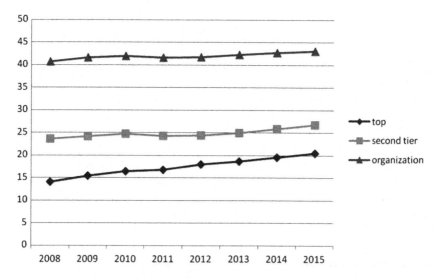

Figure 8.1 Evolution of the proportion of women at the top, second tier and overall organization, 2008–2015 (in percentages of the total number of people at the top, second tier, and overall organization; $n = 71$). *Source:* VanDoorneHuiskes en partners, Monitor Talent naar de Top 2015.

by almost one percentage point to 26.3%. It is important to include the subtop levels because they form the talent pool that is best positioned to advance into top management. Although the average percentage of total women workers increased slightly as well (from 42.4% to 42.8%), significant differences between organizations were evident. In 2015 five Charter organizations (3.2%) still had no women at the top of their organization. For organizations that signed the Charter in 2008 and 2009, we tracked performance over a longer period. The percentage of women at the top of these organizations grew slowly but steadily from 14.1% in 2008 to 20.5% in 2015 (Figure 8.1), averaging a 0.9% increase per year.

Women on Supervisory Boards

The Charter signatories are in the forefront of gender balance in regard to the boards of their organizations. Companies that have not signed the Charter show far less gender balance on their boards than do Charter signatories. The Dutch Administration and Supervision Act, which took effect on January 1, 2013, aims for at least 30% women (and at least 30% men) on the board of directors and on the supervisory board of large companies. Dutch companies predominantly apply the classical two-tier board system, comprising a management board and a supervisory board.

In 2015, an average 21.1% of the managing board seats and 26.3% of the supervisory board seats of Charter signatories were occupied by women. In supervisory boards of non-profit organizations (called *raden van toezicht*), relatively more seats were held by women: 36.6% on average. In 2015, 43.0% of the managing boards and 35.6% of the supervisory boards of Charter organizations obtained the target of a "balanced" composition (i.e., in terms of the new Act having at least 30% female seats and at least 30% male seats). The number of balanced supervisory boards of non-profit organizations is even higher: 71.8%—a much higher percentage than that found in a nationally representative sample among companies to which the Act on management and supervision applies, where women make up, on average, 9.6% of the managing board and 12.5% of the supervisory board (Pouwels & Henderikse, 2016b).

Improvement of Gender Diversity Programs

Charter organizations keep evolving and improving their diversity programs year on year. The longer that organizations are part of the "Talent to the Top" Charter, the better their gender diversity policies are developed and carried out within the organization (Pouwels & Henderikse, 2016a). Figure 8.2 shows the scores of organizations regarding the six dimensions (i.e., leadership, strategy and management, HR management, communication, knowledge and skills, and climate) in 2015.

Leadership is the most developed dimension: 43% of the Charter organizations have reached level 4, the control phase, and only 1% is still in the orientation phase, phase 1. Strategy and Management is relatively the least developed dimension: 41% of organizations are at level 2 (development) or less. Organizations that have achieved a high level of development in one dimension often have high levels of development in the other dimensions.

Every year Charter organizations score on all dimensions higher than the year before. From 2013 to 2014 Charter organizations made a big step in terms of Leadership. In addition, they developed during that period in HR Management and Climate. Between 2014 and 2015 they developed specifically in the dimension of Communication.

The Efficacy of Strategies for Diversity Management

Regarding the efficacy of diversity management programs, our analysis shows that the percentage of women at the top increases more significantly in organizations that have further developed their diversity programs. But which approaches are most effective in increasing the number of women at

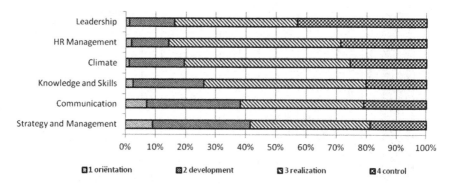

Figure 8.2 Development levels per dimension, 2015 (as a percentage of the number of Charter signatories; $n = 154$). *Source:* VanDoorneHuiskes en partners, Monitor Talent naar de Top 2015.

the top? Our regression analysis makes clear that all six dimensions are effective in raising the number of women at the top; all have an impact on the share of women at the top. High correlations were identified among the six dimensions: a high level of development on one dimension often accompanies a high level of development on the other dimensions (Table 8.1).

Only small differences were observed in the explanatory power of the six dimensions as the regression analysis shows (see Table 8.1). Climate seemed to have the greatest explanatory power and was the strongest predictor for the increase in the proportion of women at the top. HR Measures have the least explanatory power. HR Measures do have a positive effect on the increase in the percentage of women in top-level leadership roles; however, if controlled for the effect of other dimensions, the positive effect of HR Measures disappeared. In particular, Climate and Leadership eliminated the effect of HR Measures. When organizations scored high on Climate and Leadership, HR Measures showed a negative correlation, and when organizations scored low on Climate and Leadership, HR Measures had no effect. Why this is so requires further research. It is possible that a developing effect over time influenced these results; thus, HR Measures may have little effect if Climate and Leadership are highly developed and supportive of diversity.

Finally, our analysis makes clear that the *overall scale* of gender diversity management programs has a positive effect (.25) on the increase of the percentage of women at the top. Overall, it seems better to implement a broad range of measures than to search for a single measure that works.

TABLE 8.1 Efficacy of Gender Diversity Policies on the Representation of Women at the Top (OLS–Regression Analysis), 2008–2015, n = 159

| | Model 1 | | Model 2 | | Model 3 | | Model 4 | | Model 5 | | Model 6 | | Model 7 | |
| | Leadership | | Strategy and Management | | HR Management | | Communication | | Knowledge and Skills | | Climate | | Gender Diversity Management Total | |
	B	SE	B	SE	B	SE	B	SE	B	SE	B	SE	B	SE
constant	-.57	(.28)	-.38	(.24)	-.54	(.28)	-.50	(.25)	-.70*	(.27)	-.86*	(.30)	-.75**	(.28)
% women top starting year[a]	.65***	(.05)	.65***	(.05)	.65***	(.05)	.64***	(.05)	.65***	(.05)	.63***	(.05)	.64***	(.05)
Leadership	.17**	(.06)												
Strategy and management			.15**	(.05)										
HR management					.18**	(.07)								
Communication							.18***	(.05)						
Knowledge and skills									.23***	(.06)				
Climate											.24+	(.06)		
Gender Diversity management total													.25***	(.06)
adj. R²	.616		.616		.613		.628		.632		.631		.632	

*** p < .001; ** p<.01; *p<.05

[a] This variable was transformed before it was included in the model.

Note: The models are controlled for starting year, sector and organization size

Source: VanDoorneHuiskes en partners, Monitor Talent naar de Top 2015

Best Practices

Our analysis indicated that all six dimensions can be effective in raising the number of women at the top. But what do these findings mean in terms of practical implementation, and what are the lessons learned? Best practice organizations are Charter organizations that have been successful in raising the number of women at the top of their companies. These organizations meet three criteria: they pursue a successful diversity policy, realize a yearly increase in the number of women at the top, and are considered to be a "benchmark" regarding the number of women at the top among peers in their sector. Six to eight best practices are selected each year from the Charter organizations and publicized in an annual publication and presented on the Charter's yearly event. In summarizing "lessons learned," we cite examples of best-practice organizations to illustrate the implications for practice of effective interventions.

Leadership

This is the most developed dimension, as Figure 8.2 shows. Well-developed leadership with regard to gender diversity management leads to a higher share of women at the top. For Leadership to be effective, business leaders must show commitment to gender diversity and take *full responsibility* for creating gender diversity at the top. Organizations must go beyond simply saying diversity is important. Leaders must keep the organization *on track* and *encourage* the achievement of the desired goals and results. Furthermore, it is important for business leaders to *explicitly communicate* about the importance of equal representation of women at the top, to "walk the talk."

Best practice law firm Baker & McKenzie recognizes the importance of diversity in an exemplary manner. Baker's HR director thinks it is crucial to start with realizing and explicitly communicating why diversity is important for the firm:

> A reflection of society at all levels of our organization is the reason for our commitment to gender diversity. Responding to a changing labor market with more graduate women lawyers and maintaining (female) talent in the second tier is important. (Henderikse & Pouwels, 2013, p. 16)

The firm's diversity policies show a blend of ingredients that help to keep the organization on track to achieve desired results. Diversity management is led by the Diversity Council using Key Performance Indicators. Results are discussed regularly in the partner groups, which is important because close monitoring is essential for improvement (Pouwels & Henderikse, 2013).

The telecom company Vodafone takes diversity seriously. Their results show that establishing targets and adhering to clear agreements undoubtedly bear fruit (Henderikse & Pouwels, 2013). The management of Vodafone perceives that evidence of satisfying results serves as a reply to all those who are emotionally against targets for various reasons (e.g., women would be chosen to meet goals rather than based on their qualifications or merits). The organization's leadership is clearly in favor of diversity, and that contributes to achieving successful results in terms of gender equality. In fact, the CEO of Vodafone has explicitly stated, "Diversity is my great passion" (Henderikse & Pouwels, 2013, p. 23). This CEO further emphasized: "It's about the importance of clear agreements. For each position a credible woman on the short-list and sufficient talent in the pipeline." Responsible employment practices have contributed to Vodafone's achieving its goal of advancing more women into top-level leadership roles (Pouwels & Henderikse, 2013). Reflecting the composition of the population is thought to be crucial: "We aim to better reflect the population in our internal organization. More than 80% of consumer purchases are made by women and proportional representation is important from a business perspective" (Henderikse & Pouwels, 2013, p. 23).

Strategy and Management

Strategy and Management is relatively the least-developed dimension (see Figure 8.2), but the data from this study documented that organizations with high levels of Strategy and Management experience a larger increase in the proportion of women at the top. In daily work, different priorities compete for attention. Strategy and Management are, therefore, important for diversity objectives at *all levels* of the organization, specifically those related to *concrete actions* and to *anchor* these actions in the planning and control cycle of the line organization.

At the public authority of Enschede, diversity management is strongly driven by targets and agreements. Twice a year, all appointments are evaluated (Pouwels & Henderikse, 2013). Securing support from both managers and staff is important to reinforce the urgency of diversity management, as reported by Henderikse & Pouwels (2016a):

> Embedding and disseminating diversity within the organization requires not only a policy and planned approach, but also broad support in the organization. In recent years, diversity management was carried out by a separate diversity project. The objectives were achieved and diversity now has become part of organizational development under the heading of quality. (p. 17)

At biopharmaceutical company MSD Netherlands, each location has its own diversity plan. These plans contain diversity objectives and explain how the objectives will be achieved. For example, MSD Netherlands maintains a clear focus on diversity in recruitment and treats gender diversity as an important issue in discussions within the talent management and succession planning cycle (Pouwels & Henderikse, 2013). Diversity management is anchored in the regular planning and control cycle of the company as the HR Director explains: "A diversity manager is at MSD an old concept. Diversity is embedded within the line organization with a proper planning and control cycle. Through succession planning we aim for more women in important positions with a high level of visibility" (Henderikse & Pouwels, 2013, p. 21).

Knowledge and Skills

Understanding how diversity can be improved is a well-developed skill among Charter organizations. Furthermore, our analysis shows that the better the *understanding of the mechanisms* that play a role in promoting gender diversity among managers and staff, the greater this understanding is used to improve diversity management and the higher the share of women at the top (Table 8.1). This includes awareness among managers of the benefits of workplace diversity.

Airport operator Schiphol Group is another example of a corporation that is strongly committed to diversity. The Schiphol Group has placed the focus on awareness of the benefits of diversity because they realize that intrinsic motivation for diversity is of great importance. Henderikse and Pouwels (2013) quote the CEO of Schiphol, who emphasizes the importance of awareness:

> We are putting a lot of effort into it. We think this is really important. Top management was primarily interested in raising awareness; it's all about awareness, awareness, awareness. You must use resources, but it is awareness that matters. I believe very much in diversity and you passionately have to explain the "why" to the organization. (p. 22)

Climate

We proved that climate is particularly important as it shows the greatest explanatory power for the increase in the proportion of women at the top (see Table 8.1). Organizations with a positive gender diversity climate achieve a higher share of women at the top than organizations with a less-developed diversity climate. Climate is the strongest predictor for the increase in the proportion of women at the top. Equally important is to note that our analysis found that climate was likely to be affected by the dimension leadership. We assume that climate reflects the ethics of leaders, their actions and behavior, what leaders think is important, and whether or not they are able to inspire and empower people.

To achieve results in the area of gender diversity management, it is important that planning be supported by a diversity-minded organizational climate. An organizational climate that supports gender diversity is one in which gender diversity is valued throughout the organization, and attention is paid to the added value of having a diverse organizational culture. Measures and facilities that combine work with care responsibilities (e.g., part-time, flexible working hours, parental leave) are offered, accepted, and often used in the organization. Managers feel responsible for the realization of gender diversity goals. The organization is proud of what has been achieved. Stereotypes, prejudices, and discrimination are actively challenged in the organization's attitudes and code of behavior.

Another corporation that models "best practices" in regard to diversity is the Dutch energy company Essent, where room and appreciation for diverse thinking and doing are part of the corporate culture. This climate creates a safe environment to deal with diversity and to help employees feel at ease. Flexible working, in space and time, is generally accepted. At the same time, transparency of business processes is literally organized by means of design and decoration of building and workplace. Essent has created an open and innovative culture for employees supported by a variety of workplaces, from fishbowl offices, brainstorm banks, to hot spots (Pouwels & Henderikse, 2013). As the CEO of Essent explains: "The organization has a lot of tools to increase diversity. We anchor them in a safe organizational culture with open dialogue. There is room and appreciation for thinking differently, having a different view and really understand someone else" (Henderikse & Pouwels, 2013, p. 17).

The Dutch construction company Heijmans also offered examples of best practices in terms of prioritizing diversity in top-level leadership. Heijmans has paid a lot of attention to awareness and promoted an ongoing dialogue about this theme, with a "pink hat" used as a symbol for this awareness. Attention to the culture of the organization is necessary for the creation of a constructive approach in which cooperation and diversity are valued (Pouwels & Henderikse, 2013). A spokesperson for Heijmans noted, "We find it important to facilitate dialogue, as well as increase awareness of unconscious biases through training, through our women network 'La Heijmans' and using creative ways to gain attention such as the pink hat" (Henderikse & Pouwels, 2013, p. 19).

Communication

The dimension communication includes both the *visibility* of women in the organization, in word and in image, and the internal and external *communication* about the number and share of women at the top. Among Charter organizations the *visibility* of women in the organization in word and in image is highly developed and as such appears to contribute the most to a greater representation by women at the top as our analysis shows (see Table 8.1). The visibility of women in leading positions sends a clear message to other women and to girls, who represent future employees for these organizations, that they can get there too. Such visibility also demonstrates that the organization is dedicated to diversity and helps to attract a wider pool of qualified applicants.

Shifting from the corporate sector to higher education in identifying best practices, we see that Saxion University has demonstrated a de facto but also practical working commitment to gender diversity. A strong point is the conscious choice to create a balance between men and women in the executive board of the institution as one means of making it visually clear that diversity is important. Given the importance of role models, women in top management positions can inspire other women to aspire to higher-level leadership roles. The dean of Saxion University thinks this is of utmost importance and declares that "female role models are internally and externally visible in our communication" (Henderikse & Pouwels, 2013, p. 21).

Moving from higher education to other educational sectors, the school board Ons Middelbaar Onderwijs ("Our Secondary Education") pays regular attention to the theme of diversity and to the realization of targets in internal newsletters, on their website, and in their annual report. The chair of the board explains the importance of attention paid as follows: "The staff in our schools act as a model for our students. Role models can make a difference in the choices that students make in their lives" (Henderikse & Pouwels, 2015b, p. 20).

The public authority of Enschede has actively sought women for top positions. Gender diversity management is fully integrated into the organization, in part because diversity has been shown to improve the quality of decision making. Enschede currently focuses on a different method of communication and cooperation than had previously been the case (Pouwels & Henderikse, 2016a). The diversity manager of Enschede explains: "The new way (of working) can be expressed in words such as 'more equal, open, networking, content instead of power'" (Henderikse & Pouwels, 2016, p. 17), all of which are more related to the female way of working than to the male. With more women at the top, organizational leaders expect to infuse these new standards and way of working more effectively.

HR Management

HR Measures have the least explanatory power in increasing the number of women at the top. Furthermore, if controlled for the effect of other dimensions, the positive effect of HR Measures completely disappears, as we have shown. In particular, climate and leadership eliminate the effect of HR Measures. Does this finding mean we can do without HR Measures in obtaining diversity at the top of organizations? Interpreting the outcomes of our study in this direct way would not do justice to reality. Simply stated, these results indicate that HR Measures alone are not sufficient for creating diversity. Such measures by HR personnel cannot be successful without support from other leaders, a diversity minded climate, a well-planned strategy, a management plan that anchors diversity in the organizational policy, effective skills and knowledge, and sophisticated communication that expresses diversity. Or, to quote the CEO of Schiphol Group: "You have to use the resources, 'the little things' but the most important is awareness. I believe very much in diversity" (Henderikse & Pouwels, 2013, p. 22).

Determining which HR tools are the most appropriate to use will be different for each organization. Some instruments are focused on the increase of the influx of women, others on the improvement of the flow-through or pipeline and yet others are aimed at preventing talented women leaving the organization, the so-called "regretted loss." Helpful HR tools are also available that can facilitate the reconciliation of work and private life, such as offering the possibility to work part-time or facilitating working from home and working on different start and end times.

As another example of "best practices" from the corporate sector, Hotel Group Accor Hospitality Netherlands can be commended for its commitment to a transparent selection policy. Any form of discrimination is contested, and guidelines are followed in the recruitment and selection of employees to ensure objectivity. Managers receive training about various aspects of diversity via e-learning. When any vacancy occurs, managers are responsible for determining whether a woman is available, and at least two women are normally invited for the interview process (Pouwels & Henderikse, 2014a).

The new career policy of law firm Kennedy van de Laan clearly specifies the career steps employees can take at what moment and the criteria that have to be met for advancement. Significantly, the same applies to the firm's associate program. Furthermore, a new assessment system has been introduced with results and competencies that match the career stage at which lawyers find themselves, including identification of gifts and abilities. Both are relevant steps to improve career advancement of women into partnership because the path to partnership is not straight and clear, and objective measures cannot capture important elements such as internal and external reputation of junior associates (Henderikse & Pouwels, 2016). The HR manager highlights the advantages of transparency: "This will encourage everybody to develop oneself in his or her own talent. This approach is in addition to the self-evident possibility for everyone to work part-time and flexible" (Henderikse & Pouwels, 2016, p. 18).

A Wide Range of Options

Our regression analysis makes clear that each of the six dimensions proves to be effective in increasing the number of women at the top of organizations. In addition, our outcomes show that organizations having a *wide range* of policies and activities to embed diversity in the line organization achieve greater success in advancing women into senior leadership roles. The overall scale of gender diversity management has a positive effect, as we have made clear in Table 8.1. *Sustainable and continuous attention* to the issue of diversity in *various areas* appears to be critical to the success of such efforts. The CEO of the Schiphol Group advises other organizations to take the time to make the right choices:

> If a man leaves the company, you keep him in mind and hesitate to select a woman who physically and in appearance is very different. However you should not reject the female candidate but just take your time and discuss her nomination again in order to arrive at the right decision. (Henderikse & Pouwels, 2013, p. 22)

Schiphol Group actively seeks gender diversity, using a target of achieving at least 30% women at the top of the corporation. One of their strategies is the availability of a successful network called Women On Air, a Female Leadership Program. The curriculum of this Leadership Program includes training on culture awareness, and there are clear targets on recruitment, selection, and appointment. Diversity does not happen automatically; it requires continuous active steering. Diversity is clearly important within Schiphol Group's HR policies, and responsibility for diversity is also secured in the line organization with clear targets and responsibilities to deliver results, which means that line managers own the diversity strategy and are held accountable for leveraging diversity (Pouwels & Henderikse, 2014a).

Water Company Vitens also uses a wide range of measures to achieve gender diversity. Transforming people's beliefs about what is right and wrong does not happen automatically—it requires awareness and meaningful actions and measures (Henderikse & Pouwels, 2016). As the female CEO of Vitens proudly explains:

> It is self-evident that there are as many women as men at the top of the company. Vitens therefore makes a conscious decision to increase the chance of a man or woman in a (top) position. This is realized in different ways. The annual review focuses on potential talent that can contribute to diversity in the organization. For management jobs, shortlists are used with a 50% -50% ratio of men and women. Female role models are internally and externally visible in the communication. (p. 22)

CONCLUSIONS

How can we move forward to elevate gender equality in leadership? Before we can truly focus on the issue of leadership development of women, it is important that women are more visible in top-level leadership positions.

The presence of women in powerful organizational positions communicates the value of women to the organization; however, even in recent years too little progress has been made.

Our results document that gender diversity management has an effect on raising the number of women at the top of organizations. Some of our findings are in line with the results of Kalev et al. (2006), who have reported that programs such as networking and mentoring—as well as programs for reducing managerial bias through education and feedback/evaluation—have modest to no effects. Similarly, our research identified that HR initiatives alone are insufficient to create gender diversity at the top. HR measures, therefore, must be embedded in a supportive management structure and be surrounded by a diversity-minded climate.

Clearly, widespread support across various dimensions of organizational leadership is of utmost importance if real change is to occur. Therefore, leaders must not only show commitment to gender diversity but also take full responsibility for creating gender diversity at the top, keeping the organization on track, encouraging the achievement of desired outcomes, and communicating explicitly about the importance of gender equity among senior leadership and throughout the organization. Additionally, gender diversity management must be supported by a diversity-minded organizational climate that values gender diversity.

For this study, we had the benefit of access to the data of a large cross-organizational sample. However, we realize that the Charter signatories are a selective group in that they have a positive attitude toward gender diversity, are committed to setting targets and developing policies, and are highly motivated to take actions and to make gender diversity management work. We are eager to know how the results of this study would compare with data gathered from other organizations. The percentage of women at the top would probably be smaller, and the development of diversity management would likely be lower. However, the Charter signatories are leading the charge toward a gender balance in top-level leadership of organizations in the Netherlands; the organizations keep evolving and improving based on the annual data being gathered. As front runners, the Charter organizations serve as role models for non-Charter organizations and encourage them to follow. Diversity programs and practices that have been found successful within the Charter organizations can be used and adapted for use by others. While it remains beneficial to identify best practices in the organizations that were studied, these findings also call for more systematic research that evaluates the effectiveness of policies and measures that seek to increase the number of women in senior-level leadership across various types of organizations.

REFERENCES

Elmuti, D., Jia, H., & Davis, H. H. (2009). Challenges women face in leadership positions and organizational effectiveness: An investigation. *Journal of Leadership Education, 8*(2), 167–187.

Ely, R. J., & Rhode, D. L. (2010). Women and leadership: Defining the challenges. In N. Nohria & R. Khurana, *Handbook of leadership theory and practice: A Harvard Business School centennial colloquium on advancing leadership* (pp. 377–410). Boston, MA: Harvard Business Press.

European Commission. (2010). *More women in senior positions: Key to economic stability and growth.* Luxembourg, Luxembourg: Publications Office of the European Union.

European Commission. (2011). *Strategy for equality between women and men 2010–2015.* Retrieved from http://ec.europa.eu/justice/gender-equality/files/strategy_equality_women_men_en.pdf

European Commission. (2012a). *Women in economic decision-making in the EU: Progress report. A Europe 2020 initiative.* Luxembourg: Publications Office of the European Union.

European Commission. (2012b). *Women on boards: Commission proposes 40% objective.* Retrieved from http://europa.eu/rapid/press-release_IP-12-1205_en.htm

European Commission. (2015). *Gender balance on corporate boards. Europe is cracking the glass ceiling.* Retrieved from http://ec.europa.eu/justice/gender-equality/files/womenonboards/factsheet_women_on_boards_web_2015-10_en.pdf

European Institute for Gender Equality. (n.d.). *Gender equality index.* Retrieved from http://eige.europa.eu/gender-statistics/dgs/browse/gei

Farrer, J. (2004). A practical approach to diversity. *Industrial and Commercial Training, 36*(4), 175–177. doi:10.1108/00197850410542437

Foster Curtis, E., & Dreachslin, J. L. (2008). Integrative literature review: Diversity management interventions and organizational performance: A synthesis of current Literature. *Human Resource Development Review, 7*(1), 107–134.

Groeneveld, S., & Verbeek, S. (2012). Diversity policies in public and private sector organizations: An empirical comparison of incidence and effectiveness. *Review of Public Personnel Administration, 32*(4), 353–381.

Henderikse, W., & Pouwels, B. (2013). *Factsheet monitor Talent naar de Top 2012. Het zingt rond* [Factsheet Monitor Talent to the Top 2012. It sings around]. Zeist, Netherlands: Commissie Monitoring Talent naar de Top/VanDoorneHuiskes en partners.

Henderikse, W., & Pouwels, B. (2015). *Factsheet monitor Talent naar de Top 2014. De aanhouder wint* [Factsheet monitor Talent to the Top 2014. Persistence pays off]. Zeist, Netherlands: Commissie Monitoring Talent naar de Top/VanDoorneHuiskes en partners.

Henderikse, W., & Pouwels, B. (2016). *Factsheet monitor Talent naar de Top 2015. Charterbedrijven zetten de toon: Ambitie en commitment werken.* [Factsheet monitor Talent to the Top 2015. Charter companies set the tone: Ambition and commitment really work]. Zeist, Netherlands: Commissie Monitoring Talent naar de Top/VanDoorneHuiskes en partners.

148 ■ W. HENDERIKSE, A. van BEEK, and B. POUWELS

Ibarra, H., Ely, R. J., & Kolb, D. M. (2013). Women rising: The unseen barriers. *Harvard Business Review*. Retrieved from https://hbr.org/2013/09/women-rising-the-unseen-barriers

INK. (2008). *Gids voor het evalueren van organisaties (Guide for evaluating organizations)*. Zaltbommel, Netherlands: INK.

Kalev, A., Dobbin, F., & Kelly, E. (2006). Best practices or best guesses? Assessing the efficacy of corporate affirmative action and diversity policies. *American Sociological Review, 71*(4): 589–617.

Kulik, C. T. (2014). Working below and above the line: The research-practice gap in diversity management. *Human Resource Management Journal, 24*(2), 129–144.

Kulik, C. T., & Roberson, L. (2008). *Diversity initiative effectiveness: What organizations can (and cannot) expect from diversity recruitment, diversity training, and formal mentoring programs*. In A. P. Brief (Ed.), *Diversity at work* (pp. 265–317). Cambridge, MA: Cambridge University Press. doi:10.1017/CBO9780511753725.010

Marinova, J. H., Plantenga, J., & Remery, C. L. H. S. (2010). *Gender diversity and firm performance: Evidence from Dutch and Danish boardrooms*. Utrecht, Netherlands: Utrecht School of Economics Utrecht University.

Merens, A., Henderikse, W., & Pouwels, B. (2015). *Door het glazen plafond. Naar effectieve maatregelen voor meer vrouwen aan de top* [Through the glass ceiling: Effective measures for more women at the top]. *Beleid en Maatschappij, 41*(1), 6–31.

Olsen, J. E., & Martins, L. L. (2012). Understanding organizational diversity management programs: A theoretical framework and directions for future use. *Journal of Organizational Behavior, 33*(8), 1168–1187.

Pouwels, B., & Henderikse, W. (2013). *Het zingt rond. Monitor Talent naar de Top 2012* [It sings about. Monitor Talent to the Top in 2012]. Zeist, Netherlands: Commissie Monitoring Talent naar de Top/VanDoorneHuiskes en partners.

Pouwels, B., & Henderikse, W. (2014a). *Talent telt in de top. Monitor Talent naar de Top 2013* [Talent counts at the top. Monitor Talent to the Top in 2013]. Zeist, Netherlands: Commissie Monitoring Talent naar de Top/VanDoorneHuiskes en partners.

Pouwels, B., & Henderikse, W. (2014b). *Waar een wil is, is een weg. Bedrijvenmonitor 2013* [Where there is a will there is a way. Companies Monitor 2013]. Zeist, Netherlands: Commissie Monitoring Talent naar de Top/VanDoorneHuiskes en partners.

Pouwels, B., & Henderikse, W. (2015). *Topvrouwen in de wachtkamer. Bedrijvenmonitor 2012–2015* [Top women in the waiting room. Companies Monitor 2012–2015]. Zeist, Netherlands: Commissie Monitoring Talent naar de Top/VanDoorneHuiskes en partners.

Pouwels, B., & Henderikse, W. (2016a). *Charterbedrijven zetten de toon: Commitment en ambitie werken. Monitor Talent naar de Top 2015* [Charter companies set the tone: Ambition and commitment really work. Monitor Talent to the Top 2015]. Zeist, Netherlands: Commissie Monitoring Talent naar de Top/VanDoorneHuiskes en partners.

Pouwels, B., & Henderikse, W. (2016b). Waiting on the world to change. *Bedrijven monitor Topvrouwen 2016* [Companies monitor Top women 2016]. Zeist, Netherlands: Commissie Monitoring Talent naar de Top/VanDoorneHuiskes en partners.

Richard, O. C., Roh, H., & Pieper, J. R. (2013). The link between diversity and equality management practice bundles and racial diversity in the managerial ranks: Does firm size matter? *Human Resource Management, 52*(2), 215–242.

Schwanke, D. (2013). Barriers for women to positions of power: How societal and corporate structures, perceptions of leadership, and discrimination restrict women's advancement to authority. *Earth Common Journal, 3*(2), 15–28.

Seierstad, C. (2011). The use of quotas in the most equal region: Politics and corporate boards in the Scandinavian countries. In G. Healy, G. Kirton, & M. Noon (Eds.), *Equality, inequalities and diversity: Contemporary challenges and strategies* (pp. 171–194). London, United Kingdom: Palgrave Macmillan.

Seierstad, C. (2013). Gender quotas on corporate boards in Norway, necessary but not ideal. In S. Machold, M. Huse, K. Hansen, & M. Brogi (Eds.), *Getting women on to corporate boards: A snowball starting in Norway* (138–146). Cheltenham, United Kingdom: Edward Elgar.

*˅ internalized
gender
stereotypes*
p.159
*"scholarships to
attract talented
women" p. 163*

CHAPTER 9

THE LEAKY LEADERSHIP PIPELINE IN FRANCE

A Study of Career Levers and Barriers to Fostering Women's Leadership Development

Christine Naschberger, Camilla Quental, and Céline Legrand
Audencia Business School, France

Research focusing specifically on gender issues in career and leadership development has undergone an explosion in the last 20 years. From United Nations (2017) Gender statistics, we know that women represent nearly half of the working population in many developed countries. However, their careers still lag behind those of men when it comes to objective criteria for success; specifically, the leadership pipeline for women is in danger (Carter & Silva, 2010). Interestingly, communication, particularly in terms of stereotyping men and women differently, appears to be both part of the problem and part of the solution in the quest to achieve gender equality in the workplace.

Gender, Communication, and the Leadership Gap, pages 151–169
Copyright © 2017 by Information Age Publishing
All rights of reproduction in any form reserved.

151

The metaphors "glass ceiling,"[1] "labyrinth of leadership," and a "leaky female leadership pipeline" describe the complexity and difficulties of women's careers. The phenomenon referred to in this chapter as the leaky leadership pipeline[2] has raised the interest of scholars for decades. A Price-waterhouse Coopers (PwC) Report provides evidence that female talent is being lost from the pipeline, meaning that the assumption that women within organizations will desire to advance into senior-level leadership roles—and actually do so—is faulty (Global Human Capital, 2008). Multiple potential explanations of this "leakage" from the pipeline are offered in the literature: voluntary termination (Global Human Capital, 2008); work–life balance issues (Ely, Stone, & Ammerman, 2014); lack of flexibility (Sandberg, 2013); the paucity of role models, spousal support, and/or networking (Naschberger, Quental, & Legrand, 2012); self-censorship, gender stereotypes, and traditional gender roles (IMS-Entreprendre pour la Cité, 2012); a perceived "glass ceiling"; a lack of coaching/mentoring and/or cultural resistance (Heidrick & Struggles, 2015); a male-oriented organizational culture and sexism in the workplace (Grésy, 2009a); and rigid organizational structures. Women Matter Reports produced by McKinsey & Company (Barsh & Yee, 2012; Devillard et al., 2013; McKinsey & Company, 2014) have noted that "unconscious gender bias" (Davis, 2014, p. 131) embedded in cultural beliefs is holding women back. For a variety of reasons, it is clear that gender bias and differences do play a dominant role in women's advancement.

In this context, studies that appear pertinent are those addressing male and female managers' career development, those that identify gender differences in barriers and catalysts at each career stage, and those that aim to find ways to diminish these differences in career development. In addition to providing insights into barriers and levers both men and women confront in different career stages, the purpose of this chapter is to put gender differences into perspective, making a clear connection between gender and leadership, and then looking at these implications in terms of communication. More precisely, our aim is to answer the following three research questions: (a) What hinders and favors the career development of male and female managers generally, and in France specifically?; (b) What are the differences (in both barriers and levers) in career development for male and female managers?; and (c) Do barriers and levers change according to career phases and gender? Through finding answers to these questions and highlighting the communication concepts involved, this chapter contributes toward increasing gender equality and stopping some leaks in the female leadership pipeline, in particular in French companies. Although the focus is on the French context, we assume that leadership lessons may be valuable in other geographic and cultural contexts.

More specifically, this chapter seeks to contribute to a better understanding of barriers and levers of career development, as perceived and communicated by French female managers in comparison to their male counterparts, taking into account gender and age. The ultimate aim is to reduce inequalities and facilitate women's access to leadership positions by overcoming the leaky female talent pipeline. The chapter concludes with recommendations concerning career policies and managerial implications that human resource (HR) professionals and other decision makers can use to boost female managers' careers and that women may use to more effectively and actively manage their careers. In this sense, these suggestions for corporate decision makers will help those who wish to push through the "glass ceiling" and move through the career "labyrinth" more knowledgeably and effectively.

THE LEAKY LEADERSHIP PIPELINE IN FRANCE

Even though there are more women than ever before in managerial and professional jobs (Levanon, England, & Allison, 2009), they remain underrepresented in top leadership positions in organizations, and the phenomenon known as the "glass ceiling" remains a reality. There are certainly more women in highly paid, high-status jobs, and women have attained top leadership positions in many sectors. Nevertheless, these female senior-level leaders are exceptions, as is illustrated within the context of France by the paucity of women at the top of stock index companies (Belghiti-Mahut, 2004; Zarya, 2016). In order to examine potential obstacles for female top talent along the management suite, the metaphor concepts may provide a deeper insight. Metaphors are used within the communication literature to show how language structures the reality we perceive (Cheney, Christensen, Zorn, & Ganesh, 2011). More than a decade ago, Putnam and Boys (2006) demonstrated how the use of metaphors could help to formulate complex areas of social query, given that contrasting metaphors often produce different kinds of knowledge. Metaphors can also capture careers and career development (Baruch, 2004; Kram, Wasserman, & Yip, 2012). Metaphors are prevalent in the existing gender literature, and they are largely used to capture invisible (e.g., "glass ceiling," "sticky floor") or ordinary (e.g, "labyrinth, "leaky pipeline," "glass cliff") obstacles to women's careers. Furthermore, these metaphors illustrate the barriers to female career advancement (Smith, Caputi, & Crittenden, 2012); identifying them may therefore help women to overcome obstacles and move forward. In the career literature, metaphors serve as references for dialogue on careers, which are considered complex social constructs. Therefore, investigating metaphors and their multiple interpretations can help to reveal layers of meaning as well as the key role of communication at the social, organizational, and interpersonal level in either facilitating or hindering women's career development.

Some scholars have questioned the accuracy of the "glass ceiling" metaphor, arguing that it implies upward progression that is then rudely obstructed by an invisible barrier just short of the top prize (Eagly & Carli, 2007a; Prokos & Padavic, 2005). These scholars point out that, rather than a single barrier near the top that blocks women's advancement, barriers exist all the way along the route to the management suite. Eagly and Carli (2007a) proposed a different metaphor to account for the scarcity of women in top leadership positions: the "labyrinth of leadership" (p. 63)—a contemporary symbol[3] that conveys the idea of a complex journey toward a worthy goal.

The metaphors referenced above are complementary, and they try to illuminate the lack of female talent in top management positions. In attempting to address the female talent problem at the top level, countries have adopted different approaches. Some countries, the United Kingdom, for example, have preferred to adopt a voluntary and business-led approach (Heidrick & Struggles, 2015). Other countries, such as Germany and France, have implemented quota systems to help female managers progress. In the case of France, the 2011 Copé-Zimmerman law mandated that companies of the French Stock Market Index CAC 40—mainly multinational companies—have at least 40% of their corporate board seats filled by women by 2017.

In France, legislated pressure on corporations to improve gender equality in the workplace has influenced organizational and social structures. According to Cheney et al. (2011), hierarchical organizations have "a masculine bias—a set of pre-packaged, gendered assumptions about how power is to be exercised" (p. 21). For example, women are "struggling just to be heard" (Cheney et al., 2011, p. 120). Importantly, these authors specify that consciousness of gender-related aspects as well as gender roles can raise awareness of different aspects of work-life that typically are taken for granted. Some recent practices from France have illustrated how gender equality has served as a way of changing organizational structures; for example, more and more organizations are deciding to adopt inclusive working hours. As one illustration, in Trelleborg, France, increased accessibility for parents and especially women, was gained by changing the schedule of Monday board meetings from evening to morning. This example of a ban on meetings after 6:00 p.m. demonstrates how organizations implementing gender equality are opening up their company culture and redefining and shaping organizational identities in order to be inclusive; communication patterns and perceptions will be changed as a result.

Individual employees' perceptions of social reality influence their attitudes, values, beliefs, and interaction (Singer, 1998), and what individuals perceive informs what they believe about gender and leadership in organizations. Accordingly, institutional and organizational communication can help to inform how gender equality influences individuals' perceptions and understanding, and is eventually reflected in workplace behaviors and practices. This kind of evidence also strongly suggests that successful efforts toward greater equality at work will require a shift in institutional and organizational communication in matters of gender stereotyping.

RESEARCH METHODS

Empirical research was undertaken to illustrate the career development of male and female managers. The results and discussion presented in the sections that follow emerged from the administration of an online survey of 420 French female and male managers—alumni of a higher education institution. Most were employed by large companies (72%) in a diversified range of sectors, with a slight majority working in areas related to auditing, consulting, banking, or insurance. Survey data that were used for analysis were drawn from a sample that consisted of 226 women (53.8%) and 194 men (46.2%). The majority of the female and male managers surveyed lived with a companion and had on average less than two children. Specifically, 36% of those surveyed did not have children, 17% had one child, 25% had two children, 11% had three children, and the remainder had four or more children. Regarding educational attainment, all respondents had obtained at least a master's degree. The majority of the respondents in our sample belonged to dual-career couples with children.

For our analysis, the sample of male and female managers was divided into four age groups based on the Super career development model (Super, 1957); research that led to the development of this model indicated that an individual's career management primarily takes place between the ages of 27 and 45 (i.e., Super's establishment career stage). The four age categories were 27–30, 31–35, 36–40, and 41–45 years old. The survey was composed of 48 closed-ended questions (biographic data, information about the participant's job and company), and three open-ended questions that provided qualitative information about career trajectories.

The open-ended questions inquired into the managers' perceptions of their professional development, focusing on perceived barriers and levers in their careers. The answers to the open-ended questions are presented in the text of this chapter verbatim, and constituted qualitative material that we coded and analyzed to increase the trustworthiness of our findings. With regard to age, we used the technique of emerging codes to account for whether the data referred to a career lever or a barrier.

RESULTS

In this section, we describe and discuss the main findings of this qualitative study as related to gender, age, and career stage. More attention is given to the study of career development barriers, whereas the discussion of levers is developed further in the managerial implications section that follows.

Barriers to Career Development

The main career development barriers cited by men and women in France at each stage of their careers are presented in Table 9.1 by order of frequency of citation in the survey. Please note that Table 9.1 contains only those barriers cited by at least 20% of the female or male respondents.

Considerable differences were evident in the type of barriers that male and female managers reported having experienced, and in the four age-determined career phases. At the initial career stage, from 27–30, the "economic crisis" starting in 2008 was cited by both men and women. However, this crisis was cited as the most dominant career barrier for men, while for women "immaturity" was most cited. Indeed, 27–30-year-old men were more likely to mention external barriers to their careers, such as "the economic crisis" and "the reputation of the business school where I studied." Women, by contrast, more often cited barriers related to internal factors, and barriers that were more personal in nature, such as "immaturity," "maternity," "lack of self-confidence," and "work–life balance." In total, 33% of

TABLE 9.1 Career Development Barriers		
Ages	**Women**	**Men**
27–30	Immaturity Economic crisis Lack of self-confidence Work–life balance	Economic crisis Reputation of business school Lack of experience
31–35	Work–life balance Lack of networking Maternity Choice of sector (NGO, etc.) Being a woman	Ranking of business school Lack of networking
36–40	Being a woman Work–life balance	Lack of self-confidence Economic crisis Lack of networking
41–45	Maternity Priority of partner's career Work–life balance Lack of geographical mobility	Lack of geographical mobility Lack of self-confidence None

the female managers of all ages cited "work–life balance" as having been a barrier to their careers. The following responses drawn verbatim from the open-ended questions on the survey illustrate the range of internal factors cited by women of all age ranges: "finding the right balance between private and professional life," "motherhood," "motherhood first and foremost," "to create a family," "need to sacrifice one's personal life to climb professionally," "two maternity leaves and a desire to maintain work–life balance," "choice to combine work and personal life," "parenthood," and difficulty reconciling family and business trips.

In contrast, only 4% of the male participants identified "balancing career and family" as having been detrimental to their career advancement. Among those in the 36–40 age range, no man mentioned "work–life balance" as an obstacle to his career. Only one 41–45 year old man reported that the issue of work–life balance as a major obstacle to his career: "the lack of geographical mobility due to the family and the spouse's career." Thus, apart from minor exceptions, the careers of male managers in this study appeared to be less influenced by work-life-balance issues. Some respondents appeared to approve of traditional gender roles, as illustrated by a man from the 31–35 age group: "my wife has chosen to raise our child at least for now . . . some women may feel very satisfied and happy with this situation" and a woman from the 41–45 age group: "It is natural for a woman to take care of her kids and to lower her career ambitions."

The issue of a balance between work and personal life has recently gained importance and is the subject of intense debate both within companies and in academia worldwide (Tremblay, 2005). Moreover, a change in attitude can be seen in recent years, with several surveys of the "Millennial Generation" (born 1980–2000) confirming that work–life balance is one of the most decisive factors in the choice of a future employer (London Business School, 2009). Economic theories (e.g., Brines, 1994) suggest that increasing educational attainment and income of women are associated with a reduction of the number of hours invested in domestic work. However, current research findings contradict these theories. According to a recent French publication produced by the National Institute of Statistics and Economic Studies (INSEE; Champagne, Pailhé, & Solaz, 2015), over the last 25 years, French women have spent, on average, less time on housekeeping than previously but still take on the majority of domestic activities (71%) and parenting tasks (65%). The unequal distribution between partners that assigns women the role of managing family work and men that of productive work remains rooted as the prevailing mentality (Grésy, 2009b). Pursuing career goals is therefore more difficult for women who carry responsibilities in the double life of both private and professional worlds. The results of our study indicated that the 41–45-year-old women were most heavily impacted by these societal norms, which are still prevalent in the

French society. Responses reflected in the open-ended responses of women in this age group such as "priority of partner's career" and "lack of mobility" reflect this pattern. With 64% of the sample belonging to dual-career couples with children, making career decisions such as whose career comes first proved to be a big challenge.

"Being a woman" was another career barrier mentioned by many of the female respondents, ranking first for 36–40-year-old women and fifth for 31–35-year-old women. In the open-ended responses, female respondents used the following wording when referring to gender stereotypes: "prejudice against women"; "women have to over perform in order to be recognized"; "financial sector is very masculine... sex and age could be an obstacle at the beginning... but overshadowed little by little"; "my womanhood, being a woman implies being asked to do more to be recognized"; and "men are considered first for management positions... women stay behind!" Being a woman with children is sometimes complicated: "You have to invest two times more than a man to prove that you are able to take an important position, while being paid less than a man and having an equal responsibility." The "glass ceiling" really exists.

Given that the majority of the respondents worked for large French companies, this array of open-ended responses by female managers could imply that gender stereotypes are reinforced in male-oriented organizational cultures. One female respondent specifically cited this concern: "Being a woman, blond and tall, it's silly to say, but it remains an obstacle in some companies in which the management is rather patriarchal, macho." Notably, the above-illustrated expressions and verbatim comments were used only by the 31–45-year-old female managers. The fact that no woman in the 27–30 age group mentioned "being a woman" as an obstacle to her career suggests that younger female managers may not yet face or be aware of the barriers concerning gender stereotypes. These barriers seemed to be faced later in women's careers, when maternity issues and career ambitions collide and when women observe a pattern of being treated differently based on their gender.

Responses to the open-ended questions on the survey also provided evidence that being a woman also affected how others perceive and interact with one. These responses also revealed internalized stereotypes about a woman's identity and gender roles in society, for example, a woman holding back her career ambitions due to family responsibilities. Indeed, gender stereotypes can be seen as a societal factor, but also an organizational one. From an early age, social norms, beliefs, and stereotypes are acquired through education and the environment. Institutions such as school, family, and later the company in which one works, as well as influential sources such as the media, also play an important role in transmitting stereotypical images.

In contrast to the reports that "being a woman" was perceived to be a barrier by many of the women in this study, it is not surprising that no man reported that "being a man" harmed his career progress. A man from the 41–45 age group even issued a suggestion for women "to be themselves without trying to be better than men, and especially to keep their femininity, since it has a softening effect on the teams." According to Eagly and Carli (2007b) women tend to be classified into narrow stereotypical roles such as *seductive, mother, animal,* or *ironer.* Several studies (Eagly & Carli, 2007a, 2007b) highlight gender-role stereotypes as an influence in hierarchical advancement, and the findings of our study confirm this pattern. According to a recent study among French managers, perceptions of gendered skills continued to be evident: man as "leader" and woman as "support" (IMS-Entreprendre pour la Cité, 2012). The existence of these stereotypes can be a hindrance or an obstacle to the advancement of women's careers because stereotypes limit how people interact; additionally, such stereotypes act as levers for male managers.

Other career barriers that women who participated in our study self-reported as a hindrance to their career advancement included lack of self-confidence and other internalized gender stereotypes (IMS-Entreprendre pour la Cité, 2012). The youngest women (27–30) mentioned a lack of self-confidence as a career barrier, as did the two older male age groups (36–40 and 41–45). This result is interesting because lack of self-confidence is often considered to be a female attribute (Kirkwood, 2009) and our results show that men also have a lack of self-confidence.

Another career obstacle identified by one female age group (31–35) and two male age groups (31–35 and 36–40) was *lack of networking.* Some studies have reported that women typically have fewer opportunities to network than men because women are still more responsible for home tasks (e.g., family and care activities). It is mainly women who carry the "mental burden" (Tahon, 2003) of managing a household and family, characterized by "concern and availability" (Verjus & Vogel, 2009). Even if women have support at home, they typically take responsibility for managing the nanny, the cleaning lady, supervision of children's homework, and more, thus have less time to network professionally.

In conclusion, female managers do perceive and report different career barriers than men, confirming previous studies. In addition, the findings of this study indicate that these barriers vary across age ranges and career stages. Consequently, to address the leaky leadership pipeline, taking age and career stages into consideration is of primary importance, especially in the areas of internalized gender stereotypes or work-life balance, so as to encourage better customization of career development strategies and programs that address specific career barriers.

Levers to Career Development

Another aim of this study was to identify the different levers in women's and men's career development. Table 9.2 below summarizes the main career levers cited by the women and men at each stage of their careers, by frequency of citation. As with career barriers, only career levers cited by at least 20% of the female or male respondents are included in Table 9.2.

The results of this survey of 420 corporate managers indicated that both the 27–30-year-old women and men cited "mentoring" as the first career lever. However, the men also referred to "sponsoring," while the women respondents did not. Research indicates that practices such as "mentoring" and "sponsoring" are important career levers (Ibarra, Carter, & Silva, 2010). In our study, we were particularly interested in differentiating mentoring from sponsorship. Mentors offer psychosocial support (e.g., friendship, advice, assurance) for personal and professional development, plus career help that includes advice and coaching. Sponsoring, by contrast, is a strong commitment to develop a protégé's career. One characteristic in the literature that is commonly attributed to sponsors is their active advocacy for the career advancement of the individual being sponsored (Ibarra, Carter, & Silva, 2010).[4]

Analysis carried out in numerous studies by Catalyst (2015, 2017) and Ibarra, Carter, & Silva (2010) has documented that managers derive more satisfaction from being mentored but need sponsorship. Without sponsorship, a person is likely to be overlooked for promotion, regardless of his or her competence and performance. It is important to note that cultural differences related to gender exist between France and Anglo-Saxon countries concerning mentoring and sponsoring activities. According to some

TABLE 9.2 Career Development Levers		
Ages	Women	Men
27–30	Mentoring Engagement Changing of jobs International mobility	Mentoring/sponsoring International experience Self-promotion Professional network
31–35	Geographical mobility Humbleness Professional experience Risk taking	Expatriation Changing companies Mentoring and sponsoring Self-promotion
36–40	Geographic mobility Adaptability Expatriation	Ambition Personal engagement Self-promotion
41–45	Adaptability Personal engagement	Adaptability and flexibility International mobility

authors, mentoring has not yet been commonly practiced within French organizations (Persson & Ivanaj, 2009). Some studies suggest that women tend to participate and look for support in individual opportunities for the development of their competences; in contrast, men tend to find support in networking and mentoring, which are more collective practices (de Cheveigné, 2009; Ragins & Cotton, 1999). Our study confirms this last point, as illustrated in the open-ended remarks of several participants. Specifically, women tend to focus on skills development and experience, as reflected in comments in response to the career lever question such as: "adaptability and motivation to learn and diversify my skills," "professional experience," and even the "humbleness" to restart from a lower point if necessary. The surveyed female managers also tended to have invested a lot to get where they were professionally, and they expressed a belief that "chance" also played a role. For example, some of the women used terms such as: "a lot of investment and patience," "hard work, investment and luck," "ability to do a lot of work," and "chance." These results paint a picture of a "bookish" (*scolaire* in French) attitude among these French female leaders, who strategize so as to make progress through doing good work, much like being a good student, and think that they will be recognized for this kind of impression management and self-presentation. Those terms refer to the ways that individuals plan, adopt, and carry out the process of conveying an image of themselves to others. WOMEN

Clearly in contrast, the male participants in three age ranges (27–30, 31–35, and 35–40) frequently cited the importance of "self-promotion." In identifying this theme of "self-promotion," we included notions such as the French "*savoir-être*" (soft-skills in English), which concerns social/interpersonal skills, attitudes, and behavior at work. This notion of *savoir-être* emerged in our survey through certain expressions used by male managers to describe levers that had facilitated their career development.

The expressions used by the male managers that indicated *savoir-être* were "audacity," "my behavior," "know-how," "know how to show it," "seize opportunities when they arise," and "to know how to show people your work and make them recognize it." The notion of *savoir-être* also appeared to be linked to self-confidence, which is also a factor that differentiates men from women in their perceptions of career development, as explained below.

In our survey, we found that "geographical mobility" was a very important career development lever for both men and women, especially for those between the ages of 31 and 35. Interestingly, male managers also cited "expatriation" as a career lever in this age range, whereas women only cited "geographical mobility." For female managers, then, mobility exists, but not so strongly as to include "expatriation," especially for 31–35-year-old women, many of whom were likely in the life stage of becoming mothers and feeling concern about work–life balance.

Finally, "ambition" was identified as being a significant and, therefore, a very important career lever by the male managers. Ambition was cited as the first career lever by 36–40–year-old men, but was not cited by women frequently enough (i.e., at least 20% of the time) to be significant in this study. This result supports Hewlett and Buck Luce's (2005) research finding that approximately 50% of the men surveyed considered themselves extremely or very ambitious, whereas only one-third of the women considered themselves ambitious.

Only the group of 27–30-year-old male respondents cited the power of networks as a lever in managing their careers. The importance of networking was evident in the following verbatim phrases used by members of that group: "step up meetings and contacts," "creation of a network," "proposing conferences to meet experts," "development of international networks," and "to organize more meetings between professionals to enable each other to create a network." It is interesting that female respondents did not mention the role of networks as relevant to their career advancement; only the younger men did so.

In conclusion, the career levers we found are fairly similar across genders but vary according to age and career stage. As a consequence, in order to repair the leaky leadership pipeline, it appears essential to the better customization of career development strategies and programs building on different career levers, taking into consideration age and career stages, especially in the areas of career development tools (mentoring, sponsoring) and mobility aspects (geographical and international).

MANAGERIAL IMPLICATIONS FOR FRENCH HR PROFESSIONALS AND FEMALE MANAGERS

The results of this qualitative study indicated that women and men have different work experiences during their careers that are reflected in different perceptions of career barriers and levers. These barriers and levers exist at both the individual level—with impression management and self-presentation—and at the institutional and organizational levels. The reality of gender stereotypes tends to benefit men's career advancement and hinder that of women. The results of this study contribute valuable information for companies looking to foster career development and repair women's broken leadership pipeline at all levels. Four specific recommendations are offered to HR professionals for improving career management, particularly for women at the organizational level. Also, we offer strategies for female managers that can allow them to better manage their careers. Of course, a fundamental step and a necessary condition in addressing the issue of the leaky leadership pipeline involves addressing the gender stereotypes that have been perpetuated through organizational culture and interpersonal communication. Therefore, investment in awareness-building campaigns, training, and development activities are a key to fight against gender stereotypes.

Our first suggestion relates to the need for continued training and development of managers, and of women managers in particular. Traditional role models and gender stereotypes in the workplace hold French female managers back. Thus, awareness strengthening and training are key steps to achieve the goal of creating a more equal workplace. In our study, respondents emphasized the importance of training in general, but also the value of being aware of gender stereotypes. Specific diversity training (Chicha & Charest, 2009), for instance, can increase awareness of all kind of stereotypes and enhance equality in companies. In addition to offering short-term programming to raise awareness about stereotypes, some scholars (e.g., Benjamin & O'Reilly, 2011) have highlighted the benefits of long-term training for women, such as leadership development through an MBA-type training program. Especially in France, degrees from prestigious schools are career boosters. Companies, therefore, should be attentive to gender parity issues in terms of financing prestigious MBA programs for high-potential employees. In many cases, few female MBA participants receive such supportive funding, representing only 5–15% of the overall number (Internal Indicator, Audencia Business School). Further, business schools might consider offering scholarships targeted to attract talented women into their MBA programs. Women's professional networks are recognized as being another female career facilitator, including enhanced opportunities for finance training and leadership programs of the types just mentioned.

Our study found gender differences in mentoring and sponsoring, with women less frequently being sponsored. Our second suggestion is the implementation of sponsorship-based career management tools to remedy this disparity. Given that these tools are not widely used in French companies at present, alternative delivery models such as e-coaching and virtual mentoring might be appropriate solutions for managers struggling with work–life balance. Moreover, companies could organize structured opportunities for assigning role models, mentors, and sponsors as one facet of supporting women in managing their careers, especially at key stages. Establishing of goals, key indicators, and regular monitoring to track women's and men's careers would also provide data that could guide corporations in more effectively supporting highly talented employees.

Third, organizations can strengthen their internal and external networks. Career opportunities for managers can be enhanced through access to professional networks beyond the workplace. This is especially true in France, where networks are key for French graduates to get a first job (Margolis & Simonnet, 2004) and career progression is often determined by membership of the "right" network. For example, prestigious business schools have their own alumni networks that assist with navigation through the career labyrinth. Some large French companies support the development of internal networks of collaborators and such companies could thereby actively encourage and develop networking activities. The collaborative internal networks are groups composed of volunteers from a specific population, such as women or people with disabilities (Naschberger & Bellion, 2010). In France, there are several active networks of female managers acting as career facilitators: For example, MixCity of BNP Paribas, Women @ Renault Group Renault, Accenture's "Accent sur Elles," and Strong Her of Alcatel-Lucent.

Finally, our fourth recommendation is that corporate decision-makers focus on ways to support managers in achieving a more realistic work-life balance. Many authors[5] (Naschberger et al., 2012) emphasize that the solutions lie in a greater investment from men in the daily workload at home, in getting support from companies to reduce the burdens of daily life for women and men, and in the revision of family policies. For example, the new social trend in France of offering paternity or parental leave is already yielding encouraging results. Through organizational communication, companies can sensitize men and women to work–life balance and offer them support with parenthood. Indeed many HR tools already exist to foster work–life balance, such as allowances for working from home, flexible working time, on-site day care facilities, the signing of the French Parenthood Charter, avoiding evening meetings, and restricting or banning use of e-mail during the weekend. All these policies indicate support for greater gender equity in the workplace.

The results of our study indicate, however, that there is still a long way to go to achieve professional equality between women and men in French companies and to avoid losing talented women to the corporate workplace due to leaks in the leadership pipeline. Although career advancement seems to be a "given" for male managers, female managers often need to take greater control over their career development. Our study supports the notion that women's careers should be analyzed and taken into account in a different way from men's careers, given that their reported barriers and levers are not the same. This study also further confirms the important role of institutional, organizational, and interpersonal communication in changing the career advancement prospects for French women seeking leadership positions.

CONCLUSION

Previous research has found that the career experiences and advancement of women are different from those of men, with most studies finding that men advance faster, further, and with greater compensation. Several researchers have attempted to explain gender differences in career advancement. Some have confirmed that these differences cannot be explained solely by women's intermittent work-force participation (Blossfeld & Hofmeister, 2006). Despite enormous progress in professional equality in the workplace, the results of this study underline the barriers that still do exist to female managers' advancement. The purpose of this chapter was to address the leaky leadership pipeline by exploring men's and women's perceptions of barriers and levers to career advancement and their differences throughout the career cycle, and, thereby, to contribute to the advancement of women in the workplace, as well as to the necessary evolution of societies and institutions that will guarantee more equality. The results of the research reported here indicate that French female and male managers experience neither the same levers nor the same obstacles to career advancement in the workplace. Internal differences, such as self-confidence, ambition, soft skills, and perceptions of gender stereotyping affect the professional advancement of some individuals over others. Also, external differences, such as organizational, and cultural norms about work–life balance, networking, mentoring and sponsoring, preferentially advance some individuals. Furthermore, the results demonstrate the importance of taking into account the different career stages in order to analyze career development and progress, given the different priorities defined by men and women in specific periods of their working lives.

This chapter also highlights some of the metaphors that govern our social reality (in terms of perception, interaction, communication, language and/ or organizational behavior). Apart from the required shift in communication at different levels concerning gender stereotypes, which is a prerequisite for a sustainable evolution, the chapter culminates by proposing strategies that can be used by both HR professionals and female managers in tackling the problem women's career advancement into broader spheres of leadership and influence. Four strategies are proposed that could contribute to women remaining in the leadership pipeline and contributing to the future of French organizations and corporations. Although the French government has supported policies to foster gender equality, in addition to offering training and development subsidies, it is up to organizations to implement policies that can better benefit all of society. If they do so, perhaps the leaks in the leadership pipeline will more effectively be addressed, and women and men will ride the same escalator to career advancement.

NOTES

1. The expression "glass ceiling" has been coined to describe "the invisible barriers, created by behavioral and organizational prejudices, which keep women from the top responsibilities" (International Labor Organization, 1997, p. 3).

2. The "pipeline" model emphasizes a linear career progression through a series of staged roles within the professional world, with a loss of female talent at every critical transition (Etzkowitz & Ranga, 2011); it is also known as the concept of the "leaky leadership pipeline."
3. According to the authors, the "labyrinth" is a better metaphor than the "glass ceiling," as "passage through a labyrinth is not simple or direct, but requires persistence, awareness of one's progress, and a careful analysis of the puzzles that lie ahead" (Eagly & Carli, 2007a, p. 64).
4. These authors have shown, in research conducted by Catalyst, that high-potential women are over-mentored and under-sponsored compared to their male peers, and that they are not advancing in their organizations.
5. A recent study published by the Peterson Institute for International Economics documented a significant correlation between paternity leave and more women on corporate boards (Noland, Moran, & Kotschwar, 2016). In France, since 2002, men have benefited from paternity leave of three days at the time of childbirth or adoption, and another eleven days within the following four months (Bauer & Penet, 2005). In 2013, however, only seven fathers out of ten took their paternity leave (Legendre, Lhommeau, & Vincent, 2016). According to a 2016 study conducted by the Organisation for Economic Co-operation and Development (OECD), French fathers have 28 weeks of paid paternity and paid parental leave, but only 4% of them take parental leave; the figure has not changed over the last decade. The same OECD report highlights that parental leave may also help reduce discrimination against women in the workplace (2016). This is just one of many benefits of more equal social policies.

REFERENCES

Barsh, J., & Yee, L. (2012). Unlocking the full potential of women at work. *McKinsey & Company*. Retrieved from http://www.mckinsey.com/~/media/McKinsey/Business%20Functions/Organization/Our%20Insights/Unlocking%20the%20full%20potential%20of%20women%20at%20work/Unlocking%20the%20full%20potential%20of%20women%20at%20work.ashx

Baruch, Y. (2004). *Managing careers: Theory and practice*. Harrow, UK: FT-Prentice Hall/Pearson Education.

Bauer, D., & Penet, S. (2005). Le congé de paternité [Paternity leave]. *Etudes et Résultats*. 442, DREES. Retrieved from http://drees.social-sante.gouv.fr/IMG/pdf/er442.pdf

Belghiti-Mahut, S. (2004). Les déterminants de l'avancement hiérarchique des femmes cadres [Determinants of hierarchical advancement of women executives]. *Revue française de gestion, 4*(151), 145–160.

Benjamin, B., & O'Reilly, C. (2011). Becoming a leader: Early career challenges faced by MBA Graduates. *Academy of Management Learning and Education, 10*(3), 452–472.

Blossfeld, H. P., & Hofmeister, H. (Eds.). (2006). *Globalization, uncertainty and women's careers: An international comparison*. Cheltenham, England: Edward Elgar.

Brines, J. (1994). Economic dependency, gender, and the division of labor at home. *American Journal of Sociology, 100*(3), 652–688.

Carter, N. M., & Silva, C. (2010, February 1). Pipeline's broken promise. *Catalyst.* Retrieved from http://www.catalyst.org/knowledge/pipelines-broken-promise

Catalyst. (2015). Catalyst Sponsorship Guide. *Catalyst.* Retrieved from http://www.catalyst.org/knowledge/catalyst-sponsorship-guide

Catalyst. (2017, January 26). Infographic: Women on board: A Catalyst initiative. *Catalyst.* Retrieved from http://www.catalyst.org/knowledge/infographic-women-board-catalyst-initiative

Champagne, C., Pailhé, A., & Solaz, A. (2015). Le temps domestique et parental des hommes et des femmes: Quels facteurs d'évolutions en 25 ans? [The domestic and parental time of men and women: What kind of development factors have been influential over the last 25 years?]. Retrieved from http://www.insee.fr/fr/ffc/docs_ffc/ES478H.pdf

Cheney, G., Christensen, L. T., Zorn Jr., T. E., & Ganesh, S. (2011). *Organizational communication in an age of globalization: Issues, reflections, and practices* (2nd ed.). Long Grove, IL: Waveland Press.

Chicha, M-T., & Charest, É. (2009). Accès à l'égalité et gestion de la diversité: Une jonction indispensable [Access to equality and diversity: An essential relationship]. *Gestion, 3*(34), 66–73. doi:10.3917/riges.343.0066

Davis, G. (2014). Unconscious gender bias. In *Tackling gender diversity* (pp. 130–131). Retrieved from http://www.mckinsey.com/~/~/media/DE79102D452F49B-DA39AC07FB44EC9EA.ashx

de Cheveigné, S. (2009). The career paths of women (and men) in French research. *Social Studies of Science, 39*(1), 113–136.

Devillard, S., Sancier, S., Werner, C., Maller, I., & Kossoff, C. (2013). Gender diversity in top management: Moving corporate culture, moving boundaries. *Women Matter 2013.* Retrieved from http://www.mckinsey.com/~/media/mckinsey%20offices/france/pdfs/womenmatter%202013%20report.ashx

Eagly, A. H., & Carli, L. L. (2007a). Women and the labyrinth of leadership. *Harvard Business Review, 85*(9), 63–71.

Eagly, A. H., & Carli, L. L. (2007b). *Through the labyrinth: The truth about how women become leaders.* Boston, MA: Harvard Business School Press.

Ely, R. J., Stone, P., & Ammerman, C. (2014). Rethink what you "know" about high-achieving women. *Harvard Business Review, 92*(12), 101–109.

Etzkowitz, H., & Ranga, M. (2011). Gender dynamics in science and technology: From the "leaky pipeline" to the "vanish box." *Brussels Economic Review, 54*(2/3), 131–147.

Global Human Capital. (2008). The leaking pipeline: Where are our female leaders? 79 women share their stories. *Pricewaterhouse Coopers.* Retrieved from https://www.pwc.com/gx/en/women-at-pwc/assets/leaking_pipeline.pdf

Grésy, B. (2009a). *Petit traité contre le sexisme ordinaire* [*Small treaty against ordinary sexism*]. Paris, France: Albin Michel.

Grésy, B. (2009b). Rapport préparatoire à la concertation avec les partenaires sociaux sur l'égalité professionnelle entre les femmes et les hommes [Preparatory report on consultation with the social partners on professional equality between women and men]. Ministère du travail, des relations sociales, de la

famille, de la solidarité et de la ville. Retrieved from http://travail-emploi.
gouv.fr/IMG/pdf/Rapport_egalite8-07-09.pdf

Heidrick & Struggles. (2015). Women in leadership: Building a sustainable talent pipeline. Retrieved from http://www.heidrick.com/~/media/Publica-
tions%20and%20Reports/HS-Women%20in%20leadership%20pipeline.pdf

Hewlett, S. A., & Buck Luce, C. (2005). Off-ramps and on-ramps: Keeping talented
women on the road to success. *Harvard Business Review, 83*(3), 43–54.

Ibarra, H., Carter, N. M., & Silva, C. (2010). Why men still get more promotions
than women. *Harvard Business Review, 88*(9), 80–85.

IMS-Entreprendre pour la Cité. (2012). Stereotypes and gender: How to understand and tackle stereotypes in the workplace. Retrieved from http://www.
imsentreprendre.com/content/stereotypes-and-gender-how-to-understand-
and-tackle-stereotypes-in-the-workplace

International Labor Organization (ILO). (1997). La promotion des femmes aux
postes de direction [The promotion of women to leadership positions]. *Pro-
gramme des activités sectorielles*. Retrieved from http://staging.ilo.org/public/
libdoc/ilo/1997/97B09_237_fren.pdf

Kirkwood, J. (2009). Is a lack of self-confidence hindering women entrepreneurs?
International Journal of Gender and Entrepreneurship, 1(2), 118–133.

Kram, K. E., Wasserman, I. C., & Yip, J. (2012). Metaphors of identity and professional practice: Learning from the scholar–practitioner. *Journal of Applied Behavioral Science, 48*(3), 304–341.

Levanon, A., England, P., & Allison, P. (2009). Occupational feminization and pay:
Assessing causal dynamics using U.S. 1950–2000 census data. *Social Forces,
88*(2), 865–892.

Legendre, É., Lhommeau, B., & Vincent, J. (2016). Le congé de paternité: Un droit
exercé par sept pères sur dix [Paternity leave: A right exercised by seven out
of ten fathers]. *Etudes et Résultats*. 957, DREES. Retrieved from http://drees.
Social-sante.gouv.fr/IMG/pdf/er957.pdf

London Business School. (2009). The reflexive generation: Young professionals'
perspectives on work, career and gender. Retrieved from http://www.city-
women.co.uk/wp-content/uploads/2014/04/Generation-Y-Perspectives-on-
Work.pdf

Margolis, D., & Simonnet, V. (2004). Filières éducatives, réseaux et réussite professionnelle [Educational streams, networks, and professional success]. *Economie
& Prevision, 3*(164–165), 113–129.

McKinsey & Company. (2014). Tackling gender diversity. Retrieved from http://
www.mckinsey.com/~/~/media/DE79102D452F49BDA39AC07FB44EC9EA.
ashx

Naschberger, C., & Bellion, D. (2010). *Comment gérer l'emploi des personnes en situation de handicap* [*How to manage the employment of people with disabilities*]. Paris,
France: French Association of Diversity Managers (AFMD). Retrieved from
http://www.afmd.fr/documents/publication/AFMD-GUIDE-HANDICAP-
web.pdf

Naschberger, C., Quental, C., & Legrand, C. (2012). Le parcours de carrière des
femmes cadres: Pourquoi est-il si compliqué et comment le faciliter? [The

career paths of female managers: Why are they so complicated and how can they be facilitated?]. *Gestion: Revue Internationale de Gestion, 37*(3), 43–50.

Noland, M., Moran, T., & Kotschwar, B. (2016). Is gender diversity profitable? Evidence from a global survey. *Working paper, Peterson Institute for International Economics.* Retrieved from https://piie.com/publications/wp/wp16-3.pdf

Organisation for Economic Co-operation and Development (OECD). (2016). Parental leave: Where are the fathers? Men's uptake of parental leave is rising but still low. Policy Brief. Retrieved from http://www.oecd.org/gender/parental-leave-where-are-the-fathers.pdf

Persson, S., & Ivanaj, S. (2009). Faut-il adopter le mentoring en France? État des savoirs et perspectives généalogiques [Mentoring in France? State of knowledge and genealogical perspectives]. *Management & Avenir, 5*(25), 98–115.

Prokos, A., & Padavic, I. (2005). An examination of competing explanations for the pay gap among scientists and engineers. *Gender & Society, 19*(4), 523–543.

Putnam, L. L., & Boys, S. (2006). Revisiting metaphors of organizational communication. In S. R. Clegg, C. Hardy, T. B. Lawrence, & W. R. Nord (Eds.), *The Sage handbook of organization studies* (2nd ed., pp. 541–576). Thousand Oaks, CA. SAGE.

Ragins, B. R., & Cotton, J. L. (1999). Mentor functions and outcomes: A comparison of men and women in formal and informal mentoring relationships. *Journal of Applied Psychology, 84*(4), 529–550.

Sandberg, S. (2013). *Lean in: Women, work and the will to lead.* New York, NY: Alfred A. Knopf Publishing Group.

Singer, M. R. (1998). *Perception and identity in intercultural communication.* Yarmouth, ME: Intercultural Press, Inc.

Smith, P., Caputi, P., & Crittenden, N. (2012). A maze of metaphors around glass ceilings. *Gender in Management: An International Journal, 27*(7), 436–448.

Super, D. E. (1957). *The psychology of careers: An introduction to vocational development.* New York, NY: Harper & Row.

Tahon, M-B. (2003). *Sociologie des rapports de sexe* [Sociology of gender relations]. Ottawa, Canada: Presses Universitaires de Rennes.

Tremblay, D.-G. (Ed). (2005). *De la conciliation emploi-famille à une politique des temps sociaux* [From work–life balance to a social-time policy]. Québec, Canada: Presses de l'Université de Québec.

United Nations. (2017). Minimum set of gender indicators. *United Nations.* Retrieved from https://genderstats.un.org/#/home

Verjus, A., & Vogel, M. (2009). Le travail parental: un travail comme un autre? [Parental work: A job like any other?]. *Informations sociales, 4*(154), 4–6.

Zarya, V. (2016). Meet the first French women to be named CEO of a French stock index company. *Fortune.* Retrieved from http://fortune.com/2016/01/14/france-woman-ceo-isabelle-kocher/

CHAPTER 10

EMERGENT YET CONSTRAINED

Interrogating the Relationship Between Leadership, Gender, and Courage in Organizing for Peace[1]

Stacey L. Connaughton and Jasmine R. Linabary
Purdue University

Scholars have studied the relationship between leadership and communication for decades (Fairhurst & Connaughton, 2014). Yet two aspects of this relationship remain minimally addressed: (a) leadership exhibited in alternative *organizing* forms, and (b) the ways in which leadership and gender are communicatively constituted in these organizing forms. The former serves to undervalue the leadership that takes place in these settings, instead favoring formalized, hierarchical leadership in workplaces. The latter gap in the literature is also concerning, for although scholars have argued that "leadership remains a different experience for women and men" (Eagly, 2007, p. xviii), mainstream leadership literature pays scant attention to gender. To attend to the lack of research in both areas, we examine leadership and gender in the context of community-based organizing efforts to prevent political violence in West Africa.

Gender, Communication, and the Leadership Gap, pages 171–186
Copyright © 2017 by Information Age Publishing
All rights of reproduction in any form reserved.

In this chapter, we advance the notion of *courageous leadership*. To do so, we first locate gendered leadership in current literature and, specifically, within peacebuilding. Second, we outline the contexts of our study with women who lead local peacebuilding organizing in Ghana and Liberia and explore the tensions in their constructions of leadership. In doing so, this chapter contributes to understandings of the relationship between leadership, gender, and communication by interrogating how context influences the nature of this relationship.

To understand courageous leadership, we suggest positioning leadership within historical, social, economic, and political contexts as well as within gendered norms for interaction. We join scholars who seek to democratize leadership, demonstrating the value in studying leadership as everyday citizens enact it. We illustrate that leadership is not always a matter of official position, but rather a communicatively constituted phenomenon embedded within context(s). Understanding communication processes as constitutive—that the communicative (re)constitutes realities (e.g., organizing is constituted through language, symbols, and interactions; Putnam & Nicotera, 2009)—enables researchers to understand the relationships between gender, leadership, and communication.

LOCATING LEADERSHIP IN EXISTING SCHOLARSHIP

Existing scholarship primarily locates leadership within formal *organizations*. Indeed, many scholars position leadership as embodied in managers, supervisors, and executives in for-profit organizations (e.g., Bakar & Connaughton, 2010; Balogun & Johnson, 2004). Researchers also have focused on leadership in high-powered positions in public administration and government (e.g., Fairhurst, 2007; Fairhurst & Cooren, 2009). More infrequently, scholars have focused on the role of leadership in non-profit (e.g., Lewis, Hamel, & Richardson, 2001) and alternative organizations (Buzzanell et al., 1997). Taken together, the studies included in Fairhurst and Connaughton's (2014) review of leadership communication literature present a formalized version of leadership shaped by hierarchical structures embedded in organizations. Current scholarship has also been shaped by cultural expectations about *what* leadership in those settings looks like and *whose* leadership is privileged (Parker, 2005).

We argue that leadership (communication) scholars, particularly those interested in gender, should also attend to how leadership emerges organically in informal organizing. As this chapter reveals, attention to situations where women *emerge* as leaders can illuminate the ways in which gender enables and constrains leadership in these contexts. Following the scholarship of Ashcraft and Mumby (2004), we recognize gender as a "complex, ongoing, and contradictory accomplishment, unfolding at the nexus of communication and organization" (p. 115). Gender and gendered norms then are socially constructed within particular historical and cultural contexts and enacted through various discursive and material practices (Ashcraft & Mumby, 2004). Settings in which women emerge as leaders can also inform our understandings of how femininity and masculinity become reframed and reclaimed in women's leadership.

Locating Women's Leadership in Peacebuilding

In the peacebuilding literature, women's leadership is often discussed in terms of governance (e.g., Anderlini, 2007) and activism of formal women's organizations (e.g., Tripp, 2003). A smaller body of work focuses on everyday women's leadership in their communities, particularly in preventing violence (e.g., McKay & Mazurana, 2001). Much of the conversation around women and peacebuilding has focused on women's exclusion from formal decision-making and leadership positions at national and international levels (Castillo Diaz & Tordjman, 2012). Yet the local, informal ways women *do* leadership by organizing to build peace in their communities have garnered far less attention (for exceptions, see Mbabazi, 2015; McKay & de la Rey, 2001). These sites illustrate the different ways women navigate existing power structures, such as gender norms for interaction, when organizing to build peace.

Related to the development of this chapter, we posed the following research question: How do everyday women in Ghana and Liberia construct leadership in community-based, informal organizing to build peace? To address this question, we thematically analyzed data collected with six Ghanaian and Liberian women peacebuilders whom we have gotten to know through our multi-year collaborative work with them on local peace committees convened by the Purdue Peace Project (PPP), a peacebuilding initiative. We drew on focus group data collected with three female peacebuilders in Ghana and three in Liberia. Each focus group lasted approximately one hour and included questions about their experiences as women in peacebuilding and their understandings of peacebuilding and leadership. The themes presented here are grounded in these empirical data. We do not intend for these six women to represent all enactments of leadership within West Africa; rather, their voices illuminate some ways in which gender and leadership are enacted.

THE CONTEXTS OF WOMEN'S EMERGENT LEADERSHIP IN PEACEBUILDING

To understand these women's constructions of leadership, it is necessary to attend to their contexts. These women are from Monrovia, Liberia's capital, and a rural northern district in Ghana. Liberia is a country emerging from a series of civil wars (1989–2003). Post-conflict, it has seen considerable international aid and civil society organizing. Liberian women have been recognized internationally as exemplars for women's involvement in peacebuilding (Gbowee, 2011). In 2005, Liberians elected the first female president in Africa, Ellen Johnson-Sirleaf. The other three participants represented in this study are from Ghana, which is generally considered to be one of the more stable West African countries. The rural northern district where these Ghanaian women reside is a journey of approximately 14 hours by automobile from the capital. Few international non-governmental organizations are working in the region these participants represent.

The women whose voices we privilege in this chapter are everyday citizens. Of the Liberians, two work for a women's Liberian civil society organization, and the other is a market woman. Two of the Ghanaian participants have come to hold positions as queen mothers in their communities. The role of queen mother, prevalent among some Ghanaian communities, is a traditional leadership role in addition to the male chief. Queen mothers have influence particularly among other women and often command significant respect within their communities. One is also a nurse, and the other is a teacher. The third Ghanaian woman is university educated, manages the community radio station, and describes herself as a young, unmarried professional. The women in both countries are between the ages of 23 and 55. None had experience with peacebuilding before collaborating with the PPP.

Currently, these women peacebuilders view their leadership as helping prevent political violence, which we define as violence related to competing interests among two or more parties (e.g., land disputes, natural resources). They do their peacebuilding work as volunteers within local peace committees, both of which involve men and women. One female Liberian who serves as the PPP's Liberia Country Director and one female Ghanaian who serves as the PPP's West Africa Program Manager (WAPM) assist in facilitating the local peace committees' efforts.

Before we consider these women's constructions of leadership, we must be reflexive about our own positionalities, especially given our positions in relation to our participants within global power structures. Reflexivity involves constant critical interrogation of the power dynamics embedded and (re)produced in research relationships and processes (Ramazanoglu & Holland, 2002). To this end, we acknowledge our positions as White, western, middle class, educated women and recognize that we are influenced by these facets of our identities as well as western traditions of leadership studies. We have tried to attend to these positionalities actively and to acknowledge the ways they have shaped our relationships with these women peacebuilders, regarding our analyses through reflexive journaling and debriefing conversations. In writing this chapter, we hope to create openings for these women's voices to inform and advance our understandings of the relationship between leadership, gender, communication, and courage.

CONSTRUCTING LEADERSHIP IN COMMUNITY-BASED ORGANIZING TO BUILD PEACE

Rather than starting with a pre-determined definition of leadership, we followed Parker (2005); we were interested in understanding how these everyday Ghanaian and Liberian women construct leadership. Their responses reveal features of leadership that have been read as masculine and feminine in previous literature (Buzzanell, 1994; Parker, 2005). Fine and Buzzanell (2000) argued that both feminine approaches and masculine approaches have value in different situations. They posit that feminists "rewrite" masculine approaches to include what is missing, allowing for "ways of maintaining tensions among differing values and approaches [that] can be brought to the forefront of theorizing and practice" (p. 131).

Our analyses revealed that these women's constructions of leadership constituted two sets of "both/and" tensions and were constantly adapting to the situation and cultural norms they must negotiate. These "both/ands" are (a) willingness to be foregrounded and to be backgrounded, and (b) working through being targets of gendered interactions and being catalysts of productive action. We couch these "both/ands" within feminist literature that argues for transcending dualisms by disrupting artificial boundaries to embrace the dialectic (Buzzanell, 2011; Fine & Buzzanell, 2000). We contend that it is through the navigation of these "both/ands" that what we term "courageous leadership" emerges.

Leadership as a Willingness to be Foregrounded and Backgrounded

These women depict leadership as both being foregrounded and backgrounded, and they express a genuine willingness to negotiate these spaces as needed. Although this shifting between the foreground and background is in many ways consistent with what Buzzanell et al. (1997) describe in their image of dramaturgical (performative) leadership in alternative (formal) organizations, we argue that the informal leadership constructed by these West African women is also tied up in cultural and gendered norms related to voice and silence that shape instances in which women enact agency by claiming voice or creating space for others' voices.

Being Foregrounded: Signifying Leadership

In these women's constructions of leadership being foregrounded constituted: (a) being "out-front" and (b) speaking to others. First, being "out-front" refers to physical presence, being visibly present with men as they do peacebuilding work together, at times physically in front of men and being perceived by others as the leader. In this way, "out-front" functions metaphorically to signify who is leading in a particular moment. This compelling construction for cultural expectations would dictate that the feminine position is to take a more "background" role. As a Ghanaian woman peacebuilder described, "You know, we find ourselves in Africa, in Ghana, in the northern parts of Ghana for that matter; . . . tradition is very important. And, culturally our women are trained to be submissive, to be polite." Participants discussed gendered role expectations, including that women would primarily stay in the home, complete labor in service to the household, and generally stay silent while men take the primary decision-making roles.

Their leadership in peacebuilding is constructed as often deviating from those norms, as they move in public spaces, engage in voluntary labor for the community, and speak "out-front." These women found themselves pushing back against the cultural expectations placed on them. Notice the emphasis this Liberian woman peacebuilder placed on being out-front, situating this visibility within women's historical context of marginalization:

> Being a woman and working for my country, I feel so proud because for years we have been marginalized. We were sitting at the back and thinking that the women were most removed. We were women who needed to stay in the house, to take care of the children, take care of the home. But this time around, why can't the women also . . . move, knowing fully well that the women are going to have good ideas and that we put ideas together?

Second, all six women emphasized speaking to others as a hallmark of leadership. The literature often characterizes voice as something in tension with forces that seek to silence women (Houston & Kramarae, 1991). Yet note the conviction that this Liberian woman expressed when discussing her peacebuilder role and her emphasis on a spatial metaphor of being *at the front*, in talking about peace:

> If I consider myself as a peacebuilder, I shouldn't be at the back. I should be at the front talking about peace. Because I know that if we have peace, everything is fine. Even if we have peace, [we] are home, my children will sleep well, my family will be happy. So, being a peacebuilder you shouldn't just say, "Yeah, I'm making peace, talking about peace but I'm sitting at the back." I should be in the front and be the one talking about peace.

For her, building peace is tied to talk. Talking about peace *publicly* is key to leadership's constitution.

Yet having a voice, particularly in some spheres, is not a norm for West African women. Notice how cultural norms that could serve to silence women are alluded to in the following quotation, and how breaking through those cultural norms was tied to pride and bravery:

> So when our boss [a Liberian woman] really brought up that idea we felt so *proud* that, yes, indeed I'm a woman and I'm going to stand on the battlefield to say something that the men will know that a woman is speaking and she's speaking something sound. So I can be a better peacebuilder if I speak and the world will want to listen to me.... The women can be *brave*. Because we were never *brave* to stay in public to talk. We were always sitting at the back, so coming to the front now to say something for my country I feel it necessary because it gives me the strength—it gives me a good mind to always move forward. Like before, I won't sit in front of you to talk like this. I would be a shy person. Why is it that she's mute...? But for now, being a peacebuilder I'm *proud* to stand in front of anybody to say a word of peace to them.

Similarly, the Ghanaian women recognized how seeing another woman, in this case PPP's WAPM, standing in front of others, including chiefs, has encouraged them to do the same. In the words of one Ghanaian woman:

> Because of this peace committee, we can go and stand before the chiefs. And then talk to them and they will listen.... We could not have that *braveness* to approach these people. And now, we are so *brave* that if they say it is you, then they will come and talk to you.

In these quotations, the women construct their speaking as "brave," a notion that has often, at least in Western contexts, been a masculine notion tied to military service. Yet, these West African women reclaim and redefine bravery in the context of defying cultural gender norms in order to lead from the front. Jablin (2006) argued that speaking out may represent the most common form of courage within organizational contexts. This form of speaking out, however, was primarily tied to dissent and unpopular positions. In the case of these women peacebuilders, the act of "speaking out" in front is constructed as courageous not because of the content of the message *per se* but as an embodied action. Peacebuilding work gives them the space to stand before others, speak, and exhibit leadership.

Being Backgrounded: A Place of Influence

These women peacebuilders also underscore that sometimes the situation calls on them to be in the "background." Being backgrounded constitutes: (a) listening and observing and (b) reclaiming West African women's traditional roles as positions of strength and influence. While listening and observing may be interpreted as contributing to women's invisibility, these women peacebuilders reclaim the "background" as a place of influence.

First, the women peacebuilders often talked about how leaders listen. When they do so, they cast the act of listening not as a submissive position, but as an "out-front" activity essential for leadership. As one Liberian woman stated, "The thing about a leader, it should be someone who knows how to lead somebody. You *should be at the back* where you know yourself. You are a leader. You just sit quietly and watch people doing things."

Second, the Liberian peacebuilders all highlighted the PPP's female Liberia Country Director as a role model of how to be a leader and be backgrounded. They noted how she would often literally stand in the back and create space for other peace committee members to be foregrounded, as one Liberian woman described:

> I always like her [Liberia Country Director] for she always gave us the responsibility as a leader to do things on our own....At first we were ashamed to even talk in front of people. Sometimes we'd be hiding ourselves in the corner, "No, I don't want to do this." But no, she would say, "No, you do this, you do this." And gradually things started working out for us. So I must tell her, "thank you" for her work....Because I can say I can stand in front of one or two persons to . . . to express myself, and to take that leadership ability.

Finally, the Ghanaian women reported how the local peace committee's organizing form and the WAPM giving responsibility to them afforded them unique opportunities to lead. The underlying premise of the local peace committees is that any member can exhibit leadership at any time. These women stated that being a part of these committees had contributed to their development as leaders.

Reclaiming women's traditional roles as positions of strength and influence was another theme. Several of these women also spoke with conviction about their traditional roles in the home (a private space) and their emergent public roles as peacebuilders. Traditionally, the private sphere has been marked as a feminine domain, associated with caring, relationships, emotions, and the home (Buzzanell, 2011). This private domain stands in contrast to constructions of the public as a masculine domain, restricting women's visibility and mobility in these spaces (Massey, 1994).

In the context of their peacebuilding efforts, however, these women sought to (re)claim private spaces, and their associated roles, as vital to their leadership. For example, this Liberian woman evoked her identity as "homemaker" and her felt responsibility as a peacebuilder:

> To be a peacebuilder, if I hear there is something that is sparking over there that will bring a problem, I should go there. I should be the one to be able to

talk to people, and say, "This is not good. You can't live like this." I will take an example. This morning, in my yard, I was lying down. Two ladies were clashing [arguing loudly]. . . . Everybody was listening to them and didn't want to stop them. But I went there this morning, and I talked with them. I said, "It's not right. Stop doing what you are doing. It's not good for women in the community. This is not the time for confusion. This is time that we wake up and do something. It's early morning. It's time that you go to the market, buy your goods, and sell or buy your food to come and cook." And it was like, "Oh, thank you so much." And we separated. So if I'm a peacebuilder, that is [the] thing I need to be doing.

In describing this experience, this Liberian peacebuilder referenced her family and home (private domain) and used her position to enact her commitment to building peace in her community (public domain).

Leadership as Working Through Being Targets of Gendered Interactions and Being Catalysts of Productive Action

In enacting leadership, gender norms function in two primary ways. First, these women perceived that they had been targets of others' gendered expectations. Second, gendered norms in the women's interactions with others also served as catalysts for action as they worked to overcome or reimagine those expectations.

Targets of Gendered Interactions

In their peacebuilding work, traditional gendered expectations have been reinforced and communicated in their interactions with male committee members and with other men and women in the community. These women must find ways to (a) manage the gendered expectations of their peers and (b) respond to community resistance to their leadership.

First, in working with male members of the peace committee, these women have had to navigate gendered expectations that have continued to shape their interactions with others, particularly with male members who often take the lead in speaking roles in the community and at times directly and indirectly insist that certain labor should be women's responsibility. While engaged in community outreach, including setting up hand-washing stations during Liberia's Ebola epidemic in 2014–2015, one female peace committee member described working with a man as follows:

He would sit and enjoy the water. I would say, asking him, "The women there, women are empowered?" He would say he didn't get it. Because he [felt] feel that I should be the one to be fetching the water in the barrel; that's women's work.

While some, as in the example above, came up against gendered expectations that seemed immovable, one Ghanaian woman noted that although these expectations exist, the cultural assumptions may be gradually shifting, as is evidenced in her statement:

> These men are getting to know that women are also intelligent. Initially, women were not involved in decision-making. So they thought that...the kitchen was for us. So anything they are doing, they...just, ignore us. [They] only want to talk to "smart people." But lately, they have realized that women are so intelligent, so patient, and they do things at the right time....So they are getting to accept the women now.

In this way, while at times constraining their work when they found themselves ignored by male members of the committee, these women found that gendered expectations were not fixed but rather could evolve over time through their shared peacebuilding activities.

Second, gendered expectations shaped these women's interactions not just with fellow peace committee members but also with the communities in which they worked, which sometimes resulted in resistance to their peacebuilding efforts. The participants also discussed experiences with insults and intimidation as a result of their deviation from gendered expectations and norms. They reported having faced questioning and criticism for their leadership particularly in speaking to crowds or to men in positions of power. One Ghanaian woman, who was also a queen mother, discussed an incident in which she, on behalf of the peace committee, went to speak to a chief in the area. This man was of higher stature in the social order, and she had to convince him to participate in a meeting to promote peace. He attacked her for speaking in front of him and for being involved. He challenged her leadership by saying, "Because you are a queen mother, and now you can do whatever?" In talking about these experiences, she recognized that her own culture had served to perpetuate men's authoritarian views:

> And the intimidation actually is coming from our culture. Culturally, our African tradition didn't see a woman to be anything. How dare you to come and stand before a man and talk? So, it is not their [the chief's] fault anyway. But anyway, we are still forging ahead.

In such instances, these women recognized cultural norms as being at fault for men's responses, shifting blame away from the individuals involved. Particularly on issues related to land, women are not considered to have authority to speak. In speaking on these and other issues related to conflict in their communities, the Ghanaian women discussed the kind of pushback they would receive: "The men want to intimidate you because you are woman, and you want to come and stand here and talk." One woman also noted that even if they have not been the target of direct intimidation, they had come to *anticipate* it. They also suspect that people talked about them behind their backs, asking "Who is a woman to talk?"

The responses they receive are not just shaped by gender but are also tied up with other aspects of their identities, as one of the youngest of the peace committee members in Ghana illustrated:

> The number one challenge is that I am young. Number two, I'm not married. And I'm a woman. So it's sometimes difficult for people to really respect you for who you are.... [For all of] these reasons, they sometimes think that, "Oh, this small girl shouldn't be doing what she is doing."

Catalysts for Productive Action

These gendered interactions, despite offering constraints, also inspired women's leadership by both (a) instilling persistence and (b) encouraging women to enact "feminine" values in new ways.

First, what is clear from the statements of these participants was that they persisted despite the pushback they may have received for their leadership in peacebuilding. One Liberian woman illustrated the commitment to persist:

> Your words out there will not stop me from doing what I want to do. Because I have put my neck on the board that yes, we want to see this happening.... If you say everywhere "you go," [or] "you stop" because somebody insulted you,... you insulted them because you sit down, you won't go nowhere, you won't do anything. So all these things, they are challenges but it motivates you to do.... I feel the challenges are there to make us strong.

We contend that enduring and working through these gendered interactions takes defensive courage (Jablin, 2006), as does acting in ways that defy gender norms and catalyze productive action. Leadership is about moving others toward a productive end. As one Ghanaian woman said:

> It's not easy. You have to be ready for anything. Yes, have a strong heart because it's not all the times that things will go your way. Sometimes you feel like crying, cry. Sometimes you feel like sleeping, sleep. Just allow things to happen and model yourself. You have to have a strong heart to face it.... It's not easy. But you have to learn to sacrifice. Even when the going is tough, but you still have to keep going.

Second, in moving toward productive action, these women evoked and reimagined traditionally "feminine" values as they discussed leadership and peacebuilding. These included selflessness, patience, tolerance, and humility. Note the values of humility and selflessness embedded within one's interconnectedness to others that are defining features of this Liberian woman's construction of a leader:

> A leader for me, a leader is about yourself. You are not living now for yourself, but you are living for the people. . . . You should be a very humble person and not for yourself, again, not living for yourself but for your people.

These features of leadership represent traditionally feminine values and ways of knowing that formed the foundation for these women's constructions of leadership (Buzzanell, 1994).

The participants in this research spoke often about how much their felt responsibility to serve others motivated them to continue as local peacebuilders. While servant leadership has been recognized within the literature as an individual's felt obligation for improving society and action on that obligation (Greenleaf, 1977), feminist scholars have offered critiques of servant leadership because it has focused on the masculine model of a solitary, autonomous leader working for instrumental ends (Fine & Buzzanell, 2000). In their feminist "revisioning" of serving, Fine and Buzzanell (2000) argued that serving is an embodied, *ethical* stance operating in service of the greater good and involving actively engaging in co-serving with others. In light of this ethical perspective, consider this Liberian woman's words:

> A leader should have good characteristic. They should know how to talk to people, you should know how to lead people, you should know how to cool people down. You should know how to communicate with people. *You should be there for the people.* That's what a good leader [does].

Clearly, these women understood leadership to be relational and to be oriented toward other individuals and collectives (family, community, nation).

IMPLICATIONS

We began this chapter by highlighting two areas in leadership research that have not often been examined together: (a) leadership in *informal* organizing forms and (b) gender and leadership. This chapter considered contexts in which local women peacebuilders did their work and in which they emerged as leaders. Important aspects of that context are the normative constraints related to gender relations and gendered interactions as well as the historical legacies from which they emerge. Listening carefully to these women and reflecting on their constructions of leadership in context gave rise to three conclusions.

First, the informal organizing of the local peace committee created space in which women had an opportunity to emerge as leaders. The work of community-level peacebuilding produced identities of peacebuilder and leader within these everyday women, which is noteworthy because some of these women did not see themselves as leaders before beginning their peacebuilding work. Moreover, the work of community-level peacebuilding opened the space for these women to reclaim their gender identity and the influence this identity can have at the community level. Their construction of leadership as a set of "both/ands" mirrored the complexities of living in contexts where women's voices have historically been deemed most influential in the private sphere and, despite progress, where their inclusion and participation in the public sphere is still questioned. Yet as our chapter reveals, in these informal organizing forms women can *do* leadership, by owning and enacting both feminine and masculine styles of communication and leadership (Buzzanell, 1994).

Yet, second, these women's emergent leadership is still a contested domain. Recall these women's accounts of men they worked alongside expecting them to do "women's work." They had encountered resistance as they have defied gendered expectations. Even when we asked them if they perceived themselves as leaders, some hesitated. Some also were reluctant to initially be "out-front" and needed encouragement from others to do so. A cultural explanation for their hesitation may be that the very idea that women could emerge as leaders in public spaces is rare and/or seen as not being legitimate.

Third, as these women navigate these "both/ands" of leadership and the contextual constraints related to gender in which they are embedded, they teach us about leadership. Specifically, we name this phenomenon courageous leadership, which we define as *constituting and enacting with others a new way(s) of being and/or doing in order to influence (social) change within a particular context, amidst constraints on that constitutive process and outcome(s).* For us, courageous leadership is not about "heroic" behavior. We offer a different view on courage that is relationally oriented; these women's voices give rise to this understanding. For us, courageous leadership is about recognition of one's position (interconnectedness) vis-à-vis others and action for and with others, amid contexts that (sometimes) make it difficult to have such a relational orientation. In this regard, courageous leadership is not a solitary, lonely activity, nor a masculine construct akin to bravery. For us, courage is co-imagined possibility for change, and courageous leadership is the collective, co-constructed journey toward it.

Practical Implications

The experiences of these women peacebuilders also offer important practical implications for those who seek to open up opportunities for more women to emerge as leaders in and beyond peacebuilding. First, women's leadership may be encouraged through the presence and visibility of other women exhibiting leadership in different ways (e.g., the West Africa Program Manager and the Liberia Country Director) and by receiving direct invitations to get "'out-front." Second, in navigating constraints, we can see the need for developing specific communicative strategies that are culturally and contextually specific as women experience hostility when they push back against gendered constraints. In their talk, for example, these women reframed the gendered expectations of male colleagues and community members not as the fault of men but rather as part of broader cultural understandings of gender and gender roles. This reframing allowed them to continue their working relationships while persisting to effect gradual reform and to resist culturally embedded gendered expectations. Third, while responding to gendered norms can also catalyze productive action—and courageous leadership—we also wonder how this leadership can be sustained in the face of continued intimidation and threats over time. Clearly, more attention is needed regarding how to cultivate and sustain courageous leadership.

CONCLUSION

At the time of his death, Fredric Jablin (2006) was thinking deeply about courage and its relationship to leadership and followership. In his last invited lecture, Jablin alluded to several ways in which courage, which he called a "fuzzy concept" (p. 102), had been written about. At one point he proclaimed: "However, it is worth noting that our understanding of courage has not only been traditionally associated with those in the upper end of the social hierarchy but traditionally only with men" (p. 105). He then listed a host of philosophical and empirical questions:

> Is courage then a concept that is steeped in masculine ideology, and cowardice by implication feminine (at least in Western culture)? Is courage generally, and in particular in leadership and followership, a gendered concept? If so, what is the implication for women? Is the full realm of courage ideologically available to women? (Jablin, 2006, p. 106)

Our essay offers a starting point to (re)conceptualize courage within particular (gendered) contexts. Future research should examine these and related questions and the construct of courageous leadership advanced here, for both women *and* men and the contexts in which they live and work—in West Africa and beyond.

NOTE

1. This chapter is dedicated to Rosaline Baatuolkuu Obeng-Ofori (1957–2016), for her tireless, lifelong work to champion and fight for women's justice and equality in West Africa and beyond.

REFERENCES

Anderlini, S. N. (2007). *Women building peace: What they do, why it matters.* Boulder, CO: Lynne Rienner.

Ashcraft, K. L., & Mumby, D. K. (2004). *Reworking gender: A feminist communicology of organization.* Thousand Oaks, CA: SAGE.

Bakar, H. A., & Connaughton, S. L. (2010). Relationships between supervisory communication and commitment to workgroup: A multilevel analysis approach. *International Journal of Strategic Communication, 4*(1), 39–57. doi:10.1080/15531180903415939

Balogun, J., & Johnson, G. (2004). Organizational restructuring and middle manager sensemaking. *Academy of Management Journal, 47*(4), 523–549. doi:10.2307/20159600

Buzzanell, P. M. (1994). Gaining a voice: Feminist organizational communication theorizing. *Management Communication Quarterly, 7*(4) 339–383. doi:10.1177/0893318994007004001

Buzzanell, P. M. (2011). Feminist discursive ethics. In G. Cheney, S. May, & D. Munshi (Eds.), *Handbook of communication ethics* (pp. 64–83). New York, NY: Routledge.

Buzzanell, P. M., Ellingson, L., Silvio, C., Pasch, V., Dale, B., Mauro, G.,... Martin, C. (1997). Leadership processes in alternative organizations: Invitational and dramaturgical leadership. *Communication Studies, 48*(4), 285–310. doi:10.1080/10510979709368509

Castillo Diaz, P., & Tordjman, S. (2012). Women's participation in peace negotiations: Connections between presence and influence. *UN Women.* Retrieved from http://reliefweb.int/sites/reliefweb.int/files/resources/03AWomenPeaceNeg.pdf

Eagly, A. (2007). Foreword. In J. L. Chin, B. Lott, J. K. Rice, & J. Sanchez-Hucles (Eds.), *Women and leadership: Transforming visions and diverse voices* (pp. xvi–xix). Malden, MA: Blackwell.

Fairhurst, G. T. (2007). Liberating leadership in *Corporation: After Mr. Sam*: A response. In F. Cooren (Ed.), *Interacting and organizing: Analyses of a board meeting* (pp. 53–71). Mahwah, NJ: Lawrence Erlbaum.

Fairhurst, G. T., & Connaughton, S. L. (2014). Leadership: A communicative perspective. *Leadership, 10*(1), 7–35. doi:10.1177/1742715013509396

Fairhurst, G. T., & Cooren, F. (2009). Leadership as the hybrid production of presence(s). *Leadership, 5*(4), 469–490. doi:10.1177/1742715009343033

Fine, M. G., & Buzzanell, P. M. (2000). Walking the high wire: Leadership theorizing, daily acts, and tensions. In P. M. Buzzanell (Ed.), *Rethinking organizational and managerial communication from feminist perspectives* (pp. 128–156). Thousand Oaks, CA: SAGE.

Gbowee, L. (2011). *Might be our powers: How sisterhood, prayer, and sex changed a nation at war.* New York, NY: Beast Books.

Greenleaf, R. (1977). *Servant leadership.* New York, NY: Paulist Press.

Houston, M., & Kramarae, C. (1991). Speaking from silence: Methods of silencing and resistance. *Discourse & Society, 2*(4), 387–399. doi:10.1177/095792 6591002004001

Jablin, F. M. (2006). Courage and courageous communication among leaders and followers in groups, organizations, and communities. *Management Communication Quarterly, 20*(1), 94–110. doi:10.1177/0893318906288483

Lewis, L. K., Hamel, S. A., & Richardson, B. K. (2001). Communicating change to nonprofit stakeholders: Models and predictors of implementers' approaches. *Management Communication Quarterly, 15*(1), 5–41. doi:10.1177/0893318901 151001

Massey, D. (1994). *Space, place, and gender.* Minneapolis: University of Minnesota Press.

Mbabazi, P. K. (2015). Women have always had their special place in history as peace-makers: Women and peace building in the Great Lakes region. In M. van Reisen (Ed.), *Women's leadership in peace building: Conflict, community and care* (pp. 55–63). Trenton, NJ: Africa World Press.

McKay, S., & de la Rey, C. (2001). Women's meanings of peacebuilding in post-apartheid South Africa. *Peace and Conflict: Journal of Peace Psychology, 7*(3), 227–242.

McKay, S., & Mazurana, D. (2001). Gendering peacebuilding. In D. J. Christie, R. V. Wagner, & D. A. Winter (Eds.), *Peace, conflict, and violence: Peace psychology for the 21st century* (pp. 341–349). Englewood Cliffs, NJ: Prentice-Hall.

Parker, P. S. (2005). *Race, gender, and leadership: Re-envisioning organizational leadership from the perspectives of African American women executives.* Mahwah, NJ: Erlbaum.

Putnam, L. L., & Nicotera, A. M. (Eds.). (2009). *Building theories of organization: The constitutive role of communication.* New York, NY: Routledge.

Ramazanoglu, C., & Holland, J. (2002). *Feminist methodology: Challenges and choices.* Thousand Oaks, CA: SAGE.

Tripp, A. M. (2003). Women in movement: Transformations in African political landscapes. *International Feminist Journal of Politics, 5*(2), 233–255. doi:10.1080/ 1461674032000080585

CHAPTER 11

TRANSCENDING SELF

An African Girl's Journey

Rosemary M. Muriungi
Gonzaga University

Traditional African structures equipped girls with skills to transition seamlessly to adulthood. Colonization brought a way of life entirely different from that prescribed by their own cultures. The divergent world views have reshaped how African girls self-identify with the world around them. Over two decades ago, Salole (1992) suggested that "the idea of *selfhood* is the key to understanding the context in which socialisation makes sense of experience and history, and gradually equips a child with the tools and techniques that the child will need when she or he becomes an adult" (p. 6). Through the lens of communication and gender socialization, I use my experience growing up in Africa to narrate how I have navigated multiple world views to chart my own leadership path.

Gender, Communication, and the Leadership Gap, pages 187–196
Copyright © 2017 by Information Age Publishing
All rights of reproduction in any form reserved. **187**

COMMUNICATION, GENDER SOCIALIZATION, AND LEADERSHIP

Adler, Rodman, and du Pré (2014) define communication as "the process of creating meaning through symbolic interaction" (p. 5). Communication includes nonverbal facets such as tone of voice and body language, which are "largely unconscious and less likely to be manipulated or disguised by the individual" (Burley-Allen, 1995, p. 71). Listening is key to communication, given that much of what is communicated is not verbalized (Burley-Allen, 1995). In short, communication defines how we interact with the world.

According to Wood (2003) "gender grows out of cultural ideas that stipulate the social *meaning* and *expectation* of each sex" (p. 24). Gender differs from sex, which is determined by reproductive organs. Gender socialization refers to the concept of what society considers masculine or feminine. Leaper and Friedman (2007) have observed that "gender-typed practices contribute to the development of gender differences in expectations, values, preferences, and skills" (p. 561).

With respect to leadership, Burns (1978) described this as the motivation of others to work toward goals that represent the aspirations, motivations, and expectations common to them. Leadership is communicated through the value ascribed to different roles, including the opportunities and privileges a child experiences from birth. Through communication, specific roles are assigned by societies in part related to gender, including the role of leadership. These roles have a bearing on the self-identity of individuals and their place in the world. In the sections below, I narrate how communication has socialized and shaped my identity.

AFRICAN FOLKLORE AND COMMUNICATION

My earliest memories of African folklore are as a nine-year old girl seated near the fireplace in my grandmother's African hut. Family members congregated around the fireplace to share meals and life experiences. Tales from the past were regaled to children in the homestead. Around that fireplace, I learned about my language group's way of life. Across generations, culture has been transmitted in many African villages through folktales, legends, proverbs, and other forms (Sibanda, 2014). Proverbs from East Africa like *Asiyesikia la mkuu hufikiwa na makuu* (Kagwa, 2007) reminded young people of the importance of heeding the counsel of their elders. The meaning of this particular proverb is that those who do not listen to their elders receive harsh lessons in life. While folklore prevails in Africa, modern housing has changed the way families relate to one another and is eroding the sense of community and togetherness fostered by the African hut of yesteryears.

COMMUNICATION IN MODERN TIMES

Modern media has added a complexity to transferring knowledge and values to young people. I can vividly recall my family's excitement at the purchase of our first television set—my first experience with televised media—when I was a ten-year old child. As I grew older, I was greatly influenced by music and television programs from the West. I admired the lifestyles of leading movie stars and musicians of my generation. Their way of life determined what I wore and how I spoke. Not only did television influence my lifestyle and that of so many girls growing up in that era, it also shaped society's expectations of us. In urban centers where parents worked full-time jobs and left children to their own devices, the television took their place in many homes. The digital age has revolutionized the way we communicate. Social media and globalization have reshaped relationships (Morra, 2010). This revolution has transcended geographical and cultural boundaries across the globe.

COMMUNICATION AND MENTORING

Wood (2013) defines a mentor as "an experienced person who guides the development of a less experienced person" (p. 248). Protégé, French for mentee—derives from the verb *protégér* which means "to protect" in English (Protégé, n.d.). I see this concept as the essence of mentoring—protecting mentees' best interests through counsel, empowerment, and advocacy. Communication provides the platform for the sharing of knowledge and experiences in the mentoring relationship. In the following section, I describe how colonization has affected the traditional formation of African girls.

Traditional African Context

According to Hall (2007), "native communities had an organized system for educating young people, based on generations of accumulated knowledge about the natural world" (p. 14). I recall being engaged in communal activities where I learned how to do things in the tribal way. The whole community shaped young minds and behavior. This pattern has been true worldwide, as observed by Salole (1992), who noted that all adults are "responsible for assisting in inducting, training and generally helping children come to terms with the realities of this world" (p. 8). Similarly, the African concept that *it takes a village to raise a child* holds true to this day.

Modern Context

The traditional way of forming girls in Africa evolved with the advent of colonization and Christianity. Colonization institutionalized schooling that was based on the Western world. Leach (2007) has noted that "Christianization of Africa meant re-making the African in their own image" (p. 337). Some traditional roles African women played were deemed *unladylike* in Western eyes. Salole (1992) offered the following example of this tension between cultures:

> The fact that women worked in the fields did not "fit" the ideal and Europeans communicated their ideal through their so-called "civilising mission" to their hapless subjects. Africans, in the colonial context, soon learned to be embarrassed by the fact that the women were key producers and efforts were made to disguise this in statistics. (p. 7)

Colonization contributed to the collapse of age-old social structures that had been used and proven over the millennia. Consequently, Salole (1992) noted that, "as the Western models began to take root, serious gaps emerged in the indigenous repertoire" (p. 7). The identity crisis most African girls face today emerged from this. Striking a balance between African traditions and what girls learned from schools that were shaped by Western influences and the media has created challenges in mentoring African girls in modern times. Colonization of Africa would have benefitted greatly from Lao Tsu's (700 BCE) quotation, which stated, "start with what they know; build with what they have."

Mentoring and Women's Leadership

Before sharing my own story, I describe important arenas of socialization that play a role in mentoring girls and women in Africa. According to Leaper and Friedman (2007), "gender self-concepts, beliefs, and motives are informed and transformed by families, peers, the media, and schools as children grow up" (p. 561). Similar to the process of mentoring within the context of African cultures, leadership development of girls has its roots in the family. A parent's role in charting the path of a daughter contributes to who she becomes. Affirmation of girls by their fathers builds self-confidence, which allows her to navigate life with a heightened sense of self-worth. Mothers serve as role models through the nurturing only one woman can give to another. Intergenerational mentoring of girls by family relations and community members contributes to more grounded girls. A girl's sense of self is essential to understanding her identity in part because this awareness of selfhood has been influenced by communication with others (Adler, Rodman, & du Pré, 2014).

Throughout the world, the process of learning is recognized to be a lifetime undertaking that draws the best from people. According to Nathan (2005), education should "allow students to arrive at inspired new ideas for society and transformative visions of our world" (p. 148). Through advising and career guidance, girls should be encouraged to pursue careers that enhance their leadership capacity and opportunities. In addition to the influence of families and schools, the Church has a responsibility to establish mentoring platforms to support young women. Some churches in Kenya draw from women role models in their congregations to provide mentorship to young women embarking on professional life and marriage. Girls need stewardship in order to assume leadership positions.

Similarly, on the political scene, legislation on women representation in government has been introduced to increase the participation of women both in terms of numbers and in the level of engagement. A revision of the Kenyan Constitution (2010) advocated that "not more than two-thirds of the members of elective public bodies shall be of the same gender" (p. 51). This is yet to be realized for women. Gender socialization of women continues to be a major deterrent for Kenyan women with political aspirations (Mutiga, 2017). A lack of representation of women at the highest level of decision-making has a bearing on women's progress in key sectors of the economy. Archard (2013) posits that "stereotypical views about women and girls may also be perpetuated by the lack of women's and girls' political participation in society" (p. 762).

The limited participation of women on the political arena has also had an impact on the development agenda in East Africa and beyond. Dibie and Dibie (2012) have observed that "the vision of gender equality in the development process across the African continent has ultimately not been woman friendly. In most cases women continue to be perceived in terms of childbearing, procreation, and household economy functions" (p. 96). In addition, Akotia and Adote (2012) noted how women in certain cultures have been "socialized to be humble, quiet, submissive and obedient" (p. 5025). Viewed in this context, the plight of the African girl is plagued with vulnerability and disadvantage. In a way, the professional and leadership potential of girls are often nipped in the bud from childhood. Peer support and professional networks are important in nurturing leadership capacity in women. From the traditional African village to modern day reality, leadership development of girls is evolving. Not only are girls pursuing careers previously perceived as masculine, but they are also earning their rightful place in the boardroom.

AN AFRICAN GIRL'S JOURNEY

I have had wonderful mentors and role models throughout my life. The role of a parent in building confidence and self-esteem in a child cannot be underestimated. Since I was very young, my parents eased me into positions of responsibility at home and within the community. Their trust in my ability to carry out the responsibilities they assigned to me prepared me to easily assume my role in society. Playing a leadership role in the family setting also prepared me for leadership roles in the community. From my earliest years, my parents lit a fire in me for education, and thanks to their encouragement I have pursued this goal to the doctoral level. Through grit and resilience, I have balanced family, work, community responsibility, and study to achieve my dream of education attainment, refusing to give in due to challenges or financial constraints. My father believed that education was a pathway to my independence. His foresight has enabled me to take charge of my life in ways that many women in my community cannot. In situations where I have had to rise above society's expectations of women, my father's rallying call has urged me on.

Additionally, within a culture that expects women to stay home and take care of their families, my mother-in-law encouraged me to travel to a foreign country to pursue doctoral education. She believed that my responsibility as a parent should not deter me from chasing my dreams. Her pride in my achievements serves as a great inspiration and motivator. I credit my mother and my grandmothers for my spirituality, valuing family community responsibility, and for embracing my femininity. As a young girl, I accompanied my mother on visits to the sick or needy members in our community. The fact that both my mother and grandmothers blazed a trail before me by being active community members cleared a path for me to follow.

Another powerful source of inspiration was my English teacher in high school, who recognized my love for the written word and nurtured this talent. Her efforts bore fruit when I became the first student in my school to score a Distinction One in English. Her confidence in my ability demonstrated to me the impact a teacher has on students, a lesson I took with me when I became an educator. I believed in my students and motivated them to actualize their talents, and they did not disappoint! My college mentor also continues to guide me in life many years after graduation. I attended a girls-only college where students were assigned mentors to assure academic success and professional growth. My mentor has steered my professional and spiritual growth in ways that have driven me to reach beyond myself to succeed. I was privileged to serve as a mentor when I returned to teach at my alma mater. I derive great joy whenever I reconnect with my former students and see how much they have grown. Knowing that I made a difference for them attests to the power of shaping young minds.

The workplace presents opportunities to serve as both a role model and mentor to others. I have benefitted from mentors who have helped me to navigate the murky waters associated with professional life. Oftentimes, women in leadership positions face hurdles that are pegged on gender stereotypes. For example, a male colleague once told me directly: "Men don't take kindly to women administrators." Insights such as these helped me to rise above biases against women in leadership, and to focus my efforts on getting the job done well. Doing so has contributed to my professional growth.

At the community level, I held the role of "school captain" during my high school years, in addition to other leadership roles in clubs and sporting activities. I have served the church in various leadership capacities from my youth. I am a board member/sponsor in a high school in my rural home and a board director in a non-governmental organization (NGO) that advocates for women's rights and empowerment in Kenya. In the United States, I serve as a board director of a non-profit refugee organization. These opportunities have come from recommendations by community members who have seen leadership potential in me, as a woman, and have therefore supported my leadership journey.

The role of peers as mentors cannot be underestimated. Salole (1992) noted that "children are part of the socialization process everywhere, yet opportunities to allow them to play a role in `teaching' are rarely sought" (p. 9). Moving from my home in Kenya to live and study in the United States has driven this reality home for me. The concept of *Chama* ("group" in Kiswahili) is widespread in Kenya. Women friends meet regularly for moral support. How I miss the laughter and camaraderie in *Chama* meetings! Being with peers who share the same life experiences is an incredible way to build morale and uplift one another. Some *Chamas* have evolved into big investment initiatives that model the best of "women power" in the African context. It is a great joy to see women accomplishing big dreams for themselves, families, and communities

Networking opportunities increase personal mastery through self-awareness and are crucial in creating a deeper sense of self-worth as a woman. The various stereotypes girls grow up with often leave some residual effects over the course of a woman's journey through life. It is critical to have an avenue for centering oneself when self-doubt kicks in. I participated in one such program through the Alabastron Network Trust in Kenya. Alabastron was founded to coach women seeking to revamp their lives. Through its signature program—*Renewing Self: A Personal Safari*—women are taken through a journey of "identifying and overcoming self-defeating patterns so that they can live significantly, heal their families, and impact society" (Alabastron Network Trust, 2016). During my journey, I had the opportunity to witness women go through the transforming miracle that occurs when layers of destructive habits are peeled off, bringing out the beauty and potential within every woman. On a personal level, dreams that I had put on hold for years were reignited in my life after I had attended this program.

As another strategy for women's empowerment, pairing women with mentors imparts knowledge and skills needed to navigate the workplace, especially in leadership positions. The guidance and support of supervisors and professional colleagues has nurtured my talents by pointing me to career opportunities and professional engagements where my knowledge and skills would be used more optimally. The desire of these individuals to see me grow has enabled me to scale heights I never imagined. Mentorship and networking are critical to developing women leaders.

CONCLUSION

The symbolism portrayed through communication is key to bridging the leadership gap for women since it plays a role in gender socialization. As Wood (2013) argued, "Becoming aware of how our culture establishes and communicates inequities is necessary" (p. 9) if improvements to the status of women are to be achieved. Girls and women in Africa bear the brunt of poverty and other social ills in their communities. The role of communication in establishing a reality that permeates divergent world views and the leadership challenge for women in most African communities is crucial.

In order to counteract the stereotypes that tend to hold women back in Africa and elsewhere, mentoring offers a potentially helpful strategy to encourage the full realization of talents and dreams. Mentoring can help to nudge women to advance to the next level—what I refer to as transcendence of self. Women have the power within them to create new realities as individuals and for society at large. This has been my story and that of many other African women. The late Wangari Maathai of Kenya is testament to this. She advocated for environmental and human rights in Kenya, which led to her global recognition and being honored with the 2004 Nobel Peace Prize (Maathai, 2006).

I conclude with another Kiswahili saying that goes: *Mwana hufuata kisogo cha nina* (Kagwa, 2007). African women often carry infants on their backs, with the infant facing the back of the mother's head. This proverb evokes a powerful picture of the trust a child has in the mother to carry him or her safely, and within close proximity. It also depicts the responsibility older members of the community have as role models. This is the role of a mentor. While my quest for excellence has been largely for my own self-actualization, I have since realized that I carry the dreams of many girls and women from my community on my shoulders. This makes me more determined to succeed, not only for me, but for them. In their eyes, I have become their champion. As with so many other leadership responsibilities in my life, I have stepped into a leadership role I did not consciously seek. My own natural inclination may have been to stay out of the limelight and serve others in the background. Yet, in serving others and by overcoming life's challenges to realize my dreams, a pathway to leadership emerged. This is the essence of servant leadership—leaders as servants and servants as leaders (Greenleaf, 2002). This perspective offers the opportunity to see service as an avenue for leadership as opposed to servitude.

REFERENCES

Adler, R. B., Rodman, G., & du Pré, A. (2014). *Understanding human communication* (12th edition). Oxford, England: Oxford University Press.

Akotia, S., & Adote, A. (2012). The moderating effects of age and education on gender differences on gender role perceptions. *Gender and Behavior, 10*(2), 5022–5043.

Alabastron Network Trust. (2016). *Renewing self: A personal safari.* Retrieved from http://www.alabastron.org/index.php

Archard, N. (2013). Women's participation as leaders in society: An adolescent girl's perspective. *Journal of Youth Studies, 16*(6), 759–775. doi:10.1080/13676261.2 012.756974.

Burley-Allen, M. (1995). *Listening: The forgotten skill* (2nd edition). New York, NY: John Wiley & Sons, Inc.

Burns, J. M. (1978). *Leadership.* New York, NY: Harper & Row.

Dibie, J., & Dibie, R. (2012). Non-Governmental organizations (NGOs) and the empowerment of women in Africa. *African and Asian Studies, 11*(1–2), 95–122. doi:10.1163/156921012x629349

Greenleaf, R. K. (2002). *Servant leadership: A journey into the nature of legitimate power and greatness* (25th edition). New York, NY: Paulist Press.

Hall, M. (2007). Mentoring the natural way: Native American approaches to education. *Reclaiming Children and Youth, 16*(1), 14–16.

Kagwa, F. M. (2007). *Kamusi changamuzi ya methali.* Nairobi, Kenya: Moran.

Kenya Law Reports. (2010). *The constitution of Kenya.* Retrieved from http://www.kenyalaw.org/kl/index.php?id=398

Leach, F. (2007). African girls, nineteenth-century mission education and the patriarchal imperative. *Gender and Education, 20*(4), 335–347.

Leaper, C., & Friedman, C. K. (2007). The socialization of gender. In J. Grusec & P. D. Hastings (Eds.), *Handbook of Socialization: Theory and Research* (pp. 561–587). New York, NY: Guilford Press.

Maathai, W. (2006). *Unbowed: A memoir.* New York, NY: Random House.

Morra, A.-M. (2010). Women as leaders in the digital age. In K. O'Connor (Ed.), *Gender and women's leadership: A reference handbook* (pp. 780–789). Thousand Oaks, CA: SAGE.

Mutiga, M. (2017, January 6). Kenya's women struggle to end male stranglehold on power. *The Guardian*. Retrieved from https://www.theguardian.com/global-development/2017/jan/06/kenya-women-struggle-to-end-male-stranglehold-on-power?CMP=twt_a-world_b-gdnafrica

Nathan, R. (2005). *My freshman year: What a professor learned by becoming a student.* London, England: Penguin Books.

Protégé. (n.d.). In *Merriam-Webster's online dictionary*. Retrieved from https://www.merriam-webster.com/dictionary/prot%C3%A9g%C3%A9

Salole, G. (1992). *Building on people's strengths: The case for contextual child development.* (Report No. ISSN-0925-2983). The Hague, the Netherlands: Bernard van heer Foundation. Retrieved from http://files.eric.ed.gov/fulltext/ED353051.pdf

Sibanda, E. (2014). The role of folklore in African society. *International Journal of Sociological Science, 1*(1), 1–7.

Wood, J. T. (2013). *Gendered lives: Communication, gender & culture.* Boston, MA: Cengage Learning.

PART IV

INTERSECTIONS AND CONUNDRUMS

Before we can implement the six strategies for inclusive leadership from an intersectional ethic that Brenda J. Allen offers in Chapter 2 of this volume, we must understand the complexities in what is meant by both intersectionality and inclusion. Intersectionality, as first termed by Kimberlé Crenshaw (1989), refers to the interconnected social categories of identity, including race, class, and gender. An intersectional approach examines the multiple ways that these categories create overlapping systems of oppression. To consider social identity categories such as race, gender, and class, as interdependent rather than as independent, is to use an intersectional perspective. Moreover, these multiple social identity categories are socially constructed through communication. For example, Richardson and Taylor (2009) observed that "race and gender are not stable features of women of color, but rather are developed through micro-and macro-level communicative activities" (p. 255), so the two conducted a qualitative study to understand workplace sexual harassment as experienced by of women of color. An analysis of six focus groups captured "the *intersection* of race and gender, suggesting that social constructions of these categories are important throughout individuals' work experiences" (Richardson & Taylor, 2009, p. 256, emphasis in original) because of the way the construct of race was partly how these women made sense of harassment.

In addition, Richardson and Taylor's (2009) study revealed the ways organizations arc raced and gendered. The communication climate, the values, the beliefs of an organization affect how power is dispersed in organizations vis à vis race and gender. Therefore, those with less power through

Gender, Communication, and the Leadership Gap, pages 197–199
Copyright © 2017 by Information Age Publishing
All rights of reproduction in any form reserved.

both race and gender influences "the communicative possibilities for those who perceive themselves as having little power within the workplace" (Richardson & Taylor, 2009, p. 262). This study underscores how complicated identity is in organizational contexts and the importance of an intersectional approach.

In this section, chapter authors examine the multiple ways that identities intersect with leadership, and these intersections can be considered conundrums. Conundrums are difficult questions or problems that we face. Conundrums force us to look at privilege and oppression and the interlocking forces that are at play. The chapters in this section offer different examples of how scholars are grappling with conundrums. They give rise to questions such as, how do we strive for diversity when there is so much heterogeneity in positions of influence? How are institutions a factor in reproducing norms of Whiteness? If we have diversity and different perspectives in positions of power, we can solve problems more creatively. But as these chapters document, getting a seat at the table is mired in perceptions about who is and who is not a leader.

Diversity matters to leadership and business. Some companies are taking diversity seriously by hiring diversity officers, offering diversity training, and paying attention to the diversity of their hires. Yet there is criticism, as Allen (Chapter 2) pointed out, to really incorporating strategies. Diverse workplaces are good for business, as Bush and Peters (2017) found, "ethnically diverse companies are 35% more likely to outperform the national industry median, . . . [and] gender-diverse companies are 15% more likely to have better financial returns" (para. 16). Bottom line aside, diverse companies are a benefit interpersonally in building trust and contribute to productive organizational cultures through a variety of voices that produce higher quality decisions and creative ideas.

Below these surface considerations of intersectional identities and the importance of getting diversity in organizations right are conundrums Ahmed (2012) explored in her work on institutions. As she wrote, "diversity practitioners do not simply work *at* institutions, they also work *on* them" (italics in original, p. 22), so her phenomenological inquiry into what it means to be in charge of diversity in organizations revealed the conundrum of having a job that entails changing the way an organization values difference. The paradox is that organizations have become successful when diversity "ceases to cause trouble," in Ahmed's argument. In other words, "having an institutional aim to make diversity a goal can even be a sign that diversity is *not* an institutional goal" (p. 23). Like us, Ahmed located communication at the heart of the matter, saying, "diversity workers are communication workers" (p. 23). For example, "The institutional nature of diversity work is often described in terms of the language of integrating or embedding diversity into the ordinary work or daily routines of an organization" (p. 23). Her work shows the value of tracing the circulation of communication, which is important to understanding where diversity gets stuck in parts of organizations. It shows the value of what it means to identify locations in an organization where diversity is advocated. It shows what it means for relations of power when we think of the Whiteness of institutions as the welcoming hosts to diverse bodies and those bodies of difference as guests.

The chapters in this section look at intersectionality and its impact on leadership practices. From aspiring women student leaders in the classroom to rhetorical strategies of African American college women presidents, there are multiple layers of perceptions of one's self as a leader as well as cultural perceptions of leadership. These chapters highlight the ways in which women of color have been marginalized in leadership scholarship. Taken together, they offer pathways to integrate cultural values that can inform leadership practice to get beyond our current ways of doing things.

There are also opportunities to expand our framework. We note the many missing categories. Sexuality, class, religion, and age are just some areas that we should keep in mind when discussing intersectionality. These chapters can offer a springboard for studying other forms of intersectional identities since they offer critical perspectives of how power operates and how and why intersectionality and inclusion should be at the forefront of leadership scholarship.

REFERENCES

Ahmed, S. (2012). *On being included: Racism and diversity in institutional life.* Durham, NC: Duke University Press.

Bush, M., & Peters, K. (2016, December 5). How the best companies do diversity right. *Fortune.* Retrieved from http://fortune.com/2016/12/05/diversity -inclusion-workplaces/

Crenshaw, K. (1989). Demarginalizing the intersection of race and sex: A Black feminist critique of antidiscrimination doctrine, feminist theory, and antiracist politics. *University of Chicago Legal Forum, 1989*(1), 139–167.

Richardson, B. K., & Taylor, J. (2009). Sexual harassment at the intersection of race and gender: A theoretical model of the sexual harassment experiences of women of color. *Western Journal of Communication, 73*(3), 248–272.

CHAPTER 12

INTERSECTIONALITY AND FEMINIST PRAXIS

An Integrative Analysis of Diversity and Discourse in Women's Leadership

Diane A. Forbes
University of California

By 2024, the projected increase of women of color in the U.S. workforce will range from 11% for African American women to 30% for Latina women, and the projected increase in Asian women in the workforce is 24%, with a 2% projected decrease of White women. More women are in the U.S. Congress; about 25%, only 6.2% of the total number of women representatives are women of color, which includes African Americans, Latinas, and Asians (Monthly Labor Review, 2015). Although women constitute almost half of the corporate workforce, they occupy 4% and 19% of CEO and board positions, respectively (Catalyst, 2016), and although the number of women presidents in higher education has risen over the last four decades, the rate of increase has stagnated in the last 20 years. For instance, in the mid-1980s, women comprised 9% of all university presidents and in the mid-1990s,

Gender, Communication, and the Leadership Gap, pages 201–221
Copyright © 2017 by Information Age Publishing
All rights of reproduction in any form reserved.

their representation doubled to 19%; in the mid-2000s, that number rose by only 4%, from 19% to 23%. Between 2006 and 2011, the percentage of women presidents in academia increased from 23% to only 26.4%. Therefore, although there was a 100% increase in U.S. women university presidents from the mid-1980s to the mid-1990s, perhaps in part due to the effect of the women's movement decades earlier, the following decade saw only a 20% increase. From 2006 to 2016, there has been an even slower rate of increase in these numbers, and on college and university boards, men outnumber women by more than two to one (American Council on Education, 2016).

In sum, across governmental, academic, and corporate organizations, there is a gross underrepresentation of women in leadership roles and, in particular, an even more dismal picture for the representation of women of color in leadership. These statistics are troubling when we consider the projection that by 2050, women of color will be the majority of all women in the United States.

The United States is, for the most part, unprepared to meet the demographic and organizational demands of the coming decades, with little representation in leadership to mirror the societal and cultural shifts we are projected to experience. Some of the barriers that contribute to the slow or limited advancement of women of color are lack of access to informal networks, negative stereotyping, media influences that perpetuate negative images, differences in socialization and speech, "old boy" networks and the inability to read organizational and social cues made available to mostly dominant groups (Armstrong, 2008; Eagly & Carli, 2007; Oakley, 2000). There is little research on an inclusive and integrated leadership model that responds to these projections.

PURPOSE

In order to facilitate and address the existing leadership disparities and the troubling trends forecasted for the next decades, organizational scholarship and research need to be developed to inform women's leadership opportunities and disparities in access, advancement, and inclusion. As subjective knowledge and organizational experience of diverse groups are centered, a closer connection between research and praxis becomes evident, as praxis gives rise to inclusive approaches. From a Freirian perspective, praxis involves action, reflection, and action, accomplished in a cycle as people actively engage their world with a view towards transformation (Freire, 1971). Theorizing from women's perspectives shapes leadership expectations and influences understanding about the complexity of leadership. Praxis, as a reciprocal relationship between theory and practice, forges new norms and accomplishes social change (Storberg-Walker & Haber-Curran, 2017).

Praxis from feminist perspectives actively engages in disruption and a challenge of exclusive knowledge as it seeks to traverse multiple standpoints and identities in women's experiences. Feminist praxis lies at the intersection of the meanings and possibilities of complex dichotomies that can aid in our examination of the relationship between global and local, which can be seen in theory and method, individually and collaboratively produced knowledge, and academic and activist agendas (Nagar & Swarr, 2010).

Feminist theory and praxis challenge dominant systems of knowledge production and organizing that exclude the experiences of women. Active engagement in addressing the challenges of exclusion and representation of women in leadership roles facilitate changes in women's organizational and material conditions. Inclusive and integrated theoretical and practical models need to be developed to institute concrete changes that address exclusion and erasure of women's organizational leadership. Feminist theory and praxis place the diverse, nuanced, and complex lives of all women at the center of social and organizational inquiry. Blackmore (1993) conceptualizes feminist leadership in higher education research as the "doing of feminism" and leading in a way that challenges and changes hegemonic institutional practices (p. 309). Feminist leadership has at its core emancipatory politics that emerge from women's lives—their experiences, attitudes, values, and beliefs. Feminist leaders are also concerned more broadly with class, race, ability, and sexuality, a broader political and ideological agenda that opposes oppressive practices and institutions (Strachan, 1999).

Although feminists have been steadfast in their work for the advancement and equality of women, early feminists have been criticized for treating one form of oppression as more fundamental or more central than another, thus excluding women of color, international women, women of lower socioeconomic standing, less educated women, and others. Mann and Huffman (2005) discuss the difficulties of responding to and incorporating multiple oppressions, which are simultaneous, inseparable, and interlocking, and must be approached as such. Leadership research and scholarship still lack studies about diverse women in leadership, often conflating leadership to mean "male" and women to be "White."

Feminisms[1] as critical frameworks seek to accomplish social change, which is reflected through gender equality. An examination of leadership theory and practice from diverse feminist perspectives expands organizational and political discourses about the practice and process of leadership, which has been primarily centered on White, male experiences and standpoints. Inclusive feminist perspectives, such as Third and Fourth Wave Feminisms, therefore, elucidate and center diverse women's experiences and approaches as a way to resist and challenge patriarchal leadership discourse, which excludes women and underrepresented groups (Cochrane, 2013; Mann & Huffman, 2005). The overall work of feminisms involves consciousness-raising and resistance, examining and centering the conditions and experiences of women lived experiences. In sum, leadership from feminist perspectives, challenges patriarchal forms and ways of knowing as dominant and central in leadership theory and practice.

In this chapter, I propose a more inclusive and integrated framework to conceptualizing women's leadership. Drawing on both communication and leadership scholarship, I seek to ask new questions and interrogate the categories of "woman" and "leader," such that even within these categories we explore a more complicated and inclusive intersection of identities. What are the cultural influences of diverse women in leadership? How does women's socialization exclude but also serve as assets in organizing? What discursive practices demonstrate the ways in which organizations are gendered, classed, cultured, and raced, for example? How can we transform organizations to embrace diversity among and within the category "woman" to enhance leadership praxis? The chapter presents a transformative model of women's leadership through the lens of intersectionality by drawing on the diverse perspectives of women leaders to reimagine women's leadership as more inclusive and complex as it extends leadership and communication theoretical frameworks.

The discussion will first provide an overview of the conceptual framework of intersectionality and feminist praxis as a means of understanding the ways in which gender and intersecting identities influence women's leadership experiences and practice. Praxis is central to these ideas as it speaks to women's active engagement in organizational and social transformation, which is accomplished through leadership. I then discuss key intersectional identities that coexist and operate with gender to explicate diverse women's experiences in leadership to develop and expand critical organizational communication research. The study here centers women from international, varied class, and cultural backgrounds to demonstrate the ways in which gender intersects *with* these constructs and not *apart* from them. This intersectionality informs an integrative and holistic approach to women's leadership.

INTERSECTIONALITY AS FEMINIST PRAXIS

Leaders have the potential not only to influence, but also to transform organizations through discourse, such as policies and general practice; they also possess the ability to affect broader social change. Through this exploration, I suggest a keener attention to the areas of difference, complexity, and denial within feminist discourses of organizing. I discuss the ways in which difference can serve as assets to women and organizations at large, and I argue that intersectionality can strengthen and enhance analyses of leadership. Pittinsky (2010) proposes in his model of intergroup leadership that the idea of bringing subgroups together into a collective can be viewed not only as an accomplishment of a goal; rather, it must be seen as a critical step towards the achievement of organizational goals. Previous leadership studies have focused on the exclusion of women from the leadership positions, differences between male and female leadership styles; and, over the last few decades, there has been an increase in studies about women's leadership. What we still need to explore is differences within the category "woman" and "women leaders" to extend and diversify our analyses. We need to study intersectionality more closely in leadership and communication studies to meet the organizational and intellectual demands of the twenty-first century organization.

Intersectional research brings to the fore the ways in which organizational and societal members have (un)consciously participated in exclusionary practices that hinder the growth and full inclusion of diverse women in leadership in multiple contexts. These exclusionary practices also affect organizations' ability to thrive and grow in an increasingly diverse and complex environment. Such inclusive and intersectional analyses also enliven and humanize women from multiple locations and circumstances and foster greater engagement and action in the preparing of today's organizations to meet the demographic and organizational demands of the twenty-first century.

Carastathis (2013) conceptualizes identities as internally heterogeneous, complex, and constituted by dissonances and internal differences, as well as internal and external relations of power. Therefore, even within the study of women's leadership, there are nuanced, complex, and heterogeneous experiences that can inform leadership scholarship and research. Intersectionality, as a conceptual framework, addresses the multiple axes of location and rejects a singular analysis of individuals that views identities as fragmented and solitary units. Intersectionality, as conceptualized partially through Third Wave Feminism, is very much concerned with "the development of modes of thinking that can come to terms with the multiple, constantly shifting bases of oppression in relation to the multiple, interpenetrating axes of identity, and the creation of a coalition politics based on these understandings" (Heywood & Drake, 1997, p. 3).

The exploration and acknowledgement of the complexities of women's identities disrupt ways of knowing that ignore aspects of women's identities, all of which simultaneously interlock with their gender. Gender is not constructed or experienced from a unitary perspective; rather, class, nationality, sexuality, ethnicity, and race simultaneously intersect and interact with gender. Developing narratives that capture this complexity challenges singular ways of viewing women's lives. Hegemonic, one-dimensional, and essentialized identities produced and reproduced through social and organizational practices can be disrupted by the collection and dissemination of differentiated stories and narratives that focus on the complexity of identity-subjectivities and practices (Holvino, 2010). Taking women's experiences as a whole, while important, obscures the complex and nuanced experiences of women from multiple cultural, ethnic, national, class, and personal locations.

Organizational research also explores the complexity and challenge of intersectionality for women leaders, addressing the concept of gendered racism and triple jeopardy of gender, race, and ethnicity. Identity categories and experiences are not treated as autonomous in intersectional approaches; rather, intersectionality examines their connectedness to deepen leadership analyses, deconstruct hierarchies, and understand women's experiences across location and at the nexus of salient intersecting identities (Sanchez-Hucles & Davis, 2010; Ngunjiri et al., 2017; Rosette & Livingston, 2012).

Intersectional analyses need to be integrated in leadership and communication scholarship to complicate and explore the heterogeneity of "woman" and the rich knowledge and subjective positions that emerge from the study of women's leadership. Approaches towards women's leadership, then, need to include African American women, immigrant women, women leaders from various socioeconomic classes and geographic regions—women whose narratives need to shape leadership theory and practice. Intersectionality as/and feminist praxis do not approach identity as fixed, stable, and predictable constructions; rather, identities—class, race, gender, culture, and sexuality—are contextual, shifting, dynamic, and varied in particular moments in history in society, origins, and contexts.

FEMINIST PRAXIS AND WOMEN'S LEADERSHIP

Organizational communication and leadership research have established connections between local, seemingly mundane organizational practices and a broader social and global context. This approach focuses on more comprehensive and systemic analyses that examine the (re)production of unequal power relationships, close scrutiny of organizational micropractices that exclude or marginalize, and the ways in which these organizational dynamics impact change (Forbes 2009; Forbes Berthoud, 2011; Holvino, 2010; Mumby, 2010; Putnam & Mumby, 2013). To further expand and develop these ideas, a more integrative and focused analysis is needed that examines organizational discursive practices and the ways in which they (re)produce material and structural assets and disadvantages. In this study of women's leadership, I propose a keen examination of the heterogeneity of "woman" and an active engagement of intersecting and multiple shifting axes of domination, oppression, and privilege.

Moss et al. (1999) offer a model of feminist praxis that centers mentorship as a way to support women and persons of color in their navigation of organizations, the academy in particular. Mentorship as feminist praxis is predicated on values such as a focus on a woman-centered approach, feminist alliances with marginalized groups, engaging in collective decision-making processes, and dismantling oppressive organizational and systemic structures.

Mentorship has generally been linked to leadership, career, and personal success as mentees receive support, directional and personal development for leadership roles, and socialization into important networks that foster increased collaboration and productivity. Through mentorship, protégées are exposed to new learning experiences and opportunities. Leadership studies have elucidated how mentorship can support and advance organizational careers, especially for those who lack access to critical resources for their advancement—women and underrepresented groups.

As an informal organizational communication practice, mentors shape protégées' perspectives and active communication processes through the socialization process and networks internal and external to the system (Luecke & Herminia, 2004; Kogler Hill, Hilton Bahniuk, Dobos, & Rouner, 1989). Mentoring as active communication shapes organizational processes and culture, which include leadership practices, perceptions, and stereotypes associated with intersectional women's identities in these roles.

Humble, Solomon, Allen, Blaisure, and Johnson (2006), in their model of feminist mentorship, emphasize a commitment to gender equality and change, the examination of gender as a social construct, and the centrality of women's lives and experiences. A central theme in their model centers around issues of power and multiple approaches to work towards social change. These models of feminist praxis are aspects of feminist activism and progress that support women's advancement and organizational socialization.

INTERSECTIONALITY AND WOMEN'S LEADERSHIP

For the last four decades, feminisms have highlighted and challenged the lack of representation of women in multiple contexts, such as the workforce, politics, society, and organizations. Organizational strategies such as mentoring, training, and bias reduction training have been proposed as ways to support and promote women leaders. These frameworks have centered on women's experiences, subjective knowledge, and inequities in domestic and global contexts. Women's leadership studies have more recently addressed the complexities of representation in leadership and the pervasive gaps between men and women in senior positions across industries (Center for American Women and Politics, 2016; Eagly & Carli, 2007; Ruminski & Holba, 2012). These models and critiques have been gender-central, and have, in their efforts to secure progress for women, neglected to consider *all* women and to understand the intersections that complicate and enrich women's levels and the contexts within which we work.

In this section, I explore ways in which different social constructs influence women's leadership and intersect with gender in complex ways in organizational and social contexts. I draw on a review of organizational communication research that explicates women leaders' complex social and professional intersections in organizational experiences to elucidate ways in which feminist praxis is accomplished (Forbes, 2002, 2009; Parker, 2001). Through a brief personal narrative, I also offer an intersectional analysis that builds on the organizational scholarship of intersectionality and women's leadership. Organizational research in the context of women's leadership and intersectionality points to individual insights that lead to greater understanding of organizational dynamics.

Class and Women's Leadership

Intersectional analyses focus on multiple axes of identity and oppression to understand the interlocking and dynamic experiences of women and many underrepresented groups. Across these axes lie constructs such as class and socioeconomic status. The latter is closely tied to social mobility, access to financial, intellectual, social, and political capital and is determined by income level, material wealth, participation in social and educational institutions, and one's profession (Oakes & Rossi, 2003).

Although class is central to many aspects of our lives and is a primary determinant of our social, physical, professional, and financial positions/locations, public discourse and analyses in our society are largely "de-classed" (Mooney, 2008, p. 68). In U.S. society, the engagement in discourses about class and social status is somewhat uncomfortable, as this probes into people's financial standing and can "potentially disrupt deeply held beliefs about a United States where everyone is middle class and anyone can get ahead if they try hard enough" (Barak, Leighton, & Cotton, 2014, p. 84). In the United States, we therefore talk about "working families," which is all-encompassing, including families in all classes. However, such analyses do not address disparities, inequality, power relations, gender dynamics, and nuances of identities as they relate to leaders' differing, multiple, and intersecting identities.

Class is also integral in women's organizational, social, personal, and political experiences, as can be seen in ways that women from different classes approach and enact leadership, as well as the ways they negotiate relationships and manage their level of access to social, political, intellectual, and financial capital. Feminist praxis engages in reflection and action for change and explores the meaning and possibilities of complex dichotomies. Class, therefore, is an integral feature of intersectional analyses in women's leadership studies to understand women's subjective knowledge and positionality.

Sociology and economics studies reveal that there typically are clear racial and ethnic disparities in income, net worth, educational attainment, and occupation. For example, Asian Americans have the highest income, followed by Whites, as well as a higher degree of educational achievements. They were more likely to hold white collar jobs (LaVeist, 2005; Williams, Mohammed, Leavell, & Collins, 2010). U.S. Blacks and Hispanics generally have poverty levels that are two to three times higher than the poverty levels of Whites. These socioeconomic classifications also influence perceptions and organizational discourse around women from these racial and ethnic groups and shape leadership access and development.

In a 2012 study of women of color in academics, Moffitt, Harris, and Forbes conducted an intersectional analysis that included women leaders of multiple races, ethnicities, classes, and backgrounds from the United States, Latin America, and the Caribbean. The study investigated and challenged the ways in which class, race, ethnicity, culture, nationality, gender, and age operated in the women's lives. An intersectional model emerged from the study that demonstrated the shifting, intersecting, and fluid constructions of gender with other simultaneous and salient identities.

For example, one of the academic leaders in the study, a middle-aged, heterosexual, senior Latina administrator-professor, who studied at elite institutions throughout the United States, now teaches in an institution with mostly low-income and first-generation students who are African American and Latina. She has included all aspects of her studies and research in her teaching; therefore, her study of European philosophers and historians informs her contemporary pedagogy and research. In Moffit et al.'s 2012 study, this administrator associated class with increasing social mobility and a drive for excellence, and she therefore exposed her students to all the scholarship she explored in her elite institutions. She discussed having high expectations of her students and steering them towards great excellence. She explained, however, that some of her mostly White colleagues described this drive and her pedagogical approach as elitist. She decided not to change the content and pedagogical approach as she said she saw in each student "this possibility of the imagination" for which she had to make room. As an academic leader, there were ways in which her ethnicity, class, age, and gender intersect in complicated ways with the students' identities as women from lower socioeconomic backgrounds who were mostly younger African Americans and Latinas. Her pedagogical choices, beliefs about and her history in education, access and social mobility, and women's representation and knowledge production collided in complicated ways in her decision-making to participate in their advancement and leadership development.

Both students and the administrator-professor faced a structural system of doubt, pessimism, and oppression that perceived students from these backgrounds as somehow incapable of grasping such material, which might be "above their heads" or that such information and drive towards an ivy-guided curriculum may not be well-suited for this population. This woman leader "did feminism" and engaged in feminist praxis by challenging dominant systems of knowledge production and organizing that exclude these women and (re)produce their oppression. Her feminist praxis is evidenced in her choices and perspectives about access and education. Through women's narratives in organizational studies, the data reveal that racial, ethnic, and gender stereotypes also influence perceptions of competence, empowerment, and expertise (Eagly & Carli, 2007; Forbes, 2009).

Figure 12.1 proposes a more inclusive and integrated framework to conceptualize women's leadership, drawing on both communication and leadership scholarship. The diagram leads us to interrogate the categories

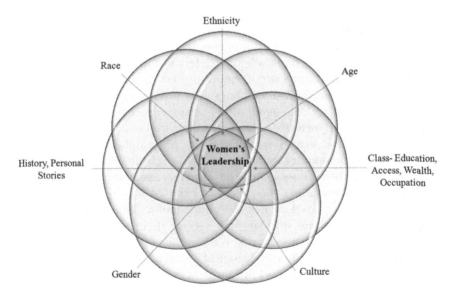

Figure 12.1 Framework to conceptualize intersectionality in women's leadership.

of "woman" and "leader" and captures a more complicated and inclusive intersection of identities beyond White and male.

Kraus and Keltner's (2009) study examined the signs of socioeconomic status (SES), focusing on the ways people signal their class or SES to others via social engagement. They also explored others' perception or judgment of the SES of others and the ways observers make judgments on the basis of displays related to SES. They found that persons with a higher SES were more disengaged socially from the persons with whom they interacted, displaying behaviors such as fidgeting with nearby objects and self-grooming during interactions. Upper SES individuals were more likely than persons from a lower SES to maintain eye contact, nod, laugh, or raise their eyebrows. In their studies of gender in these dynamics, women more frequently exhibited socially engaged behaviors, such as consistent eye contact and general responsiveness and engagement in communication interactions. Also, in their study of White American participants, there were fewer displays of engaged nonverbal behaviors than with groups of non-White and mixed ethnicity groups. Observers also made accurate assessments of participants' class from viewing their communication behaviors in interpersonal interactions. These behavioral patterns can also be linked to cultural norms and practices in communication interactions in multiple areas of organizations and society more broadly.

Nationality and Women's Leadership

Women leaders of other nationalities are also strongly influenced by national ideals, beliefs, and ways of being in the world that are uniquely part of their country's history. For example, women from Jamaica are raised in very empowering and affirming contexts where they see themselves racially and ethnically represented in public life in teachers, physicians, judges, and leaders of government, churches, and businesses. While race is not as central or salient, culture, history, class, and religion partially inform their approach to leadership and life philosophy. Previous studies highlight such stories of resilience, strength, courage, and grit (Forbes, 2002; Forbes, 2009).

In my own experience as a Jamaican-born U.S citizen, my life philosophy and approach to leadership are heavily shaped by my socialization as a Jamaican, being educated academically and musically through the U.K. system of education in Jamaica; being a descendant of Maroons, Africans who escaped slavery, resisted the British, their oppressors, and established their own free communities, governments, and infrastructure. I am shaped also by having college-educated, middle-class parents, attending private prep and high schools, U.S. universities and living in safe U.S. neighborhoods with "good" schools. However, although through education, income and occupation levels, being heterosexual, and sometimes my nationality, I hold many markers of privilege, in other ways, through race and gender in the United States, I experience marginalization and exclusion. At other times, there is privilege in holding these marginalized identities, because from academic, historical, and personal standpoints, I am able to shape decisions, policies, and research pertaining to women and people of color. Thus, through this personal reflection, as a woman leader, I offer a complicated, intersectional view of approaches to leadership, relationship to resistance, confidence in my abilities, and a collectivist orientation to work in service of others and for the empowerment, in particular, of women and underrepresented groups.

Figure 12.1 can be revised to include nationality, as U.S.-born women's standpoints sometimes differ from those of non-U.S. women. For example, culture, nationality, religion, and age become salient in the leadership of Malala Yousafzai, the young Pakistani activist whose human rights activism focuses on women's and girls' rights to education, although her age, gender, religion, and culture make her an unlikely global leader. These intersecting and dynamic identities constitute her ability to leverage her privilege and emerge as an effective and inspirational global leader.

Culture, Race, and Women's Leadership

Studies about African American leaders reveal connections between their cultural and organizational approaches to leadership. In Parker's study of African American women executives' leadership communication (2001), themes emerged such as interactive communication, empowerment through the challenge to produce results, openness in communication, and participative decision making through collaborative debate. These themes can be associated with collectivist and engaging behaviors which are demonstrated in African American culture and among women leaders generally. Other studies about African American women leaders highlight salient areas for study that include not only gendered and raced organizational dynamics, but issues of being sexualized, overlooked, disrespected, and excluded because of one's perceived class, socialization, or ethnicity (Allen, 2000; Forbes, 2009; Parker, 2001).

In my previous study of Jamaican women executives (Forbes, 2002), I theorized about the concept of internalized masculinity, in which both women and men internalize and enact masculine ways of knowing, and that women can also (re)produce and enact masculine subjectivities in organizations. The women executives revealed ways in which their socialization in a predominantly male-dominated workplace and society influenced their leadership discursive practices. One participant mentioned that emotional independence was critical in women's leadership and that women just have to "take our blows" and learn to move on, as we developed resilience and grit. This executive characterized her life, approach, and experience in male-dominated contexts as "swimming upstream with my hunting knife between my teeth" (Forbes, 2002, p. 286). In this analysis, gender, class, and personal locations emerged as more salient, as most of the executive team were Black and all were of the same nationality and culture.

This discussion of class, socioeconomic status, gender, ethnicity, and race of social actors is also closely tied to culture, histories, and notions of collectivism, individualism, and communication behaviors, which influence leadership discursive practices. Communication scholarship views culture as socially constructed and emergent, and culture and communication as intertwined in a reciprocal and causal relationship, such that culture is constituted and enacted through communication, and communication is influenced by cultural nuances and norms (Martin & Nakayama, 1999). As Mumby (1997) states in this paradigm, the "knowing mind is an active contributor to the constitution of knowledge" (p. 6). The studies cited above (Allen, 2000; Forbes, 2002; Parker, 2001) illustrate this type of constitution of knowledge based in African American cultural norms and practices and also in collectivist cultural norms of building and communicating in community.

Communication and psychology research has shown that culture has profound effects on one's development—psychological makeup, attitude, beliefs, values, prejudices, practices, rituals and rites—which then affect communication behavior. One's relatedness to the world is largely based on one's cultural background (Singelis & Brown, 1995; Triandis, 1990; Triandis, McCusker & Hui, 1990).

Collectivist cultures emphasize interdependence through a variety of norms, practices, and implicit and explicit rules. Connectedness among persons, relational harmony, empathy, and self-sacrifice are some of the central values of collectivism, whereas individualist cultures emphasize the independent self, autonomy, self-expression, and personal responsibility (Choi, 1992; Markus & Kitayama, 1994a, 1994b; Triandis, 1990). Cultural members are taught that self-expression and words are the "key to promoting individuality, autonomy, problem solving, friendship, and cognitive development" (Tobin, Wu, & Davidson, 1989, p. 189). Collectivist cultures view the self as flexible, variable, and deeply embedded in relationships and the social environment. Individualist cultures view the self as stable, and occupying a distinct position from the social context. An emphasis is placed on individual abilities, thoughts, and attributes. Directness in communication is emphasized and relational or contextual factors are not as central to assessments of performance or characteristics (Markus & Kitayama, 1991; Singelis, 1994).

Women's socialization is connected to these cultural norms as well. For example, African American women are socialized with both individualistic (U.S.) and collectivistic (African) cultural values. On the one hand, as Parker's (2001) study reveals, they exhibit communal approaches to conflict and organizing generally, and, on the other hand, because of their socialization within a society that has historically marginalized African Americans, they have been socialized to speak up and speak out—features which are antithetical to White women's socialization in the United States.

Socialization experiences differ, for example, between White women and Black women in terms of their relationships with their social and organizational worlds. White women learn to conform to social norms and standards and to practice and display appropriate etiquette while around Blacks. Black women are socialized to speak up and speak out, to develop courage, and to be resilient in the face of multiple axes of domination that impact their lives (Bell & Nkomo, 2001; Holvino, 2010). These dynamics inform organizational relationships at multiple levels as well as leadership choices and outcomes.

Women leaders' discourse can be understood more deeply through studies and applications that integrate culture and its profound influence on decision making, communication, relationship development, mentoring, activism, socialization, and organizational philosophy. For example, a woman leader may be perceived as not assertive enough or strong if she is from a collectivist culture or community. A first- or second-generation Latina may have a more central collectivist ethos, which may be in tension with a predominantly individualistic organizational ethos. Such tensions may influence relationships with and perceptions of women leaders from these cultural contexts. Another aspect of culture is evident in some communal cultures that feature distinct relationships and norms for women. For example, Latinas from various countries are reared in societies that are very matrilineal and have more direct communication styles, strong work ethic, and bolder approaches to life—work, community, and home. These attributes and values can be tremendous organizational assets. However, because of Latina women's nationalities, position as immigrants, class, and ethnicities, they may be marginalized or disregarded in organizations—even as leaders. Similar studies have integrated cultural aspects of Latina leadership highlighting these intersections (Chin, Lott, Rice, & Sanchez-Hucles, 2008; Vasquez & Comas-Días, 2007).

DISCUSSION AND IMPLICATIONS

Research has shown that organizations benefit from diverse perspectives, which lead to stronger organizational cultures, expanded creativity, increased teamwork, effective problem solving, participation, and overall stronger performance (Dwyer, Richard, & Chadwick, 2003; Eagly & Chin, 2010; Thomas, 2004; Williams, 2013). Williams (2013) offers three interconnected rationales for diversity and states that we are witnessing "the coalescence of social justice, economic, and educational aspects of diversity, achieving a kind of synergy" (p. 12). Williams discusses this idea of the "body count" and recommends that organizations move beyond this paradigm to focus instead on organizational excellence, such that we focus on diverse members' level of achievement, participation, full inclusion, and levels of representation. He argues that a number of external factors necessitate a new focus on diversity and leadership: changing demographics, the emergence of a knowledge-based global economy, increasing diverse experiences throughout the United States and beyond, and ongoing legal and political threats to diversity. Understanding and responding to these compelling forces facilitates transformative and positive societal changes (Williams, 2013, p. 32).

Leaders from underrepresented groups (e.g., women, people of color) tend to face more skepticism and shifting beliefs about their competence and effectiveness. In response to these conditions, a more resilient and superior performance may emerge as a reaction to the implicit systemic doubts (Ayman & Korabik, 2010; Cheung & Halpern, 2010; Hoyt & Blascovich, 2007). Women leaders of multiple identities and experiences, therefore, bring tremendous assets that contribute to capacity building, strategic planning, communication, and relationship building, in part, because they are related to women's socialization, intersecting identities, and perspectives. Persons from diverse identity groups also bring numerous assets to organizations, such as broader global and multicultural experiences and perspectives, because they have learned to negotiate both majority and minority cultures. Intercultural competency fosters creative and critical thinking and problem solving, adaptability and openness to change, and the ability to shift one's framework between diverse contexts (Leung, Maddux, Galinsky, & Chiu, 2008; Molinsky, 2007; Musteen, Barker, & Baeten, 2006).

Women-led organizations, therefore, stand to benefit from an investment in diversity and specifically from mentoring and promoting women from diverse cultures, races, ethnicities, classes, and experiences for leadership roles. Communication and leadership scholarship play a significant role in contributing to knowledge production and multifaceted intersectional analyses that elucidate women's multiple locations and connectedness across and within identities.

The intersectional model offered in this chapter presents a complex, nuanced, and integrative framework from which to approach women's leadership. Gender inequality and exclusion persist, in part, because of the narrow lenses from which and through which we view leadership—often White and male. Women's leadership and communication research needs to extend our analyses to include paradigms of new and different narratives that include and analyze salient identity constructs such as class, culture, nationality, race, and ethnicity, all of which often produce diverse leadership outcomes. The influences of gender on leadership practice and discourses can be more fully understood and developed through the integration and application of intersectional lenses that foster greater inclusion in women's leadership.

Taken together, interlocking and intersectional identities weave a rich tapestry of women's leadership and organizational life. However, there are areas of emerging and untapped potential, such as research about the influence of ability, sexual orientation, gender expression and identity, veteran status, and linguistic diversity.

The ways in which privilege and oppression can be co-constituted on the subjective level and the ways in which both privilege and oppression intersect in experiences need to be explored (Nash, 2008). This approach considers variations and distinct connections within and across social identities and categories, such that we explore the spectra in and across class, racial, and cultural, national, and other lines. For example, by painting any one group as wholly oppressed, we fail to consider the privilege their level of education, socioeconomic status, or leadership positions affords them and the nuances of those markers as they intersect with traditionally marginalized groups. In this chapter, I addressed some of these intersections of privilege *and* oppression to contribute to the differentiated and complex narratives of women leaders, whose age, education levels, and class may be markers of privilege, and at other times, their gender, race, or ethnicity may (not) constitute experiences of oppression and marginalization. These areas need to be explored further in the research.

This chapter discussed how intersectionality can strengthen and enhance analyses of leadership and how difference can be assets to women and organizations at large. I have offered a transformational framework to reimagine women's leadership as more inclusive and complex by examining and integrating salient areas of identity for women in leadership, such as a deeper exploration of class, culture, ethnicity, nationality, age, and gender, as they intersect with power. Since these analyses are dynamic and not comprehensive, more collective stories need to be told and diverse women's narratives centered in the research, such that in the development of feminist praxis and intersectionality, we consider differentiated stories, disrupt oppressive ideologies, and challenge dominant systems of knowledge production and organizing. Disruption and challenge move us away from treating one form of oppression as more fundamental or central than another. Some gender-centric or feminist studies have excluded women of color, international women, women of lower socioeconomic classes, and women with diverse cultural and class backgrounds—all of whom are projected to be the majority in the United States by 2050. Given this projection we, as a society, as scholars and activists engaged in feminist praxis, need to be prepared to meet the demographic and organizational demands of the coming decades by integrating and including a more expansive representation of women in organizational leadership.

NOTE

1. Feminisms is used throughout the discussion to acknowledge the distinctions among the waves of feminism, as well as other feminist perspectives that represent different ideologies and approaches to gender equality, such as Black feminism, poststructuralist feminism, and radical feminism.

REFERENCES

Allen, B. J. (2000). "Learning the ropes": A Black feminist standpoint analysis. In P. M. Buzzanell (Ed.), *Rethinking organizational and managerial communication from feminist perspectives* (pp. 177–208). Thousand Oaks, CA: SAGE.

American Council on Education. (2016, January). *New report looks at the status of women in higher education.* Retrieved from http://www.acenet.edu/news-room/Pages/New-Report-Looks-at-the-Status-of-Women-in-Higher-Education.aspx

Armstrong, L. (2008, June/July). What men say behind closed doors. *Working Mother, 31*(5), 88–90.

Ayman, R., & Korabik, K. (2010). Leadership: Why gender and culture matter. *American Psychologist, 65*(3), 157–170.

Barak, G., Leighton, P., & Cotton, A. M. (2014). *Class, race, gender, and crime: The social realities of justice in America.* Lanham, MD: Rowman & Littlefield.

Bell, E. L., & Nkomo, S. M. (2001). *Our separate ways: Black and White women and the struggle for professional identity.* Cambridge, MA: Harvard Business School Press.

Blackmore, J. (1993). "In the shadow of men": The historical construction of educational administration as a "masculinist" enterprise. In J. Blackmore & J. Kenway (Eds.), *Gender matters in educational administration and policy: A feminist introduction.* Deakin Studies in Education Series 11 (pp. 27–48). London, England: Falmer.

Carastathis, A. (2013). Identity categories as potential coalitions. *Signs, 38*(4), 941–965. doi:10.1086/669573

Catalyst. (2016). Pyramid: Women in S&P 500 Companies. *Catalyst.* Retrieved from http://www.catalyst.org/knowledge/women-sp-500-companies

Center for American Women and Politics. (2016). *Women in elective office 2016.* Retrieved from http://www.cawp.rutgers.edu/women-elective-office-2016

Cheung, F. M., & Halpern, D. F. (2010). Women at the top: Powerful leaders define success as work + family in a culture of gender. *American Psychologist, 65*(3), 182–193. doi:10.1037/a0017309

Chin, J. L., Lott, B., Rice, J. K. & Sanchez-Hucles, J. (Eds.). (2008). *Women and leadership: Transforming visions and diverse voices.* Malden, MA: Blackwell.

Choi, S. H. (1992). *Communicative socialization processes: Korea and Canada.* Birmingham, AL: Swets & Zeitlinger.

Cochrane, K. (2013). *All the rebel women: The rise of the fourth wave of feminism.* London, England: Guardian Shorts.

Dwyer, S., Richard, O. C., & Chadwick, K. (2003). Gender diversity in management and firm performance: The influence of growth orientation and organizational culture. *Journal of Business Research, 56*(12), 1009–1019.

Eagly, A. H. & Carli, L. (2007). *Through the labyrinth: The truth about how women become leaders.* Boston, MA: Harvard Business School Press.

Eagly, A. H., & Chin, J. L. (2010). Diversity and leadership in a changing world. *American Psychologist, 65*(3), 216–224.

Forbes, D. A. (2002). Internalized masculinity and women's discourse: A critical analysis of the (re)production of masculinity in organizations. *Communication Quarterly, 50*(3–4), 269–291.

Forbes, D. A. (2009). Commodification and co-modification: Explicating Black female sexuality in organizations. *Management Communication Quarterly, 22*(4), 577–613.

Forbes, D. A. (2011). Education for global leadership: A leadership agenda for women. In E. L. Ruminski & A. Holba (Eds.), *Communicative understandings of women's leadership development: From ceilings of glass to labyrinth paths* (pp. 57–71). Lanham, MD: Lexington Press.

Freire, P. (1971). *Pedagogy of the oppressed.* New York, NY: Herder and Herder.

Heywood, L., & Drake, J. (Eds.). (1997). *Third wave agenda: Being feminist, doing feminism.* Minneapolis, MN: University of Minnesota Press.

Holvino, E. (2010). Intersections: The simultaneity of race, gender and class in organization studies. *Gender, Work & Organization, 17*(3), 248–277. doi:10.1111/j.1468-0432.2008.00400.x

Hoyt, C. L., & Blascovich, J. (2007). Leadership efficacy and women leaders' responses to stereotype activation. *Group Processes and Intergroup Relations, 10*(4), 595–616. doi:10.1177/1368430207084718

Humble, Á. M., Solomon, C. R., Allen, K. R., Blaisure, K. R., and Johnson, M. P. (2006). Feminism and mentoring of graduate students. *Family Relations, 55*(1), 2–15.

Kogler Hill, S. E., Hilton Bahniuk, M., Dobos, J., & Rouner, D. (1989). Mentoring and other communication support in the academic setting. *Group & Organization Studies, 14*(3), 355–368.

Kraus, M. W., & Keltner, D. (2009). Signs of socioeconomic status a thin-slicing approach. *Psychological Science, 20*(1), 99–106.

LaVeist, T. A. (2005). Disentangling race and socioeconomic status: A key to understanding health inequalities. *Journal of Urban Health, 82*(3), 26–34.

Luecke, R., & Herminia, I. (2004). *Harvard business essentials: Coaching and mentoring: How to develop top talent and achieve stronger performance.* Boston, MA: Harvard Business School Press.

Leung, A. K., Maddux, W. W., Galinsky, A. D., & Chiu, C. (2008). Multicultural experience enhances creativity: The when and how. *American Psychologist, 63*(3), 169–181.

Mann, S. A., & Huffman, D. J. (2005). The decentering of second wave feminism and the rise of the third wave. *Science & Society, 69*(1), 56–91.

Markus, H. R., & Kitayama, S. (1991). Culture and the self: Implications for cognition, emotion, and motivation. *Psychological Review, 98*(2), 224–253.

Markus, H., & Kitayama, S. (1994a). A collective fear of the collective: Implications for selves and theories of selves. *Personality and Social Psychology Bulletin, 20*(5), 568–579.

Markus, H. R., & Kitayama, S. (1994b). The cultural construction of self and emotion: Implications for social behavior. In S. Kitayama & H. R. Markus (Eds.), *Emotion and culture: Empirical studies of mutual influence* (pp. 89–130). Washington, DC. American Psychological Association.

Martin, J. N., & Nakayama, T. K. (1999). Thinking dialectically about culture and communication. *Communication Theory, 9*(1), 1–25. doi:10.1111/j.1468-2885.1999.tb00160.x

Moffit, K., Harris, H., & Forbes, D. (2012). Present and unequal: A third-wave approach to voice parallel experiences in managing oppression and bias in the academy. In G. G. Muhs, Y. F. Niemann, C. G. González, & A. P. Harris (Eds.), *Presumed incompetent: The intersections of race and class for women in academia* (pp. 78–92). Boulder, CO: University Press of Colorado.

Molinsky, A. (2007). Cross-cultural code switching: The psychological challenges of adapting behavior in foreign cultural interactions. *Academy of Management Review, 32*(2), 622–640.

Monthly Labor Review. (2015, December). Labor force projections to 2024: the labor force is growing, but slowly. *Bureau of Labor Statistics.* Retrieved from https://www.bls.gov/opub/mlr/2015/article/labor-force-projections-to-2024.htm

Mooney, G. (2008). "Problem" populations, "problem" places. In J. Newman & N. Yeates (Eds.), *Social justice: Welfare, crime and society* (pp. 97–128). Maidenhead, England: Open University Press.

Moss, P., Debres, K. J., Cravey, A., Hyndman, J., Hirschboeck, K. K., & Masucci, M. (1999). Toward mentoring as feminist praxis: Strategies for ourselves and others. *Journal of Geography in Higher Education, 23*(3), 413–427. doi:10.1080/03098269985371

Mumby, D. K. (1997). Modernism, postmodernism, and communication studies: A rereading of an ongoing debate. *Communication Theory, 7*(1), 1-28. doi:10.1111/j.1468-2885.1997.tb00140.x

Mumby, D. K. (2010). *Reframing difference in organizational communication studies: Research, pedagogy, and practice.* Los Angeles, CA: SAGE.

Musteen, M., Barker, III, V. L., & Baeten, V. L. (2006). CEO attributes associated with attitude toward change: The direct and moderating effects of CEO tenure. *Journal of Business Research, 59*(5), 604–612. doi:1016/j.jbusres.2005.10.008

Nagar, R. & Swarr, A. L. (2010). Introduction: Theorizing transnational feminist praxis. In A. L. Swarr & R. Nagar (Eds.), *Critical transnational feminist praxis* (pp. 1–22). New York, NY: SUNY Press.

Nash, J. C. (2008). Re-thinking intersectionality. *Feminist Review, 89*(1), 1–15.

Ngunjiri, F. W., Almquist, J. M., Beebe, M. Elbert, C. D. Gardiner, R. A., & Shockness, M. (2017). Intersectional leadership praxis: Unpacking the experiences of women leaders at the nexus of roles and identities. In J. Storberg-Walker & P. Haber-Curran (Eds.), *Theorizing women and leadership: New insights and contributions from multiple perspectives* (pp. 249–264). Charlotte, NC: Information Age.

Oakes, J. M., & Rossi, P. H. (2003). The measurement of SES in health research: Current practices and steps toward a new approach. *Social Science and Medicine, 56*(4), 769–784.

Oakley, J. G. (2000). Gender-based barriers to senior management positions: Understanding the scarcity of female CEOs. *Journal of Business Ethics, 27*(4), 321–334.

Parker, P. S. (2001). African American women executives' leadership communication within dominant-culture organizations: (Re) conceptualizing notions of collaboration and instrumentality. *Management Communication Quarterly, 15*(1), 42–82.

Pittinsky, T. L. (2010). A two-dimensional model of intergroup leadership: The case of national diversity. *American Psychologist, 65*(3), 194–200.

Putnam, L. L., & Mumby, D. K. (Eds.). (2013). *The SAGE handbook of organizational communication: Advances in theory, research, and methods.* Thousand Oaks, CA: SAGE.

Rosette, A. S., & Livingston, R. W. (2012). Failure is not an option for Black women: Effects of organizational performance on leaders with single versus dual-subordinate identities. *Journal of Experimental Social Psychology, 48*(5), 1162–1167. doi:10.1016/j.jesp.2012.05.002

Ruminski, E.L., & Holba, A.M. (2012). *Communicative understandings of women's leadership development: From ceilings of glass to labyrinth paths.* Lanham, MD: Lexington Books.

Sanchez-Hucles, J. V., & Davis, D. D. (2010). Women and women of color in leadership: Complexity, identity, and intersectionality. *American Psychologist, 65*(3), 171–181.

Singelis, T. M. (1994). The measurement of independent and interdependent self-construals. *Personality and Social Psychology Bulletin, 20*(5), 580–591.

Singelis, T. M., & Brown, W. J. (1995). Culture, self, and collectivist communication linking culture to individual behavior. *Human Communication Research, 21*(3), 354–389.

Storberg-Walker, J. & Haber-Curran, P. (2017). Theorizing women's leadership as praxis: Creating new knowledge for social change. In J. Storberg-Walker & P. Haber-Curran (Eds.), *Theorizing women and leadership: New insights and contributions from multiple perspectives* (pp. 1–18). Charlotte, NC: Information Age.

Strachan, J. (1999). Feminist educational leadership: Locating the concepts in practice. *Gender and Education, 11*(3), 309–322. doi:10.1080/09540259920609

Thomas, D. A. (2004, September). Diversity as strategy. *Harvard Business Review, 82*(9). Retrieved from https://hbr.org/2004/09/diversity-as-strategy

Tobin, J., Wu, D., & Davidson, D. (1989). *Preschool in three cultures: China, Japan, and the United States.* New Haven, CT: Yale University Press.

Triandis, H. C. (1990). Cross-cultural studies of individualism and collectivism. In *Nebraska Symposium on Motivation, 37*, 41–133.

Triandis, H. C., McCusker, C., & Hui, C. H. (1990). Multimethod probes of individualism and collectivism. *Journal of Personality and Social Psychology, 59*(5), 1006–1020.

Vasquez, M., & Comas-Díaz, L. (2007). Feminist leadership among Latinas. In J. L. Chin, B. Lott, J. K. Rice, & J. Sanchez-Hucles (Eds.), *Women and leadership: Transforming visions and diverse voices* (pp. 264–280). Malden, MA: Blackwell.

Williams, D. A. (2013). *Strategic diversity leadership: Activating change and transformation in higher education.* Sterling, VA: Stylus.

Williams, D. R., Mohammed, S. A., Leavell, J., & Collins, C. (2010). Race, socioeconomic status, and health: Complexities, ongoing challenges, and research opportunities. *Annals of the New York Academy of Sciences, 1186* (1). doi:69-101. 10.1111/j.1749-6632.2009.05339.x

CHAPTER 13

SHE JUST DOESN'T
SEEM LIKE A LEADER

African American Women College
Presidents and Rhetorical Leadership

Dorine L. Lawrence-Hughes
University of Southern California

Recently, I taught a public speaking course at my university in which only women were enrolled. During one memorable session, I played recorded speeches of two prominent business leaders, Ginni Rometty, Chairman, President, and CEO of IBM, and Indra Nooyi, Chairman and Chief Executive Officer of PepsiCo. After showing excerpts of their speeches (Nooyi, 2009; Rometty, 2014), I opened the floor for discussion. One student criticized Nooyi's address to the Economic Club of Washington, saying that Nooyi just did not "seem like a leader" to her. I pressed the student to elaborate, but she was unable to provide a more thoughtful analysis. For whatever reason, no one leveled the same critique at Rometty. The discussion was vexing. What does it mean for a woman of color to "seem" like a leader? Nooyi, a woman of South Asian descent, had earned an MBA from

Gender, Communication, and the Leadership Gap, pages 223–241
Copyright © 2017 by Information Age Publishing
All rights of reproduction in any form reserved.

the Yale School of Management and held several high-level positions before advancing to CEO of PepsiCo.

Unfortunately, if recent statistics are to be believed, a strong academic record, stellar business credentials, and extensive work experience are not enough to garner the credibility one needs to be perceived as a leader. One report noted that while women held more than "half of [the] managerial and professional occupations in the U.S." (Pew Research Center, 2015, p. 7) in 2013 (52.2%), women held only 22% of senior management positions in 2014 (Pew Research Center, 2015). The numbers for African American women are even more dismal. Only 1.2% of executive/senior level officials and managers in S&P 500 companies are Black women, and they hold only 0.2% of CEO positions (Catalyst, 2016). Granted, significant differences exist between higher education and corporate environments (Madsen, 2008), but the representation of women in higher education presidencies is equally disappointing. The American Council on Education (ACE) reported in 2012 that 26% of college presidents were women; a scant 4% were women of color (Cooper, 2015).

The purpose of this chapter is to examine the inaugural speeches of three African American women presidents of predominantly White colleges and universities to determine how they use language to legitimize their leadership. Bucklin (2014) found that female college presidents identified effective communication as being "critically important" for leadership (p. 176); however, a review of educational leadership literature reveals little discussion dedicated to providing women specific guidance for developing their public oratory skills within the context of higher education leadership. As Duffy and Leeman (2005) stated, "[P]ublic oratory remains the means by which democratic societies renew their values and create solidarity" (p. xii). More pointedly, Morse (2012) noted that one's call to leadership in higher education is also embodied in public spaces where these leaders are expected to "represent the institution" (p. 71). Although the study of public address "kindles thoughts . . . of classical antiquity" (Duffy & Leeman, 2005, p. xii), it remains an important vehicle through which college presidents can connect with broad audiences to advance institutional agendas, increase institutional visibility, galvanize stakeholders in times of crisis, and even build their own personal brand.

According to James Freedman, a former president of Dartmouth College, "More people listen to your inaugural address than any other" (as cited in Bornstein, 2003, p. 184). As such, inaugural ceremonies provide new leaders with an opportunity to garner trust and influence behavior. Valerie Smith, the first African American president of Swarthmore College; Fayneese Miller, the first African American and second woman president of Hamline University; and Joanne Berger-Sweeney, the first African American and first woman president of Trinity College (CT), used rhetoric in their inaugural addresses to socially construct themselves as leaders. A transcript and video of President Smith's October 2015 inaugural speech, "Changing Lives, Changing the World," remains posted on Swarthmore College web pages (Smith, 2015). President Miller's address to Hamline University, "Preparing Leaders for Tomorrow," can be read and viewed on the Hamline University President's Office website (Miller, 2015). Trinity College maintains a website dedicated to the inauguration of President Berger-Sweeney containing a link to her speech, "Bold, Engaged, in a Complex Learning Network" (Berger-Sweeney, 2014). A rhetorical analysis of these speeches assesses both the substantive and stylistic communication choices of each speaker and identifies emerging themes that may be helpful in understanding how ground-breaking college presidents use savvy communication strategies to establish leadership credibility.

LEADERSHIP COMMUNICATION AND AFRICAN AMERICAN WOMEN IN HIGHER EDUCATION

When we think of effective leaders, we may initially conjure up images of strong male leaders who "take charge" (Catalyst, as cited in Bucklin, 2014, p. 171). Trait-based theories of leadership undergird the notion that masculine values—strength, self-efficacy, control, and authority—are commonly associated with good leadership and therefore reinforce masculine models of leadership (Malkowski, 2012; Northouse, 2007; Parker, 2005). As a result, "women lack the presumption of competence enjoyed by White men" (Kellerman & Rhode, 2014, p. 27) to be perceived as effective leaders. To re-envision women's leadership traits and communication through feminine/feminist viewpoints, Helgesen and Johnson (2010) and Gilligan (1982) have posited that women's communicative practices foster connection and collaboration. Madden (2005), conversely, cautions against the dualism associated with adopting the notion that women leaders, by virtue of being women, have a distinct leadership style and instead advocates a more feminist approach that acknowledges and confronts the bias women leaders face. Nonetheless, Koenig, Eagly, Mitchell, and Ristikari's (2011) study of leadership stereotypes found that masculinity remains the primary image of leadership and that women leaders who are competent and qualified may still be unable to overcome perceptions that they "are not well equipped to lead" (p. 637).

Scholars of women's communicative leadership increasingly recognize the need for a more interdisciplinary approach for identifying effective leadership communication. Ruminski and Holba (2012) note that "[a]s singular disciplines, women's studies, leadership studies, and communication studies each invite interdisciplinarity" (p. 6). Also, recent scholars have

documented the paucity of women's communicative and leadership literature addressing race and ethnicity, particularly the leadership language of
women of color (Lloyd-Jones, 2011; Ospina & Foldy, 2009; Parker, 1996,
2001, 2005; Scott, 2013). Parker (2005) and Byrd (2008) have criticized
seemingly race-neutral mainstream leadership literature, including the new
gendered theories, because the scholarship was based almost exclusively on
men and White women. In 2012, McClinton and Dawkins noted that Black
women's exclusion from "traditional understandings of leadership" resulted in "the majority of research conducted on Black women in leadership
positioning them as the subgroup or comparison group in a broader study"
(p. 21). Additionally, in higher education, barriers such as stereotypical attitudes and racial discrimination have been found to limit access to top roles
for female minorities (Jackson & Harris, 2007). The number of African
Americans in chief academic positions (the position most-frequently cited
as the immediate position prior to the presidency) declined from 3.7% in
2008 to 2.3% in 2013 (Kim & Cook, 2013), and the number of African
American women assuming the leadership mantle at non-HBCU, co-edu-
cational, four-year colleges and universities has dwindled (Catalyst, 2016).

Nonetheless, the resilience of African American women who become college and university presidents gives insight into their successful communicative
practices. Their intersectionality "between gender, race, and other categories
of difference in individual lives, social practices, institutional arrangements,
and cultural ideologies and the outcomes of these interactions in terms of power" (Davis, 2008, p. 68) calls for a leadership theory which, in Parker's (2005)
words, embraces "multiple subjectivities" (Byrd, 2008, p. 107).

INAUGURATIONS AND INAUGURAL ADDRESSES: THE RHETORICAL SCENE

The examination of presidential rhetoric, specifically inaugural speeches,
has produced a rich body of literature (Black, 1994; Campbell & Jamieson, 1985; Holman, 2016; Vigil; 2013; Zarefsky, 2004). As Campbell and
Jamieson (1985) noted, a presidential speech "evinces presidential leadership by the very fact of its delivery" (p. 401). Black (1994) also observed
the importance of language choice in presidential speeches, stating that
rhetoric "brings speech close to magic, not in the sense that words alone
are expected to alter physical reality, but rather in a sense that words are
expected to be constitutive, performative" (p. 29). University presidential
inaugural speeches are no less performative: "Colleges and universities are
inherently political organizations, and many scholars argue that they are
becoming more political over time" (Kezar, 2008, p. 411). Consequently,
college presidents become "political leaders" who "need to learn the skills

of persuasion, helping people to understand different perspectives and values outside their own narrow interests" (Kezar, 2008, p. 413).

Higher education inaugural ceremonies are imbued with institutional culture, history, and tradition (Bornstein, 2003); notably, the inaugural address may be the first time stakeholders witness how a newly appointed president can embody an institution's culture, history, and tradition and still articulate a new vision for the institution. As such, the inaugural address provides new presidents with the opportunity to demonstrate to internal and external constituencies their worthiness of their new role—to establish legitimacy as leaders through the performative act of public address. However, the expectations of a newly appointed female president may be higher (Bornstein, 2009). Bornstein (2009) notes "the first woman president is an oddity, a novelty, even a cultural misfit. Constituents may feel that she does not look or act like a president" (p. 214). Assuming this to be true, how much more challenging is it for new African American women presidents to "seem" like leaders at predominantly White institutions if our construct of leadership is not only gendered (Acker, 1990) but also racialized? I hypothesize that the intersectionality of race, class, and gender may affect the language choices of new African American women presidents who must legitimize their role as institutional leaders, and I hope to add to what Ruminski and Holba (2012) called the "increasing texture in our personal and public perceptions and representations of leadership" (p. 16) by calling attention to the rhetorical leadership exercised by women of color. By focusing on inaugural speeches, we avoid what Dow (2016) refers to as a conventional focus on the "holy trinity" of women's public address: "social movement leaders, political leaders, and First Ladies" (p. 61). Instead, I hope to contribute to existing efforts to broaden the scholarship of leadership communication by including the discourse of speakers of color who occupy rhetorical spaces intransigently dominated by White men.

METHOD OF ANALYSIS

The way leaders craft messages for particular audiences is important; thus, leadership and communication are interrelated (Bligh & Kohles, 2008). Conger (1991) asserts that the ability of leaders to "sell themselves and their missions" largely "depends on highly effective language skills" (p. 32). A traditional rhetorical analysis reveals how leaders use language to influence their audience's belief and behavior by observing the speaker, the message, the audience, and the context in which the message is presented (Hill, 2016). By studying the rhetorical strategies of others, women and students of leadership communication may benefit from what Fairhurst (2011) refers to as a "heighten[ed] sensitivity to language" (p. 92) that, in turn, may encourage leaders to make more nuanced and effective communication decisions.

Rhetorical analysis scrutinizes discourse to determine whether "observable, explicable, and predictable rhetorical commonalities occur" (Benoit, 2009, p. 77). For example, Benoit (2009), noted that "presidential inaugural addresses are an instance of situational genre" (p. 86) because, by their very nature, inaugurations guide the rhetorical choices of the rhetor. Studies of university inaugural addresses have revealed that the rhetorical choices of new presidents are similarly guided, resulting in common themes and rhetorical strategies (Khwaja, 2015). Observing that studies comparing the leadership styles and rhetoric of female and male presidents of four-year universities are scarce, Khwaja's (2015) dissertation, *The Language of Leadership: A Feminist Poststructural Discourse Analysis of Inaugural Addresses by Presidents of High-Profile Research Universities,* analyzed 34 inaugural speeches, cataloging the rhetorical differences between men and women presidents. Anastasia's (2008) examination of university presidents' use of metaphor provided additional insight into the rhetorical choices of new leaders. Regardless of the rhetorical strategies a speaker employs, it is important for leaders to remember that even in formal public oratory situations in which speakers rarely respond to audience feedback, communication is a transactional process wherein audience members assess, consciously or unconsciously, the credibility of the speaker and the connectivity of the message.

ANALYSIS

The following constitutes an analysis of five themes that emerged from the inaugural addresses of Smith (2015), Berger-Sweeney (2014), and Miller (2015), including: (a) recognition of inaugural speech norms, (b) identification of common values, (c) communication of competence, (d) articulation of vision and mission, and (e) fostering of community. All three addresses employ persuasion tactics, including storytelling, the use of symbols, appeals to expertise, and connecting relevant issues to something meaningful to their audiences (Bolman & Deal, 1997) to bolster credibility and establish legitimacy. This analysis yielded additional patterns including: (a) express identification as the institution's leader, (b) express mention of bona fides, (c) willing subjectivity (Black woman as leader), and (d) the importance of diversity. While this analysis is neither normative nor prescriptive, it can be instructive for women and women of color who aspire to lead institutions and for anyone seeking diverse representations of effective leadership communication—representations that reflect gender and racial diversity in leadership.

Inaugural Speech Norms

Khwaja (2015) finds similarities among the inaugural addresses of men and women presidents of select research universities, including (a) acknowledgments and expressions of thankfulness, (b) articulations of the institutional mission and their vision, (c) statements of the "significance of higher education as a public good" (p. 215), and (d) affirmations of higher education's responsibility to society. All four themes emerge from the inaugural speeches of Smith (2015), Miller (2015), and Berger-Sweeney (2014), thus supporting Khwaja's (2015) assertion that these patterns are to be expected, "given similar leadership roles in somewhat similar contexts" (p. 216). For example, Smith (2015) begins by thanking those who participated in the inaugural celebration: faculty, staff, students, speakers, performers, and inauguration planners. Miller's (2015) gratitude extended to "the Methodist community for their continued support" (para. 2) of the university's mission and to her colleagues in academic and professional circles. All three acknowledge the presence of key political representatives, including governors, mayors, government representatives, and city council members, and all three acknowledge family members, both present and absent. Berger-Sweeney's (2014) acknowledgments are most brief, one paragraph, but her gratitude is evident in her phrase, "I can't name you all, but you are all in my heart" (para. 1).

Identification and Storytelling

The speakers rely on narrative to serve several functions. Gardner (1995) explains that storytelling is a core leadership skill. Narratives and stories help people make sense of the world; they are rhetorical strategies that allow speakers to connect with audiences. Meaning is generated as stories invite the listener to connect through familiar elements (Natelle & Bodenheimer, 2004). The more authentic the story feels to the audience, the more likely the audience is to trust the storyteller (Anderson, 2012). In the inaugural addresses, narrative and storytelling provided a platform for the leaders to express their own subjectivity and intersectionality as African American women leaders with values and life experiences to which the audience can relate. Moreover, narrative also provided each an opportunity to identify and share common values with her audience.

All three of these new presidents share stories about their parents. Miller (2015) recalls her parents' "active involvement in the Civil Rights Movement and [her] father's service as the secretary of the local NAACP" (para. 8), and Berger-Sweeney (2014) and Smith (2015) expressly recall their own parents' participation in the Great Migration of African Americans who were searching for better opportunities. For example, Berger-Sweeney (2014) re-counts her parents' decision to leave Washington, DC for Los Angeles: "Fam-ily lore has it that on the day my father graduated from law school in 1954, he packed up his bags to drive cross-country to set up life [as a professional] in Los Angeles. My mother and the two boys took the train west to join my father a little later" (para. 10). Smith (2015) recounts this story about her parents: "Born and raised in Charleston, South Carolina, they were part of the second great migration that took African Americans from the south to the north. . . . In their case, they left Charleston for Harlem" (para. 9). The ap-peal to family is universal, and it increases identification with listeners; family stories humanize speakers so that audiences better identify with them.

Additionally, narrative serves an argumentative function, allowing speak-ers to transmit values likely shared by their audience. When used effectively and ethically, rhetoric adjusts ideas to people and people to ideas (Bryant, 1953). Each speaker identified values instilled by her parents. Smith (2015) described her parents as "retired educators" who "placed a high value on academic achievement" (para. 9). Berger-Sweeney (2014) explained that her journey to the presidency was a reflection of her parents' "pioneering spirits" (para. 17). Miller (2015) explained how her activist parents encour-aged her "to speak up, when the urge was to remain silent because to be silent meant that I was giving my voice and rights to another" (para. 8).

Moreover, each speaker used narrative framing to situate her personal history squarely within the larger narrative of American history. The deci-sion to share vignettes of African American migration and the struggle for civil rights affirmed historical values associated with the American mythos. Miller's (2015) reminder that she was "a part of a democracy, a civil society" (para. 8) and Smith's (2015) recollection of her parents' "extraordinary sacrifices" (para. 9) imbued the speakers with American values such as sac-rifice, achievement, social mobility, risk-taking, and even discovery—cultur-ally shared narratives of the nation's pioneering spirit.

Finally, all three of the presidents used narratives as a platform for ac-knowledging their own positionality and intersectionality. By thanking members of their immediate family—including spouses, siblings, children, parents both living and dead, cousins, and even nieces and nephews—these women reaffirmed their connectedness with others and underscored their positionality as someone's child, wife, mother, sister, aunt, and cousin. This pattern contrasts with Khwaja's (2015) observation that, with the excep-tion of Rensselaer Polytechnic Institute's President Shirley Ann Jackson, no other women of color in her study called attention to their gender or ethnic identities, which was attributed to "continued unease with gender and race in the context of research universities" (p. 221). In contrast, both Berger-Sweeney (2014) and Miller (2015) referenced themselves as Afri-can Americans and as women leaders. Miller noted that she was "the first

African-American and the second woman" to serve as president of Hamline University (para. 11). Berger-Sweeney (2014) noted that she was the "first woman president and the first African American president of Trinity College" (para. 17). Smith (2015) did neither although she, too, is the first African American and the second woman to serve as Swarthmore's president. She may have felt that there was no need to do so, considering that inaugurations are documented public events and, with electronic media, such information can easily be obtained.

Leadership Qualifications: Cultivating Credibility

Bornstein (2003) posited that when an individual becomes the leader of a higher education institution through a "well-handled" search process, immediate, albeit fragile, legitimacy is conferred upon the new leader (p. 24). Because the inaugural address is one of the first opportunities for new leaders to bolster that immediate legitimacy, it is no surprise that all three speakers include a public acknowledgement of the Board of Trustees or a similar governing body that approves presidential appointments. For example, Smith (2015) expressly thanked the Board of Managers and the presidential search committee for "design[ing] a rigorous and thoughtful process to select Swarthmore's 15th president" (para. 5). Miller (2015) thanked the Board and the Hamline community "for believing in and trusting me to do what will continue to make us a strong leader in the higher education community" (para. 10). The speakers' mention of receiving the approval and the trust of their Boards comports with the genre of the inaugural speech; formal selection by an institution's governing body signals to the audience that their presidency is legitimate.

To strengthen credibility, all three speakers shared their qualifications with the inaugural audiences, identifying themselves with what audiences may consider to be desirable leadership traits, such as boldness (Berger-Sweeney, 2014; Miller, 2015) and intelligence (Smith, 2015). Each also included what Bornstein (2009) referred to as academic "bona fides," reaffirming their qualifications to lead an academic institution (p. 210). Early in her address, Berger-Sweeney (2014) identified herself as a "neuroscientist, by training" and later intertwined her identity as an African American woman with her identity as an academic who took the traditional route to the presidency (para. 3). She noted, "I was one of the only African Americans graduating from Johns Hopkins with a science doctorate my year. I was the first African American woman to move through the ranks to become a tenured full professor in biology at Wellesley College" (para. 17). Similarly, Miller (2015) noted her time spent as a post-doctoral fellow at Yale University and mentioned other organizations and institutions in which she had worked and cultivated friendships, including Brown University, the American Council of Education, and the American Psychological Association. Although Smith (2015) avoided referencing her academic resume, she, too, mentioned her extended network of family and friends from Bates, the University of Virginia, UCLA, and Princeton—all institutions where she studied or held positions.

All three of these presidents referenced past university leaders or acknowledged their presence at the inauguration ceremony, which is typical of inaugural speeches. Bornstein (2003) noted that inauguration ceremonies are symbolic in that new leaders are welcomed "while paying homage to the institution's history and former presidents" (p. 184). Mentioning past leaders also allowed each speaker to enhance her credibility by associating herself with other leaders. However, each speaker made different rhetorical choices. Miller (2015) mentioned her work with Ruth Simmons, the first Black president of Brown University, and Tom Sullivan, the president of the University of Vermont. She also referred to three past presidents— "Linda, Chuck, and Jerry"—by their first names (para. 6). Smith (2015) acknowledged by name the presence of three former Swarthmore presidents as "special guests" attending the inauguration ceremony (para. 4). Several current and former college presidents spoke on behalf of Berger-Sweeney (2014) during her ceremony and she acknowledged the "past presidents of Trinity College" (para. 1).

Finally, all three referred to themselves as "leaders" of their institutions, a departure from Khwaja's (2015) finding that women presidents do not talk about themselves as leaders. Berger-Sweeney (2014) noted that "now it is my time to lead this great institution into the future, with your help" (para. 37), while Miller (2015) stated that she was "humbled by your support and embrace of me as a person, a scholar, and a leader" (para. 10). Smith (2015) expressed gratefulness for the forces in her life that "prepared me to lead this college" (para. 3). Although gender norms often prevent women from touting their accomplishments (Smith & Huntoon, 2014), these three presidents embraced the opportunity to do just that in their inaugural addresses.

Communicating Institutional Vision Through Metaphors and Framing

Communicating an inspirational vision is essential for transformational leaders (Conger 1991), and for women leaders, articulating a vision also constitutes an important, ongoing theme of leadership philosophy (Madsen, 2008). In their inaugural speeches, all three addressed the role of higher education and shared their visions of their institutions, which is consistent with the themes found in other inaugural speeches (Khwaja, 2015). To advance their ideas and their agendas, the presidents employed metaphors and framing.

The Vision in Metaphors

Of the three, only Berger-Sweeney (2014) and Smith (2015) used extensive metaphors to communicate their respective visions. In an analysis of metaphors in inaugural addresses by women college presidents, Anastasia (2008) explained that a metaphor "is a comparative analysis that utilizes a rhetorical image to aid in further understanding by the audience" (p. 6). As noted by Holman (2016):

> Metaphors and frames serve a variety of psychological functions, including increasing persuasion and motivating listeners to understand and remember messages, promoting an emotional reaction, and giving "structure to cognitive content." (pp. 503–504; see also Deason & Gonzales, 2012, p. 255, the source of the internal quotation)

Berger-Sweeney's (2014) reference to Trinity College as a "complex learning network" was the most consistent metaphor of the three addresses. By interweaving her personal biography, including her background as a neuroscientist, with her vision of the university, Berger-Sweeney invited her audience to think of Trinity College as a "learning network in a very complex environment" similar to the interconnected neurons in our neurological system (para. 38); she used similar metaphorical language at least a dozen times during the speech, always emphasizing complexity. Her reference to the university as a "complex learning system" implies that Trinity College will be stronger because of its complexity—just as individuals are able to learn more when we are challenged. Berger-Sweeney's network metaphor was extensive; it prepared the audience for her vision of the college that included "experimentation," "innovation," and "engagement" (para. 38). Berger-Sweeney's expansion of the neurological system metaphor also allowed her to display her scientific knowledge, thereby enhancing her credibility because the audience was reminded of her intellect and her academic achievements.

Smith (2015) employed a similar strategy, encouraging her audience to view Swarthmore's campus as a series of spaces that invite contemplation and transformation. She shared a "story of place" (para. 14) by figuratively taking her audience on a tour of the campus; her descriptions of the buildings and public spaces personified the campus. For example, Smith stated that as she stood at what she called the town center of Swarthmore, "the College spoke to me, and I had an unmistakable sense that I could be home here" (para. 12). She also wove together descriptions of familiar campus landmarks with college-founding narratives that included Quakers, abolitionists, and feminists. By mentioning these narratives, Smith encouraged the audience to identify with shared values such as social responsibility and activism. She painted a picture of the Swarthmore campus as a place where the public spaces allow for what she called "the familiar and the unknown" (para. 15). By explaining that "the landscape of the campus tells the story of a life adventure that begins with the safety of being held . . . and ends with the invitation to step out into the unknown" (para. 17), Smith conveyed her vision of Swarthmore as a place of transformation.

Framing Diversity

All three presidents presented institutional visions that included goals for achieving diversity and inclusivity. According to Kezar (2008), leaders can help others "see the value of an idea" (p. 413) through reframing. Framing is a rhetorical technique that allows us to shape a message in such a way as to emphasize certain things over others. In *The Power of Framing: Creating the Language of Leadership*, Fairhurst (2011) contended that framing "involves the ability to shape the meaning of a subject" (p. 3) in order to align the interests of others with our own interests. The three presidents framed diversity and inclusion as moral imperatives, essential for student success, reinforcing that diversity and inclusion encourage global citizenship. Doing so is consistent with Holman's (2016) argument that female leaders may use moral frames to establish their credibility.

In discussing the importance of learning to work through difference, Miller (2015) alluded to the need for diversity and inclusion at Hamline University without ever directly uttering those words. Instead, she quoted Robert Putnam, who observed in *Bowling Alone* that "there is a decline in 'bridging capital,'" which allowed Miller (2015) to explain that her vision for students includes what she calls "social education" (para. 25). By telling her audience that they "must be just as deliberate about our students' social education, as we deliberate about their academic education" (para. 25), Miller signaled to her audience her belief that adopting an agenda to increase diversity through access must also include a willingness to teach students about difference.

Smith (2015) took a more humanistic approach, framing diversity and inclusion in terms of the improvement and advancement of humanity and society. For Smith, diversity should be considered a means to an end— something that will ultimately benefit the institution. She cautioned her audience to not perceive diversity efforts merely to be "charitable" acts (para. 20). Instead, they should view diversity as a mechanism for improving the Swarthmore community because allowing for different perspectives creates opportunities to generate new knowledge. She explained that both the humanities and the arts are "all enhanced when we earnestly engage with others whose perspectives and experiences differ from our own" (para. 21). Smith also adopted a moral frame by equating a commitment to diversity with a commitment to democracy. She explained that "the future of our democracy depends upon our ability to create inclusive and equitable communities to which everyone is invited to contribute their ideas, gifts, and enthusiasms to enhance the human enterprise" (para. 22) For Smith, "true engagement" occurs only if "we respect and value difference" (para. 22).

Berger-Sweeney's (2014) discussion of diversity was shorter than that of the other two, and her framing of the issue was more conventional. Although she briefly acknowledged that academia benefits from "openness to different viewpoints" (para. 25), she plainly stated that advancing an agenda of diversity means making college more accessible and affordable: "To be a great college, we must ensure that we have financial resources to allow a diverse set of students to attend this institution without regard to their ability to pay full tuition" (para. 25). Although Berger-Sweeney's treatment of diversity in her speech is brief, her agenda surrounding diversity is clear.

One could argue that addressing diversity and inclusion in an inaugural address made the issue of diversity more salient for the audience, yet two of the presidents' rhetorical choices reflected an attempt to "package" the message in a way that more broadly appealed to the shared values of the audience. These presidents used language to construct a reality in which students who learn in diverse environments will be better equipped to work in a complex world characterized by difference and, sometimes, conflict. The ultimate value proposition for the audience becomes one of preparedness and citizenship, and instead of seeing diversity as an issue fraught with politics and conflict, it was reframed as a means for achieving desirable goals.

Community Engagement and Collaboration

Each president discussed the institution's relationship with the surrounding community. Again, carefully chosen language framed their college's presence in the community as being integral to the community's success. Connective rhetorical choices appeal to the community and invite those who are "affected" by the institution's actions "to see themselves as a community with shared concerns and one capable of action" (Olson, 2011, para. 7). Berger-Sweeney (2014) envisioned rising prominence for Trinity College and implied that the accomplishment of this mission will require the cooperation of the community. She sought assent for this goal by framing her institution's involvement with its local community as a privilege for the college, noting that "most academic institutions do not have a chance to play such an integral role in the life of their city or town" (para. 28). She referred to Hartford "as a trusted neighbor" and listed a number of community engagement initiatives as evidence of Trinity College's continued commitment to serving the community (para. 28). Smith (2015) reaffirmed her vision of Swarthmore as a college that values "community," "collaboration," and "connect[tedness]" (para. 31). Miller's (2015) speech was peppered with references to "society," "democracy," and "civic engagement"; she also provided several examples of how Hamline students had become a part of the St. Paul community through civic engagement (paras. 8, 16, 19). Interestingly, all three presidents employ anaphora, or the schematic repetition of words and phrases in successive sentences, to create a memorable cadence for their audience. Berger-Sweeney (2014) repeatedly asked the audience, "How many selective liberal arts colleges...?" to call attention to Trinity's institutional uniqueness. She asked, "How many selective liberal arts colleges have a Community Learning Initiative...?" How many selective liberal arts colleges have the groundbreaking Center for Urban and Global Studies?" (paras. 31–34). Berger-Sweeney ended her speech with a collective appeal: "Let us dream big. Let us go boldly. Let us be engaged. Let us embrace the complexity" (paras. 42–45). Smith employed a similar refrain, "let us build together," both as a stylistic device and as a call to action to the stakeholders to support the Swarthmore community. She called out, "Let us build together a Swarthmore that provides a rich and vibrant community," and, "Let us build together a Swarthmore that houses academic and co-curricular programs and residential experiences" (para. 31). Miller's reliance on John Wesley's Methodist refrain, "Do all the good you can, by all the means you can, in all the ways you can, at all the times you can, to all the people you can as long as ever you can" (para. 32), with each phrase ending with the words, "you can," reminds the audience of Hamline's commitment to civic engagement and empowers the audience to share in the vision.

SUMMARY AND DISCUSSION OF THE CONTRIBUTION

To a certain extent, the intersectionality of race, class, and gender did affect the communication choices of these three African American women presidents. Although all three heeded, consciously or unconsciously, the conventional norms of university inaugural addresses by identifying values held in common with the audience, articulating a vision for the institution, and fostering a sense of community, they also took steps to legitimize their leadership without subverting their identity. Smith (2015), Berger-Sweeney (2014), and Miller (2015) asserted themselves as institutional leaders, demonstrated that other leaders recognized their leadership, associated themselves with great leaders of the past, and conveyed to the audience their qualifications for leadership. Yet, they also shared rich family narratives, and two of the presidents called attention to their own ethnicity and gender.

This study has both theoretical and practical implications for current and emerging leaders. First, leadership communication research should focus on women of color instead of relegating them to a subset of a broader research sample; doing so attests to the leadership community that the communication of women of color is not derivative. Second, women—and women of color—must be encouraged to develop communication competency in public address. Developing a language of leadership requires a deliberate effort to understand how language can be powerful and influential. Third, women of color who seek leadership positions must find their own voice in order to be authentic leaders. Marshall and Wingfield (2016) advise aspiring leaders of color to "crack" the code of executive presence by "acting, speaking, and dressing the part" of a leader (p. 70). However, they acknowledge that women and people of color often resent this conformance to White male leadership norms (p. 72). The more leaders of color find their authentic voice, the more broadly we can construe our social constructions of leadership. As Bligh et al. (2010) noted, charismatic leadership can "straddle or transcend the double-bind of gender stereotypes" (p. 828). By making both conventional and unconventional rhetorical choices in their inaugural addresses, Presidents Smith (2015), Berger-Sweeney (2014), and Miller (2015) both straddle and transcend the fence to establish leadership legitimacy while reaffirming their identities as women of color.

As Bornstein (2009) contended, greater diversity among presidents will allow us to "expand our conceptions of the presidency" (p. 234) and perhaps broaden our ideas about who is qualified to be a leader. Because public address and the scholarship surrounding leadership communication have traditionally been the domain of "prominent white men with political power" (Dow, 2016, p. 61), I hope this examination will help us expand our understanding that what it means to "seem" like a leader has much to do with whether we "sound" like leaders. We must make sure that we include in our leadership communication toolkit examples of public oratory presented by a diverse set of speakers.

Although I have not again had the pleasure of teaching an all-women public speaking course, my experience with that class gave me pause to reflect on the examples of public speaking that I share with students. I am now more conscientious of what I identify as exemplars of public address. To the extent that those with the power to help women and women of color advance to leadership positions do the same, we will all be the better for it.

REFERENCES

Acker, J. (1990). Hierarchies, jobs, bodies: A theory of gendered organizations. *Gender & society, 4*(2), 139–158.

Anastasia, T. T. (2008). Analysis of metaphors used by women college presidents' inaugural addresses at coed institutions. (Unpublished doctoral dissertation). Colorado State University, Fort Collins, CO.

Anderson, P. S. (2012). Tell me a story: Using an old tool to sustain culture, embrace change, and envision a bold future. In K. A. Longman (Ed.), *Thriving in leadership: Strategies for making a difference in Christian higher education* (pp. 99–120). Abilene, TX: Abilene Christian University Press.

Benoit, W. (2009). Generic elements in rhetoric. In J. A. Kuypers (Ed.), *Rhetorical criticism: Perspectives in action* (1st ed., pp. 77–95). Lanham, MD: Rowman & Littlefield.

Berger-Sweeney, J. (2014, October 26). Bold, engaged, in a complex, learning network [speech] Retrieved from http://www.trincoll.edu/Inauguration/Pages/address.aspx

Black, E. (1994). Gettysburg and silence. *Quarterly Journal of Speech, 80*(1), 21–36.

Bligh, M. C., & Kohles, J. C. (2008). Negotiating gender role expectations: Rhetorical leadership and women in the US Senate. *Leadership, 4*(4), 381–402. doi:10.1177/1742715008095187

Bligh, M., Merolla, J., Schroedel, J. R., & Gonzalez, R. (2010). Finding her voice: Hillary Clinton's rhetoric in the 2008 presidential campaign, *Women's Studies, 39*(8), 823–850.

Bolman, L. G., & Deal, T. E. (1997). *Reframing organizations: Artistry, choice, and leadership.* San Francisco, CA: Jossey-Bass.

Bornstein, R. (2003). *Legitimacy in the academic presidency: From entrance to exit.* ACE/Praeger series on higher education. Westport: CT: Greenwood Publishing Group.

Bornstein, R. (2009). Women and the quest for presidential legitimacy. In D. R. Dean, S. J. Bracken, & J. K. Allen (Eds.), *Women in academic leadership: Professional strategies, personal choices* (pp. 208–237). Sterling, VA: Stylus.

Bryant, D. C. (1953). Rhetoric: Its functions and its scope. *Quarterly Journal of Speech, 39*(4), 401–424.

Bucklin, M. L. (2014). Madame president: Gender's impact in the presidential suite. In K. A. Longman & S. R. Madsen (Eds.), *Women and leadership in higher education,* (pp. 169–185). Charlotte, NC: Information Age.

Byrd, M. (2008). Negotiating new meanings of 'leader' and envisioning culturally informed theories for developing African-American women in leadership roles: An interview with Patricia S. Parker. *Human Resource Development International, 11*(1), 101–107.

Campbell, K. K., & Jamieson, K. H. (1985). Inaugurating the presidency. *Presidential Studies Quarterly, 15*(2), 394–411. Retrieved from http://www.jstor.org/stable/27550215

Catalyst. (2016). *Women of color in the United States.* Retrieved from http://www.catalyst.org/knowledge/women-color-united-states-0

Conger, J. A. (1991). Inspiring others: the language of leadership. *The Executive, 5*(1), 31–45.

Cooper, K. J. (2015, 17 March). ACE preparing female minorities for higher ed presidencies. *Diverse Issues in Higher Education.* Retrieved from http://diverseeducation.com/article/70776/

Davis, K. (2008). Intersectionality as buzzword: A sociology of science perspective on what makes a feminist theory successful. *Feminist Theory, 9*(1), 67–85. doi:10.1177/1464700108086364

Deason, G., & Gonzales, M. H. (2012). Moral politics in the 2008 presidential convention acceptance speeches. *Basic and Applied Social Psychology, 34*(3), 254–268.

Dow, B. J. (2016). Authority, invention, and context in feminist rhetorical criticism. *Review of Communication, 16*(1), 60–76. doi:10.1080/15358593.2016.1183878

Duffy, B. K., & Leeman, R. W. (2005). *American voices: An encyclopedia of contemporary orators.* Westport, CT: Greenwood Press.

Fairhurst, G. T. (2011). *The Power of framing: Creating the language of leadership.* (2nd ed.) San Francisco, CA: John Wiley & Sons.

Gardner, H. (1995). *Leading minds: An anatomy of leadership.* New York, NY: Basic Books.

Gilligan, C. (1982). *In a different voice.* Cambridge, MA: Harvard University Press.

Helgesen, S., & Johnson, J. (2010). *The female vision: Women's real power at work.* San Francisco, CA: Berrett–Koehler.

Hill, F. I. (2016). The traditional perspective. In J. A. Kuypers (Ed.), *Rhetorical criticism: Perspectives in action* (2nd ed., pp. 69–90). Lanham, MD: Rowman & Littlefield.

Holman, M. R. (2016). Gender, political rhetoric, and moral metaphors in state of the city addresses. *Urban Affairs Review, 52*(4), 501–530. doi:10.1177/1078087415589191

Jackson, S., & Harris, S. (2007). African American female college and university presidents: Experiences and perceptions of barriers to the presidency. *Journal of Women in Educational Leadership, 5*(2), 119–137.

Kellerman, B., & Rhode, D. L. (2014). Women at the top: The pipeline reconsidered. In K. A. Longman & S. R. Madsen (Eds.), *Women and leadership in higher education* (pp. 23–39). Charlotte, NC: Information Age.

Kezar, A. (2008). Understanding leadership strategies for addressing the politics of diversity. *The Journal of Higher Education, 79*(4), 406–441.

Khwaja, T. (2015). *The language of leadership a feminist poststructural discourse analysis of inaugural addresses by presidents of high-profile research universities* (Unpublished doctoral dissertation). The College of William and Mary, Williamsburg, VA. Available from ProQuest Dissertations & Theses database. (Order No. 3662991).

Kim, Y. M., & Cook, B. J. (2013). On the pathway to the presidency: Characteristics of higher education's senior leadership. Washington DC: American Council on Education.

Koenig, A. M., Eagly, A. H., Mitchell, A. A., & Ristikari, T. (2011). Are leader stereotypes masculine? A meta-analysis of three research paradigms. *Psychological Bulletin, 137*(4), 616–642. doi:10.1037/a0023557

Lloyd-Jones, B. (2011). Diversification in higher education administration: Leadership paradigms reconsidered. In J.-M.Gaëtane, B. Lloyd-Jones (Eds.), *Diversity in higher education: Vol. 10: Women of color in higher education: Changing directions and new perspectives* (pp. 3–18). Bingley, England: Emerald Group.

Madden, M. E. (2005). 2004 Division 35 presidential address: Gender and leadership in higher education. *Psychology of Women Quarterly, 29*(1), 3–14.

Madsen, S. R. (2008). *On becoming a woman leader: Learning from the experiences of university presidents.* San Francisco, CA: John Wiley & Sons.

Malkowski, J. A. (2012). Women's leadership in the academy: Identifying, evaluating, and rewarding feminine contributions. In E. L. Ruminski & A. M. Holba (Eds.), *Communicative understandings of women's leadership development: From ceilings of glass to labyrinth paths* (pp. 135–153). Plymouth, England: Lexington Books.

Marshall, M., & Wingfield, T. (2016). *Ambition in black and white: The feminist narrative revised.* Los Angeles, CA: Rare Bird Books.

McClinton, M. M., & Dawkins, L. S. (2012). Essential skills for the leadership path. In T. B. Jones, L. S. Dawkins, M. M. McClinton, & M. H. Glover (Eds.), *Pathways to higher education administration for African American women* (pp. 18–26). Sterling, VA: Stylus.

Miller, F. (2015, October 2). Preparing leaders for tomorrow [speech]. Retrieved from https://www.hamline.edu/uploadedFiles/Hamline_WWW/Offices_-_Admin/President/Documents/FM%20Installation%20Address%2010-02-2015.pdfl

Morse, M. (2012). Leading from the center: Body and place. In K. A. Longman (Ed.), *Thriving in leadership: Strategies for making a difference in Christian higher education* (pp. 59–77). Abilene, TX: Abilene Christian University Press.

Natelle, E. J., & Bodenheimer, F. R. (2004). *The woman's public speaking handbook.* Belmont, Canada: Wadsworth.

Nooyi, I. (2009, March 12). *Speech at the Economic Club of Washington, D.C.* [Video file]. Retrieved from https://www.youtube.com/watch?v=V4WSRJajg-w

Northouse, P. G. (2007). *Leadership theory and practice* (4th ed.). Thousand Oaks, CA: SAGE.

Olson, K. M. (2011). What is rhetorical leadership?: My perspective, statement, revised September 2011. Retrieved from https://uwm.edu/rhetorical-leadership/wp-content/uploads/sites/322/2016/02/whatisrl.pdf

Ospina, S., & Foldy, E. (2009). A critical review of race and ethnicity in the leadership literature: Surfacing context, power and the collective dimensions of leadership. *The Leadership Quarterly, 20*(6), 876–896. doi:10.1016/j.leaqua.2009.09.005

Parker, P. S. (1996). Gender, culture, and leadership: Toward a culturally distinct model of African-American women executives' leadership strategies. *The Leadership Quarterly, 7*(2), 189–214. doi:10.1016/S1048-9843(96)90040-5

Parker, P. S. (2001). African American women executives' leadership communication within dominant-culture organizations: (Re)conceptualizing notions of collaboration and instrumentality. *Management Communication Quarterly, 15*(1), 42–82.

Parker, P. S. (2005). *Race, gender, and leadership: Re-envisioning organizational leadership from the perspectives of African American women executives.* Mahwah, NJ: Lawrence Erlbaum Associates.

Pew Research Center. (2015, January 14). Women and leadership: Public says women are equally qualified, but barriers persist. *Washington, D.C.: Pew Research*

Center. Retrieved from http://www.pewsocialtrends.org/2015/01/14/women-and-leadership/

Rometty, G. (2014, March 12). *A new era of value: A conversation with Ginni Rometty, NRF 2015 keynote*. [Video file]. Retrieved from https://www.youtube.com/watch?v=whwRMzwGXIQ

Ruminski, E. L., & Holba, A. M. (2012). Introduction. In E. L. Ruminski & A. M. Holba (Eds.), *Communicative understandings of women's leadership development: From ceilings of glass to labyrinth paths* (pp. 1–17). Plymouth, England: Lexington Books.

Scott, K. D. (2013). Communication strategies across cultural borders: Dispelling stereotypes, performing competence, and redefining Black womanhood. *Women's Studies in Communication, 36*(3), 312–329. doi:10.1080/07491409.2013.831005

Smith, J. L., & Huntoon, M. (2014). Women's bragging rights: Overcoming modesty norms to facilitate women's self-promotion. *Psychology of Women Quarterly, 38*(4), 447–459. doi:10.1177/ 0361684313515840

Smith, V. (2015, October 3). Inaugural address [speech]. Retrieved from http://www.swarthmore.edu/inauguration-valerie-smith/valerie-smith

Vigil, T. R. (2013). George W. Bush's first three inaugural addresses: Testing the utility of the inaugural genre. *Southern Communication Journal, 78*(5), 427–446. doi:10.1080/1041794X.2013.847479

Zarefsky, D. (2004). Presidential rhetoric and the power of definition. *Presidential Studies Quarterly, 34*(3), 607–619.

CHAPTER 14

I *AM* VERSUS I *WILL BE* A GREAT LEADER

Using Critical Race Feminism to Explore Gender Differences Among College Students of Color

Annemarie Vaccaro
University of Rhode Island

Melissa J. Camba-Kelsay
University of Rhode Island

Many higher education institutions claim that developing leaders of the future is central to their mission and purpose (Dugan, 2006). As such, enhancing the leadership skills of college students has become an increasing focus of colleges and universities (Dugan & Komives, 2011; Komives, Longerbeam, Owen, Mainella, & Osteen, 2006). Correspondingly, the number of formal (and informal) leadership development programs for college students has proliferated in higher education institutions. However, little attention has been paid to differences in the leadership perspectives and

Gender, Communication, and the Leadership Gap, pages 243–262
Copyright © 2017 by Information Age Publishing
All rights of reproduction in any form reserved.

experiences of racially diverse men and women who participate in these programs, nor have leadership scholars used critical race feminism (CRF) to examine the narratives of men and women college student leaders.

Drawing from a five-year study of students in a college-level leadership course, this chapter uses CRF theory (Wing, 2003) and the methodological tradition of narrative analysis (Daiute & Lightfoot, 2004; Reissman, 1993) to begin to fill the gap in the literature about gender differences for college student leaders of color. Our study findings revealed that women undergraduates of color eschewed the label of leader, did not exude leadership confidence, and were trying to find a leadership voice in the context of a "catch-22" regarding weakness and aggression. Conversely, men of color expressed confidence in their leadership skills and proudly proclaimed themselves to be effective leaders.

LITERATURE

Not only do colleges and universities prepare college students to be employees of tomorrow, but also as leaders of the future by offering formal (e.g., courses, minors) and informal (e.g., workshops, trainings) leadership development programs (Dugan & Komives, 2011; Komives et al., 2006). Since the United States is fast becoming more diverse, colleges and universities have an obligation to produce leaders who understand, and are responsive to, the needs of diverse communities. Some critical scholars even contend that it is important for leaders to come from, or at least to share, some of the same cultural backgrounds as the communities that they lead (Stovall, 2006).

To accomplish the goal of producing leaders from diverse cultural backgrounds, Roberts and Ullom (1989) argued that campus leadership programs "should be designed and directed to meet the needs of various special populations that exist in a specific institution" (p. 69) such as students of color and women. Dugan and Komives (2007) suggested the need for specific leadership programs for particular social identity groups (e.g., women of color) where students could explore how their social identities inform their leadership perspectives and practices. Yet, recruiting students from diverse gender and cultural backgrounds to leadership development programs is only part of the solution to diversifying the pool of future leaders. What undergraduates learn in leadership development programs is equally important. If leadership curriculum and training materials do not reflect diverse perspectives, women and people of color will get the message that leadership does not include people like them. For instance, popular leadership theories that emerged between the nineteenth and mid-twentieth centuries typically portrayed leadership as hierarchical, emphasizing leadership as power enacted through traits or formal positions—often held by White men (Dugan & Komives, 2011). Scholars have criticized the fact that these traditional leadership theories were often written by, and for, those in power (i.e., White men). In fact, Larson and Murtadha (2002) lamented how traditional paradigms about leadership have "blocked researchers from envisioning theories of leadership that went beyond a White, middle-class, male standpoint" (p. 138).

In their book, *Herstories: Leading With the Lessons of the Lives of Black Women Activists*, Alston and McClellan (2011) document how women of color have been left out of leadership history, despite their accomplishments. However, it is not merely historical or traditional leadership literature in which diverse leaders (especially women and people of color) are excluded. As student leadership programs have proliferated, contemporary research about student leadership has also increased (Dugan & Komives, 2007; Komives & Wagner, 2012). Yet, much of this research has not been conducted with diverse samples. Dugan, Kodama, and Gebhardt (2012) lamented how literature on college student leadership has taken a color-blind approach. Similarly, Chin (2010) argued most leadership research is "silent on issues of equity, diversity, and social justice" (p. 150).

In the few studies that include diverse samples, researchers have found that women and people of color often eschew the label of leader (Arminio et al., 2000; Kezar & Moriarty, 2000). Specifically, Kezar and Moriarty (2000) found Black and White men were more likely than women to label themselves as leaders. However, gender differences in leadership go beyond the act of self-labeling. An unwillingness to assume the label of leader may be related to women's capacity to see themselves reflected in representations of leadership. Indeed, there is a large body of literature explicating how all women—especially women of color—have historically been silenced or treated as if they were invisible (Alston & McClellan, 2011; Hayes & Flannery, 2000; Lewis, 1993; Lorde, 1984; Luke, 1994; Sadker, Sadker, & Zittleman, 2009; Wing, 2003). This legacy of silencing and disempowering women negatively affects women's self-esteem, self-confidence, achievement, and also prompts them to use powerless speech (O'Barr & Atkins, 2011; Sadker & Sadker, 1994; Sadker et al., 2009).

Two studies with undergraduate students suggest that women may indeed feel invisible, silenced, and, in turn, exude less confidence or fail to see themselves as effective leaders. In a study of 9,731 students at 352 colleges and universities, Kezar and Moriarty (2000) found that men were more likely to highly rate growth in their own leadership abilities. In another multi-institutional study of more than 63,000 college students from 52 higher education institutions, Dugan and Komives (2007) found that despite higher levels of leadership competence, women reported less self-confidence in their leadership abilities than men. To fully comprehend these findings, we must delve into empirical and theoretical literature about women's silence and voice, paying special attention to the ways women are socialized not to speak up or tell their stories.

For decades, scholars documented the phenomenon of women being silenced in society in general, and educational settings in particular (Hayes & Flannery, 2000; Lewis, 1993; Lorde, 1984; Luke, 1994; Sadker et al., 2009). Lewis (1993) explained how "inequalities become profound daily experiences, marked fundamentally by disempowerment, the struggle to survive, and silencing" (p. 11). Similarly, Luke (1994) contended that women's subjugated social status directly results in women's voices being silenced. Feminists of color (e.g., Black, Chicana, Critical Race, Third World, womanists) have long argued that voice and silence can only be understood in the context of multiple systems of oppression such as sexism, racism, classism, and heterosexism (Crenshaw, 1989; Hill Collins, 1991; hooks, 2000; Moraga & Anzaldúa, 1981, 2002; Wing, 2003). Women of color are silenced by interlocking forms of gender and racial oppression (hooks, 2000; Moraga & Anzaldúa, 1981, 2002; Wing, 2003). Second wave feminism and critical race theory are the scholarly areas that illuminate these intersections. Critical race feminists and other women writers of color (hooks, 2000; Moraga & Anzaldúa, 1981, 2002; Wing, 2003) explicate how predominately White feminist writings and largely male-dominated critical race theory literature "have permitted women of color to fall between the cracks, so that they become, literally and figuratively, voiceless and invisible" (Wing, 2003, p. 2). In both these cases, the narratives of women of color were excluded—suggesting that women of color were somehow not leaders in either of these social justice movements. Unfortunately, erasing the leadership contributions of women of color has a long history in the United States (Alston & McClellan, 2011).

Notions of voice and silence have been described in both literal and metaphorical manners. Reinharz (1994) explained, "Voice means having the ability, the means, and the right to express oneself" (p. 180). Others understand voice as more than the act of speaking and inseparable from subordination, empowerment, and identity. For instance, Reinharz described voice as a "megametaphor representing presence, power, participation, protest, and identity" (p. 183). Correspondingly, voice has been equated with empowerment and healthy identity development while silence has been associated with marginalization.

The silencing of women begins early in life. In a classic educational (Sadker & Sadker, 1994) and follow up study (Sadker et al., 2009), scholars found that teachers praised boys for being confident and assertive while they encouraged girls to assume submissive and silent roles. During classroom observations, Sadker et al. (2009) found "no girl called out. Like the passive little princess, their voices were also frozen and unheard" (p. 98).

Patterns of silence continue into post-secondary environments, where women are marginalized by faculty and peers (Johnson-Bailey, 2001), interrupted by peers and instructors during classroom conversations (Komarovsky, 1985), or ignored by male administrators when they demand equity (Vaccaro, 2009). Johnson-Bailey (2001) described how women learn cultural scripts of disempowerment and, in turn, internalize oppressive messages and become silent. This silencing may be subtly noticed in the words women use to describe themselves and their leadership capabilities. In fact, Hayes and Flannery (2000) claimed "the act of naming our experiences is an integral part of establishing who we are; in many ways, we *are* our experiences; . . . the act of giving voice can be transformative" (p. 92). Conversely, being silenced is disempowering.

The study presented in this chapter explores the narratives of students who were enrolled in a course where naming their leadership experiences and finding voice were central. Despite the efforts to empower women of color through the use of transformational counterstories, most women of color still had difficulty viewing themselves as leaders, exuding leadership confidence, finding their leadership voice, and navigating the catch-22 regarding racial and gender stereotypes of weakness and aggression. Men of color, however, did not express any hesitation in touting their leadership capabilities or claiming a leadership title. These differences between men and women of color are detailed in the findings section of this chapter.

THEORETICAL FRAMEWORK

A theoretical framework "offers suppositions that inform the phenomenon under study" (Jones, Torres, & Arminio, 2014, p. 22). In this case, critical race feminism (CRF; Wing, 2003) informed our study. CRF builds upon, and critiques, basic tenets (Solórzano, 1997) of critical race theory (CRT). Solórzano (1997) described five central tenets of CRT. First, racism is endemic to society and centering race in contemporary life is imperative. As critical race feminists, we contend racial *and* gender oppression are pervasive in society in general, and in leadership development programs, in particular. Second, CRT and CRF scholars expose and challenge dominant ideologies such as meritocracy, race neutrality, colorblindness, and equal opportunity. Dominant ideologies are hegemonic narratives that normalize the experiences of the majority (e.g., men, White people) while silencing and/or distorting the realities of women and people of color (Solórzano & Yosso, 2001). To combat the silencing of people of color, CRT and CRF scholars draw upon a third tenet, which is valuing experiential knowledge (Solórzano, 1997). Often, experiential knowledge is collected in the form of counternarratives or counterstories whereby women and people of color debunk dominant ideologies and deficit stereotypes through personal accounts of oppression, struggle, and triumph. Through our qualitative case study we documented the experiential knowledge and counterstories of men and women student leaders of color.

A fourth tenet of CRT is often labeled as an interdisciplinary or intersectional approach to examining oppression (Solórzano, 1997). While race is a central concept in CRT, contemporary scholars acknowledge the importance of other social identities such as gender and class (Solórzano, 1997; Solórzano & Yosso, 2001). Women writers of color, including critical race feminists, have argued that many CRT writings—often authored by men—do not adequately address the intersections of race, gender, and social class (Crenshaw, 1989; Wing, 2003).

The fifth tenet of CRT is a commitment to social justice (Solórzano, 1997). Critical race scholars do not merely think about oppression, they seek to combat it through scholarship and activism. This tenet aligns with our passion for conducting research that has the potential to lead to greater equity in collegiate student leadership programs. Through praxis, critical race feminists seek to remedy the silencing, invisibility, and disempowerment of women of color. Critical race feminist praxis is a concept that highlights the importance of empowerment and action through scholarship (Wing, 2003). When counterstories are central to a classroom learning environment, students can "become empowered participants, hearing their own stories and the stories of others, listening to how the arguments are framed, and learning to make the arguments themselves" (Solórzano, Ceja, & Yosso, 2000, p. 64). As we describe in the next section, encouraging students to tell their stories was a central aspect of the leadership course we examined in our research.

THE SISTER STORIES CLASS AND CASE STUDY

We used a holistic, multiple-case study (Yin, 2014) as our research method. The main research question for the study was: How do students enrolled in an undergraduate leadership course about the historical and contemporary experiences of women of color describe their classroom experiences and learning in general, and their leadership journeys in particular? In other words, what stories do men and women of color tell about themselves as leaders? The leadership course—which we refer to by the pseudonym Sister Stories—was situated at one mid-sized public university. The official Sister Stories course description read:

This elective is designed for students that are interested in an exploratory and introspective look at the issues affecting women of color. Students will explore cultural identity and leadership theories through readings and other media as well as learn about a variety of issues, including historical perspectives, which continue to affect women of color today. (University website, n.d.)

As noted earlier, CRF scholars often use counterstories to center the experiences of people who have historically been marginalized (e.g., women of color; Darder, Baltodano & Torres, 2003; Wing, 2003). Because of this, the Sister Stories curriculum was almost exclusively comprised of counterstories by women of color. Course readings included first-person narratives from diverse women of color. The format of the counterstories ranged from traditional academic book chapters and articles to guest presentations, first-person narratives, poetry, and spoken word art from women of color. Through classroom conversations, online discussions, and assignments, Sister Stories students were invited to wrestle with the ways course materials related to their everyday lives. One major Sister Stories assignment asked students to begin crafting their own counterstory. In this paper, they were prompted to write about who they were and who they hoped to become. As a step toward crafting their leadership narrative, or counterstory, students were invited to answer questions such as: "Who am I? What do I value? What are my strengths? and What does leadership mean to me?"

In holistic, multiple case studies, research is bound by setting and time (Yin, 2014). In this case, our project was bounded by a unique leadership course at one institution (setting) and five separate spring semesters of data collection (time). During our five-year research project, we collected data from a total of 57 students. Participants self-identified as White ($n = 8$), Black ($n = 26$), Latina/o ($n = 14$), Asian/Pacific Islander ($n = 2$), and bi or multi-racial ($n = 7$). All students self-identified as cisgender men ($n = 14$) or cisgender women ($n = 43$). The racial and gender composition varied by semester, but overall, the course was mostly comprised of women and men of color. Because of space limitations and the limited data yielded from the small number of White students ($n = 8$), we focus exclusively on the leadership narratives of men and women of color in this chapter. All participants cited in this paper were assigned pseudonyms to protect their identities.

As CRT and CRF scholars note, there is immense value in focusing solely on the lived realities of men and women of color. For instance, Parker and Stovall (2004) argued that the experiences of people of color "merit intellectual pursuit because of the uniqueness of the cultural, historical, and contemporary experiences of persons of color [and] the historical and contemporary experiences of people of color can prove instructive about human interactions" (p. 174). An exclusive focus on men and women of color is also important since almost no collegiate leadership studies have centered the voices of racially diverse men and women. Analyses of narratives from the eight White Sister Stories participants can be found elsewhere (Vaccaro, 2017; Vaccaro & Camba-Kelsay, 2016).

To gather rich evidence, case study researchers utilize multiple modes of data collection (Yin, 2014). We used data from student papers, participant observations, and focus groups. Throughout the semester, the course instructor (Camba-Kelsay) conducted participant observations and wrote field notes. After grades were submitted, the instructor asked students for permission to utilize written course work (e.g., reflection papers, online discussion posts) as case study evidence. The researcher (Vaccaro), visited the class multiple times and also wrote field notes. At the end of the semester, Vaccaro conducted focus groups with students asking them to reflect upon their experiences over the semester. Semi-structured focus group questions included: What are your general reflections on the leadership class experience?; What was your biggest learning moment?; Do you consider yourself a leader?; Why or Why not?; and How did this course influence your thoughts about leadership?

Both the researcher and instructor coded student work, focus group transcripts, and field notes. For this research study, we used an inductive (or "ground up") analytic process to allow themes to emerge (Yin, 2014). As critical race feminists, we paid special attention to subtle issues of gender inequality embedded in narratives from students of color. Because case study data can be analyzed in a variety of ways (Yin, 2014), we drew upon the methodological tradition of narrative analysis (Daiute & Lightfoot, 2004; Reissman, 1993) to understand gender differences in the leadership stories of college students. Narrative analysis is a format for "conceptualizing the storied nature of human development" (Daiute & Lightfoot, 2004, p. x). A strength of narrative analysis is that it allows a researcher to holistically explore a person's identity, relationships, and emotions, all within a larger cultural and social context (Daiute & Lightfoot, 2004; Reissman, 1993). As we reviewed the leadership counterstories of men and women of color, we saw connections to their identities, sense of self, and relationships. We also heard their emotions come through. Moreover, through the analytic process we recognized the ways student narratives were situated within the larger cultural and social context where all women—especially women of color—have been silenced (hooks, 2000; Moraga & Anzaldúa, 1981, 2002; Wing, 2003). Our analysis involved multiple rounds of coding for micro concepts related to self-identity, confidence, and emotions as well as macro concepts like power, marginalization, voice, and silence.

Trustworthiness and credibility are essential to effective qualitative research (Jones et al., 2014). In this study, we used seven strategies to achieve trustworthiness and credibility: trust building with participants, researcher reflectivity, inter-rater reliability during coding, discrepant case analysis, triangulation of data sources, member checking, and peer validation of findings (Jones et al., 2014; Merriam, 2009; Yin, 2014).

FINDINGS

In the following pages, we explicate patterns of gender differences and inequities that emerged from written and verbal counterstories from men and women undergraduate students of color in the Sister Stories leadership course. Although students described Sister Stories as an empowering course (Vaccaro & Camba-Kelsay, 2016), most women of color still had difficulty viewing themselves as leaders, exuding leadership confidence, finding their leadership voice, and navigating the catch-22 regarding stereotypes of weakness and aggression. Men of color, however, did not express any hesitation in claiming a leadership title or touting their leadership capabilities. Details of these emergent themes are described below.

Am I a Leader?

Whether or not they held multiple (or no) formal leadership roles on campus and despite enrollment in a leadership course, women of color consistently described how they were leaders in training. They viewed themselves as having the potential to be great leaders someday in the future. Instead of proclaiming their skills and talents, women viewed themselves as works in progress. They expressed a need to hone leadership skills before they could become effective leaders. Carmen explained, "I haven't gained all those leadership skills. That's why I'm in this class—to learn how to become more of a leader." For Lauren, the Sister Stories course was only the first step on her leadership learning journey. She intended to declare a leadership minor so she could continue to develop and hone her leadership skills. Lauren said: "In the future, I hope to . . . attain more characteristics of being a leader. I plan to be a leadership minor and develop more skills to take along with me in my career."

Even women who were relatively confident in their leadership skill base felt they had to continue to grow if they wanted to truly be effective leaders. Ife stated:

> I would love to be better at [leadership] in the future, . . . to become better at being more outspoken when I am in a big group. I would also like to work on my attitude, which I have been working on and I plan to keep on working on it. And although I do feel like my leadership skills are up to par, there is absolutely nothing wrong in making it better and being stronger at what I do.

Claire also expressed the importance of leaders knowing their strengths and working on areas of growth:

> How can you lead others if you don't have your own act together? A leader is someone who knows themselves.... In order for me to fully consider myself, as a leader, I feel that I need to further my [own] development in the future. I need to... refine skills... like time management, organization, self-care, self-discipline, perseverance, developing and maintaining family, interpersonal, and intimate relationships.

Even women who possessed leadership skills, sometimes needed the validation of external authorities (e.g., faculty, staff, family, peers) before they viewed themselves as leaders. Women of color in our study often eschewed the label of leader until an external authority told them they were leaders. Only after validation from these external authorities did women feel confident calling themselves leaders instead of good followers. Lucy explained:

> [As an athlete who was] just a little bit older than some of my other classmates,... I was put in a leadership role. I have always been like, "I can't do it, I don't want to be a leader." I've always said that I'm a really good follower, and everyone who's met me or dealt with me in some type of like classroom or sports field are like, "Lucy, no you have leadership qualities." I just felt like, I didn't know what to say, I didn't know how to say it. That's why I'm a good follower because if you tell me something to do, I'll do it and I'll be a good example.

Similarly, Ana only began to consider herself a leader when professors began to label her as such. She claimed the title of leader only after instructors "really saw that I was a leader. [Then] I [felt I] could become a really good leader." Hanna recently began labeling herself as a leader because "now I am viewed as a leader to some people such as my friends." In essence, women of color tended to consider themselves leaders only after receiving praise, encouragement, and validation from others.

Conversely, men in our study did not seem to need validation from others in order to view themselves as leaders. They were quick to list their leadership strengths and rarely talked about areas where they needed improvement. Men did not speak of external authorities and seemed quite confident claiming a leadership title without the validation from anyone else. Harry explained, "I see myself as a leader because I am very certain of myself, and I think that I can help people who aren't." Diego felt he was born to lead—no one had to tell him he was a leader. He shared:

> I feel like I was put in this earth to help people and this is what *I am* doing, every day of my life. I think it's safe to say that *I am* a mentor.... Men would say I have "Swagg," in other words, [I am] confident. *I am* "a real laid back dude,"

which are both so true! I myself see myself as a man in the middle. Came from the bottom and currently on my way to the top. (emphasis in original)

Not only was Diego self-confident and needed no external validation, he also was able to list a number of qualities that made him a good leader. This was consistent among most of the men of color in the class. They did not hesitate to confidently proclaim the characteristics, strengths, and skills they believed made them effective leaders. Men proudly described themselves as "change agents" whose leadership had "positive effects." They also described themselves as "confident, inclusive leaders" who "communicated well." Men believed they were leaders who "set the right example" for peers and family members. Men proclaimed that they were indeed leaders in the present tense—meaning they saw themselves as leaders today. For instance, Diego stated: "I am not a follower. I try to lead in everything I do. I know what I need to do to get where I need to go." In short, men rarely spoke about the importance of learning to become better leaders. Like Diego, they "know what [they] need" to be good leaders. They believed that they already possessed the skills they needed to be good leaders. They did not need to learn more to be effective, nor did they need external authorities to affirm or validate their leadership identities.

In sum, men of color expressed confidence that they were indeed leaders of today because they already possessed the skills, talents, and characteristics of effective leaders. Women of color, on the other hand, felt they needed to develop their skills in order to be effective leaders in the future. Moreover, women were more apt to rely on the validation and affirmation of external agents before they were confident enough to claim the title of leader. In our study, men proudly proclaimed, "*I am* a leader," while women thought they would learn to become great leaders someday. Drechsler and Jones Jr. (2009) argued that: "a first step to becoming a change agent is to claim the personal empowerment to recognize oneself as a leader" (p. 401). If this is true, women of color were steps behind their male counterparts on the path toward becoming a leader and agent of change. However, educators might argue that women surpassed their male counterparts in openness to lifelong learning—an essential factor in human growth and development—and an important foundation for ongoing leadership development.

Voice and Silence

Through an analysis of their narratives we came to see that many women of color felt silenced and disempowered before taking the Sister Stories course (Vaccaro, 2017; Vaccaro & Camba-Kelsay, 2016). Through Sister Stories, women learned that there were many ways to be an effective leader.

Once they learned to challenge traditional and androcentric notions of leadership that suggested the use of power and authority were ideal behaviors for effective leaders, women of color started to realize that they could indeed be leaders. For instance, Lucy unlearned stereotypical perspectives (e.g., controlling, loud, inflexible) of how leaders should act. New learning inspired by the Sister Stories curricular focus on successful women leaders of color prompted Lucy to see herself as a leader for the first time. She said,

> Taking this class has really helped reinforce that I do have those qualities and that I can be a leader. I can voice my opinion, and I can take charge and I can be in control. . . . A lot of times I don't want to be a leader because my experiences with leaders have been—you know—combative and very controlling, loud, angry. And that's something I *never* want to be.

Liza was also socialized to believe that leaders had to be loud and outspoken to be effective. As a self-described naturally "shy and quiet" person, she wondered if she could ever be an effective leader. Through the Sister Stories course, she began to unlearn narrow stereotypes about hierarchical and power-based leadership and came to see that she was indeed a leader. Liza said:

> I may not be the loudest, outspoken, bravest leader there is, but I know that I am [one]. I have always grown up being shy and quiet. I have grown so sick and tired [of remaining silent] because I do have a lot to say! I do want to have my word heard.

Through the Sister Stories course, women began to realize that they had a voice and they should put that voice to use via leadership. Lena shared:

> I got a lot more than I bargained for from [Sister Stories]. I never expected to feel as empowered as I did. . . . More importantly, I was reminded of the impact that my voice can have if I just speak up. If there was one thing that I learned overall, it was that I can make a difference.

Possibly because of a history of racial and gender oppression—combined with participants' lived experiences of being silenced and disempowered (Sadker & Sadker, 1994; Sadker et al., 2009; Wing, 2003)—women of color expressed how important it was for leaders to ensure that everyone's voices were heard and opinions valued. Lucy said: "I think this class has really taught me that there's other ways to lead effectively where everyone has a voice." For Claire, effective leadership meant "broadening her perspectives to understand others" by listening to their voices. Ana also felt she was a better leader after taking Sister Stories because she learned how important it was to "be aware" and affirm that people have "different lenses" through which they view the world. Elsy concurred, saying, "To be a leader, you need to be open-minded and understand other people's perspectives." Women of color like Elsy, Ana, Claire, and Lucy learned that to truly understand others, leaders had to listen to, and affirm, the diverse voices of followers.

Men's written work and focus group comments suggested that they did not arrive at Sister Stories feeling silenced or disempowered. In fact, they felt powerful and used their authority to make leadership decisions—even when others disagreed. Although some men claimed to be open to the ideas and opinions of others, their comments suggested that they might hear other people out, but ultimately made leadership decisions based upon their own opinions. Moreover, men emphasized the importance of speaking and being listened to more often than listening to others. Brian stated:

> [The course] taught me to open up to a lot more opinions.... [In the past], I was kind of open but I was still in my own place.... Basically [I] hear out others. [But] I have a voice. I am able to speak and I will be listened to.

Like Brian, it seemed that men felt effective leaders not only foregrounded their own voices and ideas but sometimes even ignored the ideas and opinions of others. Brandon explained how leadership "feels very powerful...because...people will listen and hear me out. Even if they don't think my opinion is valid, I said it and it's out there." Brandon also emphasized the power of his own voice by saying: "I will preach to the younger generations coming up behind me." These quotes suggest that men were more interested in speaking than listening. Correspondingly, men of color often ignored the voices, or silenced the perspectives, of others—including women of color. Marginalization of the voices of women of color by men is an oppressive reality that critical race feminists have long lamented (Wing, 2003). Men's tendency to speak instead of listening also aligns with social justice writings about privilege. As scholars have argued, privilege often manifests in men feeling the right, and claiming the verbal space, to speak their minds (Johnson, 2006; McIntosh, 2003).

The Catch-22

Women of color in Sister Stories realized that they were in a catch-22 in regard to traditional, androcentric, White, and hierarchical notions of leadership. We contend that a catch-22 is a dilemma or difficult situation mired by contradictory rules and double standards. While the traditional leadership literature suggests effective leaders have certain traits or behaviors that make them effective, those same traits and behaviors form the foundation of negative and stereotypical images of women of color (Hill

Collins, 1991). For instance, Hill Collins (1991) noted how women of color are often portrayed negatively as angry, domineering, or overly aggressive. Rose explicated how aggressiveness—a trait that might be viewed as positive for White and/or male leaders—is a negative one when used to describe women of color. Rose lamented the catch-22 for women of color: effective leaders supposedly show assertiveness not weakness, but women of color who are aggressive are viewed negatively. She explained:

> As women of color, personally, I feel as though society is always looking to highlight our faults rather than our intelligence. The readings on leadership pinpointed how if a woman of color attempts to take the role of a leader, she could be criticized for being overly aggressive or trying too hard. If she sits back pleasantly, however, she is not strong enough or even too weak-minded to be in her position.

Men of color were not faced with this leadership catch-22. They viewed themselves as effective leaders precisely because they possessed some of the traditional, aggressive, and power-laden characteristics they believed leaders should have. For instance, Brandon felt he had "a bright future ahead of me. Once I make it to where I want to go, wherever that may be, I want people to recognize that I did it my way because I have never been the type to conform to social roles or expectations." In essence, Brandon thought he was a good leader because he aggressively resisted societal conventions and did leadership "my way." Diego was not worried that his assertiveness and resistance to authority would lead others to question his leadership abilities. In fact, his words suggest he believed that those qualities made him a good leader. Diego seemed to view the assertion of power as key to his leadership style. He stated, "I am someone who stands for what they believe in and someone who doesn't let people bring me down. I know what I need to do to get where I need to go.... It's a good quality." As the quote suggests, Diego felt that assertiveness was a positive aspect of his leadership. If he were a woman of color, he might have experienced the catch-22 and felt differently.

In short, men of color did leadership "my way" and often did "not care" what others thought about them. Their words suggested that they equated leadership with assertiveness, aggressiveness, power, and authority. Women of color had also been socialized to view leadership through a lens of power and authority. However, they recognized a catch-22 whereby women of color were considered ineffective leaders if they attempted to exude powerful, aggressive, or "loud" styles of leadership. They were also considered weak and ineffective if they were not assertive. They were in a no-win situation framed by what Patricia Hill Collins referred to as the matrix of domination (1991) wherein women of color are oppressed by intersecting racial and gender stereotypes. In short, women of color in Sister Stories attempted to make sense of their leadership identity within the matrix of domination and found themselves in a catch-22: they would be negatively viewed as a stereotypical aggressive or "angry" woman of color if they were assertive, but seen as a weak and ineffective leader if they were not.

DISCUSSION

Critical race feminists have long argued that despite the efforts of critical race theory to expose racial oppression, much literature has failed to recognize intersectionality and, thus, address disparities between men and women of color—often rendering women of color "voiceless and invisible" (Wing, 2003, p. 2). In this chapter, we combined our critical race feminist lens with the tradition of narrative analysis to examine the disparities between men and women of color in an undergraduate leadership course. Striking differences in the leadership narratives from students in our study suggest that we have a long way to go before we achieve equity in leadership among men and women undergraduates of color.

Even after enrolling in a course that emphasized the historical and contemporary accomplishments of women leaders of color, most women had difficulty viewing themselves as leaders, exuding leadership confidence, finding their leadership voice, and navigating the catch-22. Conversely, men of color were confident in their leadership capabilities and expressed no hesitation claiming the title of leader. These gender differences will no doubt contribute to the already existing gender gap in leadership—with women of color potentially eschewing both the leader label and leadership roles while men of color confidently accept them.

Our data suggested that women and men had been exposed to (and possibly internalized) stereotypes and power-laden notions of leadership. As such, men and women of color seemed to make meaning of themselves and their leadership capabilities in very different ways. Admittedly, we did not conduct a life history or quantitative study that could show causation. Therefore, we cannot say with confidence that gender bias and power-laden beliefs about leadership caused these findings. However, student narratives presented in this chapter align with decades of theoretical and empirical literature about the presence of gender bias and its negative effects on women's voice, self-confidence, self-esteem, and academic success (Sadker & Sadker, 1994; Sadker et al., 2009). The narratives are congruent with literature from critical race feminists (and other women writers of color) who have documented the unique forms of intersectional race and gender oppression experienced by women of color (Hill Collins, 1991; Wing, 2003). We contend that a lifetime of experiencing silencing and disempowering oppression affected women of color so pervasively that it even appeared in women's narratives *after* taking a semester-long course about the accomplishments of women leaders of color. Women described how the Sister Stories course put them on the path toward becoming "a really great leader" (Ana). Moreover, as Lena explained, the course also helped women begin to feel empowered and realize that their voices were powerful. The historical silencing of women of color cannot be undone in one semester. However, as women's quotations suggest, the Sister Stories course was a step in the right direction.

Since we focused heavily on gender differences in leadership narratives, some readers could assume women merely need to catch up to men. That is not our intention. For instance, we would not encourage women to adopt some of the hierarchical and power-laden approaches to leadership that men use (e.g., not listening to followers). Nor would we suggest that the extreme confidence in leadership skills possessed by men was necessarily a good thing. In fact, women of color end up in a catch-22 when they are perceived as either submissive or domineering leaders (Hill Collins, 1991). Moreover, college is intended to be a place where students grow and develop. Fostering the motivation for lifelong learning is arguably an implicit goal of higher education (Mayhew, Wolniak, & Pascarella, 2008; McCombs, 1991). McCombs described lifelong learning as a natural propensity to, and foundational motivation for, human growth and development. When men approach leadership courses with the beliefs like, "*I am*" already a great leader, they might not be open to learning new perspectives and enhancing their leadership skills. Moreover, they may be exhibiting a lack of openness to lifelong learning. When viewing men and women's leadership narratives from this perspective, we could argue that women held a lifelong learning orientation and were focused on continuous improvement—not stagnation. In sum, our critical race feminist lens prompted us to lament how women hesitated to take on the label of leader and exude leadership confidence. However, as educators we applaud women's desire to focus on improvement through lifelong learning. As women like Claire suggested, all leaders could use a love for continual learning to "further [their] development [and] . . . refine skills."

Implications for Praxis

As critical race feminists and leadership scholars, we are passionate about conducting research that leads to equity for men and women of color in collegiate leadership programs. Through critical race praxis, we also hope to empower women undergraduates of color. As such, we conclude this chapter with a number of practical recommendations.

First, we encourage higher education institutions to focus on the empowerment of women of color. Leadership development educators must be aware of the history of silencing of women of color and offer venues where they can find and use their voice. Instructors should be intentional about selecting course readings, videos, and guest speakers that highlight the counternarratives of confident and successful women leaders of color so students can learn from empowered women leaders of color who look like them. As we learned from our data, instructors should not expect to undo a lifetime of disempowerment and silencing of women in one course. However, they can encourage women to take the initial steps on a lifelong path toward leadership empowerment. As our data suggest, most women were eager to begin their journey of leadership development. Post-secondary institutions should consider offering extracurricular workshops and academic courses—like Sister Stories—to empower women leaders of color.

Second, we encourage instructors to call attention to gender disparities not only in the leadership research (e.g., Dugan & Komives, 2007; Kezar and Moriarty, 2000) but also in student leadership narratives. Since our work was part of an ongoing research project, we did not fully analyze student narratives until after the courses concluded. As such, we missed the opportunity to draw student attention to, and discuss the implications of, gender differences in classroom conversations about leadership. We encourage instructors to listen carefully for gender disparities in student writings and in-class conversations. Educators have an opportunity to interrupt the cycle of oppression when men exhibit confidence while women express difficulty viewing themselves as leaders, exuding leadership confidence, or finding their leadership voice while navigating the catch-22. Educators can engage students in classroom conversations about the power of socialization, the legacy of women being silenced, and the implications of racial and gender oppression on twenty-first-century leadership. Inviting students to reflect upon gender differences that emerge in their own classroom can lead to insightful conversations. Educators can also invite students to reflect more deeply upon these topics (and what they mean for their lives) in papers, portfolios, or multi-media projects.

Third, educators should focus on student strengths and encourage men and women to learn from each other. Women of color might be empowered by listening to the perspectives of their male counterparts. Encouraging men to talk about why and how they developed leadership confidence might offer valuable lessons to women of color. On the other hand, men can benefit from adopting a lifelong learning orientation (Mayhew et al., 2008; McCombs, 1991). By drawing attention to women's openness to continuous leadership growth and development, educators can help men learn the importance of lifelong learning.

In conclusion, we hope that this chapter offers insight to leadership educators interested in combatting the subtle (and not so subtle) oppressive forces that can negatively influence lifelong leadership development for undergraduate women (and men) of color. By combatting the matrix of domination, challenging oppressive stereotypes about women of color, empowering women of color to claim a leadership identity, inspiring women of color to find and use their voice, and fostering a learning orientation in all students, educators can begin to close the leadership gap between men and women of color.

REFERENCES

Alston, J. A., & McClellan, P. A. (2011). *Herstories: Leading with the lessons of the lives of Black women activists*. New York, NY: Peter Lang.

Arminio, J. L., Carter, S., Jones, S. E., Kruger, K., Lucas, N., Washington, J.,... & Scott, A. (2000). Leadership experiences of students of color. *NASPA Journal, 37*(3), 496–510.

Chin, J. L. (2010). Introduction to the special issue on diversity and leadership. *American Psychologist, 65*(3), 150–156. doi:10.1037/a0018716

Crenshaw, K. (1989). Demarginalizing the intersection of race and sex: A Black feminist critique of antidiscrimination doctrine, feminist theory, and antiracist politics. *University of Chicago Legal Forum, 1989*(1), 139–167.

Darder, A., Baltodano, M., & Torres, R. D. (2003). Critical pedagogy: An introduction. In A. Darder, M. Baltodano, & R. D. Torres (Eds.), *The critical pedagogy reader* (pp. 1–21). New York, NY: Routledge.

Daiute, C., & Lightfoot, C. (Eds.) (2004). *Narrative analysis: Studying the development of individuals in society*. Thousand Oaks, CA: SAGE.

Drechsler, M. J., & Jones, Jr., W. A. (2009). Becoming a change agent. In S. R. Komives, W. Wagner & Associates (Eds.), *Leadership for a better world: Understanding the social change model of leadership development* (pp. 397–443). San Francisco, CA: Jossey-Bass.

Dugan, J. P. (2006). Explorations using the social change model: Leadership development among college men and women. *Journal of College Student Development, 47*(2), 217–225. doi:10.1353/csd.2006.0015

Dugan, J. P., Kodama, C. M., & Gebhardt, M. C. (2012). Race and leadership development among college students: The additive value of collective racial esteem. *Journal of Diversity in Higher Education, 5*(3), 174–189. doi:10.1037/a0029133

Dugan, J. P., & Komives, S. R. (2007). *Developing leadership capacity in college students: Findings from a national study*. A Report from the Multi-Institutional Study of Leadership. College Park, MD: National Clearinghouse for Leadership Programs.

Dugan, J. P., & Komives, S. R. (2011). Leadership theories. In S. R. Komives, J. P. Dugan, J. E. Owen, C. Slack, W. Wagner & Associates (Eds.), *Handbook for student leadership programs* (pp. 35–58). San Francisco, CA: Jossey-Bass.

Hayes, E., & Flannery, D. D. (2000). *Women as learners: The significance of gender in adult learning*. San Francisco, CA: Jossey-Bass.

Hill Collins, P. (1991). *Black feminist thought: Knowledge, consciousness, and the politics of empowerment.* New York, NY: Routledge.

hooks, b. (2000). *Feminist theory: From margin to center* (2nd ed.). Cambridge, MA: South End.

Johnson, A. G. (2006). *Privilege, power, and difference* (2nd ed.). New York, NY: McGraw Hill.

Johnson-Bailey, J. (2001). *Sistahs in college: Making a way out of no way.* Malabar, FL: Kreiger.

Jones, S. R., Torres, V., & Arminio, J. (2014). *Negotiating the complexities of qualitative research in higher education: Fundamental elements and issues* (2nd ed.). New York, NY: Routledge.

Kezar, A., & Moriarty, D. (2000). Expanding our understanding of student leadership development: A study exploring gender and ethnic identity. *Journal of College Student Development, 41*(1), 55–69.

Komarovsky, M. (1985). *Women in college: Shaping new feminine identities.* New York, NY: Basic.

Komives, S. R., Longerbeam, S. D., Owen, J. E., Mainella, F. C., & Osteen, L. (2006). A leadership identity development model: Applications from a grounded theory. *Journal of College Student Development, 47*(4), 401–418. doi:10.1353/csd.2006.0048

Komives, S. R., Wagner, W., & Associates. (Eds.). (2012). *Leadership for a better world: Understanding the social change model of leadership development.* Hoboken, NJ: Wiley.

Larson, C. L., & Murtadha, K. (2002). Leadership for social justice. *Yearbook of the National Society for the Study of Education, 101*(1), 134–161.

Lewis, M. G. (1993). *Without a word: Teaching beyond women's silence.* New York, NY: Routledge.

Lorde, A. (1984). *Sister outsider: Essays and speeches.* New York, NY: The Crossing Press.

Luke, C. (1994). Women in the academy: The politics of speech and silence. *British Journal of Sociology of Education, 15*(2), 211–230.

Mayhew, M. J., Wolniak, G. C., & Pascarella, E. T. (2008). How educational practices affect the development of life-long learning orientations in traditionally-aged undergraduate students. *Research in Higher Education, 49*(4), 337–356.

Merriam, S. B. (2009). *Qualitative research: A guide to design and implementation* (2nd ed.). San Francisco, CA: Jossey-Bass.

McCombs, B. L. (1991). Motivation and lifelong learning. *Educational Psychologist, 26*(2), 117–127.

McIntosh, P. (2003). White privilege and male privilege: A personal account of coming to see correspondences through work in women's studies. In M. S. Kimmel & A. L. Ferber (Eds.), *Privilege: A reader* (pp. 147–160). Boulder, CO: Westview Press.

Moraga, C., & Anzaldúa, G. (Eds.). (1981, 2002). *This bridge called my back: Writings by radical women of color* (3rd ed.). Berkeley, CA: Third Woman Press.

O' Barr, W. M., & Atkins, B. K. (2011). "Women's language" or "powerless language"? In J. Coates & P. Pichler (Eds.), *Language and gender: A reader* (2nd ed., pp. 451–460). Chichester, England: Wiley-Blackwell.

Parker, L., & Stovall, D. O. (2004). Actions following words: Critical race theory connects to critical pedagogy. *Educational Philosophy and Theory, 36*(2), 167–182.

Reinharz, S. (1994). Toward an ethnography of "voice" and "silence." In E. J. Trickett, R. J. Watts, & D. Birman (Eds.), *Human diversity: Perspectives on people in context* (pp. 178–200). San Francisco, CA: Jossey-Bass.

Reissman, C. K. (1993). Narrative analysis. *Qualitative Research Methods Series* (Vol. 30). Newbury Park, CA: SAGE.

Roberts, D., & Ullom, C. (1989). Student leadership program model. *NASPA Journal, 27*(1), 67–74.

Sadker, M., & Sadker, D. (1994). *Failing at fairness: How America's schools cheat girls.* New York, NY: Simon & Schuster.

Sadker, D., Sadker, M., & Zittleman, K. R. (2009). *Still failing at fairness: How gender bias cheats girls and boys in school and what we can do about it.* New York, NY: Scribner.

Solórzano, D. G. (1997). Images and words that wound: Critical race theory, racial stereotyping, and teacher education. *Teacher Education Quarterly, 24*(3), 5–19.

Solórzano, D. G., Ceja, M., & Yosso, T. (2000). Critical race theory, radical microaggressions, and campus racial climate: The experiences of African American college students. *Journal of Negro Education, 69*(1–2), 60–73.

Solórzano, D. G., & Yosso, T. J. (2001). Critical race and LatCrit theory and method: Counter-storytelling. *International Journal of Qualitative Studies in Education, 14*(4), 471–495.

Stovall, D. (2006). Forging community in race and class: Critical race theory and the quest for social justice in education. *Race Ethnicity and Education, 9*(3), 243–259.

Vaccaro, A. (2017). Does my story belong? An intersectional critical race feminist analysis of student silence in a diverse classroom. *The Journal About Women in Higher Education, 10*(1), 27–44.

Vaccaro, A., & Camba-Kelsay, M. J. (2016). *Centering women of color in an academic counterspace: A critical race analysis of teaching, learning, and classroom dynamics.* Lanham, MD: Lexington.

Wing, A. K. (2003). Introduction. In A. K. Wing (Ed.), *Critical race feminism: A reader* (2nd ed., pp. 1–19). New York, NY: New York University Press.

Yin, R. K. (2014). *Case study research: Design and methods* (5th ed.). Los Angeles, CA: SAGE.

CHAPTER 15

MEXICAN AMERICAN WOMEN LEADERS

Filling a Gap in the Study of Gender, Communication, and Leadership

Yolanda Chávez Leyva
The University of Texas at El Paso

Patricia Dennis Witherspoon
The University of Texas at El Paso

Hispanics, or Latinos, are the fastest-growing minority in the United States today, projected to possibly become one-third of the nation's population by 2050. They comprise 20% of Millennials, one in five school children, and one in four newborns (Bordas, 2013). More than 60% of this increasingly influential demographic group traces their roots to Mexico. Yet there is almost no research on Mexican American leaders' behaviors in general, and those of Mexican American women, specifically.

The purpose of this chapter is to add to the body of research findings about Mexican American women's leadership and communication

Gender, Communication, and the Leadership Gap, pages 263–285
Copyright © 2017 by Information Age Publishing
All rights of reproduction in any form reserved.

behaviors. We first briefly discuss the relevant research that informs and contextualizes this study. Second, we describe the study and our ten Mexican American women interviewees. Third, we present the major themes that emerged from our interviews, the perspectives that were clearly shared by these women whose sites of leadership differ but whose efficacy is significant and sustained. Fourth, we discuss the themes as they inform, or add to, previous research. Finally, we suggest future research questions for the study of Mexican American women and leadership communication.

The U.S. Census Bureau defines "Hispanic" as people whose origins are in Mexico, Puerto Rico, Cuba, South or Central America, or other Spanish cultures. A 2011 report by the Pew Research Center revealed that 51% of "Latinos" or "Hispanics" in the United States preferred to label themselves based on their country of origin, despite more than 40 years of government and media emphasis on using the broader terms (Taylor, Hugo Lopez, Martínez, & Velasco, 2012, p. 1). This report reflects a historical reality that Latinos often identify most closely with their countries or regions or even hometowns, harkening back to the 19th century when individuals called themselves "Tejano" or "Californio." While umbrella terms like "Latino" or "Hispanic" serve a purpose, it is important to understand the specificity of distinct Latino groups reflected in the preference. "Latinas" are not a monolithic group. There are differences in the Spanish they speak, foods they eat, celebrations in which they participate, heroes they honor, and holidays they observe. There are multiple components to their unique cultures, fostered by their country of origin. This chapter focuses on women leaders of Mexican descent.

A review of the research literature on gender and leadership will find almost no scholarly monographs or journal articles on the leadership communication behaviors of Latinas in general, or of Mexican American women specifically. Indeed, there is no body of literature on their communication in interpersonal or organizational contexts. The literature on communication behaviors of women leaders of color began to develop in the 1990s, when women scholars of color, interested in the topic of leadership, emerged from doctoral programs, became members of the professoriate, and began publishing their research. As many higher education administrators are aware, there are few Latinos/as in doctoral programs of any discipline at the present time, and even fewer are in the ranks of assistant and associate professor. This is one critical reason why there is little published research on the leadership communication behaviors of Mexican American women leaders. As leadership and history scholars, and administrators, at the largest Mexican American majority university in the United States, we are well aware of the lack of research on American women leaders, the dearth of literature on interpersonal and organizational communication behaviors of Latinos, and the need for increased research on Mexican American women leaders because of the changing demographics of the United States. Through in-depth interviews with Mexican American women leaders in national, regional, and local organizations, and through questions seeking information about leadership and communication behaviors in corporate, governmental, social justice, and community outreach contexts, we provide the results of a qualitative study that will inform other studies of Mexican American women's leadership communication. The findings of this study will help to narrow the gap in gender, leadership, and communication research.

REVIEW OF RELEVANT LITERATURE

Gender and Leadership

While many of her examples of the relevant literature are in corporate America, rather than diverse sites of leadership in non-profit, governmental, and community contexts, the study of gender and leadership has benefited greatly from the work of Alice Eagly. Her 2007 book with Linda Carli offers a new metaphor to replace the "glass ceiling." According to Eagly and Carli (2007), women now must traverse the circuitous routes of "a labyrinth," which has different pathways, and barriers, to different jobs and careers. There are also various types of organizations that require different routes to a preferred position, which may not be at the top of a company but as the head of a workplace team, a work unit, or an international task force. Eagly and Carli (2007) describe two basic principles to help women navigate the labyrinth. One principle is to blend agency with communion, that is, to take credit for accomplishments, negotiate effectively, and feel authentic in leadership roles (Eagly & Carli, 2007). In other words, use instrumental behaviors to move the task, the team, and the organization forward, yet also create opportunities for collaboration, participative decision-making, collegially developed decisions and solutions, and a sense of community among diverse constituents (Eagly & Carli, 2007). The second principle is a recommendation to build social capital, by creating and sustaining relationships and networks that will develop, implement, and support new solutions to problems, new goals, and development of constituents' personal and professional goals. Eagly and Carli (2007) offer a critical observation germane to our study:

> The effects of gender on leadership style may vary depending on the cultural context. Ideally, there would be many cross-cultural studies to explore this issue, but such studies are rare. There are also few studies that have taken subcultures into account by considering race and ethnicity along with gender. (p. 131)

Jean Lipman-Blumen's seminal article, "Connective Leadership: Female Leadership Styles in the 21st Century Workplace," was published in 1992. Her 1996 book, *Connective Edge,* focuses on leadership in a changing world, extending her discussion of gender and leadership to societies trying to balance independence and interdependence as they face issues created by increasingly global influences. Lipman-Blumen (1992) describes connective leadership as that which "connects individuals to others and *others'* goals, using a broad spectrum of behavioral strategies" (p. 184). Moreover, she observes, "It shares responsibility, takes unthreatened pride in the accomplishments of colleagues and protégés, and experiences success without the compulsion to outdo others" (Lipman-Blumen, 1992, p. 184). Lipman-Blumen's 1992 article posited that connective leadership was a gendered form of leadership, as the title indicates. However, the 1996 book (Lipman-Balumen, 1996) launched a more in-depth description and analysis of this new conceptualization of leadership, needed in a different world than that of the twentieth century, where the notions of "great men," leadership traits, and "command and control" in formal, hierarchical organizations dominated academic and applied discussions of leadership. Connective leaders, Lipman-Blumen (1996) emphasizes, will operate from an ethical base and join their vision to the dreams of others; strive to overcome mutual problems; create a sense of community in organizations and societies; encourage colleagues at all levels to assume responsibilities; join with other leaders, even former adversaries, as colleagues; and demonstrate authenticity through dedication to goals that go beyond self-interest. The studies that are available on Latino/a leaders and leadership suggest that these individuals exhibit several of the behaviors Lipman-Blumen (1992, 1996) identifies as characteristics of connective leaders.

As we have noted, there are few contributions to the literature on leadership communication as enacted by Mexican American women, or Latinas of any national origin. Bordas' two books on multicultural and Latino leadership do not focus on leadership communication, yet the ways most leaders exhibit leadership is through a repertoire of communication behaviors. Accordingly, we added to our interview questions an item on how our interviewees communicate as leaders. As qualitative methodologists, we have seen numerous examples of interviewee responses to questions that were not asked, but were prompted by a line of inquiry, and that happened in our study. In addition to the specific question on the use of communication in their leadership, several of our interviewees mentioned communication behaviors in answer to other questions we asked.

Observations to Date on Latina and Mexican American Women's Leadership and the Role of Communication Within It

For more than 25 years, the study of gender and leadership focused almost solely on Anglo women by Anglo scholars. In 2011, Jean Lau Chin added another voice to the importance of gender and leadership studies in cultural contexts:

> [I]t is increasingly clear that cultural worldviews, socialization of gender roles, and different life experiences do contribute to one's resulting philosophy and style of leadership. Authenticity as a leader is more challenging when needing to negotiate multiple and intersecting identities. Women from diverse racial and ethnic groups might lead in different ways more aligned with their different worldviews and cultural perspectives. They may identify not only as leaders, but also as women, as racial/ethnic individuals, as mothers, etc., all of which intersect with one another. These include the challenges of work-family balance, caretaking responsibilities, gender role expectations, connectedness, and affiliation with multiple communities while exercising their leadership. (p. 4)

The notion of "intersectionality," or overlapping and interdependent systems of discrimination faced by minority women, is relevant to a study of Latinas (Crenshaw, 1991). For instance, Ella Bell (1990) once described the phenomenon of "double jeopardy," facing prejudice if one is African American *and* a woman. As she explains, "black professional women divest themselves of their culture of origin, the black community," and "attempt to fit into the dominant white community" when they go to work (Bell, 1990, p. 462). These women may not only experience the differential treatment at work that White women may experience, including exclusion from both formal and informal organizational networks, they also are constantly attempting to maintain ties to the community in which they live, "where they assume active roles with their families, significant others, and in social groups" (Bell, 1990, p. 475). Intersectionality means African American women still face issues as a result of both their gender and their race. Understanding the role that intersectionality plays in the study and practice of leadership, Sánchez, Hucles, Sánchez-Hucles, and Mehta (2007) have observed: "We must . . . strive to develop more culturally distinctive leadership theories that recognize the unique experiences of diverse women," emphasizing that "diverse women leaders will finally become part of the definition of leadership" (p. 241) because of the behaviors and strategies they exhibit. As Vasquez and Comas-Diaz write (2007): "Although not all Latinas share the same values, there are a core set of Latino cultural values, including centrality of family, messages received about gender roles, and a collective identity that emphasizes social responsibility and service" (p. 266). It is to these values and characteristics of Latino leadership that we now turn to provide part of the context for our findings about Mexican American women as leaders.

Bordas (2013) has written that Latinos/as are creating a new philosophy and practice of leadership, one that does not focus on leadership by individuals but by "the Many" (p. 173). The "*we*" culture of Latinos/as has a strong sense of belonging, a focus on working together for mutual benefit, a focus on people and on the collective and on benefiting the whole before the individual (Bordas, 2012). Having learned to contribute to their families and communities at an early age, she emphasizes that Latinos value collaboration as leaders because collaborative and activist leadership depends on *fuerza*, or the strength "of many hands and many voices" (Bordas, 2013, p. 173). For centuries, those who practiced and studied leadership focused on individual leaders, their lives, traits, successes and failures. In the last half of the twentieth century, however, Bordas (2012) reminds us that phenomena such as the civil rights movement, globalization, changing demographics, democratic values, and higher education levels are redefining leadership as a participatory, collegial, and collaborative process that is group-centered not "I-focused" (p. 82). This transformative series of influences is occurring at the same time that Latinos/as are increasingly identified as leaders of the many in social action/social justice organizations and groups. As Arturo Vargas, Executive Director of the National Association of Latino Elected and Appointed Officials, emphasizes: "It's thousands of leaders. It's thousands of movements in thousands of communities across the country, whether it's the immigrants who are organizing at a local level or the head of a nonprofit organization that is mobilizing his community" (as cited in Bordas, 2013, p. 173). Such leadership is being identified as essential for the twenty-first century because of demographic trends and expectations that people will have more control over their own destinies in the future than has been in the case in many world societies in the past.

In *The Power of Latino Leadership: Culture, Inclusion, and Contribution,* Bordas (2013) reminds us that Latino power is derived from the community, and it represents a diversity of countries. Particularly important to this study is the observation that one-third of the United States was once part of Mexico, and the Mexican American prides himself or herself on being a "mestizo/a," the product of the joined relationship of Spanish and indigenous peoples in what is now Mexico and the United States. The Spanish heritage itself includes diverse populations, including Moors, Arabs, Jews, Romans, Germans and Celts, and descendants of this heritage, and indigenous peoples, are aptly suited to appreciate, work with, and lead populations of diverse peoples. As Bordas (2013) writes, "Latinos are bound together by the Spanish language, a shared history, a spiritual tradition, and common values that stem from both their Spanish and their indigenous roots" (p. 99).

Bordas (2013) offers several Latino Leadership Principles, rooted in the importance of family and community. These include:

- *Personalismo.* The character of a leader, which is also the relational component of leadership.
- *Destino.* The distinct life path and purpose of a Latino, which includes an appreciation of family history and traditions.
- *La Cultura.* A "we" orientation that comes from Latinos as a culture, which values simpatico, or being congenial and likeable.
- *De Colores.* Many cultures and heritages which come from 26 different countries, typified by the "self-identification" that characterizes Latinos—the collective identity forged from diversity.
- *Juntos.* An emphasis on "union," on working in a group and side by side, which results in leadership being conferred by the community.
- *Sí Se Puede.* The roots of leadership in social activism, community organizing, and coalition-building to effect social change.

With its emphasis on working with people from diverse backgrounds and cultures, its resultant focus on collaboration and shared decision-making, its appreciation of the need for many leaders, not one person or one group, to effect change, Latino/a leadership reflects the contemporary notions of leadership described by Greenleaf (1970), Lipman-Blumen (1996), George (2003), Wheatley (2006), and others who have focused on the leadership of change in new and ever-changing national and organizational contexts. Some ethnic minority leadership models come from the civil rights movement and its work, characterized by leadership behaviors exhibited by Martin Luther King, Cesar Chavez, Dolores Huerta, Barack Obama, and most of the Mexican American women we interviewed. Community and social justice organizing requires the ability to bring people together to solve common problems, manage conflicts, motivate volunteers, and build and sustain coalitions. As a result, critical communication skills needed are listening, using persuasion, communicating in a person-centered manner that leads to relationship-building, and creating identification and common ground with audiences and individuals. These are behaviors that reflect a focus on followers and a leader's multiple constituencies.

None of the scholars cited here focus their work on leadership communication. Indeed, few scholars to date have written specifically about leadership *and* communication. Those contributions tend to be course texts, although Fairhurst (2007, 2010; Fairhurst & Sarr, 1996) is a notable exception with her scholarly work on discursive leadership and her applied texts on framing (Hackman & Johnson, 2013; Northouse, 2016; Witherspoon,

1997). Our study also adds to the body of literature that explores cultural effects on the exercise of leadership communication.

MEXICAN AMERICAN WOMEN LEADERS: HISTORICAL OVERVIEW

Mexican American women have assumed leadership positions in their communities throughout the history of Mexican-origin people in the United States. Twentieth-century trailblazers are the precursors to today's leaders, and many of those individuals continue to work in the same areas as their predecessors, especially education, employment, housing, and the pursuit of freedom from violence. Then, as today, women often worked on multiple issues, and across borders, understanding that their communities faced a web of challenges that worked together to limit opportunities. Women's work at the forefront of civil rights and labor organizations refutes the long-held stereotypes of Mexican American women as docile and submissive.

In 1939, Luisa Moreno organized the first national Latino civil rights gathering, *El Congreso de Pueblos de Habla Española*, with more than 1,000 delegates representing more than 120 organizations. They called for an end to segregation in schools, improved employment, and better housing. While they urged immigrants to become U.S. citizens, they also declared the right of immigrants to work in the United States without fear of deportation (Ruiz, 2008). A more recent labor organizer, Dolores Huerta, is frequently mentioned in conjunction with Cesar Chavez, with whom she co-founded the United Farmworkers Union. Her leadership, however, preceded their work together. In 1955, she began organizing with the Community Service Organization in Stockton, California. She credited her mother, who owned a restaurant that served farmworkers, with inspiring her and raising her consciousness about civil rights. Huerta's work as a schoolteacher in Stockton also motivated her. She related that she could not stand seeing hungry children arriving at school every morning so she thought she could do more for them by organizing their farmworker parents. In 1960, she co-founded the Agricultural Workers Association, and in 1962 she co-founded the National Farm Workers Association (later known as the United Agricultural Workers Organizing Committee or UAWOC), both with Chavez. When she negotiated a contract between the UAWOC and a wine company, it became the first time farmworkers successfully bargained with a commercial employer (Garcia, 2008).

Elizabeth "Betita" Martinez was born in 1925 in Maryland, to a father who had immigrated to the United States eight years earlier and a Euro American mother. After graduating with a history degree from Swarthmore College in 1946, she began working at the United Nations in 1947. In the

1960s, she became involved in the Black civil rights movement, working in the Student Non-Violent Coordinating Committee, traveling the country speaking about civil rights. In 1968, she founded one of the most influential Chicano movement newspapers, *El Grito del Norte*. During the 1960s and 1970s, she was involved in the most important organizations and actions of the Chicano Movement. In 1973, she founded the Chicano Communications Center to use photography and other media to educate Chicanos about their history. She founded the Institute for Multi-Racial Justice in 1997 in an effort to bring people of color together to fight for human rights (Ruiz & Sánchez Korrol, 2006).

Mexican American women's leadership is not new. Its roots lie in the injustices and lack of rights experienced by previous generations. Its roots are equally deep in the desire for equality, opportunity, and social justice. However, scholarly attention to these women as leaders and communicators has been rare. The study of leadership and leadership communication behaviors of Mexican American women has received little attention by leadership scholars.

This study is one step toward recognizing that there are Mexican American women leaders in a variety of important economic, educational, political, and social contexts. The study completes one step in closing a significant gap in gender and leadership communication research.

THE STUDY

As we have noted, there is a dearth of research literature on Mexican American women's leadership communication. When one of the authors received notice about the development of this volume, she contacted an historian with significant research and insight into Mexican American women leaders, a scholar who also has many years of experience in oral history interviewing, and in studying the people of the U.S.–Mexico borderlands and the issues they face. We believe this chapter benefited from an interdisciplinary view, from an historian representing the humanities and from a social scientist whose work on leadership communication has been situated in the White House, corporate, and governmental organizations. We developed interview questions that reflected both our training. Following the interviews, which were carried out both in person and via phone, we received release forms. The interviews have been deposited with the University of Texas at El Paso Institute of Oral History for use by future researchers. As oral histories, the interviews were exempt from IRB review by the university's policy. We also posit that our grounded theory review of qualitative data benefited from our different cultural backgrounds, one Anglo and one the child of Mexican and indigenous peoples.

The lenses used by scholars who work in qualitative methodologies are critically important to the review and constant comparison techniques used in a study. Historically, in the study of gender and leadership, those lenses have lacked the benefit of diverse cultural experiences and backgrounds—with resultant perspectives. We decided to pursue this study because of our *mutual* interest in Mexican American women and their increasing contributions at regional and national levels in social, economic, and political contexts. We soon realized our approaches to developing the project were very different, from the interview questions we each developed to the interviewees we recommended to each other. However, we think the study benefited from our combined approaches and orientations to academic research, or what emerged as an interdisciplinary partnership.

While the case has been made for the importance of a single example, a one-person case study, for in-depth knowledge about a subject we determined to interview women from different cities, different sizes and types of organizations, and different ages and life experiences. All allowed us to use their names. We interviewed ten Mexican American women leaders, including presidents and directors of national educational and political organizations. The interviewees also included corporate executives, community organizers, and social justice advocates for farmworkers and others who lost jobs in the U.S. manufacturing industry. Some of the women were born in Mexico; others are the daughters or granddaughters of immigrants. Their education and socio-economic status vary. All of the interviewees spoke English, but some felt more comfortable speaking Spanish in the interviews.

Major themes emerged from a constant comparison technique in which we independently reviewed the recordings of all interviews and individually identified themes that emerged from them. Then we compared the themes that each of us saw as emergent ones from the interviews.

IN THEIR OWN WORDS: EMERGENT THEMES FROM THE INTERVIEWS

The similarity of our identified themes was striking, and we combined them into the themes discussed below.

Leadership as Advocacy in Service to Others (La Responsable)

The very definition of leadership among our interviewees is rooted in communication. To them, leaders are advocates, spokespersons, for the groups they lead or the causes they champion. They view themselves as the responsible ones, *la responsable*, who by selection, election, or their own commitment to a cause or a community enact leadership through public speaking, interpersonal persuasion, and group decision-making skills.

An overarching idea that connected the ideas of leadership among our interviewees was that leadership and communication is based on relationships with others. Dr. Catalina Garcia's notion of leadership is as "spokesperson for whatever I've seen that needed to be done." She recalls, "I didn't speak up in med school," concerned that some issues she might have wanted to address might damage her career as a pioneering Mexican American female in an Anglo, male- dominated environment. So she waited until she had a medical degree and title, then proceeded to be an advocate for minority students in the 1980s in one of the state's largest school districts, reminding the school board about the changing demographics in that district. Garcia, born and raised in El Paso's *Segundo Barrio*, was one of the first Latinas to graduate from the University of Texas Southwestern Medical School, and is co-founder of the Dallas Women's Foundation.

Bea Villegas, indigenous spiritual leader and activist who was born in Ciudad Juárez and lived her adult life in El Paso, observed, "Because we have been oppressed being Latinos, being Hispanos, being Mexican, then when we hear 'leader' we think 'someone who is going to tell us what to do' even though that is not what the word means." Recently retired from the El Paso Community College, Villegas engaged with thousands of students over the course of several decades. Engaging in leadership is motivated by a sense of responsibility to family and, later in one's development, to community.

Alicia Marentes, social activist, suggested, leadership "is not about being above others; it is about what you did for others." She thoughtfully commented, "Do everything you can for the people;...that is leadership." Enriquez observed that leadership is "contextual," "purposeful," and "relationship-based."

Rosa Guerrero emphasized "A leader has to open doors for others." Guerrero is a nationally known educator, artist, and dance historian who recently retired at the age of 80 and has indeed opened doors for generations of students.

Janet Murguia observed that it is a sign of leadership when "you are representing the interest of others, when you are seen as a champion, an advocate, for others, when you are working on behalf of a community." Born in Kansas City, Kansas, Murguia has served as the President and CEO of the National Council of La Raza since 2005.

Carmen Rodriguez co-founded a Mexican American student advocacy organization as a university student and equates leadership with taking action, with "having strong opinions, being able to articulate them, and being willing to work." Deciding she could be a successful change agent by attaining a law degree, she also co-founded the Texas Rural Legal Aid (now Texas Rio Grande Legal Aid), helping farm laborers and garment workers, and eventually working in labor law. She continues to be a political activist.

As a communicator, Murguia reflected, a leader "gives voice on behalf of others." That statement encapsulates the kind of communication that enacts leadership for our interviewees.

Influence of Mexican American Values

The values that have permeated Mexican American families for generations remain the foundation on which leadership development is based among our interviewees. Mexican American women are key leaders in families, instilling cultural and often religious values, and emphasizing the importance of earning an education. Dr. Blanca Enriquez, national Director of Head Start, emphasized that as Mexican American women move into leadership roles, they do not forget their duties as mothers, wives, and daughters. Almost all of the interviewees stressed the importance of family in the Mexican American culture and the genesis of their own leadership in a familial context.

Working for decades with some of the nation's most exploited laborers as co-founder and director of social work for the 30-year-old Border Farmworkers Center in El Paso, Marentes stated: "I feel more like the workers are my family than I feel that I am a leader. If there is no money for a funeral, we all come together to give what we can."

Christine Ortega, Senior Adviser to Southwest Airlines in International Community Affairs, emphasized that African American women leaders also have a sense of leadership that is "deeply rooted in family, a personal nexus around which leadership blooms." Raised in San Antonio, Ortega is an alumna of Notre Dame University and serves on the board of the Smithsonian Latino Center.

We also heard multiple references to the importance of service to the neighborhood, or the church, the poor, the elderly, and the young, or women workers as communities of need. For example, Marentes talked about the situation of women farm workers who experienced sexual assault in the fields by employers and other workers. The health effects of being sprayed with pesticides and deaths from cancer were other common stories. Marentes said, "The women would tell me what happened in the fields. I would cry with them. Everything stays here inside. We have to keep working for women to be respected." Communication gives voice to Mexican American values, in familial, community, and work contexts.

Economic Struggle

An emphasis on effective leadership communication is especially important to Mexican American women who view communication as a survival skill and a skill used to achieve upward mobility. While one does not have to be poor to become a leader, several interviewees stated that this experience helps individuals empathize with those who are struggling economically in the United States. Wealth can be a barrier to understanding some leadership contexts and people who are part of those contexts, as Rodriguez observes. Socio-economic status is also directly related to women's relationship to communication, as is shown below. Speaking about some women leaders who are raised in Mexico and who are born into wealthy families, Ortega emphasized that they always have been able to speak their own language without fear of punishment by teachers or criticism from non-Hispanics, have no resultant self-concept issues, and therefore have greater self confidence in public leadership contexts when they come to the United States as visitors or leaders with dual citizenship. Ortega observed that for Mexican American women leaders "the experience of poverty may be motivating," although not all women can overcome its challenges. She reflected on poverty's costs: "I wonder how many in poverty never make it out to be leaders." Lorena Andrade described wealthy women from Mexico as "negating the experiences" of working-class Mexican American women. Andrade, born and raised in Boyle Heights in Los Angeles, has served as director of La Mujer Obrera for over five years, having worked with the women's advocacy organization since the 1990s.

The experiences of these women are based on economic, social, and political inequity, and the totality of resulting experiences has molded the values and behaviors that have fostered leadership emergence among them. As Villegas observed, "People who have less and a more difficult life communicate better because they have learned out of necessity or out of sacrifice" that communication is a process to achieve a mutually desired goal. Guerrero emphasized that "people need to live six weeks in a barrio to be true leaders" so they can identify with those they serve who in great part are not the wealthy members of the community. She was influenced by the words of her father: "It is a sin to be lazy. It is not a sin to be poor."

All of our interviewees held jobs as teenagers, in retail and hardware stores, agricultural fields, ice cream shops, and other sites of hourly work. Economic struggle helped mold their attitudes toward education, the importance of work, and the need for leadership to improve economic opportunity for those whose struggles continue.

Listening as a Key Communication Behavior

These women use listening as they work with others to enact change, mediate conflicts among groups, and move people toward the goals "the people" have espoused. In conflict mediation, several of the interviewees discussed the importance of listening first, to both (or more) sides, and focusing the interplay of ideas on negotiation, or conflict management. Ortega observed that listening is not only important as a way to understand people, it helps leaders understand the environment in which they are working. In community leadership, she suggested, a leader's focus on listening encourages individuals to express their concerns and ideas is a key communication behavior of servant leaders. Enriquez praised the process of listening as a way to identify an organization's strengths and develop a strategy for its evolution. Rodriguez emphasized that listening allows leaders to acknowledge the opinions of others, validating those opinions, and perhaps facilitating the process of reaching consensus.

Communication is their tool to motivate, inspire, and persuade, to move others in efforts to improve social and economic justice. In other words, communicating leadership for these individuals constitutes a focus on others, not on "me." Communication choices that foster collaboration are part of the leadership behaviors of these women. As Georgina Celia Perez, elected to the Texas State Board of Education in 2016, observed: "When we collaborate, our outcomes are far better." An emphasis on effective leadership communication is especially important to Mexican American women, who view communication as a survival skill and as a skill used to achieve upward mobility. As a communicator, Murguia reflected, a leader "gives voice on behalf of others." That statement encapsulates how communication enacts leadership for our interviewees. Leaders listen, they emphasize; leadership is not solely about talking. When they are engaged in the processes of motivating and inspiring, they make their cases in personal ways, "engaging through personal stories and anecdotes to make a connection," as Murguia suggested. Leadership is often associated with rhetorical ability, the power to persuade through speech. The women we interviewed emphasized that leaders must also listen to those they seek to serve, those for whom they seek to advocate, and those who are shared partners in the process of change.

The Use of Narrative Strategies

While listening was clearly a critical leadership communication behavior discussed by these women, they also mentioned the importance of narrative strategies. Leadership interaction may begin with a story, a song, an opening question, as well as statistics and data. Garcia and Enriquez emphasized the importance of data, including statistical information, in building a case for solutions in work and professional contexts. However, in her own community, Garcia observed, "I use personal examples from family and the history we share." When they are engaged in the processes of motivating and inspiring, our interviewees make their cases by "engaging through personal stories and anecdotes to make a connection," as Murguia suggested. These are culture-based strategies to initiate the leadership process. Communication behaviors of particular importance to these Mexican American women, in both large/hierarchical and smaller/emergent organizations, include the use of narratives or storytelling and asking questions during the process of conflict management to ascertain areas of agreement and disagreement. Murguia, Enriquez, and Ortega emphasized the importance of using personal stories and anecdotes to establish "common ground" with individuals in formal organizational contexts and with individuals in smaller, emergent, social action organizations.

The indigenous peoples of Mexico and the United States value storytelling as a way to share history and culture and lessons of survival. Its importance in Mexican American families and communities continues, as a form of cultural transmission and as a way to initiate and lead change in organizations, communities, and segments of American society.

Influence of Parents

Parents served as influential role models for these women leaders. As role models, they raised children; some worked outside the home, and all spent time teaching their daughters about the importance of getting an education as well as the importance of "family" in one's life. Most of the parents had no more than an eighth-grade education, yet they taught our leaders life skills, such as money management. As Guerrero recalled, her mother taught her about persistence: "If you fall three times, get up five." Others recalled how grandmothers had transmitted cultural knowledge: "She gave me a sense of identity." The communication of familial and cultural values by these individuals underscored Bordas' (2012; 2013) Latino/a leadership principle of *destino* (an appreciation of family history and traditions).

The influence of parents and grandparents was felt through memories of stories, face-to-face conversations, and communication at family celebrations. The narrative tradition was very important in remembering and recalling parental influence.

Recognition of Bordas' Latino Leadership Principles

This study provides evidence of leaders illustrating some of the Latino Leadership Principles discussed by Bordas (2013). As Andrade stated: "We always have our history in front of us." Preparing for a meeting or event, she observes, "I study the history of our organization and read our principles to guide decision making." She is also continually mindful of the vision and mission of the organization. The leadership of those we interviewed is also influenced by a belief in the importance of education and striving to attain a better life for their families (the ones they create and the ones into which they are born) and for those in in their community. Murguia emphasized that as a Mexican American woman she benefits from two cultures, from the values and culture of her Mexican heritage and the beliefs and values learned from being born in the United States, including the importance of getting an education and working hard to achieve a better life. That diversity, she observed, is an asset. Her comments reflect of *la cultura*, a "we" orientation that comes from Latinos/as as a culture.

Furthermore, the women's pride in Mexican American culture does not deter them from appreciating others. Marentes urged Mexican Americans to: "Feel proud of your culture and support other cultures. It's all one struggle. . . . Fighting for housing, for children, for women. We have to support each other. Our culture should not stop us from supporting others." Rodriguez, who has served as a leader on boards and in civic organizations in addition to her work as a leader in legal contexts, emphasized that Mexican American women do communicate differently than other women, that their culture values establishing empathy with others, and communicating with others on a personal level facilitates such empathy. And, while culture may affect communication among Mexican American women leaders, Rodriguez observes that educational attainment can be an equally great influence on Mexican American women's leadership development and resultant positive consequences when that education is used to improve social conditions in communities. These comments and those of other interviewees reflect *destino*, an appreciation of family history and traditions, and *si se puede*, leadership beyond the family, in social activism and community organizing to effect social change.

Leadership, as defined and described by our interviewees, is clearly connective, authentic, and has a goal of serving others first. It is collaborative and collegial and values leadership from many, not a single, dominant person. As Perez told us: "Everyone is a leader in some capacity. In this, . . . I am no more a leader than anyone else. . . . I'm a human and I work to make things better than I found it." As founder of *Tu Libro*, she has contributed over 30,000 books to El Paso's rural and impoverished students who do not have access to libraries in her effort "to make things better." Leadership is also hopeful. Andrade, describing the philosophy of La Mujer Obrera, said: "When we dream it, we call it something, and we begin working on it. And make it happen."

DISCUSSION

The women interviewed in this study are leaders in multi-hierarchical, large organizations and in small, emergent, organic organizations with distributive leadership.

All of these individuals understand the importance of collaborative and connective leadership, regardless of organizational size or purpose. Lipman-Blumen's (1992) notion of bringing people together to solve problems resonates in many of the comments we heard about the goal and purpose of leadership. Greenleaf's (1970) focus on serving others first also is present in the work, and language, of these leaders. We saw that in the multiple comments defining leadership *as* service. Such service includes advocacy for those whose voices are not attended to, or heard, and becoming a spokesperson, the one responsible for those who cannot speak for themselves. This philosophy is not only espoused by our interviewees. It was practiced continuously by Cesar Chavez and Dolores Huerta as they led migrant farmworkers in demonstrations for better pay and as they chose rhetorical symbols (Virgin de Guadalupe) and words to effect social change.

The Mexican American values guiding these women leaders are certainly embedded in their leadership communication that uses the metaphor of "family," as several interviewees observed. To Mexican Americans, communities are often extended families, as we also heard from the interviewees, reminding us of Vasquez and Comas-Díaz (2007) comments in the research literature that there is a core set of Latino cultural values, including centrality of family and the collective identity that emphasizes service and social responsibility.

The pervasive presence of "economic struggle" as a theme among the women leaders was not surprising when one considers the history of Mexican Americans in this country. As we observe in the historical section of the chapter, most Mexican Americans are not from wealthy Mexican families and earned their educations, positions, and financial resources over a period of time with hard work. The importance of work, of serving the poor, of advocating for social justice for all, and of getting an education to increase one's economic position in life are messages heard in our interviews. Indeed, these messages illustrate that the content of communication is an important dimension of leadership communication—often as significant in the persuasion process as rhetorical strategy or style.

Leadership communication is often regarded as the domain of a single leader and his or her abilities to persuade. Our interviewees voiced what many communication professors try to impart to their students. Among multiple communication behaviors, listening may be the least used and most important in the conduct of everyday life. It is certainly a behavior one sees in the processes of servant leadership, and connective, collaborative, and team leadership. Leaders of the twenty-first century, in almost any venue, initially find common ground, identification, with those they seek to lead; and one does that through the process of listening. That also is a skill first learned, and used, in families, as several of our leaders recalled.

Indigenous peoples throughout the world use storytelling to transmit to subsequent generations the lessons of survival, group identification, goal-setting and task achievement. Our interviewees' initial use of narrative strategies, whether a story, a listing of facts and figures, or a joke to gain attention is a common set of strategies among leaders, particularly those engaged in change. Stories seize and hold attention, communicating across different sets of references. They can help move people toward mutually held goals, as several of our leaders of both large organizations and small community groups realized early in their leadership development.

The sources of those early stories were parents, and the influence of their parents on these Mexican American women leaders is undimmed by time. The influence is the result of interaction, frequent and sustained, so that memories were contained in a saying or quotation, either originating with the parent or passed down by him or her from a previous generation. In some cases, we heard that the women were conduits of messages to the succeeding generation, their children.

Finally, this study may be one of the first to see Bordas' Latino Leadership Principles emerge from qualitative data, from interviews with individuals leading in large governmental and corporate organizations with multiple races, ethnicities and generations, and with individuals mobilizing people in relatively small emergent, community-based groups with homogenous members. We did not phrase any questions to seek comments about Bordas or her principles, but examples emerged in virtually every interview that reflected one or more principles described in the chapter. Of particular note were references to the importance of serving one's people, taking pride in one's culture, and striving for social justice and the improvement of social conditions locally, regionally, and nationally.

QUESTIONS FOR FUTURE RESEARCH

Looking at the comments of our interviewees, the overarching themes that emerged from these comments, and the research literature that framed the study, we offer several observations to guide future studies and questions they may wish to include.

One observation that emerged during our review of the literature and the planning of this study is that scholarly inquiry into gender and leadership should not be conducted solely in formal organizational contexts, much less in corporate contexts. In the twenty-first century, women, and certainly women of color, are leading in political, community, governmental, and non-profit organizations, and we encourage researchers to go into those places as well. What are the predominant leadership communication behaviors used by Mexican American women to lead people in emergent, informal, social justice, and community organizing groups?

A second observation is that we now know that cultural influences on the exercise of leadership deserve more research time and effort, including the study of ethnic and racial cultural influences. As the demographics of the United States change, it is critically important for leadership researchers to study the influence of gender, and various Hispanic cultures, on this phenomenon, and to continue the study of African American women, Asian American women, and Native American women as leaders. There is increasing intermarriage among races and ethnicities in this nation, and that, too, has implications for the study of leadership communication in multiple contexts. Future research should look at leadership among women who literally embody multiple cultures, races, and/or ethnicities. What are the similar, and different, leadership communication behaviors used by Mexican American women, compared to those exhibited by African American women, Asian American women, and Native American women?

As we discussed in the survey of current research literature, Latinas from different countries of origin may differ in the exercise of leadership. Mexican American women have different experiences from those of Latinas from other countries of origin. These differences are due in part to the history of Mexico and in part to the history of the Mexican Americans who trace their roots to the combination of Spanish and indigenous blood and who are proud of their mestizo heritage. Some Latinas did not grow up thinking that speaking Spanish was a "bad thing," as Mexican American children were once told in some American public schools where they were punished for speaking their native language. Some Latinas did not grow up poor, as many Mexican American women have because of their start in a poor country, prejudice and bigotry in this country, and denial of access to participate in school. How do leadership communication behaviors differ among various groups of Hispanic women from different nations of origin? To what can those differences be attributed?

Finally, the word "leader" may not adequately embody twenty-first-century leadership in an increasingly multicultural society. "Leader" is a word intrinsic to the dominant Anglo culture in American society, and to all of our interviewees, it means, "the one who will tell us what to do." As we observed early in this chapter, Latinas have expressed the view that Latina leadership is leadership from the many, not one or a few. Our interviewees talked about being "spokespersons," or "being the responsible one," or people in service to others, emphasizing a connective, collaborative philosophy about leadership. We have considered whether a different word better describes "leadership" among Mexican American women (e.g., *la responsable*), the Spanish reference to "the responsible one." Andrade, in describing the work of La Mujer Obrera, talked about how each woman served as *la responsable* for her area of work. Together, they lead as a community. How does an understanding of communication, as a set of behaviors and processes that enact leadership, change our understanding of leadership in the twenty-first century? How does it change our approach to studying gender and leadership? Culture and leadership?

We have begun a journey to study whether the notion of "leader" is different as we enter the third decade of the twenty-first century, and whether there are other words or names for the process that now more aptly describe one who enacts purposeful activity and communicates influence that moves people and their goals forward. History, and the events of the present, are teaching us that the exercise of leadership by women is vital to a democratic and progressive society and one that will offer opportunity to all.

APPENDIX: Interviewees			
Name	**Organization**	**Current City**	**Birth City**
Lorena Andrade	Director, La Mujer Obrera	El Paso, Texas	Boyle Heights, California
Dr. Blanca Enriquez	National Director, Head Start	Washington, DC	El Paso, Texas
Dr. Catalina Garcia	Physician and co-founder of the Dallas Women's Foundation	Dallas, Texas	El Paso, Texas
Rosa Guerrero	Educator (retired) and cultural advocate	El Paso, Texas	El Paso, Texas
Alicia Marentes	Assistant Director, Border Farmworkers Center	El Paso, Texas	Ciudad Juárez, Mexico
Janet Murguia	President and CEO of the National Council of La Raza	Washington, DC	Kansas City, Kansas
Christine Ortega	Senior Advisor for Community Affairs & Grassroots, Southwest Airlines	Dallas, Texas	San Antonio, Texas
Georgina Cecilia	Educator and member of the Texas State Board of Education	El Paso, Texas	El Paso County, Texas
Carmen Rodriguez	Attorney and activist	El Paso, Texas	
Beatriz Ilhuicatlahuili Villegas	Indigenous ceremonial grandmother and teacher, retired from El Paso Community College	El Paso, Texas	Ciudad Juárez, Mexico

REFERENCES

Bell, E. L. (1990). The bicultural life experience of career-oriented black women. *Journal of Organizational Behavior, 11*(6), 459–477.

Bordas, J. (2012). *Salsa, soul, and spirit: Leadership for a multicultural age* (2nd ed.). San Francisco, CA: Berrett-Koehler.

Bordas, J. (2013). *The power of Latino leadership: Culture, inclusion, and contribution.* San Francisco, CA: Berrett-Koehler.

Chin, J. L. (2011). Women and leadership: Transforming visions and current contexts. *Forum on Public Policy Online, 2011*(2). Retrieved from https://eric.ed.gov/?id=EJ944204

Crenshaw, K. (1991). Mapping the margins: Intersectionality, identity politics, and violence against women of color. *Stanford Law Review, 43*(6), 1241–1299.

Eagly, A. H., & Carli, L. L. (2007). *Through the labyrinth.* Boston, MA: Harvard Business School Press.

Fairhurst, G. T. (2007). *Discursive leadership: In conversation with leadership psychology.* Thousand Oaks, CA: SAGE.

Fairhurst, G. T. (2010). *The power of framing: Creating the language of leadership.* San Francisco, CA: John Wiley & Sons.

Fairhurst, G. T., & Sarr, R. A. (1996). *The art of framing: Managing the language of leadership.* San Francisco, CA: Jossey-Bass.

Garcia, M. T. (Ed.). (2008) *A Dolores Huerta reader.* Albuquerque, NM: University of New Mexico Press.

George, B. (2003). *Authentic leadership: Rediscovering the secrets to creating lasting value.* San Francisco, CA: Jossey-Bass.

Greenleaf, R. K. (1970). *The servant as leader.* Cambridge, MA: Center for Applied Studies.

Hackman, M. Z., & Johnson, C. E. (2013). *Leadership: A communication perspective* (6th ed.). Long Grove, IL: Waveland Press.

Lipman-Blumen, J. (1992). Connective leadership: Female leadership styles in the 21st century. *Sociological Perspectives, 35*(1), 183–203.

Lipman-Blumen, J. (1996). *The connective edge.* San Francisco, CA: Jossey-Bass.

Northouse, P. G. (2016). *Leadership: Theory and practice* (7th ed.). Los Angeles, CA: SAGE.

Ruiz, V. L. (2008). *From out of the shadows: Mexican women in twentieth-century America.* New York, NY: Oxford University Press.

Ruiz, V. L., & Sánchez Korrol, V. (2006) *Latinas in the United States: A historical encyclopedia.* Bloomington, IN: University of Indiana Press.

Sanchez, P., Hucles, P., Sanchez-Hucles, J., & Mehta, S. C. (2007). Increasing diverse women leadership in corporate America: Climbing concrete walls and shattering glass ceilings. In J. L. Chin, B. Lott, J. K. Rice, & J. Sanchez-Hucles (Eds.), *Women and leadership: Transforming visions and diverse voices* (pp. 228–244). Malden, MA: Blackwell.

Taylor, P., Hugo Lopez, M., Martínez, J., & Velasco, G. (2012, April 4). When labels don't fit: Hispanics and their views of identity. *Pew Research Center: Hispanic Trends.* Retrieved from http://www.pewhispanic.org/2012/04/04/when-labels-dont-fit-hispanics-and-their-views-of-identity/

Vasquez, M., & Comas-Díaz, L. (2007). Feminist leadership among Latinas. In J. L. Chin, B. Lott, J. K. Rice, & J. Sanchez-Hucles (Eds.), *Women and leadership: Transforming visions and diverse voices* (pp. 264–280). Malden, MA: Blackwell.

Wheatley, M. J. (2006). *Leadership and the new science: Discovering order in a chaotic world.* San Francisco, CA: Berrett-Koehler.

Witherspoon, P. D. (1997). *Communication leadership: An organizational perspective.* Boston, MA: Allyn & Bacon.

PART V

IN THE ETHER: DIGITAL LEADERSHIP

Digital leadership is an emerging area and lends itself to a broader discussion of how women can use these new forms of communication for leadership. Social media, such as blogs and social networking sites (SNS), allow for two-way, interactive forms of communication and thus women can become more effective at managing their online presence, as can be seen in the research presented in this section. Women can set their own agendas through the use of Twitter rather than being stereotyped or limited by mainstream media, or, they can use their blogs to challenge normative power structures.

At the same time that online communication can be empowering, it is important to pay attention to the differences in how online communication is used. Online communication has a limited number of what Walther and Parks (2002) call cues filtered in and out. Cues are verbal and nonverbal forms of communication that give off information about individuals. Thus users need to be more adept at understanding how to use a variety of text-based and image-based forms of communication to manage identity. As Thrasher points out in this section, using online media poorly can limit leadership potential. In her forum, she offers insight into how to use the online portfolio system LinkedIn to create and maintain a sense of professionalism.

Erving Goffman's (1959) work on how we attempt to use communication for how others see us, known as impression management, is a useful frame for understanding these online dynamics. He compares our interactions to life on stage. In this framework, there is a front stage on which we perform and manage identity, and there is a back stage. The front stage includes

Gender, Communication, and the Leadership Gap, pages 287–289
Copyright © 2017 by Information Age Publishing
All rights of reproduction in any form reserved.

verbal and nonverbal communication and is a strategic negotiation between the individual and the audience. The back stage, then, is where users can drop their guard and be more authentic. As Goffman (1959) writes, "when an individual enters the presence of others, they commonly seek to acquire information about him or bring into play information about him already possessed" (p. 1). Online forms of communication allow users to negotiate and manage their impressions through online profiles or interactive communication on social media platforms (Cunningham, 2013). In some ways, users have more control over the impressions they make online because they can consciously choose images and text to create a specific image. However, forms of online communication are also interactive, and thus impression management necessarily includes forms of negotiation. Impression management includes the ability to manipulate text and images to create a favorable public image. As Paul and Perrault show in their chapter, "Leader or Lady? The Visual Rhetoric of Hillary Clinton's Twitter Images" (see Chapter 18, this volume), Hillary Clinton was able to create Twitter images that showed her in different frames, including as both a mother and a leader. These images were counter to mainstream media images of Clinton, which often framed her as unfeminine. Instead, the ability to use Twitter helped her control her campaign image.

Social media outlets have grown in the past few years, and it is important for women to understand how to use different platforms for positive impression management. Impression management is especially important for women leaders who are able to use these sites for self-promotion. Self-promotion is a strategy with which women leaders struggle (Holmes, Marra, & Lazzaro-Salazar, 2017). Avoiding self-promotion can be a hindrance to career advancement (Waung, Hymes, Beatty, & McAuslan, 2015). Indeed, as Ibarra and Petriglieri (2016) found, as junior women in leadership craft identity strategies in their organizations to advance into more senior roles, these roles became unattainable. Ibarra and Petriglieri (2016) use the term "impossible selves" to refer to the struggle that women face to remain authentic while also conforming to masculine norms of the organizations they work in (p. 1).

The chapters in this section offer some guidance for how women can use social media to overcome some of these leadership challenges. In her chapter on LinkedIn, Thrasher offers best practices for constructing and maintaining a robust portfolio. As she points out, a poorly constructed profile can lead to a lack of credibility.

A common thread throughout this section is how to use interactive media to promote women's leadership. As Sorenson-Lang points out in her chapter on women church bloggers (see Chapter 19, this volume), these women are able to challenge some of the dominant power structures within the church to offer alternative viewpoints and perspectives. These bloggers are framing a counternarrative that can be powerful for women members of the church.

In addition to the forms of communication that social media affords, it is also important to pay attention to the new forms of work that results from these new technologies. As Hardey finds in her chapter on Tech Cities (see Chapter 16, this volume), these new forms of work can result in amplifying gender inequality under new ideologies that high tech work is more casual and playful. This lack of structure, taken as freedom at face value, could reify gender inequality by requiring more work hours under the guise that there is more independence. The women in Hardey's study also spoke about gender inequality when they looked for investment funding for their startup companies. Here, many of them spoke about the difficulty of not being taken seriously.

Taken together, the chapters in this section offer insight into some of the ways that gender differences in communication occur online and how these differences can help or hinder women in leadership. While we are just scratching the surface of this new area, the research helps provide direction for future studies in digital leadership.

REFERENCES

Cunningham, C. (Ed.). (2013). *Social networking and impression management: Self-presentation in the digital age.* Lanham, MD: Lexington Books.

Goffman, E. (1959). *The presentation of self in everyday life.* New York, NY: Doubleday.

Holmes, J., Marra, M., & Lazzaro-Salazar, M. (2017). Negotiating the tall poppy syndrome in New Zealand workplaces: Women leaders managing the challenge. *Gender and Language, 11*(1), 1–29. doi:10.1558/genl.31236

Ibarra, H., & Petriglieri, J. (2016, March 4). Impossible selves: Image strategies and identity threat in professional women's career transitions. INSEAD Working Paper No. 2016/12/OBH. Retrieved from SSRN: https://ssrn.com/abstract=2742061

Walther, J. B., & Parks, M. R. (2002). Cues filtered out, cues filtered in: Computer-mediated communication relationships. In M. L. Knapp & J. A. Daly (Eds.), *The handbook of interpersonal communication* (3rd ed., pp. 529–563). Thousand Oaks, CA: SAGE.

Waung, M., Hymes, R., Beatty, J. E., & McAuslan, P. (2015). Self-promotion statements in video resumes: Frequency, intensity, and gender effects on job applicant evaluation. *International Journal of Selection and Assessment, 23*(4), 345–360. doi:10.1111/ijsa.12119

.

CHAPTER 16

THEORIZING AND RESEARCHING GENDER AND DIGITAL LEADERSHIP IN "TECH CITIES"

Mariann Hardey
Durham University

One manager in Silicon Valley (California, USA) stated,

> I am the only female manager in the Tech group where I work. I am the lowest paid, the last one to get asked questions, and I work the longest and the hardest (in my opinion), etc. They [her colleagues] look at me as "mom." I could never be their equal, let alone a mentor, investor, or CEO. Wait until you get older, fatter, and grey :-)—then you're really invisible.

The purpose of this chapter is to identify how social media and digital work environments impact leadership effectiveness for women workers and entrepreneurs who work in "Tech Cities." The chapter benefits from longitudinal data collected from women working in Tech Cities known as London's *Silicon Roundabout,* New York's *Silicon Alley,* and California's *Silicon Valley.* The chapter sets out in identifying the attitudes towards and

Gender, Communication, and the Leadership Gap, pages 291–310
Copyright © 2017 by Information Age Publishing
All rights of reproduction in any form reserved.

expectations of professional roles and behavior of women among these communities and significance for various cultures of professional work, organization, and behavior across the tech industry.

Among other topics, the chapter's focus is on the identity of, and access to, women engineers, game developers, and chief executive officers (CEOs) whose career progression reveals a complex hierarchy and dynamics of working in a Tech City. Tech Cities provide important social, commercial, and professional spaces. The economic impact of tech companies and the dot.com boom has become a familiar story in the media. This story also features as entertainment, such as HBO's comedy series *Silicon Valley*, which reinforces the "hyper-masculine alpha-bro" heritage of internet companies (Raftery, 2016, para. 6). The idea that vested interests, including the power investment and enterprise of business, have an important role to play in shaping women's leadership positions in technology may seem obvious to those involved with the digital and technology-based industries. However, very few would readily associate the sector with equality or a shining beacon of ideals and practices around gender. To give some context, many companies and organizations are only just beginning to look at equal rights or to take action to address inequality. According to the Silicon Valley Index (Joint Venture, 2015), men in the Silicon Valley earned as much as 61% more than their female counterparts. In 2016, Suzanne McGee, writing for *The Guardian*, launched a blistering attack on a patriarchal technology industry, writing, "Anyone who has looked in even a cursory fashion at the economics of the technology universe shouldn't be surprised by the existence of a gender pay gap" (para. 9). In other words, McGee, like many others, accused those working in Silicon Valley of endorsing the harassment of women in the name of a "brogrammer" culture (para. 18).

In the context of this edited volume about women and leadership, a key feature of the chapter is to give a voice to the women who are the workers within these Tech Cities. The women involved with this research experience tech networks that are teeming with sexism and chauvinism. To ensure this narrative is straightforward for the reader, a degree of story-like reflection is required. To begin, we hear accounts from three different women, each of whom is a CEO, holds a significant leadership position, and has established a business in a Tech City. Each sets out her individualized narrative, but taken together, the collective experiences reveal how gendered categories and leadership positions are lived by "women in tech" in Tech Cities.

WHY TECH CITIES?

Technology and, by extension, the "tech industry" are often lauded in a socially liberal rhetoric that emphasizes the way they allow multiple methods of working, networking, and commercial experience that help to improve business opportunities that otherwise would not have been possible. Yet, there are significant variations in the social and cultural contexts that define the "workplace," and our very perception of gendered roles share common perspective with a substantial body of theory based in the premise of co-construction of work and methods of working, for example, Jackson, Poole, and Kuhn (2002) and more recently the experiences of new technologies by women and their use for "work," by Webster (2013). In part because of the rate of emergence of new technologies and, thus, the conditions of work, we lack the adequate resources to understand and assess technologies' relationships to our work, to our organizations (Grint & Woolgar, 2013), and to our experiences within tech communities. Most recently, Irani (2015) identifies with the culture of "microwork" to refer to the division of labor and kinds of workers produced in an information-rich society. In this context, Tech Cities provide an interesting site for inquiry into emerging cultures of work and relationships.

The area of California's Silicon Valley holds a reputation as a place for startups, entrepreneurs, and the elite in tech. Recently, two other sites of interest have emerged designed to repeat the success of "The Valley": London's Silicon Roundabout and New York's Silicon Alley. The context for this discussion is taken from data collected at each of the three sites from women who work in technology.

METHODS

Having pointed out the culture and location of Tech Cities, along with the numerical dominance of men in high-achieving roles (e.g., CEO, Angel Investor) in the tech sector, this section outlines the methodological approach to extract the data for this study. A research grant from the Durham University Business School, United Kingdom, allowed for interviews to be conducted face-to-face, as well as over Voice over Internet Protocol (VoIP) with women in leadership positions from each Tech City area. Women in positions of leadership and/or who had experience of running their own company were recruited through snowball sampling that included the launch and promotion of the study through the research website that was launched in 2014.[1]

The data collection also included a series of seminars and workshops that took place at various marketing and conference events at each of the sites over a two-year period. To date, 268 women have been interviewed. Interview questions were free forming and open, designed to capture different work aspirations along with the educational and career choices of the interviewees. The existence of a significant gender gap in tech was a key departure point for discussion, though other representations of women and men in particular roles formed an important part of the interview themes. This research forms part of a larger study that includes ethnographic data taken from eight CEOs over the course of two years.

Regarding the geography of Tech Cities, I have worked in this area, and gender theory was part of the motivation to study the environment and to perform the interpretative analysis. In terms of contextual approach, there was not any boundary around the ways in which patterns of divisions of labor had been reported prior to the data collection. However, this information acted as "scene-setting" for some of the discussions and business rhetoric around Tech Cities as sites for commercial activity and professional relationships more generally. The three women featured in this chapter were selected from the data as a modest attempt to reflect, in greater depth, the ways that some women have experienced working in Tech Cities. The narratives intersect through a process of coming closer to different issues—such as the relationship between competency, leadership, equality, and gender—and at the same distancing themselves from "trouble-makers" who "make it difficult to avoid subjecting themselves to sexism." This final aspect is complex, highlighting a need to voice "a problem," and revealing a particular set of deficiencies that other women may have who "like to draw attention to themselves."

In this chapter, the three narratives are not intended to be representative, but indicative of the culture and professional roles experienced by these women. Using their narratives in this way allows specific dimensions to emerge around fluctuating personal and professional investment in leadership and business. Each of these women has worked within large tech companies (of more than 500 employees), has set up her own business, and is currently positioned as a CEO with at least one business in a Tech City. To protect the identities of the women, all names and identifying information have been changed.

THE NARRATIVES FROM TECH CITIES

At the foundations of the Tech Cities are a set of gendered expectations, physical and digital spaces, and behavior. The prevailing theme is a profound and acutely felt set of hierarchal relations. The three women I have spoken to describe themselves as leaders and hold leadership roles.

Narrative 1: Working With Toxic Masculinity

I begin by focusing on the experience of Natalie (Tech City, London), who before becoming a CEO and launching her own tech company in 2014 based in London's Shoreditch tech village, had held a series of junior roles as a marketing executive, social media manager, and event organizer. In Natalie's own words:

> I hope that my experience doesn't troll (see below) as something like an "all men are like this" response. Most of the behaviors I have come across are from entitled (juvenile) men cashing in on their level of affluence and influence in the tech industry. I came to Shoreditch to learn everything I could about the tech business, and so I could set up and be in charge of my own startup. It was never the plan to be working for someone else. So I had to do a lot of networking. I started at the drinkabouts where it's about just meeting people after work. This was a continuation of work as I was trying to meet the right kinds of people who could invest in my business. I had a few false starts; one guy who I thought was interested in my business idea was (and I quote) "in it for the great lay." Something I was supposed to take away as a compliment. The idea of there being equal opportunities and pathways in tech must be known and acknowledged as one of the main causes of the toxic masculinity that exists, especially at the investment pitches. Often you're the only woman in the room who is pitching. Other women cover the social media and marketing and PR.

Natalie mentioned a concern about her experience being "trolled." To give some context, the phrases, "troll," "trolling," and "to be trolled," refer to the way an internet post along with the author's identity are reposted, commented upon, and made fun of in order to upset the original author and to provoke a response from others. There have been a number of recent cases in which women have been subject to abuse from other internet users when they have spoken out against sexism in the workplace, particularly in the tech industry (see Kasperkevic, 2016). A few of the women I talked to have offered tantalizing insight into the importance of networks, and this is often comprised of outsiders' perspectives of her leadership position and her professional experience within which her leadership and subsequent networks are known. The resulting imbalance, made up of often inappropriate and condescending behavior as an indication of "where one cornerstone of equality in tech should be" (Natalie speaking), forms part of the negative culture and has created a bad environment.

Narrative 2: Making "The Pitch"

For the next perspective, Rachel (Silicon Alley, New York) is a CEO of a games company based in Silicon Alley and was set up in 2014 with angel investment of $1.4 million. In Rachel's own words:

There's a lot of posturing when making a pitch. You prepare and rehearse, but what it comes down to is the investor's "gut" instinct on the day. Whatever you do in this business you have to be able to think on your feet pretty quickly and make things a matter of professionalism. I've been asked so many times what my boyfriend/partner/husband thinks of my business plan and "about my children." When I am pitching, my method is to deal with the business side of things and keep the personal to a minimum. Faced with the question, "Do I think that my business will succeed?" I have answered, "I'm bringing up five children, so I can face any challenge day or night." That shuts them up. Since that time my mentor has advised against mentioning anything personal. I think we need to tackle the whole culture here. Although carving out enclaves is important, our networks mean that we are a sum of larger parts and we need to make the whole network good, not just parts of it.

The virtue of being in touch over a long period of time (more than three years) with the women in this study is that their experiences draw attention to the professional and social-level relationships, and it reveals the emergence of new dimensions of behavior. We turn now to Julia's narrative; Julia had experienced some of the more negative and oppressive aspects of her working environment in the ecology of Tech Cities.

Narrative 3: The Definition of Prohibited Behavior

In the final narrative, Julia's (Silicon Valley, California) experience is about the extent to which rules about leadership might protect prohibited behavior of the kind at tech events and across social media and networks. Julia is a game developer and designer and has been based in Silicon Valley for 15 years. In Julia's own words:

This is my experience; in fact, after I left my last job, I had to change my Twitter handle just to stop the negativity. After I had gone through *a lot* [speaker's emphasis], I found other women who had faced the same negativity in the same places. The tech industry is expanding its definition of prohibited behavior, but this doesn't go far enough: What about reporting threats of violence to any official authority? And the authorities, I dunno, [do not know] DOING something about it? No one's going to do anything at ground level, not here [Silicon Valley] and certainly not from VCs [Venture Capitalists]. I don't want to sound too dire or pessimistic, but I've asked myself (and others), who are "the authorities" and what are we expecting from them?

In my role now, I can't imagine this going down where I work, but then I'm a VC. Surely the best steps for prevention of any kind of discrimination are (1) avoidance (though you can't avoid being saddled with the label "woman in tech," you can take precautionary measures to protect your identity), (2) observation (you are always being on yellow alert in your day-to-day activities), and (3) self-defense preparedness (whether that means martial arts training, or training with and carrying a weapon like a knife, or a handgun). Yes, I am serious. I can't stress enough that any "authority" will be little help in preventing what amounts to criminal behavior, only responding to it and trying to prosecute those responsible. Even then the system doesn't work so well. Don't rely on the system for the safety of yourself or your family. Turn to the community instead.

The distribution of equality across the Tech Cities is complex. The three narratives above offer a snapshot into experiences and situations that are not uncommon. Some organizations have started to publish survey data about the number of their employees who are the "women in tech." The message appears to suggest that more women in tech means more equal opportunities. Finally, participation in technology by women is clearly influenced by the availability of leadership posts that offer flexible working.

WORK, WOMEN, AND TECH CITIES

Sheryl Sandberg (2013) stated in *Lean In,*

> As more women lean in to their careers, more men need to lean in to their families. We need to encourage men to be more ambitious in their homes. We need more men to sit at the table . . . the kitchen table. (p. 120)

Research on who are (as in how many, at what stage of their career, and why we might label them in this way) the "women in tech" is relatively new, where this gap might be filled is the literature around women in computing and interventions to support diverse working groups (see Aspray, 2016; Craig, 2016; Vitores & Gil-Juárez, 2016). The stories from Natalie, Rachel, and Julia highlight how gender relations have become a central aspect of functioning in professional spaces and of their businesses. While there is a noticeable division of labor—including for men to populate the most sought-after leadership roles as Venture Capitalists (VCs) and CEOs, while women face more marginal roles at the organization's, administrative, and marketing levels—the narratives in the last section draw on the experience of successful women who run their own businesses where the apparent gender discrimination is increasingly viewed as a "necessary evil" of Tech City life.

Sheryl Sandberg's (2013) *Lean In* highlighted the lack of equality between women and men in the tech industry. The women I spoke to found the attitude of Sandberg, the Chief Operating Officer of Facebook, to be "off-putting," "repugnant," "uninspiring," and "unrealistic." The image of Sandberg—a well-known "woman in tech" at the height of her career—was viewed critically by the women interviewed and made more pronouced the difference in men's and women's experience working in the tech sector. Sandberg's success also points to the strength of her professional networks rather than her ability to overcome the inequality in the tech workplace or her professionalism in a leadership role. The women interviewed for this research were aware of Sandberg's (2013) and Huffington's (2016) reputations and the effect of the popular media in drawing attention to their success as "women in tech" and /or an indication of "what women in tech should *look* like." To return to Julia, during our interviews, her focus was on "the insertion and assertion of women's worker rights. . . . I am happy to agree that things are more equal, but that doesn't end the discussion, it points to the very little progress we have had." Reflecting on Sandberg's attitude, we should take issue with such out-dated duality, and one would hope that we are gaining distance from the instrumental arena of feminine and masculine occupations (e.g., Cockburn, 1991; Hochschild, 1983; Hollway, 1984). Of course, given the narratives above, Tech Cities are seen to harbor preconceived orientations in the tech industry that *lean in* to dominant ideas about technology and masculinity. At the same time, there is also a "revolt against" (as Natalie described) why these spaces have been, should be, and are continuing to be experienced as "feminine" or "masculine." Whether such duality exists or not had "left a bad taste" in Julia's mouth about her experience of Silicon Valley. Speaking to me six months after we first met, Julia spoke of how there was "too much effing around the edges of 'equal opportunities' . . . and still they [the event organizers] get strippers for tech events." Rachel was the first to talk about "a vague opposition" to dominant masculinized ideology. Like other women interviewed, Rachel talked openly about her feelings of the "endless cycle" of debate and disappointment in what "are supposed to be life enhancing" careers in tech, "but are pretty depressing at times." An important part of this chapter is to encourage recognition of this breaking up of male domination and masculinity, and also to highlight the difficulties of characterizing a group of women and a group of men under the very large umbrella of tech.

In the wider work and organization literature, conceptions about a socially situated construction of gender discrimination have (thankfully) replaced previous static theory about women and men reproducing roles in the workplace as a result of biology or uniform macro forces (see Acker, 1992; Alvesson, 1998; and Alvesson & Billing, 2009 for more on this discussion). To understand the relationships and networks in Tech Cities, we can turn to social constructivist ideas that "create gender, including gendered forms of subjectivity" (Alvessson, 1998, p. 970). The categorizations of male and female/man and woman are unclear and loose and increasingly viewed as a social construction and function of linguistic meaning (Flax, 1987; Hollway, 1984). This context is important when we consider that the women in tech, like the men in tech, are not simply clocking-in in a conventional manner to a "9–5 job," but they put a lot of emotion, meaning, and personal identity into the work that they do. As a result, the spaces of Tech Cities are often indistinct in the formation of work and social spaces. The women interviewed related to a city-space that Julia described as "held together by networks of networks; of networking of networks . . . a pattern of lifestyle." This point is interesting in terms of how Tech Cities are being experienced as discursive spaces with both physical and digital boundaries to cross and remain, as Rachel observed, "locked into." The social dimensions of Tech Cities and the networking opportunities influence the women working here. Settings are often based on social spaces, offering access to lots of natural light, quasi-communal, and domestic settings.

Natalie talked at length about the design features of her warehouse space. Our first meeting was on site at a viewing of a potential new workspace. We met at a top floor studio in Central Shoreditch, a former warehouse with a large roof terrace with the emphasis on this being "it's outstanding feature as a light, airy and open plan workspace to play in . . . if you're going to sacrifice your home life . . . better in a beautiful environment." Given the fluidity of work space in Tech Cities—often open-plan and communal by design—there is an interesting tendency for these spaces to be based on play and the specific transfer of skills and ideas by a flexible workforce. Certainly all the women interviewed had worked in such warehouse spaces, though their involvement had shifted as they progressed into higher leadership roles. Natalie spoke of her experience:

> Work quickly becomes a floorshow. . . . Okay, there are some aspects of this I wish to clarify: The only part of this I can reply to is that it feels like the use of a "power gesture." I had this kind of issue with one of the directors I used to work for and the degree he kept the company from being fun for me, even though it was the "hot company" everyone was supposed to be into. I don't know how much of this was his lack of experience working with women high up in the business versus his lack of sufficiently distinct character. He oozed the kind of dominant masculine culture typical here, and this fed into my creative space. It's this kind of dominant culture that feeds itself, . . . then this kind of harassment becomes invisible. . . . In other words, you can't say that's what's going on, cos [because] the deal you've made is by not saying anything means that they can't harass you. It's a subtle form of control that ensures you always identify with the harasser and it's grossly enabling—though they make out they're being charming. Working as a CEO today, I rarely have the same problem with my team. There's definitely an art form/design to creating the right work environment.

McRobbie (2011) reminds us of the many articles and books written recently on the topics of the "precarious labor" and "affective labor" that are understood within the over-arching frame of post-Fordist regimes of production and the difficulty of being able to talk about equality and/or to highlight the significance of divisions defined by gender. The physical spaces of Tech Cities and the combination of thinking about women and employment reflect McRobbie's observation. For example, Rachel's "office" was modeled on the workspace of Facebook's headquarters with meeting rooms made up of beanbags and game consoles to give an informal work environment by combining business and play activities. Talking to women in Tech Cities, we can see how there are efforts to occupy a "secure" and professional space, particularly to protect women from unwanted sexual advances or interactions. The caveat here is particularity: This is not to argue that every woman and man experiences these spaces in an obtusely gendered or sexualized way. However, these spaces reveal gendered and sexual principles, characteristics, expectations, and values. To give an example, the women included in this research have mentioned the ways in which women are given roles that involve "getting their top off" as advertising and promotion at networking and tech events. Working in a Tech City, an area of concern was the way in which women—particularly those in leadership positions—felt that they "had to . . . be in control" of close friendships and relationships so as "not to mislead and end up fighting off an investor when he had another idea." In all this, there are hidden hierarchies of power joined with financial control of the running, ownership, and coordination of tech companies in Tech Cities. Taken together, the experiences at the bottom of the ladder can be, as Rachel disclosed early on in our exchanges how she felt

> limited with what you can do because of the view of women [and] you're unlikely to be going up the ladder, or if you do get there it's because a man got you there. I don't think it's a gender thing, so much as how the tech culture just is.

Given such experiences, we might speculate as to the different impacts women in leadership positions hold in Tech Cities. At this level, Saskia Sassen's (2002) work on global cities and civil society enables us to think about the influence of multiple localizations of social and cultural artifacts that are part of global circuits and trans-boundary networks.

The three women leaders interviewed here report two main sources of tension in Tech Cities: the expectation around the professional roles and leadership positions of both women and men, and the endemic culture that one interviewee said "acts like a glass cliff." A particular issue is the values most visible reproduce sexist cultural stereotypes (e.g., events hosted by bikini-clad women along with entertainment by strippers), all male-panels leading discussion and debate, and male-dominated control of investment and employment. Together these heighten tensions and practices within and around Tech Cities in terms of the promotion of equality, expectations in the kinds of working practices available, and how these both combine, as one interviewee, speaking after a tech event in Silicon Valley, observed, "with more complexity and more sexism." With very little visible or impactful counter messages, Tech Cities seem to be spaces that indicate an interest in gender equality without any proper legislation or support to the women and men in tech who want to achieve a fairer balance. The business, organization, and work literature about the tech community has traditionally addressed this unequal balance through recommendations for direct and instrumental measures from policy makers. What we are trying to do here is to investigate and critically address the experience of "women in tech" as they are situated within professional and social networks. While this is not an entirely pessimistic scenario—the women discussed here *are* successful and highly influential—there continue to be reports of the "insignificant improvement" in the proportion of women working in technology or those deployed in work that requires computer science background (see Vitores and Gil-Juárez, 2016, pp. 666–667). In short, generating theoretical discussion and providing new policy for the future of the Tech Cities and relationships therein requires more than a theory of business, work, organization, and technology.

SYMBOLISM IN TECH CITIES

Doing the research of Tech Cities occupies social, cultural, and professional spaces well beyond the appropriation of organization and business networks. Simply put, the "women in tech" label does not tell us anything specific about equality or what makes for a positive or negative experience. After all, a set of relations within physical and digital environments would still encompass women in tech regardless of their characterization. For clarity, it would be useful to return to the first discussion point in this chapter about how we approach a problem that has a clever marketing and media name, "women in tech," but little understanding of the social, cultural, and professional environment within which the "women in tech" work. This is, I argue, a necessary step in order understand how the spaces of Tech Cities define the experiences of individuals.

An interesting incident took place during one of my interviews at a startup in California while the annual company photo was taking place. Founded in 2013, the company is a mobile video marketing company that designs software to promote consumers' use of in-app navigation and in-browser video promotion. The company photo that year had male tech workers standing up and the women workers periphery or kneeling at the front on the floor of the picture. I was struck by this symbolism and asked the CEO about it, who replied that the composition that "it was unintentional" and where individuals were placed "had been up to the photographer." Speaking to some of the women who were included in the image, one said, "I wish we were more integrated as a workforce; it feels like we're being put at the front [of the picture] to make a point, and it is a bit staged." Another made the point that this activity (like many others) "is a misguided promotion thing, I don't think I've seen a company photo that didn't look the same." Talking about equality for workers in tech around the label "women in tech," another colleague added:

> I don't think people will pursue this far enough; like today it's been funny to point out, and I think it's important to even point out the small stuff like this [staff photo], even in passing, to demonstrate the larger point that being a part of the label as a "woman in tech" is often exhausting because there's SO much of the small stuff (micro-aggressions, micro-sexism, micro-flirting and so on etc. etc.).

To say that investigations of equality in the tech industry may be condensed into the sum of the experiences of those who can be labelled as the "women in tech" completely ignores the sum of the experiences and actions of individuals as well as the pathways and flows that relationships within and across the Tech Cities create. The sequence of events at the company above is in some ways a very small incident, yet it signals an important and impactful reinforcement of potential for boundaries between women and men in these spaces. The environment of Tech Cities appears to offer a compelling (and often convincing) account of the future of tech and, in particular, the pervasive dissolution of the boundary around women in tech (see Baldry, et al.'s volume on the meaning of work). There is also growing literature focusing on the education of technology and the opportunities open to young people based on promoting equality (see Henwood, 2000). The dissolution is professional, social, physical, and digital; the informal or professional relationships seem to recognize there are many nuanced and subtle limits on the sorts of experiences that can be fostered in Tech Cities that this study highlights. The symbolism of these spaces also provides a rich, evocative characterization of the so-called "small stuff" harms (such as those noted above) caused by external scrutiny. One male CEO's objection to the sheer unfairness of "being judged" by one staff photo rings true in this case. Yet, again, it is the way this event and its symbolism moves beyond being one incident and is reflected in a pattern of networking events, marketing emails, and invitations to an "exclusive club" based on "gentleman's events," as well as online activities that offer new opportunities for how we might unpack the environment of Tech Cities beyond the physical walls of workspace.

I AM A "WOMAN IN TECH"

In conducting this research, I draw inspiration from other feminists, social scientists, and organization and management theorists who have been inspired by their personal experience and interest in patterns of gender inequality (see Knipfer, Shaughnessy, Hentschel, & Schmid, 2016). Research on Tech Cities is primarily concerned with the tech industry as a whole and is only just becoming an important research field. One does not have to spend very long in the tech community to notice that both the physical and digital spaces of Tech Cities by no means stand for the equality strivings of technology. According to data from the U.S. Department of Labor, the percentage of women working in management positions in computer and information systems remains at around 27.2% (Torpey, 2017). A closer look at the number of women in leadership roles shows significantly fewer women occupying positions to influence a company's strategic direction, research and development, and leadership (CEOs and investors). Recognizing a new turn and/or "revolution" in the field of technology is not merely about the hardware and the software; it requires a deeper understanding of their digital and physical environments. The values of what Castells (2011) identifies as those of the "information age" are those in which individuals are defined through their choices as consumers and users of technology and how they share information. These everyday behaviors show how our actions as situated subjects are manifest and repeated across a number of dimensions and, indeed, the tools with which important policies and legislations may "claim shelter" (see Cohen, 2012a, 2015). If we turn to the liberal and cosmopolitan contexts of business and workers' rights, up to now, typically these have not paid "attention to the *processes* by which power relations are encoded in technologies and artefacts" (emphasis added, Cohen, 2012b, pp. 148–149). The argument being highlighted here is the way in which subject-formation holds both creative and spatial significance with varying levels of transparency and power-knowledge. As an indication, the narrative of these Tech Cities is incomplete; the tech industry has been highly vocal in the media, in making claims about the clarity of equality and "grassroots" solutions (e.g., Winley, 2017). However, the enduring unequal opportunities craft limitations on top of such initiatives as the "Women in Microsoft," "Women Tech Makers" (partnered with Google), and President Obama's "ConnectED Initiative" (sponsored by Apple), because the tech industry is structurally unable to address the wide range of systemic issues women in the sector raise. From the larger study one woman investor noted a "culture of sexism" as a common barrier to business success. This type of argument has a myriad of foundations but generally assumes that Tech Cities provide opportunities to raise people up, depending upon what is considered to be the prevailing culture of the time. It was felt that providing women with extra resources and initiatives would encourage them to solve their (to quote a CEO from California) "own problems."

The focus in this study is women's experiences of leadership in Tech Cities. In the context of the interviews, the label "women in tech"—referring to any woman who might choose to work on computer hardware, software or the flow of digital information systems—was treated negatively. From the analysis of the interview data, the gender equity programs used to provide support and promote the visibility of women working across the tech industry were generally welcomed. However, the characterizations of women's participation gave rise to related concerns in the following areas:

1. First, it was felt that the major companies (e.g., Microsoft, Apple, Google, and Yahoo) that had increased the quota of women employees were, as one CEO put it, "undeserving" of the accolade they received in supporting the long-term participation of women in the tech sector.
2. Second, a board director noted that the observation that women were significantly less likely to "have the time" to commit to leadership positions was misleading, and it was noted that there was a considerable lack of support in this area, especially for women with families.
3. Third, a venture capitalist from Silicon Valley realized that there were common misapprehensions about the way that women work and the roles they were expected to undertake, "often to fulfill the marketing requirements."

In summary, women in this study felt optimistic about the opportunities within Tech Cities because of the geography of networks and visibility of professional connections. Yet, it was also felt that within these sites there were often misaligned processes to support equality, and the same issues had taken on greater significance since the investment in, and identification of, locations supporting high-tech SMEs.

DIVISION OF LABOR IN TECH CITIES

The way in which researchers might be interested in the productivity of companies based in the Tech Cities requires further investigation, and we can make a strong case to widen the professional context of work and the workers in these spaces (see, for example, Crick & Spence, 2005). A significant factor for this research has been the absence of women in long-term leadership roles and the inclusion of women onto boards to fill what one interviewee referred to as "the silk on seats" quota. This sense of absence and displacement implies that women do not have a place at the highest positions nor are they seen to make important decisions. The widespread gender difference reflects a particular kind of power-knowledge at the heart of work-spaces, and there is an important history around the workplace, the visibility of gender and power (e.g., Hochschild, 2003), and, more recently, entrepreneurship and networking (Scarmozzino, Corvello, & Grimaldi, 2017).

In the context of this research, it was felt that within the Tech Cities, certain roles, tasks, spaces, and events were gendered. To give an example, one interviewee who attended the well-known annual security and hackers conference *DefCon* in Las Vegas felt there were "very strong" female and male dimensions, and certain events were deliberately marketed to appeal (to quote the interviewee) to "masculine tastes" (e.g., bikini-clad event). Another woman interviewed related how, at one of the conferences she attended, they gave all the women "game cards" each with a different female action figure on it to play and offer favors to the male attendees as a "getting to know you" icebreaker. From the larger study, every woman had observed and mentioned the presence of bikini-attired hosts and noted that it was typical to see all-male panels. The experiences of these women reveal that there are implicit gender hierarchies at play in these spaces (see also Hacker, 2017).

The research showed the striking gap between the status of men and women in the Tech Cities, which suggests that breaking down these barriers is problematic—and doing so is often the task of women (e.g., Roberts 2016). Something similar may be identified from other creative and prosperous industries (e.g., advertising, PR, service, and financial sectors). These sectors have corresponding roles for women and men in which a version or form of a feminine or masculine identity is central (classic literature that has informed this research includes Alvesson, 1998; Cross and Bagilhole, 2002; see also Simpson's 2004 work on the experiences of men in female-dominated professions). The recent work of Faulkner (2007, 2009) contextualizes the interrelationship between technical and social boundaries and the impact on identity; Hatmaker (2013) also explores similar themes among engineers and considers how identity impacts on women working "in a gendered profession" (p. 382). In addition to these studies, there are opportunities to understand similar context in the emerging spaces and culture of Tech Cities. Perhaps the environment to which we should be looking, not only for inspiration but also for our analysis, should include the physical world of work across the tech communities as well as the social movements that intersect with culture, identity, and equality. We can also consider these intersections by looking at the ways in which Tech Cities enrich diversity and support opportunities for many people to participate in tech communities. Recent initiatives—for example, Women at Microsoft, IAMCP Women in Technology Network (Microsoft Partner Network), Association for Computing Machinery–Women, Anita Borg Institute (ABI),

EdTechWomen, Girls Who Code, Hackbright Academy, Ladies Learning Code, Women's Coding Collective, and Women in Technology International—may demonstrate a pro-women stance, yet it is difficult to assess their impact and transference of support in the right areas to achieve equality. Natalie's observation about deepening sexism in the community is telling:

> Yea [sigh and a long pause], it is hard to tell how much sexism is hurting tech... since *all* gender issues are overshadowed by a history of chauvinism and elitism. Also that the media use the concept of "women in tech" as nothing more than a marketing tool to manipulate men doesn't help. Many [women and men] have screamed sexism in one of the most progressive periods working in this industry in recent history and whipped supporters into an attack on anyone who questions these issues. We should be ashamed of using [these] real issues as nothing more than a way to attack other women that "don't fall in line";... *it is disgusting.* Some of the worst sexism I've seen has come from other people working in tech. Like when they dismissed anyone who supports "women in tech" as "just wanting to get laid." (emphasis from original interview)

CONCLUSION

A provocative book on gender can influence the tech community; however, even when part of the theory has been very well developed, key issues can be missed through a lack of context. To make sure this is avoided, the major contribution of this chapter has been to highlight important hermeneutic principles and detail their application to the context of gender and work across social media and in digital environments. If we are to take seriously the ideals of equality and openness of opportunities that technology offers, the answers we provide must remain linked to the realities of lived experiences of women and men working together in Tech Cities. We must find a way to describe what individuals encounter in these environments to enable them to establish and create successfully—and to see beyond the limitations and immediacies of restricted access and sexist marketing stunts to the larger social and cultural patterns. Given the womens' descriptions of women working in Tech Cities, the study of leadership in these spaces is especially problematic for researchers because scholarship in this area is at the nexus of a number of methodological and theoretical anxieties that working in a digital economy highlights acutely. Taking research in this area forward, it will be important to specify whether it is the individuals (both women and men) or the broader patterns of leadership that should be the primary focus for analysis and, thus, the appropriate data and analytical approach for evaluating leadership within Tech Cities. For this study, there was tension between understanding the different versions of leadership and the identifying opportunities afforded by the work environment of Tech Cities. The former included the critical review of the linear and hierarchical vision of leadership. The latter revealed very complex relationships around the culture of tech entirely and methods to support equality and the promotion of women into leadership roles. Each of these points might be criticized for being predicated on a false dichotomy—an extension of the gender-essentializing argument and the not uncommon trap of attributing "male" and "female" characteristics to different roles and behaviors. However, the differences are important to note because they reflect (all the promotion of equality aside) the often-diverging experiences of women and men in Tech Cities and raise fruitful questions regarding the interactions between tech, leadership, and culture. Questioning those experiences opens up the way for new approaches that enable a more concrete concentration of the kinds of commitment, participation, and processes that should attend leadership in Tech Cities. Such approaches, in turn, point toward a more sustained engagement with digital and leadership culture that, up to now, scholars have largely overlooked.

While Tech Cities may radically alter the social bases of traditional work relationships and conventional gender constraints of social interaction, there remain significant gender divisions. However, the picture is not entirely bleak; there is evidence of new opportunities and leadership roles for women. The issues that arise can be addressed as questions of emerging structures of "work" and reorganization of social boundaries that can occur through the mediated interactions on which the community is based, including the culture of "event-based" networking. To take this research forward, my stance is to problematize the category of "women in tech" and to make more visible the positive impact of spaces within and around Tech Cities. The scope of future research is ambitious, seeking to take issue with assertions in key literature that "women in tech" is a useful description of gendered dynamics and, thus, that women's presence in these spaces is a threat that can displace or disrupt professional and leadership success. In taking issue with such questions, it is hoped that we can address key aspects of gender and agency in such highly dynamic social, business, and leadership contexts.

NOTE

1. Gender in Tech Cities (GiTC). http://gitc.io/

REFERENCES

Acker, J. (1992). Sex roles to gendered institutions. *Contemporary Sociology, 21*(5), 565–569.

Alvesson, M. (1998). Gender relations and identity at work: A case study of masculinities and femininities in an advertising agency. *Human Relations, 51*(8), 969–1005.

Alvesson, M., & Billing, Y. D. (2009). *Understanding gender and organizations* (2nd ed.). London, England: SAGE.

Aspray, W. (2016). *Women and underrepresented minorities in computing: A historical and social study.* Cham, Switzerland: Springer.

Baldry, C., Bain, P., Taylor, P., Hyman, J., Scholaros, D., Marks, A.,...Bunzel, D. (2007). *The meaning of work in the new economy.* Basingstoke, England: Palgrave Macmillan.

Castells, M. (2011). *The rise of the network society: The information age: Economy, society, and culture* (Vol. 1). New York, NY: Wiley.

Cockburn, C. (1991). *In the way of women: Men's resistance to sex equality in organizations.* Ithaca, NY: ILR Press.

Cohen, J. E. (2012a). What privacy is for. *Harvard Law Review, 126,* 1904–1933.

Cohen, J. E. (2012b). Configuring the networked citizen. In A. Sarat, L. Douglas, & M. M. Umphrey (Eds.), *Imagining new legalities: Privacy and possibilities in the 21st century* (pp. 129–153). Stanford, CA: Stanford University Press.

Cohen, J. E. (2015). Studying law studying surveillance. *Surveillance & Society, 13*(1), 91–101.

Craig, A. (2016). Theorising about gender and computing interventions through an evaluation framework. *Information Systems Journal, 26*(6), 585–611. doi:10.1111/isj.12072

Crick, D., & Spence, M. (2005). The internationalisation of "high performing" UK high-tech SMEs: A study of planned and unplanned strategies. *International Business Review, 14*(2), 167–185. doi:10.1016/j.ibusrev.2004.04.007

Cross, S., & Bagilhole, B. (2002). Girls' jobs for the boys? Men, masculinity and non-traditional occupations. *Gender Work and Organization, 9*(2), 204–226. doi:10.1111/1468-0432.00156

Faulkner, W. (2007). "Nuts and bolts and people": Gender-troubled engineering identities. *Social Studies of Science, 37*(3), 331–356.

Faulkner, W. (2009). Doing gender in engineering workplace cultures. II. Gender in/authenticity and the in/visibility paradox. *Engineering Studies, 1*(3), 169–189. doi:10.1080/19378620903225059

Flax, J. (1987). Postmodernism and gender relations in feminist theory. *Signs, 12*(4), 621–643.

Grint, K., & Woolgar, S. (2013). *The machine at work: Technology, work and organization.* New York, NY: John Wiley & Sons.

Hacker, S. (2017). *Pleasure, power and technology: Some tales of gender, engineering, and the cooperative workplace.* London, England: Routledge.

Hatmaker, D. M. (2013). Engineering identity: Gender and professional identity negotiation among women engineers. *Gender, Work & Organization, 20*(4), 382–396. doi:10.1111/j.1468-0432.2012.00589.x

Henwood, F. (2000). From the woman question in technology to the technology question in feminism: Rethinking gender equality in IT education. *European Journal of Women's Studies, 7*(2), 209–227.

Hochschild, A. R. (1983). *The managed heart.* Berkeley: University of California Press.

Hochschild, A. R. (2003). *The managed heart: Commercialization of human feeling.* Los Angeles, CA: University of California Press.

Hollway, W. (1984). Women's power in heterosexual sex. *Women's Studies International Forum, 7*(1), 63–68.

Huffington, A. S. (2016). *The sleep revolution: Transforming your life, one night at a time.* New York, NY: WH Allen.

Irani, L. (2015). The cultural work of microwork. *New Media & Society, 17*(5), 720–739.

Jackson, M. H., Poole, M. S., & Kuhn, T. (2002). The social construction of technology in studies of the workplace. In L. A. Levrouw & S. Livingstone (Eds.), *Handbook of new media: Social shaping and consequences of ICTs* (pp. 236–253). London, England: SAGE.

Joint Venture. (2015). 2015 Silicon Valley index. *Silicon Valley Institute for Regional Studies.* Retrieved from https://www.jointventure.org/images/stories/pdf/index2015.pdf

Kasperkevic, J. (2016, January 12). Sexism valley: 60% of women in Silicon Valley experience harassment. *The Guardian.* Retrieved from https://www.theguardian.com/technology/2016/jan/12/silicon-valley-women-harassment-gender-discrimination

Knipfer, K., Shaughnessy, B., Hentschel, T., & Schmid, E. (2016). Unlocking women's leadership potential: A curricular example for developing female leaders in academia. *Journal of Management Education, 41*(5), 272–302.

McGee, S. (2016, March 6). Silicon Valley's gender problem extends beyond pay gap. *The Guardian.* Retrieved from https://www.theguardian.com/money/us-money-blog/2016/mar/06/silicon-valley-women-tech-industry-gender-pay-gap-bias

McRobbie, A. (2011). Reflections on feminism, immaterial labour and the post-Fordist regime. *New Formations, 70,* 60–76. doi:10.3898/NEWF.70.04.2010

Raftery, B. (2016). The *Silicon Valley* boys aren't just brilliant—they're part of a comedy revolution. Retrieved from https://www.wired.com/2016/03/silicon-valley-new-comedy-economy/

Roberts, T. (2016). Women's use of participatory video technology to tackle gender inequality in Zambia's ICT sector. In *Proceedings of the Eighth International Conference on Information and Communication Technologies and Development* (article number 6). ACM. June. doi:10.1145/2909609.2909673

Sandberg, S. (2013). *Lean in: Women, work, and the will to lead.* New York, NY: Alfred A. Knopf.

Sassen, S. (2002). Global cities and diasporic networks: Microsites in global civil society. In Helmut Anheier et al. (Eds.), *Global civil society 2002* (pp. 217–238). Retrieved from http://transnationalism.uchicago.edu/Diasporic%20Network.pdf

Scarmozzino, E., Corvello, V., & Grimaldi, M. (2017). Entrepreneurial learning through online social networking in high-tech startups. *International*

Journal of Entrepreneurial Behavior & Research, 23(3), 406–425. doi:10.1108/IJEBR-12-2015-0302

Simpson, R. (2004). Masculinity at work: The experiences of men in female dominated occupations. *Work, Employment & Society, 18*(2), 349–368. doi:10.1177/09500172004042773

Torpey, E. (2017, March). Women in management. *United States Department of Labor.* Retrieved from https://www.bls.gov/careeroutlook/2017/data-on-display/women-managers.htm

Vitores, A., & Gil-Juárez, A. (2016). The trouble with 'women in computing': a critical examination of the deployment of research on the gender gap in computer science. *Journal of Gender Studies, 25*(6), 666–680. doi:10.1080/09589236.2015.1087309

Webster, J. (2013). *Shaping women's work: Gender, employment and information technology.* London, England: Routledge.

Winley, B. (2017, March 29). A grassroots approach to solving diversity in tech. *Forbes.* Retrieved from https://www.forbes.com/sites/richwinley/2017/03/29/a-grassroots-approach-to-solving-diversity-in-tech/#9a1d1a53e930

CHAPTER 17

THE LINKS OF LINKEDIN

Impression Management
on Professional Social Media

Evelyn H. Thrasher
Western Kentucky University

In a series of leadership development workshops held from 2015 to 2016, participants were asked to describe a leader. The groups included male and female participants, crossing generational boundaries and representing diverse backgrounds. The list generated from their responses included perseverance, influence, desire, caring, willingness to work, upfront, collaboration, support from above, ability, knowledge, born, learned, genuine, vision, history, trust, situational, timing, steadfast, consistent, empowering, motivating, intelligent, humility, and enable. While much of this list is dependent upon face-to-face encounters with the leader, technology affords us the opportunity to get to know leaders through a number of means unavailable as recently as 10 to 15 years ago. Arguably, most are more accurately assessed during face-to-face interactions, yet the evolution of social media means an online persona is more critical today than at any other point in time. But, how does a person convey or demonstrate leadership qualities

Gender, Communication, and the Leadership Gap, pages 311–325
Copyright © 2017 by Information Age Publishing
All rights of reproduction in any form reserved.
311

effectively on social media? And, does the individual's gender bias our perceptions of him or her on social media? If we argue that our impression of a leader is also affected by his or her communication style and ability, then forming an impression of a leader based on a social media profile becomes increasingly difficult. Yet, in today's world, many organizations seek out potential leaders online and form a first impression based on a digital profile.

This chapter explores the concept of impression management as it relates to leadership, especially highlighting the nuances of impression management related to gender. Furthermore, this chapter discusses LinkedIn, a social media platform designed for professional networking, the sharing of business and industry news, and the creation of a professional portfolio. With that in mind, the chapter offers a series of suggested actions to assist leaders and aspiring leaders with the creation of an effective LinkedIn profile that supports impression management and assists with reducing gender bias. Each characteristic given above is tied to one or more of the suggested actions within LinkedIn to further illustrate the power of social media, particularly LinkedIn, to broaden one's network and to afford a person the opportunity to reach a far broader audience than is possible with face-to-face communication.

IMPRESSION MANAGEMENT AND LEADERSHIP

Impression management is "the process of controlling how one is perceived by other people" (Leary, 1996, p. 2) and "any behavior by a person that has the purpose of controlling or manipulating the attributions and impressions formed of that person by others" (Tedeschi & Riess, 1981, p. 3). Goffman (1959) originally conceived of the idea of impression management when he wrote about the presentation of self and his idea that we are all simply actors creating a performance. He suggested that individuals will act in ways that are appropriate for the setting, audience, and situation. Thus, one may act in a professional manner while in the workplace, but act in a more informal manner in a casual setting with friends or family. In other words, people will adapt their behaviors to the context presented them. Goffman (1959) tells us that people, also called performers, "offer their observers an impression that is idealized" (p. 35). While impression management was originally conceived of for face-to-face encounters, Becker and Stamp (2005) found that impression management also occurs online and through digital communication. And, interestingly, social media is perfectly suited to the idea of self-presentation through performance (Goffman, 1959).

Social media affords us the ability to be whomever we choose through our online persona. Kuznekoff (2013) suggests that people engage in impression management on social media for one or more of the following reasons. First, the individual may desire to be perceived a certain way for a specific context, a way that is in keeping with the context of the social media. Second, the individual may desire to display his or her ideal persona, a persona that may be an exaggerated version of him or herself but that will be better perceived than a more honest representation. Third, the individual may desire an impression that is consistent with the purpose of the chosen platform.

Regarding Kuznekoff's suggestions, gender may influence one's approach to impression management. In fact, "around one-half of the 'digital divide' between men and women on the Internet is fundamentally gender related" (Bimber, 2000, p. 868). At the time of Bimber's (2000) research, the digital divide attributed to gender centered on the idea that men were more likely to use the Internet than women. However, in more recent years, researchers have suggested that the gender-related digital divide is more accurately depicted as a difference in how, rather than whether, the Internet is used (Haferkamp, Eimler, Papadakis, & Truck, 2012; Manago, Graham, Greenfield, & Salimkhan, 2008; Torres-Díaz, Duart, Gómez-Alvarado, Marín-Gutiérrez, & Segarra-Faggioni, 2016). For instance, Jackson, Ervin, Gardner, and Schmitt (2001) found that women tend to exhibit online behaviors that are more focused on interpersonal communication and relationships, while men tend to exhibit online behaviors that are more focused on information gathering and task completion. Similarly, Haferkemp et al. (2012) found that men tend to put more emphasis on context because they use social media to find friends and gather information, while women tend to put more emphasis on creating the ideal persona because they often use social media to compare themselves to others. These observed tendencies may influence a person's choice of social media and whether or not to use social media at all (Haferkamp et al., 2012). The tendencies observed on social media are not significantly different from the behaviors observed of males and females in face-to-face encounters. Studies conducted prior to the advent of social media described the face-to-face impression management of males and females in much the same way, suggesting that men are more task-oriented and more focused on gathering information, while women tend to be more social and more focused on cultivating interpersonal relationships (Dolgin & Minowa, 1997, Sattel, 1976; Williams, 1985).

Impression management plays a vital role for leaders in any organization. "Leadership is classically defined as the function of a leader—one who guides, influences, or directs a group" (Friedman, 2013, p. 14). Traditional leadership structures provide a context for impression management that places the leader at the top of a hierarchy with a chain-of-command vertical communication structure. This structure provides the leader with a power of voice and an opportunity to be viewed clearly as a person of authority.

This structure also provides a fairly accurate image of the organizational leadership for those outside the organization, further strengthening the impressions of the leader and affording him or her the power to influence the perceived culture of the organization. However, social media has brought about new leadership challenges, as it allows a more horizontal flow of communication across both internal and external boundaries, making it increasingly difficult to maintain a vertical communication structure. Thus, Friedman (2013) suggests that social media has altered the role of the leader to "empower the group rather than tell it what to do" (p. 14) and to "demonstrate leadership" rather than to "have organizational authority" (p. 14). He further suggests that today's leaders must be comfortable with social media and must lead through "horizontal communications, relationship-building, and context-setting rather than vertical control" (p. 14). If we tie these suggestions back to the work of Jackson et al. (2001) and Haferkamp et al. (2012), we can see that leaders may be equally advantaged and disadvantaged in these new roles based on the impression management tendencies of males to focus on context and females to focus on interpersonal relationships.

Social media affords male leaders the opportunity to define the context and to adapt their communication to best suit the context and to best portray their leadership qualities. The idea of defining the context may be more challenging for female leaders. Yet, leading in a time of social media also requires strong relationship building, a noted strength for female leaders and a weakness for male leaders. Thus, while male and female leaders are traditionally strong relative to one or more aspects of social media-influenced leadership, neither is expertly positioned to address all opportunities and challenges (Haferkamp et al., 2012; Jackson et al., 2001).

Regarding leadership and impression management, social media affords a leader the opportunity to create the image he or she desires others to see. When created and maintained correctly, a digital profile is an opportunity to convey an impression that pushes aside gender norms, stereotypes, or biases that may be exacerbated in face-to-face situations. However, Thomson and Murachver (2001) suggest that gender may still be evident in digital communication because individuals tend to adapt gender-specific language patterns and vocabulary from spoken communication for use in various forms of digital communication. Across the more casual social media platforms, such as Facebook and Instagram, women are more apt to give the impression of being attractive and stylish, while men convey the impression of strength and power (Manago et al., 2008). Women demonstrate a more interpersonal interaction online, while men tend to be more concerned about the completion of tasks or the gathering of information (Haferkamp et al., 2012). Yet, despite the assumption that many embellish or censor their online presence, research suggests that users actually desire to create an authentic online presence that mimics their true persona (Haferkamp et al., 2012).

Tufekci (2008) found that, as in the face-to-face realm, women tend to be more concerned with their existing network of friends and with cultivating relationships on social media, while men tend to be competitive both on- and offline and desire to increase their network. This may pose a challenge for female leaders on LinkedIn, since LinkedIn is intended for the creation of professional networks that may include both old and new acquaintances. This may be easier for men, since they desire to meet new people. Interestingly, though, women tend to spend more time preparing their online profiles than men (Haferkamp et al., 2012), and this may be important, as LinkedIn encourages completeness, thoroughness, and explicit professional identities that will require a dedication to nurturing one's online presence.

IMPRESSION MANAGEMENT ON LINKEDIN

The mission of LinkedIn is "to connect the world's professionals to make them more productive and successful" (How LinkedIn Can Help You, 2017). In April 2017, the site had more than 467 million members worldwide, and claims to be "the world's largest professional network on the Internet" (About LinkedIn, 2017, p. 1). Unlike other social media, such as Facebook, most view LinkedIn as an electronic repository for resumes, biographies, portfolios, and experiences (Liberman, 2013). LinkedIn provides leaders and aspiring leaders a unique opportunity to exercise professional impression management and self-presentation, beyond what is possible only within his or her organization (Liberman, 2013). In fact, Liberman (2013) suggests that LinkedIn is users' way of "ultimately publicizing their identities" (p. 122) and that "self-presentation is perhaps the foremost function of LinkedIn" (p. 122). This selective presentation of oneself on social media is in line with Walther (1996) and Dominick (1999), who found that computer-mediated communication, in general, enables individuals to take advantage of this context to present a more ideal image of themselves. Eagly and Carli (2003) have suggested that effective leadership today is described as communal, interactive, and empowering. Holden and Raffo (2014) suggest that these are characteristics that are traditionally described as feminine. Generational differences may also be playing a role in the changes in characterizations of effective leaders, as the most recent generation (called Generation Y) tends to value leadership characteristics that include fun, informal, and technologically savvy (Holden & Raffo, 2014). LinkedIn allows leaders and aspiring leaders to embrace a more informal presentation of his or her skills, values, and abilities using a digital medium

(Walther, Van der Heide, Kim, Westerman, & Tong, 2008), thus, potentially increasing their appeal to a younger generation of professionals. It is important for a leader to maintain a social media presence that is in keeping with his or her face-to-face presence. For a leader, the LinkedIn presence goes beyond a great profile and an impressive photo. A leader should share his or her insights, link to important literature, and emphasize his or her expertise in a chosen discipline. Just as the bar of professionalism and expertise is raised for leaders in a face-to-face setting, the same is true on social media. Similar to the findings of Dominick (1999) regarding poorly constructed, incomplete personal web pages, a neglected or incomplete LinkedIn presence can be more detrimental to a leader than having no LinkedIn presence at all. A leader should recognize that new professionals may want to connect with him or her, so it is important to be responsive to those requests. Because a leader is generally viewed as an expert in his or her field, it is important to follow the leading trade publications and to share pertinent articles from those publications (Liberman, 2013). Joining industry-related groups and groups designed for specific professional roles will encourage networking and can create an environment of support and professional development. Most will want a leader to demonstrate a commitment to continual professional growth and development, and many will look to that leader's LinkedIn profile to find resources to promote his or her own growth (Liberman, 2013).

As described above, LinkedIn provides a unique medium for professionals at all stages of their careers to connect with other professionals and to make their credentials available for all to see (Thew, 2008). Much like a virtual resume, LinkedIn is an effective outlet for practicing impression management and creating the desired professional image (Liberman, 2013; van Dijck, 2013). LinkedIn is designed to help individuals be professional among a network of peers, colleagues, and mentors; thus, the sections that follow will provide advice and best practices for establishing, building, and maintaining an effective LinkedIn presence. Using many of the characteristics listed in the workshops mentioned in the introduction, the next section looks at how those can best be conveyed on LinkedIn. Each time a characteristic from this list is used, it will be italicized.

Be Trustworthy and Genuine

Dominick (1999) found that a poorly constructed or maintained personal web page created a negative impression of the page's author as either incompetent with digital communication or unprofessional. The same may be true for LinkedIn and the impressions of leaders who fail to maintain their accounts (Singh, 2013). Thus, if an individual cannot, or does not wish to, devote the time necessary to properly populate and maintain a LinkedIn profile, it is best to continue without one (Singh, 2013). While creating the LinkedIn profile, it is best to keep the profile settings private and refrain from adding connections until the profile is sufficiently populated and ready to be viewed and used. As with any other media, the first impression is important. So, publishing a profile while it is still under construction may create a negative first impression, as it will appear sparsely populated and inaccurate. Use the meter available in LinkedIn to know when the profile is close enough to complete to be made available for others to view (Singh, 2013).

The profile picture should convey as much as possible about the leader's style and characteristics. Ragan (1982) analyzed 1,296 yearbook photos and found differences across genders. For instance, females smiled more often and more expansively than males. In addition, females tilted their heads more often and were photographed without glasses more often than males. Interestingly, in 2013, McDermott found similar differences on social media. McDermott (2013) tells us that men are more likely than women to post a full-body photo or a photo that includes at least the upper body, which he attributes to a lack of confidence among females. Thus, women tend to post close-up photos with a head tilt or an attempt to appear approachable (McDermott, 2013). According to McDermott (2013), men will capture their adventures in a profile photo, while women will capture moments or emotions. While these images may be completely appropriate for social networks such as Facebook or Instagram, LinkedIn is intended to reflect professionalism and leadership ability. Thus, according to researchers, regardless of gender, the profile picture should be an accurate representation of the individual as a leader (McDermott, 2013). A professional portrait taken close enough to capture the face and shoulders down to just below the collarbone is generally preferred and conveys a sense of power and control (Rose et al., 2012). A smile is appropriate, as it allows a leader to appear as an expert but also as approachable and human (McDermott, 2013). If a professional head shot has been published through other outlets, such as a current employer's website or for speaking engagements or other publicity, use of that photo will build continuity across LinkedIn and other media (van Dijck, 2013).

Media scholars describe a phenomenon called "drench hypothesis" that suggests that exposure to consistent media representations can lead to an adoption of those representations as accurate and expected (Ezzedeen, 2015; Gerbner, Gross, Morgan, & Signorelli, 1986; Gordon, 2008). Tannen (1993) describes this phenomenon as being "marked" and suggests that women's attire, hairstyle, and makeup mark them, regardless of choice. In other words, the style and color of a woman's attire, including clothing and shoes, may be perceived as professional or not based on preconceived notions of what a female leader should wear. Women have a wide range of attire from which to choose, and each choice conveys a certain message about a woman, depending upon the perceptions of those who see her. The drench hypothesis would suggest that the media plays a significant role in defining the markedness associated with women's attire and styling (Ezzedeen, 2015). Thus, unlike their male counterparts, it is not possible for a woman to choose attire and styling that are unmarked (Tannen, 1993). For example, television and movies most often portray female leaders in an arguably masculine ensemble that includes a dark suit, dark shoes, a white blouse, and a conservative hairstyle such as a bun or ponytail. Something with more color or a more modern look may be perceived as less professional or inappropriate for a female leader. Considering the drench hypothesis and markedness, it may be in the best interest of leaders and aspiring leaders to choose attire for the LinkedIn profile photo that is consistent with media representations. A suit will likely be preferred; but, if desired, a female might consider a colored blouse underneath to add a bit of fun and informality that enhances the image of approachability and *genuineness* (McDermott, 2013; Tannen, 1993).

Schramm (2014) found that, as is generally true for a resume, most executives will not look past the headline and summary of a LinkedIn profile unless they are compelled to do so. Thus, the author suggests that the headline and summary should be informative, especially since these are publicly viewable. Schram (2014) further suggests that the summary should include the person's area(s) of expertise, responsibilities, current position and organization, and any keywords that are commonly used in the specific field or discipline. If the individual's current job title is unique and not easily interpreted, then ensure that the summary clarifies the current position and responsibilities. A gender-neutral vocabulary will aid in removing gender bias from the evaluations of the profile (Schramm, 2014).

Scholars have noted that the most effective professional pages populate and maintain all applicable sections of LinkedIn, including honors, awards, skills, education, and organizations (Leiser, 2013; Singh, 2013). According to the research, presenting one's professional journey on LinkedIn will demonstrate *perseverance* and will *motivate* others who aspire to be leaders. Any remaining profile content may help to demonstrate *history, knowledge,* the *learned* aspects of leadership, *situational* leadership, and the individual's *desire* to grow as a leader (Leiser, 2013; Singh, 2013). In addition, commonalities with others on LinkedIn can lead to stronger connections, increased credibility, and *collaboration.* Keep all profile information up-to-date. This does not mean that updates are necessary every day, but perhaps consider adding a task list item for the same day of each month as a reminder to make any necessary updates (Leiser, 2013; Singh, 2013).

Be Active

Connections in LinkedIn, just as in business, can be important for building one's reputation as a leader. In general, men are better at building connections, as they tend to use social media to increase their network. Women, on the other hand, tend to prefer smaller networks that allow for the cultivation of relationships (Jackson et al., 2001; Haferkamp et al., 2012). However, while women may have to work harder in this area of LinkedIn, it is important for leaders to have a larger number of connections. Whether warranted or not, *influence* and successful leadership ability are often judged by the number of connections (i.e., followers). Experts in a field are likely to have at least 500 connections (Schramm, 2014). In addition, connections with both similar and differing points of view will show a breadth of networking. A diverse network can send a more powerful message to others because it suggests a willingness to *collaborate* with a variety of people and a desire to expand one's ideas by connecting with those who are different (Liberman, 2013).

In addition, connections with young professionals can demonstrate a desire to mentor new leaders. As social media platforms have moved from a focus on connectedness to the size and composition of a person's virtual network, a varied and large LinkedIn network may serve to create a positive impression of the leader's circle of influence (Liberman, 2013; van Dijck, 2013). Growing one's LinkedIn network also helps to increase his or her leadership visibility and credibility as the followership increases and expands outside the organization. Further, as young professionals share items of interest, an opportunity exists to *learn* about what is important to the next generation of professionals and to be in tune with what they find interesting, thereby enhancing one's ability to remain relevant as a leader (Singh, 2013).

Active participation will generally be easier for women, as they prefer to cultivate relationships and collaborate (Jackson et al., 2001; Haferkamp et al., 2012). It is important for leaders to seek continuous professional development and to stay abreast of the latest news and developments in his or her field and industry. Joining groups on LinkedIn may provide an opportunity for *collaboration* and *learning*, may lead to increased exposure in a field and/or industry, may provide an introduction to additional professional organizations, and may provide additional means to stay informed (Pollard, 2014). Building a positive reputation within one or more groups will lead to increased credibility within the field or industry (Schramm, 2014).

Diana (2011) noted that it is simply not enough to have a well-constructed LinkedIn profile. A leader will be looked to on social media just as in face-to-face to be a thought leader and an expert in his or her field. So, in much the same way one might share insights, books, readings, and ideas with followers and peers in the workplace, consider doing this on LinkedIn. This provides the leader or aspiring leader a unique opportunity to demonstrate *intelligence* and *knowledge*, while reaching out to a much broader audience from a diverse set of industries and backgrounds. With that said, everything shared should be professional and pertinent to leadership development in one's field or industry, or to leadership in general. LinkedIn is not the venue for sharing politically charged posts, funny or questionable posts, or the types of humorous things one might share on another social media. Pollard (2014) explained that if there is any doubt about how something might be perceived, consider carefully if it will create the desired leadership image.

LinkedIn offers the opportunity for users to seek recommendations and endorsements from their connections to add credence to their claims of skills and abilities. To get started with endorsements, Adams (2012) and van Dijck (2013) advise that individuals should choose skills from the list provided on LinkedIn, choosing those skills most important for the role of a leader in the specific field or organization. Once the list is created, the leader may ask colleagues, superiors, clients, and other knowledgeable peers to consider providing endorsements. Adams (2012) found in her research that endorsements can be a quick way to strengthen a LinkedIn profile and to show that one is respected for certain skills or characteristics. Additionally, van Dijck (2013) suggests that endorsements from specialists are often more valuable than those of strangers or novices.

Similar to endorsements, recommendations are provided by connections and are intended to highlight a person's strengths as a leader (Luscher, 2015). However, recommendations carry more weight than endorsements because they are written testimonials to the person's skills and abilities, and they take greater effort to create (van Dijck, 2013). A LinkedIn recommendation is similar to a written letter of recommendation; however, it is generally less formal (Luscher, 2015). It is particularly important to have a recommendation from a current or former superior and from those who have witnessed the person's abilities (van Dijck, 2013). Those recommendations show *support from above* and can speak directly to one's *willingness to work, consistency,* and any number of characteristics observed about this person (Luscher, 2015). Because one's LinkedIn profile will potentially reach a large audience of people, most of whom will be strangers, having positive entries on the profile that speak to the person's character and leadership abilities can significantly enhance their impression management (Luscher, 2015; van Dijck, 2013).

Be Clear

In a face-to-face conversation or discussion, an individual is generally able to state his or her position on an issue and then explain his or her reasoning (Rose et al., 2012). In that setting, verbal and nonverbal cues may help to ensure that the position has been stated clearly and that it was received as intended. In addition, in face-to-face communication, the sender can make adjustments as needed for culture, context, audience, and other factors (Rose et al., 2012). Social media reduces the amount of interactivity driven by nonverbal cues and provides very limited information regarding the audience, thereby making clear communication difficult (Rose et al., 2012; van Dijck, 2013). There is no guarantee about who the recipients of the communication will be, and one must assume that there will be recipients far removed from the intended audience. Further, the opportunity does not always exist to explain a position or opinion in a way that will ensure it is interpreted correctly. One should assume that posts, shared items, and profile entries might be misinterpreted. Thus, it is best to use due diligence when choosing to post or share, so that, even without further explanation, the post captures the intended point of view and is not left to risky interpretation by those who see it (Rose et al., 2012; van Dijck, 2013).

CONCLUSION

Social media has brought about new opportunities and challenges for leaders. Because social media encourages a more horizontal flow of information, the more traditional vertical communication channel is challenged. On the other hand, the horizontal flow of information enables a more constructive, multi-dimensional conversation among a much wider audience. With that said, today a digital presence is common and expected; impression management plays a significant role in how that digital presence is created and maintained. Having an active, dynamic, and well-respected profile on LinkedIn can help boost an individual's reputation as a leader and remove barriers often linked to gender. As this chapter has discussed, it is certainly possible for a leader or aspiring leader to convey many of the characteristics on social media for which a leader is identified. In fact, LinkedIn, a social media platform dedicated to professional networking, provides all the necessary options for a leader to portray himself or herself in a very authentic and genuine way. In addition, the leader can create a very informative portfolio of his or her professional journey. When created and maintained correctly, a leader's digital profile is an opportunity to convey an impression that pushes aside gender norms, stereotypes, or biases that may be exacerbated in face-to-face situations. However, as the literature has noted, just as a good profile can be effective, a poorly maintained profile can be detrimental. The impact of LinkedIn for a leader begins with the decision as to whether or not to have a social media presence at all. The research and ideas presented in this chapter have suggested a plan for developing a more effective LinkedIn presence, one that will more accurately represent the skills and abilities of the leader.

While LinkedIn affords a leader a far broader audience than he or she will likely have within their organization, one disadvantage of LinkedIn is that the leader is exposed to an audience filled with people he or she does not know. So, exercising impression management in light of an unknown audience can be exceedingly difficult (Jackson et al., 2001; Rose et al., 2012). In addition, because social media eliminates many of the nonverbal cues available for face-to-face communication, leaders must find ways to communicate their viewpoints and knowledge to ensure understanding.

Further study is necessary to examine the impact of LinkedIn use for leadership development and career opportunities. Although we are told that Generation Y believes a good leader will have technology skills in addition to the other, more traditional leadership characteristics, little research exists to assess the overall importance placed on technology skills in relation to the other leadership skills.

In conclusion, this chapter has examined the issues of impression management as they relate to leadership, gender differences, and social media. Specifically, this chapter explored LinkedIn as an effective social medium for leadership and offered a series of actions that are encouraged for all leaders using LinkedIn. The chapter discussed potential differences across gender with regard to how LinkedIn may be used; but, by its very nature as a professional networking tool, LinkedIn encourages a professional profile and image that tends to transcend gender. As an extension of a leader's real life persona, LinkedIn provides a textual representation of the leader's skills, abilities, and accomplishments, much like a virtual resume. With advances in technology and digital communication, an effective virtual presence has gained importance for leaders across industries, thereby affording leaders a wider, more global audience than is possible via purely face-to-face means.

REFERENCES

About LinkedIn. (2017). *LinkedIn.* Retrieved from https://press.linkedin.com/about-linkedin

Adams, S. (2012, December 4). Everything you need to know about LinkedIn endorsements. *Forbes.* Retrieved from https://www.forbes.com/sites/susanadams/2012/12/04/everything-you-need-to-know-about-linkedin-endorsements/#22ee596b1026

Becker, J. A. H., & Stamp, G. H. (2005). Impression management in chat rooms: A grounded theory model. *Communication Studies, 56*(3), 243–260. doi:10.1080/10510970500181264

Bimber, B. (2000). Measuring the gender gap on the Internet. *Social Science Quarterly, 81*(3), 868–876.

Diana, A. (2011, March 17). Executives flock to LinkedIn. *Information Week*. Retrieved from http://www.informationweek.com/software/social/executives-flock-to -linkedin/d/d-id/1096690?

Dolgin, K. G., & Minowa, N. (1997). Gender differences in self-presentation: A comparison of the roles of flatteringness and intimacy in self-disclosure to friends. *Sex Roles, 36*(5), 371–380. doi:10.1007/BF02766653

Dominick, J. R. (1999). Who do you think you are? Personal home pages and self-presentation on the world wide web. *Journalism & Mass Communication Quarterly, 76*(4), 646–658.

Eagly, A. H., & Carli, L. L. (2003). The female leadership advantage: An evaluation of the evidence. *The Leadership Quarterly, 14*(6), 807–834. doi:10.1016/j.leaqua.2003.09.004

Ezzedeen, S. R. (2015). Portrayals of career women in Hollywood films: Implications for the glass ceiling's persistence. *Gender in Management, 30*(3), 239–264. doi:10.1108/GM-07-2013-0073

Friedman, P. (2013, January). Social leadership. *Leadership Excellence Essentials, 30*(1), 14.

Gerbner, G., Gross, L., Morgan, M., & Signorelli, N. (1986). Living with television: The dynamics of the cultivation process. In J. Bryant & D. Zillman (Eds.), *Perspectives on media effects* (pp. 17–40). Hillsdale, NJ: Erlbaum.

Goffman, E. (1959). *The presentation of self in everyday life*, New York, NY: Doubleday.

Gordon, M. K. (2008). Media contributions to African American girls' focus on beauty and appearance: Exploring the consequences of sexual objectification. *Psychology of Women Quarterly, 32*(3), 245–256.

Haferkamp, N., Eimler, S. C., Papadakis, A., & Truck, J. V. (2012). Men are from Mars, women are from Venus? Examining gender differences in self-presentation on social networking sites. *Cyberpsychology, Behavior, and Social Networking, 15*(2), 91–98. doi:10.1089/cyber.2011.0151

Holden, K. E., & Raffo, D. M. (2014). A potential generation gap: Perspectives on female leadership. *Gender in Management, 29*(7), 419–431.

How LinkedIn Can Help You. (2017). *LinkedIn*. Retrieved from https://www.linkedin.com/help/linkedin/answer/45/how-linkedin-can-help-you?lang=en

Jackson, L. A., Ervin, K. S., Gardner, P. D., & Schmitt, N. (2001). Gender and the Internet: Women communicating and men searching. *Sex Roles, 44*(5–6), 363–379. doi:10.1023/A:1010937901821

Kuznekoff, J. H. (2013). Comparing impression management strategies across social media platforms. In C. Cunningham (Ed.), *Social networking and impression management: Self-presentation in the digital age* (pp. 15–34). Lanham, MD: Lexington Books.

Leary, M. R. (1996). *Self-presentation: Impression management and interpersonal behavior*. Boulder, CO: Westview.

Leiser, T. (2013, November 17). How franchise professionals should use LinkedIn. *Franchising World*. Retrieved from http://franchisingworld.com/franchise-professionals-use-linkedin/

Liberman, C. J. (2013). Branding as social discourse: Identity construction using online social and professional networking sites. In C. Cunningham (Ed.),

Social networking and impression management: Self-presentation in the digital age (pp. 107–128). Lanham, MD: Lexington Books.

Luscher, K. F. (2015, April 7). Not all LinkedIn recommendations are created equal. Retrieved from http://www.marketleadership.net/not-all-linkedin-recommendations-are-created-equal/#sthash.xoYT47vt.dpbs

Manago, A. M., Graham, M. B., Greenfield, P. M., & Salimkhan, G. (2008). Self-presentation and gender on MySpace. *Journal of Applied Developmental Psychology, 29*(6), 446–458. doi:10.1016/j.appdev.2008.07.001

McDermott, J. (2013, November 20). How to create a CEO-level LinkedIn profile [Web log post]. Retrieved from http://blog.careerintelligence.com/create-star-linkedin-profile/

Pollard, C. (2014, December 11). How to use LinkedIn to build your thought leadership [Web log post]. Retrieved from http://www.huffingtonpost.com/catriona-pollard/how-to-use-linkedin-to-bu_b_6299230.html

Ragan, J. M. (1982). Gender displays in portrait photographs. *Sex Roles, 8*(1), 33–43. doi:10.1007/BF00287672

Rose, J., Mackey-Kallis, S., Shyles, L., Barry, K., Biagini, D., Hart, C., & Jack, L. (2012). Face it: The impact of gender on social media images. *Communication Quarterly, 60*(5), 588–607. doi:10.1080/01463373.2012.725005

Sattel, J. W. (1976). The inexpressive male: Tragedy or sexual politics? *Social Problems, 23*(4), 469–477. doi10.1525/sp.1976.23.4.03a00090

Schramm, J. (2014, June 5). LinkedIn for CEOs: What your profile should say about you. Retrieved from https://www.linkedin.com/pulse/20140605144800-96757-linkedin-for-ceos-what-your-profile-should-say-about-you

Singh, S. (2013, February 5). LinkedIn is about connecting talent with opportunity at a massive scale: Deep Nishar, VP. *The Economic Times.* Retrieved from http://articles.economictimes.indiatimes.com/2013-02-05/news/36764514_1_linkedin-premium-subscriptions-deep-nishar

Tannen, D. (1993, June 20). Wears jump suit. Sensible shoes. Uses husband's last name. Retrieved from http://www.sallymundo.com/kimberly/425/readings/jumpsuit.pdf

Tedeschi, J. T., & Riess, M. (1981). Identities, the phenomenal self, and laboratory research. In J. T. Tedeschi (Ed.), *Impression management theory and social psychological research* (pp. 3–20). New York, NY: Academic Press.

Thew, D. (2008). LinkedIn—A user's perspective: Using new channels for effective business networking. *Business Information Review, 25*(2), 87–90. doi:10.1177/0266382108090810

Thomson, R., & Murachver, T. (2001). Predicting gender from electronic discourse. *British Journal of Social Psychology, 40*(2), 193–208.

Torres-Díaz, J., Duart, J. M., Gómez-Alvarado, H., Marín-Gutiérrez, I., & Segarra-Faggioni, V. (2016). Internet use and academic success in university students. *Comunicar, 48*(24), 61–69. doi:10.3916/C48-2016-06

Tufekci, Z. (2008). Can you see me now? Audience and disclosure regulation in online social network sites. *Bulletin of Science, Technology & Society, 28*(1), 20–36.

van Dijck, J. (2013). You have one identity: Performing the self on Facebook and LinkedIn. *Media, Culture, & Society, 35*(2), 199–215. doi:10.1177/0163443712468605

Walther, J. B. (1996). Computer-mediated communication: Impersonal, interpersonal, and hyperpersonal interaction. *Communication Research, 23*(1), 3–43.

Walther, J. B., Van der Heide, B., Kim, S. Y., Westerman, D., & Tong, S. T. (2008). The role of friends' appearance and behavior on evaluations of individuals on Facebook: Are we known by the company we keep? *Human Communication Research, 34*(1), 28–49.

Williams, D. G. (1985). Gender, masculinity-femininity, and emotional intimacy in same-sex friendship. *Sex Roles, 12*(5–6), 587–600.

CHAPTER 18

LEADER OR LADY?

The Visual Rhetoric of
Hillary Clinton's Twitter Images

Newly Paul
Appalachian State University

Gregory Perreault
Appalachian State University

The 2016 election will be remembered as the "social media revolution" election (Bellstrom, 2015). Candidates from both the Democratic and Republican sides used Twitter to inform, fundraise, attack, and microtarget voters. Donald Trump, who uses the Twitter handle @realDonaldTrump, amassed 13 million followers during the course of the campaign, while Hillary Clinton, who tweets using the handle @HillaryClinton had 10.2 million followers.

Over the past decade, social media, especially Twitter, has become an integral part of political campaigns. Tweets have the power to persuade people (Jansen, Zhang, Sobel, & Chowdury, 2009), influence followers to take action (Havey, 2010; Sarno, 2009), and help amplify media coverage

Gender, Communication, and the Leadership Gap, pages 327–338
Copyright © 2017 by Information Age Publishing
All rights of reproduction in any form reserved.

(Donia, 2010). Campaigns use Twitter mainly to mobilize voters, attract media attention, and help establish a candidate's leadership credentials. Since Twitter is a free campaigning tool, it is especially beneficial for women candidates who might not have support for extensive fundraising drives.

Political campaigns often post viral content on Twitter. This includes information about candidates' positions on non-controversial issues and information about their personal life that is likely to encourage emotional attachment from supporters (Bronstein, 2013). One of the indications of viral content on Twitter is the number of times it gets retweeted—a behavior that indicates the users' perceived importance of the tweet (Starbird, Palen, Hughes, & Vieweg, 2010). Using photos causes an average of 35% boost in retweets—more than videos, quotes, hashtags, or statistics (Rogers, 2014).

Given that Twitter users engage more with images rather than text, and that campaigns often use visuals to influence our understanding of events and candidates (Gilliam & Iyengar, 2000; Todorov, Mandisodza, Goren, & Hall, 2005), we examined the visual rhetoric of Hillary Clinton's primary campaign on Twitter using the lens of Symbolic Convergence Theory (SCT) and its related method of Fantasy Theme Analysis (FTA). Visual rhetoric is the study of symbols or images that are created by humans and are used specifically to communicate with an audience (Foss, 2005). Given that the ability to communicate effectively is an important leadership trait, it is important to understand how the deliberate juxtaposition of images, colors, camera angles, and subjects' expressions are combined with textual messages to influence the audience. We focus on Clinton's candidacy because it was novel. Not only was she the first woman Democrat nominee for the office of President, but she also carried a unique set of experiences that differentiated her from other women candidates. Given her 30-plus years in public service and her tenure as Secretary of State and First Lady, she overcame traditional obstacles related to lack of experience and name recognition that many women candidates faced. In this study, we examined the relationship between gender and communication on social media. Specifically, we identified the fantasy themes that emerged from the most retweeted images on Hillary Clinton's Twitter account and examined their shared rhetorical vision about the role of a female presidential candidate.

GENDER AND CAMPAIGNS

Campaigns use gender as a strategy to appeal to voters' gender-stereotypic expectations (Dittmar, 2015). These expectations are derived from roles that men and women have historically played in society. Since women have traditionally been nurturers and caregivers, voters tend to associate women candidates with feminine characteristics such as empathy and caring, and expect them to be better at handling issues such as education and childcare (Huddy & Terkildsen, 1993; Kahn, 1996). Men, on the other hand, have traditionally been leaders and protectors, and are perceived as confident, tough, and naturally suited to handle taxes and national security issues (Dolan, 2014; Kahn, 1996).

Given these gendered expectations, women candidates often use feminine communication styles to appeal to voters. For example, in their political ads, they focus on character traits rather than issues, appear with their families, dress formally, use surrogates to vouch for their credibility (Bystrom, Banwart, Kaid, & Robertson, 2004; Dabelko & Herrnson, 1997; Larson, 2001), and refrain from attacking their male opponents (Kahn & Gordon, 1997).

Recent studies, however, have found a declining reliance on gender stereotypes. These studies indicate that voters are more likely to rely on cues such as party identification and incumbency to cast their votes (Dolan, 2014, Hayes & Lawless, 2015). Scholars have attributed the lack of gender appeals online to voters' changing attitudes and to the freedom afforded by the web, which allows candidates to communicate directly with voters, bypassing the gendered expectations of the media and party elites (Evans & Clark, 2015).

In the 2016 elections, gender became salient on several occasions, and Hillary Clinton's campaign reflected the "double-bind" that many women candidates face. Despite her "unsurpassed name recognition, unprecedented fundraising ability, and the right resume" (Lawrence & Rose, 2009, p. 102), Clinton was considered unlikeable and faced doubts about her fitness for an office that has never been occupied by a woman. Our analysis examined the fantasies revolving around her use of Twitter visuals and how they indicate a shared rhetorical vision of what it means to be a woman candidate.

VISUAL IMAGES ON TWITTER

Campaigns regularly use visual images in political ads, speeches, and press conferences to portray candidates favorably and influence public opinion (Grabe & Bucy, 2009; Schill, 2009). According to Schill (2012), visuals have ten important functions in politics: "They serve as arguments, have an agenda setting function, dramatize policy, aid in emotional appeals, build the candidate's image, create identification, connect to societal symbols, transport the audience, and add ambiguity" (p. 122) to the candidate's controversial messages. Images capture nonverbal human experiences that are nonlinear and multidimensional, and work alongside text to produce comprehensive messages (Foss, 2005).

In addition to these functions, visuals on Twitter are designed to go viral. Usually, this occurs by retweets—a practice that implies agreement, endorsement, or a desire to draw attention to the message. Some messages attract more retweets than others. Those that contain emotional appeals, humor or violence, feature children and celebrities (Golan & Zaidner, 2008; Southgate, Westoby, & Page, 2010), contain URLs and hashtags (Suh, Hong, Pirolli, & Chi, 2010) or incorporate topics, videos, and images that are already chaining on social media (Yang & Wang, 2015) are more likely to be retweeted.

According to political analysts, the Clinton campaign used popular Twitter messaging techniques to combat her unemotional image and portray her as an authentic candidate (Przbyla, 2016). Since joining Twitter in June 2013, her campaign used humor, pop culture references, selfies, and sarcasm to build a loyal fan following of 7.35 million people. During the 2016 elections, Clinton's campaign combined regular tweets with snarky videos and GIFs (a type of image that is static or animated, but usually doesn't have sound) to post quick retorts to Trump's statements (Scola, 2016), thereby inserting her into media coverage. As several campaign strategists noted, the strategies worked—Clinton appeared more relatable on Twitter than in interviews or on the campaign trail (Scola, 2016).

THEORY

Sharing visuals on Twitter amounts to more than mere re-creation because through sharing, audiences indicate an understanding of the visual's inner code. This understanding helps create a shared sense of identity and a feeling of shared issue positions between candidates and the audience. Page and Duffy (2016) argue that interaction on social media "is not merely the sounding and sharing of opinions, it is a political socialization process that nurtures shared worldviews and spurs political action" (p. 25). SCT builds on the concept of the social construction of reality and argues that through the ways in which symbols converge, people create a social reality (Bormann, 1985). Symbols can be thought of as a sort of *inside joke*, in which the reader must understand the code written into the symbol in order to appreciate the joke. Sharing Hillary Clinton visuals may not indicate agreement with the nature of the visual per se—Twitter users at times share materials for the purposes of critique and criticism—but it certainly indicates the degree to which the audience has understood the visual's inner code. Through SCT and its partner method of fantasy theme analysis, researchers can identify various fantasy themes that contribute to a shared rhetorical vision.

In order to assess whether a fantasy is resonating with a social media public, researchers measure what in SCT terminology is referred to as *chaining* (Bormann, Cragan, & Shields, 2003). Chaining is the process by which symbols are shared through a community. In SCT, chaining has occurred through email chains, Twitter, and Facebook, but in all of them it acts as a process of political socialization (Duffy, Page, & Perreault, 2014). By sharing these symbols—memes, photographs, cartoons, graphics—individuals are indicating their agreement with, or at least understanding of, the symbol's inner code. Hence, symbols that tend to chain more heavily are worthy of analysis in that it is then indicative of a shared ideology (Duffy et al., 2014). For Twitter, assessing the *chaining* of an image can be done through measuring retweets and favorites (Duffy et al., 2014; McKewon, 2012). Images that chain more heavily resonate well with the public. Through its shared method of fantasy theme analysis, SCT can help pinpoint the fantasies written into the inner code of these visuals and help uncover paradigmatic values on given issues or people. For example, this method was used to uncover latent racism in tweets following the statements of Seattle Seahawks player Richard Sherman (Page, Duffy, Frisby, & Perreault, 2016), latent political values regarding credibility and expertise in visual messaging from the 2012 elections (Page & Duffy, 2016), and rape imagery used in order to shape youth audience perceptions of Obamacare in Obamacare ads (Duffy et al., 2014).

Following this tradition, we collected the 10 most chained visuals from Clinton's Twitter account from February to July 2016. Early images in the primary campaign received few retweets, whereas near the conclusion of the primaries, they were retweeted thousands of times. A few factors likely contributed to this: a shrinking of the primary field as it became clear Sen. Bernie Sanders would not be able to get the number of delegates necessary to win, an increased focus on the historicity of her nomination, an increased focus on responding to the claims of Trump, and perhaps an increased resonance of her images.

FINDINGS

Fantasy of the Presidential Image

The first fantasy theme showed Clinton as the perfect picture of a U.S. president. Each image under this theme framed her from the shoulders up, with no bust visible in the frame, a method commonly used in portraits of presidents (Lee, 2016; Verser & Wicks, 2006). The images deemphasized her femininity, yet simultaneously linked her visually to the credibility of prior American presidents. The images also placed her above the viewer, looking down at them. This can be judged by her gaze, which focused over the top of the viewer in the visuals. Again, similar to the official images of Presidents Obama and Bill Clinton, Clinton's picture used the American flag in the background. By placing her in well-recognized visual frames, the subtle argument being made was that Clinton was presidential material.

The accompanying text to these images also emphasized her leadership role. The message, "I'm with her," put Clinton in the driver's seat. The viewer was not leading; the message was not that Hillary was with "us," but rather pointed to Hillary as the leader. Similarly, we saw the historicity of her candidacy stressed in the text, "History made," and, "For the first time in our history, a woman is a major party's presidential nominee for President of the United States." This cast Hillary in the role of hero, breaking boundaries for all others.

Other images that were part of this fantasy theme featured Barack Obama as the central figure. In the text accompanying these images, Obama lauded Clinton's credentials for president. Though Clinton did not appear in some of these images, the visual reference to her was implicit. In some images, Clinton and Obama were pictured side by side, with arms outstretched toward the crowd. An underlying message of these images was that Obama and Clinton have a shared mission and shared values.

Fantasy of the Relatable and Reliable Candidate

Another fantasy theme that emerged from the most re-tweeted images was that of Hillary Clinton as a *relatable candidate*. An image posted by the campaign on June 7—the last date for the primaries and also the date when Clinton's path to the Democratic nomination appeared clear—showed her dancing and clapping with a Black child, while other women looked on approvingly. Unlike her other images, which often look posed and focus only on her face, this image was a full-body shot and portrayed her as playful and spontaneous. Though we associate black and white visuals with the past, the use of these colors added to the poignancy of the image, and the women surrounding Clinton in the picture signaled their support for her candidacy. In addition, by sharing space with women of various races and ages, Clinton reminded the audience of her women-centric campaign platform, and implied that she was fighting on behalf of all of them. The text above the picture drove home the symbolism: "To every little girl who dreams big: Yes, you can be anything you want—even president. Tonight is for you." This tweet was signed "H," denoting that it was a personal message from Hillary Clinton, not one composed by the campaign.

Another theme that emerged from Clinton's most chained images was that of her as a *reliable candidate* whose traits and issue positions stood in direct contrast to those of the Republican candidates. In one such image that exemplified this fantasy theme, Republican (also known as the Grand Old Party or GOP) candidates were shown arguing with each other at a Republican primary debate, while Clinton's photo, taken from the October 2015 Benghazi hearings, showed her as thoughtful and serious. The picture emphasized the body language of the candidates, and in doing so it compared the disorder and discord in the Republican camp with Clinton's poise and control. Other tweets used visuals from the same Benghazi hearing and showed Clinton's exasperation at the issues raised in the Republican debate. These Twitter images focused entirely on her; the image and the accompanying text—How many more of these do we have to sit through? Asking for a friend. #GOPdebate—exuded sarcasm and appeared to give a subtle, sympathetic nod to people impatient with the tenor of the GOP debate. The tone of the tweet and the hashtag were intentional. They highlighted the negative tone and lack of substantive discussion in the GOP debate and helped Clinton insert herself into Twitter discussions that were trending at the time.

Another image that portrayed Clinton as a reliable candidate, showed her against a background composed of gay pride colors. This tweet responded to the gay marriage issue raised in the GOP debate and juxtaposed Clinton's acceptance of the Supreme Court's decision on gay marriage with the GOP's reluctance. The image showed her with eyes closed, a content smile on her face, and her head swaying to music, signaling her complete acceptance and approval of the "law of the land."

DISCUSSION AND CONCLUSION

Our analysis of Clinton's most popular tweets showed two primary fantasy themes—the *presidential image* and the *relatable and reliable candidate.* The first linked her implicitly and explicitly with past presidents, and in the second, she was humanized and portrayed as more reliable than the GOP candidates. Taken together these suggested a rhetorical vision that envisioned Clinton as the *grown-up* in the midst of a campaign of children. This was done by drawing a dichotomy between the Republican candidates and reducing their arguments to absurdity through the use of GIFS and by showing her in very adult settings—in the structure of presidential photographs and interacting with actual children in a kind manner.

Surprisingly, the image that chained the most showed Clinton surrounded by women and a young child, as compared to the images that portrayed her as mature and presidential. This could have two implications: first, Twitter users relate well to images of Clinton as a traditional woman candidate—exuding warmth and familiarity, rather than emphasizing her presidential qualities; second, Twitter users respond well to emotions (Stromer-Galley, 2014). In this case the hopeful message that Clinton's candidacy is historic, signaling progress for women and children. Both these images showed Clinton in natural poses, as opposed to her tightly scripted media appearances, and helped audiences relate to her. The Clinton campaign found success through the use of candid images that showed an "unedited" political candidate. In particular, aged images of Clinton and her family were popular. Indeed, as the campaign progressed, Clinton used more vintage images of herself to make her more "relatable" so that she appeared like an "average person" (Karni, 2015). Michelle Obama also found social media success sharing vintage and candid images with her own Twitter account (Paul & Perreault, 2016). It is possible that Michelle Obama and Clinton tapped into the social media voice for women politicians. This strategy of using vintage and candid images could be of value to future women candidates.

The second most retweeted was one that visually compared her with the GOP candidates—while she appeared calm and composed, the GOP candidates were pictured yelling at each other. Though this image focused on her maturity as a candidate, employed sarcasm, and showed Clinton in a candid pose. As in previous research, we saw evidence of Twitter's preference for emotions and humor rather than a controlled image (Southgate et al., 2010). Overall, the visuals that resonated the most with the masses used simple and direct rhetoric, and portrayed Clinton in a relatively gender-stereotypic role.

The visuals also performed the traditional rhetorical functions outlined by Schill (2012). First, and most importantly, they *served as arguments*. One instance where they achieve this is in the juxtaposition of Clinton's image with gay pride colors that suggested connections with the salient election issues. The visuals also created a sense of uniqueness about the candidacy by tapping into the audience's historical and cultural knowledge, and the facial expressions helped create cues about the candidate's traits and issue positions. The visual rhetoric also signaled the issues—for example, women's empowerment and gay marriage—that are the most salient in the election. In doing so, the tweets helped set the audience and the news agenda (Messaris & Abraham, 2001). Clinton's visual on gay marriage served the *dramatization* function and also helped *create identification*, or a sense of similarity in issue position between her and the audience. As Schill (2012) argued, politicians often used visuals with drama and aesthetic qualities to draw attention to policies and assert their significance, and the visual achieved this end with its dramatic use of the gay pride colors juxtaposed against Clinton's image. Almost every tweet analyzed in this sample contains positive *emotional appeals*, and using these appeals helped *connect the candidate to the people*. As Stromer-Galley (2014) pointed out in her analysis of the 2012 Obama campaign, it is essential that campaigns develop "a parasocial relationship with supporters" (p. 179) in order to motivate them to support the campaign. Clinton's campaign aimed to use current topics, visuals that are likely to relate to voters of all ages, and feel-good emotions in order to build up support. The images also helped *build the candidate's image* as a mature and capable leader by contrasting her with the Republican candidates.

Lastly, Schill (2012) pointed out that visuals have the power to *transport the audience* to "a particular spatial, emotional, or virtual space" (p. 131), and Clinton's use of Obama as a surrogate achieved this end. The images that showed her sharing space with Obama were meant to transport the audience back in time, exude feelings of nostalgia and hope, and drive home the message that Clinton is an appropriate choice to carry on Obama's legacy.

In conclusion, our study of Clinton's Twitter visuals showed a deliberately crafted image that portrayed her leadership qualities as well as her femininity. While the news media dwell on her public persona—which often appears guarded—social media allowed her campaign to produce a counter narrative that toggled between her public and private persona and helped create the image of a well-rounded leader. Given that media narratives of women candidates often tend to be sparse, negative, stereotypical, and focused on traits, family, and physical appearance (Conroy, Oliver, Breckenridge-Jackson, & Heldman, 2015; Dunaway, Lawrence, Rose & Weber, 2013), Clinton's ability to use social media to shape an alternate image points to a useful strategy that could be employed by women running for public office.

REFERENCES

Bellstrom, K. (2015, December 1). This is why social media will decide the 2016 election. *Fortune.* Retrieved from http://fortune.com/2015/12/01/social-media-2016-election/

Bormann, E. G. (1985). Symbolic convergence theory: A communication formulation. *Journal of Communication, 35*(4), 128–138. doi:10.1111/j.1460-2466.1985.tb02977.x

Bormann, E. G., Cragan, J. F., & Shields, D. C. (2003). Defending symbolic convergence theory from an imaginary Gunn. *Quarterly Journal of Speech, 89*(4), 366–372. doi:10.80/0033563032000160990

Bronstein, J. (2013). Like me! Analyzing the 2012 presidential candidates' Facebook pages. *Online Information Review, 37*(2), 173–192. doi:10.1108/OIR-01-2013-0002

Bystrom, D. G., Banwart, M. C., Kaid, L. L., & Robertson, T. (Eds.). (2004). *Gender and candidate communication: Videostyle, webstyle, newstyle.* New York, NY: Routledge.

Conroy, M., Oliver, S., Breckenridge-Jackson, I., & Heldman, C. (2015). From Ferraro to Palin: Sexism in coverage of vice presidential candidates in old and new media. *Politics, Groups, and Identities, 3*(4), 573–591. doi:10.1080/215655 03.2015.1050412

Dabelko, K. L. C., & Herrnson, P. S. (1997). Women's and men's campaigns for the U.S. House of Representatives. *Political Research Quarterly, 50*(1), 121–135. doi:10.2307/449031

Dittmar, K. (2015). *Navigating gendered terrain: Stereotypes and strategy in political campaigns.* Philadelphia, PA: Temple University Press.

Dolan, K. (2014). Gender stereotypes, candidate evaluations, and voting for women candidates: What really matters? *Political Research Quarterly, 67*(1), 96–107. doi:10.1177/1065912913487949

Donia, L. (2010, March 23). A look at Cory Booker, the social media mayor. *Techpresident.* Retrieved from http://techpresident.com/blog-entry/ look-cory-booker-social-media-mayor

Duffy, M., Page, J., & Perreault, G. (2014, August 8). *Sticking it to Obamacare: A rhetorical analysis of Affordable Care Act advertising and social media.* Paper presented at the Association for Education in Journalism and Mass Communication. Montreal, Canada.

Dunaway, J., Lawrence, R. G., Rose, M., & Weber, C. R. (2013). Traits versus issues: How female candidates shape coverage of senate and gubernatorial races. *Political Research Quarterly, 66*(3), 715–726. doi:10.1177/1065912913491464

Evans, H. K., & Clark, J. H. (2015). "You Tweet like a girl!" How female candidates campaign on Twitter. *American Politics Research, 44*(2), 326–352. doi:10.1177/1532673X15597747

Foss, S. K. (2005). Theory of visual rhetoric. In K. Smith, S. Moriarty, G. Barbatsis, & K. Kenney (Eds.), *Handbook of visual communication: Theory, methods, and media* (pp. 141–152). Mahwah, NJ: Erlbaum.

Gilliam, F. D., & Iyengar, S. (2000). Prime suspects: The influence of local television news on the viewing public. *American Journal of Political Science, 44*(3), 560–573.

Golan, G. J., & Zaidner, L. (2008). Creative strategies in viral advertising: An application of Taylor's six-segment message strategy wheel. *Journal of Computer-Mediated Communication, 13*(4), 959–972. doi:10.1111/j.1083-6101.2008.00426.x

Grabe, M. E., & Bucy, E. P. (2009). *Image bite politics: News and the visual framing of elections.* New York, NY: Oxford University Press.

Havey, N. (2010, June 8). Can Act.ly keep Sen. Brown green? *Huffington Post.* Retrieved from http://www.huffingtonpost.com/nathan-havey/can-actly-keep-sen-brown_b_530470.html

Hayes, D., & Lawless, J. L. (2015). A non-gendered lens? Media, voters, and female candidates in contemporary congressional elections. *Perspectives on Politics, 13*(1), 95–118.

Huddy, L., & Terkildsen, N. (1993). Gender stereotypes and the perception of male and female candidates. *American Journal of Political Science, 37*(1), 119–147. doi:10.2307/2111526

Jansen, B. J., Zhang, M., Sobel, K., and Chowdury, A. (2009). Twitter power: Tweets as electronic word of mouth. *Journal of the American Society for Information Science and Technology, 60*(11), 2169–2188. doi:10.1002/asi.21149

Kahn, K. F. (1996). *The political consequences of being a woman: How stereotypes influence the conduct and consequences of political campaigns.* New York, NY: Columbia University Press.

Kahn, K. F., & Gordon, A. (1997). How women campaign for the U.S. Senate: Substance and strategy. In Norris, P. (Ed.), *Women, media, and politics* (pp. 59–76). Oxford, England: Oxford University Press.

Karni, A. (2015, Sept. 15). How Hillary Clinton is using old photographs to make herself more 'relatable.' *Politico.* Retrieved from http://www.politico.com/story/2015/09/hillary-clinton-2016-vintage-images-nostalgia-213615

Larson, S. G. (2001). Running as women? A comparison of female and male Pennsylvania assembly candidates' campaign brochures. *Women & Politics, 22*(2), 107–124. doi:10.1300/J014v22n02_04

Lawrence, R. G., & Rose, M. (2009). *Hillary Clinton's race for the White House: Gender politics and the media on the campaign trail.* Boulder, CO: Lynne Rienner.

Lee, J. (2016). Presidents' visual presentations in their official photos: A cross-cultural analysis of the U.S. and South Korea. *Cogent Arts & Humanities.* Retrieved from https://www.cogentoa.com/article/10.1080/23311983.2016.1201967.pdf

McKewon, E. (2012). Talking points ammo. *Journalism Studies, 13*(2), 277–297. doi:10.1080/1461670X.2011.646403

Messaris, P., & Abraham, L. (2001). The role of images in framing news stories. In S. D. Reese, O. H. Gandy, Jr., & A. E. Grant (Eds.), *Framing public life: Perspectives on media and our understanding of the social world* (pp. 215–226). Mahwah, NJ: Erlbaum.

Page, J. T., & Duffy, M. E. (2016). What does credibility look like? Tweets and walls in U.S. presidential candidates' visual storytelling. *Journal of Political Marketing,* 1–29. doi:10.1080/15377857.2016.1171819

Page, J. T., Duffy, M., Frisby, C., & Perreault, G. (2016). Richard Sherman speaks and almost breaks the Internet: Race, media, and football. *Howard Journal of Communications, 27*(3), 270–289. doi:10.1080/10646175.2016.1176969

Paul, N., & Perreault, G. (2016, May). Michelle Obama, first lady of social media: The symbolic convergence of social media visuals. Paper presented at the International Communication Association, Fukuoka, Japan.

Przbyla, H. M. (2016, January 18). Clinton media campaign follows BuzzFeed model. *USA Today.* Retrieved from http://www.usatoday.com/story/news/politics/elections/2016/01/18/hillary-clinton-social-media-trump-twitter-facebook/78856358/

Rogers, S. (2014, March 10). What fuels a tweet's engagement? *Twitter Blog.* Retrieved from https://blog.twitter.com/2014/what-fuels-a-tweets-engagement

Sarno, D. (2009, February 18). Twitter creator Jack Dorsey illuminates the site's founding document. *Los Angeles Times.* Retrieved from http://latimesblogs.latimes.com/technology/2009/02/twitter-creator.html

Schill, D. (2009). *Stagecraft and statecraft: Advance and media events in political communication.* Lanham, MD: Lexington Books.

Schill, D. (2012). The visual image and the political image: A review of visual communication research in the field of political communication. *Review of Communication, 12*(2), 118–142. 10.1080/15358593.2011.653504

Scola, N. (2016, June 10). How Clinton aims to trump Trump on Twitter. *Politico*. Retrieved from http://www.politico.com/story/2016/06/hillary-clinton-trump-twitter-224197

Southgate, D., Westoby, N., & Page, G. (2010). Creative determinants of viral video viewing. *International Journal of Advertising, 29*(3), 349–368. doi:10.2501/S0265048710201221

Starbird, K., Palen, L., Hughes, A. L., & Vieweg, S. (2010, February). Chatter on the red: What hazards threat reveals about the social life of microblogged information. Paper presented at the Computer Supported Cooperative Work conference, Savannah, Georgia. Doi: 10.1145/1718918.1718965

Stromer-Galley, J. (2014). *Presidential campaigning in the Internet age*. New York, NY: Oxford University Press.

Suh, B., Hong, L., Pirolli, P., & Chi, E. H. (2010). Want to be retweeted? Large scale analytics on factors impacting retweet in Twitter network. *IEEE International Conference on Social Computing*. Retrieved from www.parc.com/content/attachments/want-to-be-retweeted.pdf

Todorov, A., Mandisodza, A. N., Goren, A., & Hall, C. C. (2005). Inferences of competence from faces predict election outcomes. *Science, 308*(5728), 1623–1626.

Verser, R., & Wicks, R. H. (2006). Managing voter impressions: The use of images on presidential candidate web sites during the 2000 campaign. *Journal of Communication, 56*(1), 178–197. doi:10.1111/j.1460-2466.2006.00009.x

Yang, H. C., & Wang, Y. (2015). Social sharing of online videos: Examining American consumers' video sharing attitudes, intent, and behavior. *Psychology & Marketing, 32*(9), 907–919. doi:10.1002/mar.20826

CHAPTER 19

HER GOSPEL TRUTH

Bloggers Rewriting Grand Narratives of Women of Faith in Church Leadership

Karen Sorensen-Lang
California State University Channel Islands

This discussion briefly describes and analyzes the movement of women Christian egalitarian and intersectionality bloggers addressing gendered church leadership norms and male-authority narratives through online, digital leadership. Egalitarian writers support equality for women and men in church, work, and home, and they believe women should have full access to church leadership based on giftedness and calling, not gender. Intersectionality bloggers make visible and understood the overlapping aspects of people's identities and how sexism, racism, classism, able-ism, and all forms of bias intersect as layered oppression for individuals. The goals of this discussion include examining digital leadership in an online women's movement building momentum as it advocates for full participation for women in church leadership, feminist theological knowledge-making, and shared-power models for home life. It explores the intersectionality of women leaders as women of faith, examining the ways in which women

Gender, Communication, and the Leadership Gap, pages 339–348
Copyright © 2017 by Information Age Publishing
All rights of reproduction in any form reserved.

navigate the common bifurcation of their identities when they move from empowerment in the workplace or civic contexts into traditional or patriarchal communities of faith that deny their leadership abilities and authority.

The interviews and brief content analysis shared here document the rhetorical practices and self-reported impacts of women bloggers who utilize virtual platforms as change agents to sidestep the gatekeepers and to offer counter-narratives and language that value women's leadership in patriarchal Christian church systems and related domestic roles. The necessity of counternarratives and the influence of social media to disseminate them arises from the platform's "democratic nature" (Kasana, 2014, p. 246). The very design of blogs and other social media platforms is that of a powerful decentralizing force to diffuse dominate narratives that are reinforced by those controlling the traditional communication channels and meaning-making. Kasana (2014) notes that digital media both "ferments and catalyzes discourses" (p. 246), making it a friendly medium for those needing to be heard.

The project reports a list of dominant struggles and topics that emerge in the movement, describes the role of women's mentoring via blogging and the gap that blog platforms fill for women's leadership development, and examines the tensions inherent in faith-based egalitarian and intersectionality women's blogging movement.

UNDERSTANDING THE BACKDROP
OF MALE-LEADERSHIP TRADITION

Egalitarian and intersectionality bloggers offer a counternarrative to traditional faith-based claims of "biblical gender roles" and the ongoing exclusion of women from church leadership. Modern Christian faith communities host a widely accepted belief system with standpoints that women should not aspire to top leadership positions in the church—they are to submit to their husbands' leadership—and because of patriarchal interpretations of scripture, in many cases women are not permitted to teach men or serve in any level of leadership in church institutions other than pastoring children. Complementarianism is a widely held Christian view that God made men and women to have separate roles that complement each other, primarily maintaining that men are commissioned by God to lead the home and the church.

The bloggers in this project are re-writing this narrative using their platforms to lead the discussion about egalitarian and mutual-submission theology accompanied by an alternative domestic design that empowers women in the home to positions of influence and decision-making to be shared with spouses. The movement these bloggers usher forward translates academic feminist theology to everyday language that is shareable on social media and approachable to non-academic audiences whose curiosity is piqued regarding interpretations that do not prop up church-sanctioned male privilege or leave out half the church from leadership and pastoral influence.

THE WOMEN BEHIND THE BLOGS

The bloggers interviewed include four noteworthy Christian bloggers who identify as either egalitarian or intersectionality bloggers. On her blog, Sarah Bessey (http://sarahbessey.com/blog) identifies as a writer telling stories about the intersection of those things that a woman is not to discuss "in polite company," including women's issues, theology, social justice, politics, and the sacredness of everyday life and mothering. She began blogging in 2005 and has two million visitors a year to her site. Her book *Jesus Feminist* is a central part of her platform and notoriety. The mission statements of two participants' blogs, The Junia Project (http://juniaproject.com/blog/) and Breaking the Glass Steeple (http://jorymicah.com/blog/), explicitly focus on the advocacy work of reducing patriarchy in faith communities and opening up access to all leadership positions and policy-making bodies in Christian institutions, mainly evangelical denominations and churches. The Junia Project's main avenue for advocacy is paved in educational content and translating feminist theological academic work to everyday audiences toward the goal "to encourage the study of egalitarian theology within a supportive online community" (Juinia Project, n.d., para. 3). The Junia Project has just under 10,000 followers on Facebook and another 4,000 on Instagram. Jory Micah's Breaking the Glass Steeple blog is characterized by activist tones, refutations of famous evangelical leaders, and mentoring of young women who feel called to Christian ministry or who feel injured by the Christian church's disempowering of women. She has 25,000 followers on social media. Kathy Khang's intersectionality blog (http://www.kathykhang.com/) makes no explicit mission to "smash patriarchy" as others in the study, but she writes from the position of an egalitarian and counter-racism advocate embodying the values of the movement and bringing to voice the stories and perspectives of an evangelical, Asian-American woman working in Christian leadership. The blog started in 2014 and has just over 2,000 followers. Her most popular posts publicly challenge famous Christian leaders who stereotype or fail to acknowledge Asian-American Christians experiences.

INTERVIEWS AND BLOG CONTENT

These leaders took part in in-depth interviews and content analysis on the top two posts from each site and were also included in the discussion for this forum. The following questions guided the interviews:

1. How do egalitarian or intersectionality blogs contribute to the development of women leaders?
2. What gaps in development and support of women leaders does your blog fill?

READERS' DOMINANT NEEDS AND QUESTIONS

When asked about the most popular blog content and posts that were most important to them as writers, the bloggers reported several top topics and recurring issues in their writing and leadership (see Table 9.1). The topics are listed in related categories in order to provide practical examples of the communication topics and leadership development generated by the blogs.

The Cost of Male-Dominant Faith Leadership

When biblical passages that focus on women leaders and women of action go widely underutilized in sermons and teaching, those counted among the faithful who question the erasing of these biblical heroes can make an easy case to call out injustice about the blind spots of male-generated communication and leadership. Illiteracy about women in scripture is widespread among churchgoers, and when egalitarian bloggers educate readers about a biblical womanhood that includes warriors, judges, prophets, elders, spies, and apostles, some followers express a shock, asking, "How is it I've spent my whole life in church, but never heard about these women?" The bloggers in this study are addressing this gap in literacy and the injustice of women's untold stories—narratives about ancient women and women of today.

What is missing in male-dominated faith leadership? The bloggers spoke of losing a richer understanding of who God is in the doctrine and sermons that make up Christian life. Some bloggers used words such as Christian leaders are "not honoring the fullness of God's image" and they are disenfranchising women when the "only voice they hear on Sunday is male." One blogger expressed that the Christian church loses out on being sensitive to and resourcing outreach toward social ills that women typically give voice and energy to, such as sex slavery and labor abuse. She suggested that by its nature of promoting passivity in women, complementarianism is not raising up strong and risk-taking women of faith to combat global evils. As long as male eyes are reading the world and deciding the agenda for response, women's issues and oppression will never rise to the level of urgent needs for leaders to address. When patriarchal church and domestic leadership persists, it also fails to acknowledge that not all men are "wired" to be leaders in the church

TABLE 19.1   Most Common Blog Topics Generated by the Writers in This Project

Blog Topic	Examples
Feminist Biblical and Theological Interpretations Posts	• interpreting difficult passages in Christian scripture that have been interpreted to silence women • providing talking points for the egalitarian case (i.e., top 5 reasons to be egalitarian) • facing illiteracy regarding women in Bible stories • addressing limited exposure to mutual submission theology and alternatives to "biblical gender roles"
Leadership and Mentorship Posts	• mentoring women feeling called to leadership and egalitarian living • building familiarity and comfort as traditional behaviors and leadership norms in church are discarded • telling personal stories and real-life examples for shared-power and mutual marriages • hiring women for staff and leadership positions in churches, and unconscious workplace bias • responding to male pastors writing in to ask how to empower the women in their churches
Women's Identities Posts	• voicing resistance to traditional authority and women having voices in their homes and churches • discussing the clash between personal or cultural values and advocacy messages or increased freedom for women • addressing sex and marriage topics and women's sexuality, specifically impacts of the "purity movement" that directs people to restrict sex and sexual behavior within marriage • identifying women's mental health issues amid pressures to perform and behave in varied socio-cultural circles • amplifying readers' admission that they want to leave the church because of woundedness connected to women's oppression and exclusion

or in their homes, and this leads to fatigue for men and diminishment of giftedness for women when they shrink to be followers or assistant helpers.

DISCUSSION

The bloggers' rhetorical acts of disruption and producing counternarratives are theory-making acts in process. Their texts and rhetorical impact mirror Foss, Foss, and Griffin's articulation of theory as "a way of framing an experience or event—an effort to understand and account for something and the way it functions in the world" (as cited in Ryan, 2010, p. 97). The blog platforms generate theories about women pastors, the roles of women, new readings on religious texts, and how to make sense of phenomena and gendered cultural habits and behaviors.

Feminist rhetoricians often resist academic strongholds on theory that privilege academic Theory with a capital T and opaque academic writing. They instead claim theory-making as a feminist process to outline the landscape in which the feminisms are voiced and the experiences of women are made sense of in an everyday way. The defining of women in church leadership that the bloggers do is "a valuable means of enacting agency and promoting reform" (Ryan, 2010, p. 100). Ryan suggests that redefinition as a part of theorizing can transform and adapt definitions toward the goal of change, specifically when feminist perspectives are applied. In this project, the bloggers are theorizing or meaning-making about such issues as normalizing women's leadership by going around the gatekeepers, modeling critical questions, asking questions, and mentoring young women via social media. Their rhetorical acts are creating a new order for gender justice in church leadership.

Sidestepping Gatekeepers

Emerging from a defined culture where the well-known voices of authority are male, these bloggers are sidestepping the gatekeepers who decide what voices get keynotes at conventions, publish well-promoted books, and get the radio waves. A clarifying blog that helped launch one participant's platform includes this powerful declaration:

> I have a tremendous well of hope for the voice of women in the church. The men at the table may be loud but the pockets of hope and love and freedom are spreading like yeast. I see it. I feel it in the ground under my feet. More and more of us are sick of waiting for a seat and so we are simply going outside, to freedom, together. And here, outside, we're finding each other and it's beautiful and crazy and churchy and holy. (Bessey, 2011, para. 5)

These writer-advocates are amplifying women's voices via their unregulated platforms, and, on any given day, reach far more audience members than an institutionalized male voice in a pulpit on Sunday. "We become the place that shares in normalizing the language of equality," explained one blogger in an interview. They offer to their readers the educational content and the power of naming. Phrases like "mutual submission," "women preachers," "spiritual abuse," "male privilege," and "gender justice," become normalized and visible to the online seeker positioned in a complementarian community.

Asking Critical Questions

The topics of the many blog posts generated from the participants' sites often share a common factor of asking hard-hitting and critical questions. The freedom to "cause a ruckus" and challenge established authority is not one that female readers, or even the bloggers at times, can always feel comfortable doing. Norms of politeness and expectations on women to be harmonious create the pressure-filled expectation that women should not generate disruptive speech. Their act of posing questions and challenges to male authority is a crucial element in women's development and advancement. In an interview, one participant names "question-asking" as the key charge she issues to readers. She encourages readers to ask,

> Who are the women at the table? Who are the men at the table? Ask about yourself, your friendships, your mentors. Ask why the stigma [is] here on this or that issue for women of color compared to White women. Ask why we are told to "pray away" our depression or why women and stereotypes of races are permitted to be the punchline for the pastor's joke in church.

The bloggers also address the key question of how women who function as leaders in the workplace and in civic context step into their faith communities to then take a secondary role to men, based not on abilities or strengths, but simply on gender. One woman said,

> Women who are okay with that compartmentalization have to ask the question of what this is doing to our souls. How does our faith integrate into our whole lives, and could we carry that complementarianism into the other arenas of our lives?

While all women leaders of faith navigate a split existence, White egalitarian bloggers may find it easier to navigate than intersectionality bloggers. Women of color communicate about this with nuanced language and deep, personal familiarity. They are keenly aware of their bi-cultural and multi-location survival strategies and code-switching among groups. Still, in an interview, one intersectionality blogger questions, "What kind of Gospel are we living? What are these distinct spaces for? What purposes do they serve for you, your family, and community?"

When Women Can't Be What They Can't See

The bloggers and the guest writers, who often are women in church leadership, are the role models to women and men who do not and might never encounter egalitarianism in their communities. In women's empowerment conversations, the expression that "you can't be what you can't see" is a motivational saying that explains, in part, why egalitarian values have been slow to gain ground in the church at large. There are very few women pastors, elders, and preachers functioning as examples to people of Christian faith. Few girls and young women are exposed to the option to be a church leader or to bring their full selves to domestic decision-making and behaviors because they have not seen women do these things.

The genre of lifestyle blogging particularly welcomes role modeling as a tool for leadership development. The posts on these sites written by women preachers are often readers' only avenue for encountering and learning from women church leaders. Echoes of "I have never heard that preached" speak to the need for women's issues and identities to be magnified in sermon teachings. Women's embodied experiences are often denigrated or scandalized by male biblical interpretations and male communication in the pulpit. When women preach, they engage the experiences and needs that are central to women, even into such details as suffering and bleeding or childbirth and barrenness.

EMERGING TENSIONS

White Egalitarianism and Women of Color Bloggers

At the onset of this research, a tension became apparent about the label "egalitarian." When the researcher was contacting popular women bloggers, a distinction emerged of White writers identifying as egalitarian, while women of color most often did not claim that label, even though, by definition, they embody and write about egalitarian values. The blogs of women of color do not as definitively isolate one issue in equality work, but they address the intersectionality of race, socio-economics, sexuality, and multiple layers of oppression and identity. Intersectionality was referenced several times in interviews with bloggers. For example, one intersectionality blogger discussed the inability to separate her gender from her ethnicity: "White women's stories are not universal. My story as a woman of color is not just a *little* different." She points out that the major voices and blogs in egalitarian work continue to be White women. "Maybe for the sake of progress, White men will listen to White women more, but women of color know when we are being included on White blogs as tokens." The group identity formation of intersectionality and egalitarian advocates very much run parallel to the ongoing discussion in the women's movement at large; womanist and White feminist activists organize around different key values. When women of color partner with White feminists, they often do so with a measure of self-protection and guardedness, looking out for appropriation of their stories or overextending the narrative that White voices represent all women's voices.

In interviews, all of the bloggers mentioned that the first step to addressing the egalitarian movements' majority White voices would be for White bloggers and readers to follow women of color bloggers. For example, one said, "The conversations about intersectionality even between feminism and theology would not be happening beyond academics without bloggers. I never would have access because of my location to women of colors' voices and storytelling without blogs." Two White bloggers validated the critique that much of egalitarian leadership has involved mostly White women. One said, "Even the basic truth that the women of the Bible we are educating people about are women of color, that is a fact that does not get emphasized in biblical study when it should be."

Involving Men in Women's Advocacy Work

Another tension in how to approach advocacy for women's leadership in faith communities is the positionality of men in the conversations. The concerns are in part that including and highlighting men in the movement can become a reiteration of the bias that men's voices matter more than women's or that women need men's support to validate their claims. In what ways should men be invited into the blog spaces and conversations? One blog includes posts by both men and women in order to deepen all readers' understanding of women in the Bible and to help develop egalitarian biblical interpretations. In an interview, one blogger explains that "men need to lose something to let women into the available leadership positions." Another blogger points out, "We have to include the people who have the power to change things." She often challenges men in her writing, suggesting they are "called to empower women" to protect and be protected by women.

CONCLUSION

Sidestepping limiting gendered communication expectations is a key advocacy act for the women bloggers included in this investigation. Their theorizing about equality for women in church leadership and domestic roles are feminist rhetorical acts working to advance the status of women. Online digital leadership is a vital factor of egalitarian and intersectionality Christian women's representation and empowerment, and the women bloggers introduced here are active voices in the power of naming key terms and ideas crucial to rewriting gendered norms for women of faith leaders. Is their egalitarian and intersectionality blogging a movement? It maintains its growth with increasing followers and voices, a growing body of literature and published books, popular podcasts and forums, and resources and bibliographies all forming noteworthy pockets of new conversations and new worldviews for a message of inclusion for women of faith that both resists and rewrites gendered leadership scripts.

REFERENCES

Bessey, S. (2011, December 10). In which I am done fighting for a seat at the table [Blog post]. Retrieved from http://sarahbessey.com/in-which-i-am-done-fighting-for-seat-at/

Junia Project (n.d.). About the Junia Project. Retrieved from http://juniaproject.com/about-2/

Kasana, M. (2014) Feminisms and the social media sphere. *Women's Studies Quarterly, 42*(3/4), 236–249.

Ryan, K. J. (2010). Making pathways: Inventing textual research methods in feminist rhetorical studies. In E. E. Schell & K. J. Rawson (Eds.), *Rhetorica in motion: Feminst rhetorical methods & methodologies* (pp. 89–103). Pittsburgh, PA: University of Pittsburgh Press.

ABOUT THE EDITORS

Carolyn M. Cunningham is Associate Professor of Communication and Leadership Studies at Gonzaga University, where she teaches classes in communication theory, communication technologies, and women and leadership. She is the editor of *Social Networking and Impression Management: Self-Presentation in the Digital Age.* Her research interests lie in the intersections of gender and technology. Her research has been published in journals including *New Media & Society, The Journal of Children and Media,* and *Explorations in Media Ecology.*

Heather M. Crandall is a member of the faculty at Gonzaga University. She is Associate Professor in the Master of Arts program in Communication and Leadership Studies and an Affiliate Faculty member in the Women's and Gender Studies Department. She teaches courses in the following areas: women, communication and leadership, theorizing communication, small group and interpersonal communication, rhetoric, organizational communication, and media literacy. Heather is active in the discipline of communication, serving on the editorial board of the *Western Journal of Communication* and on the Executive Council of Western States Communication Association. She edited the Northwest Communication Association's journal for three years and reviews regularly for the *Journal of Communication and Media Studies, Western Journal of Communication,* and *Communication Research Trends.* She has co-written a chapter on how to teach community-engaged courses from a feminist perspective in a digital age, and she is part of a team that offers workshops on gender and communication, and on inclusive classroom teaching in STEM fields.

Gender, Communication, and the Leadership Gap, pages 349–350
Copyright © 2017 by Information Age Publishing
All rights of reproduction in any form reserved.

Alexa M. Dare is Assistant Professor of Communication Studies at the University of Portland. She researches what can broadly be characterized as "embodied action," focusing in various ways on how bodies organize and are organized, especially in activism and social change initiatives. She has written about memes, protest, and police violence; the embodied dimensions of transnational collaboration; the implications of disembodied online education; and the way that pregnant workers negotiate work spaces. She is currently working on a project that draws from posthumanist theories to think about the interaction of human and nonhuman actors in natural resource confrontations in Oregon and North Dakota. She teaches classes in organizational communication, collaborative leadership, and environmental communication.

ABOUT THE CONTRIBUTORS

Brenda J. Allen is Vice Chancellor for Diversity and Inclusion and Professor of Communication at the University of Colorado Denver and the Anschutz Medical Campus. Her scholarship and teaching focus is on organizational communication and social identity (e.g., gender, race, sexuality, age, ability, nationality, and social class), with an emphasis on diversity in higher education. Among her publications is the groundbreaking book, *Difference Matters: Communicating Social Identity*. She presents keynote speeches, conducts workshops, and provides consultation on topics such as implicit bias, inclusion in the workplace, strategic planning, culturally-responsive teaching, mentoring, and diversity hiring practices.

Melissa J. Camba-Kelsay is a coordinator for student leadership and instructor in the minor in Leadership Studies in the Center for Student Leadership Development at the University of Rhode Island. Before that she served as Assistant Director in the Marshall Center for Intercultural Learning at Wheaton College in Massachusetts. She received her Master of Science degree in Student Affairs in Higher Education from Colorado State University and her Bachelor of Arts in English, with a minor in Human Development, from the State University of New York College at Geneseo. Melissa's professional expertise includes leadership development, inclusion, and social justice.

Yolanda Chávez Leyva is Associate Professor of History at the University of Texas at El Paso, where she specializes in Mexican American, borderlands, and public history. She is the director of the Institute for Oral History and

Gender, Communication, and the Leadership Gap, pages 351–358
Copyright © 2017 by Information Age Publishing
All rights of reproduction in any form reserved.

the Borderlands Public History Lab. She has published on the history of Mexican American women, children, and public history.

E. Anne Christo-Baker is Associate Professor of Organizational Behavior and Leadership in the College of Business at Purdue University Northwest. Her teaching experience and research interests include leadership, organizational behavior, personality, gender, and diversity. She is an engaged member of several academic and professional organizations, including the Academy of Management, International Leadership Association, North American Management Society, and Society for Human Resource Management. She also currently serves as the head of the Managerial Studies Department and oversees programs in management, human resources, marketing, entrepreneurship, and leadership. Dr. Christo-Baker provides consultation and employee development services to various organizations both nationally and internationally. She is also a member of the Board of Directors of the Chicagoland Immigrant Welcome Network. Before embarking on an academic career, Dr. Christo-Baker had more than two decades of experience in the public and private sectors.

Stacey L. Connaughton is Associate Professor and Associate Head in the Brian Lamb School of Communication at Purdue University. Her research examines leadership and identification in distributed organizing forms, particularly in the contexts of virtual teams and peacebuilding. Her research has been funded by the National Science Foundation, the Carnegie Foundation, and the Russell Sage Foundation, and she has published in *Journal of Communication, Management Communication Quarterly,* and *Small Group Research,* among others. She is the Principal Investigator and Director of the Purdue Peace Project, an externally funded political violence prevention initiative in West Africa and Central America.

Diane Forbes is Assistant Vice Chancellor of Equity, Diversity, Inclusion at the University of California (UC), San Diego. Her most recent position was as the Director of the Sixth College Practicum program and a lecturer in Communication, Leadership, and Civic Engagement at UC San Diego. Previously, she was Associate Professor of Organizational Communication and Department Chair at Trinity Washington University. She has held faculty positions at George Washington University and George Mason University in Virginia, and was a lecturer at Howard University, where she received her PhD in Organizational Communication and Social Psychology. Dr. Forbes has been awarded several faculty fellowships in the areas of women's leadership, community-based research, public policy, and dialogue. Her research focuses on gendered, raced, intersectional processes of organizing, and explores creative ways to expand pedagogy in leadership studies. One of her recent works appears in Communicative Understandings of Women's

Leadership Development: From Ceilings to Labyrinths, a Lexington Press publication. She is currently researching Adaptive Leadership and Group-as-a-Whole pedagogy and design applied in the RISE Urban Leadership Fellows program in California.

Tammy J. Halstead is Director of Alumni Advising & Development at Franklin & Marshall College. Dr. Halstead's background includes corporate training and development, business operations, recruiting, and human resources. She is a member of the Alumni Career Services Network, where she serves on the Executive Board and is the co-chair of the Career and Workplace Topic Network for the Society for the Study of Emerging Adulthood. She has presented nationally and regionally. Her research areas of interest include self-efficacy in career transitions, women in leadership, professional development programs, and emerging adulthood.

Mariann Hardey is Joint-Director of the Institute for Advanced Research in Computing (iARC) and Lecturer in the Durham University Business School. Her research interests have long been concerned with mediated relationships and digital communications; she strives to bring a richer comprehension of opportunities around working in technology into the leadership process, focusing on supporting gender equality in technology. Early in her career, she applied digital interaction ethnographic research to marketing and business development for startup companies. In 2014 she secured funding to develop approaches for understanding how leadership is communicated and understood in Tech Cities. This work continues and feeds into new projects to investigate the emergent capabilities of women leaders working in Tech Cities along with the legal and commercial issues regarding the now-infamous "women in tech" (WIT) label.

Sally Helgesen is author of six books, most recently *The Female Vision*, which explores how women's strategic insights can strengthen their careers and benefit their organizations. Her best-selling book, *The Female Advantage: Women's Ways of Leadership*, is hailed as "the classic work" on women's leadership styles and has remained in print since 1990. *The Web of Inclusion: A New Architecture for Building Great Organizations* was cited in *The Wall Street Journal* as one of the best books on leadership of all time and is credited with bringing the language of inclusion into business. She delivers leadership programs for corporations, partnership firms, universities, and nonprofits around the world.

Wilma Henderikse is Director and Associate Partner at VanDoorneHuiskes and Partners, a research and consultancy company recognized for its expertise in the field of equal opportunities and diversity issues. Wilma is an educational sociologist and has more than 30 years of experience in research, consultancy, and training regarding diversity issues; she has numerous publications in this field. Wilma is also Vice-Chair of the Humanist Center of Ethical and Worldview Education.

Dorine L. Lawrence-Hughes is Clinical Assistant Professor in the Annenberg School of Communication at the University of Southern California. She teaches foundational communication courses, such as public speaking, argumentation and advocacy, and small-group communication. Her research interests include higher education leadership and leadership communication with a focus on race, gender, and equity. She has presented her work on stakeholder management and communication and conflict at the annual conferences of the International Association for Conflict Management, the American Educational Research Association, and the Association for the Study of Higher Education. Before teaching, Lawrence-Hughes practiced law full time in California and provided legal advice to public entities, non-profits, and corporations.

Céline Legrand is an Associate Professor in the Department of Management at Audencia Business School in France. Legrand was educated in France and Canada and holds a Doctorate in Management from HEC Montréal, Canada. Legrand coaches managers on career transition and development. Her research interests include CEOs and top executives, managers' practices, and careers. She has been published in ranked journals.

Jasmine R. Linabary is a PhD candidate in the Brian Lamb School of Communication at Purdue University. Her emphasis is on organizing, new media, and social change, with particular interests in gender and participatory methodologies. Her dissertation is a participatory action research project examining the potentials and limitations of digital space for transnational feminist organizing. She is also a research assistant with the Purdue Peace Project, a locally-led peacebuilding initiative in Ghana, Liberia, Nigeria, and El Salvador. Her work has been published in the *Journal of International and Intercultural Communication* and *Communication Teacher*.

Kelly Lynch McKenzie is Academic Advisor for Interdisciplinary Studies students, Exploratory Studies students, and International Studies minors in the Department of Academic Enrichment and Learning at East Stroudsburg University. She also teaches First Year Experience courses and supervises Interdisciplinary Studies research projects. She has presented at regional, national, and international conferences, and she has taught in France and Mexico. Her most recent publications focus on women leaders and on organizational climate and communication. Her research interests include organizational communication and climate, women in leadership, and advising exploratory and interdisciplinary studies students.

Steve Mortenson is Associate Professor in the Department of Communication at the University of Delaware. His research and teaching focus on cross-cultural communication, social support, emotional management, leadership development, and interpersonal effectiveness. He has published research in national journals such as *Communication Research*, as well as international journals such as *Journal of Cross Cultural Psychology* and *The Journal of Intercultural and International Communication*. He has presented award-winning research at the annual conferences of the International Communication Association, the National Communication Association, and the Association of Leadership Educators. He designs and conducts leadership seminars for the Blue Hen Leadership Program on his home campus and for the U.S. State Department's international programs for young leaders in the Middle East and for women leaders from Sub-Saharan countries. In addition to his academic work, he conducts educational credit seminars on effective communication for educators, pediatricians, psychiatrists, and licensed therapists.

Rosemary M. Muriungi is a PhD candidate in the Department of Leadership Studies at Gonzaga University. Muriungi has more than 20 years' experience in the private sector, international non-governmental, and multi-lateral organizations advocating for girl education, children's rights, sustainable development, and human rights. Before her doctoral studies, she was Deputy Head of Human Resources Management at the United Nations Development Program in Kenya. Muriungi is a board member/sponsor at a secondary school in her rural home in Kenya and board director of a non-governmental organization advancing women's rights and economic empowerment. In the United States she is a board director of a non-for-profit refugee organization in Spokane, Washington, and her passion is talent development.

Anne Murphy is an educator, researcher, and consultant who works in a wide range of educational and organizational settings in Europe and the Americas. Murphy has been engaged in development work for more than 30 years, and her expertise is in organizational learning and communication. She is co-author of *Managing International Partnerships and Alliances* and *The Partnering Imperative: Making Business Partnerships Work*. She blogs regularly at https://englishandpower.wordpress.com

Christine Naschberger is Associate Professor in the Department of Management at Audencia Business School in France. Naschberger was educated in Austria, Germany, and France; she holds a Doctorate in Human Resource Management. Naschberger's research focuses on diversity and inclusive practices in an organizational context. More specifically, she studies women's careers, work–life balance issues, disability in the workplace, genera-

356 ■ About the Contributors

tional issues, and LGBT inclusion. She has been published in many ranked journals, and her research receives a high level of media coverage, both nationally and internationally. She has also published several book chapters and a number of books. Naschberger is passionate about people: their differences and uniqueness.

Newly Paul is Assistant Professor of Journalism at Appalachian State University. Her research focuses on political advertising, political communication, and race and gender in the media. Her work has appeared in *Political Research Quarterly, PS: Political Science & Politics,* and *Information, Communication and Society.* Previously, she worked as a news and entertainment reporter in India in New Delhi and Mumbai as well as in Los Angeles, California. At Appalachian State, she teaches classes on media writing, copyediting, and minorities in the media. Her website is newlypaul.weebly.com

Gregory Perreault is Assistant Professor of Multimedia Journalism at Appalachian State University. His research involves the operation of media paradigms. His work has appeared in the *Journal of Media & Religion, Howard Journal of Communication,* and *Journalism: Theory, Practice and Criticism.* He worked as a sports journalist before entering academia. He teaches classes on media writing, multimedia journalism, and mobile media. His website is gregperreault.com

Babette Pouwels is Director and Associate Partner at VanDoorneHuiskes and Partners. She is a sociologist who received her PhD in economics at Utrecht University in the Netherlands. Her main research interests are gender and diversity in organizations, equal opportunities and non-discrimination in the workplace, corporate governance, and the reconciliation of work and private life. Her current projects include women in top managerial positions, the efficacy of gender diversity policies, and the gender pay gap. She is co-author of the annual *Dutch Monitor Talent to the Top* and the *Dutch Company Monitor Women on Boards.*

Camilla Quental is Assistant Professor and Researcher in Management, Human Resources, and Organizational Behavior at Audencia Business School, France. She received a Master's of Sciences Po Paris and a PhD in Management from HEC Paris. Quental's research interests include identity, women and men's careers in professional services firms, and gender and diversity in organizations. She has published a number of articles and chapters on these subjects and is Coordinator of the Management Discipline for the global repository of the United Nation's Principles for Responsible Management Education on gender equality.

Sarah E. Riforgiate is Assistant Professor in the Department of Communication Studies at Kansas State University. Her research and teaching concentrate on organizational and interpersonal communication to increase understanding and develop practical solutions to improve interactions. Research projects focus on the intersections between paid work and private life, including topics pertaining to work–life tensions, leadership, emotions in organizations, conflict, and policy communication. Her work has been published in *Communication Monographs, Journal of Family Communication, Management and Communication Quarterly, Western Journal of Communication,* and the *Electronic Journal of Communication.*

Emily M. Ruder is a masters student in the Department of Communication Studies at Kansas State University. Her research focuses on leadership communication with a special interest in understanding the socialization of women in leadership and nonprofit leadership. She has presented her research at several conferences including, the National Communication Association and Central States Communication Association.

Karen Sorensen-Lang is a feminist rhetorician and service-learning scholar. She teaches communication courses at California State University Channel Islands and is the founder of SparkVoice, a mentoring and writing program for teen girls in Ventura County, California.

Evelyn H. Thrasher is Associate Professor in the Gordon Ford College of Business at Western Kentucky University. She teaches courses in information systems at the undergraduate and graduate levels. Dr. Thrasher also serves as the Knicely Faculty Fellow in Leadership for the Center for Leadership Excellence at Western Kentucky University, where she assists with executive leadership education, community outreach, and physician leadership development. She has published in numerous information systems journals and presented her work at global information systems conferences. Before joining academia, Dr. Thrasher worked as an advanced systems analyst for Eastman Chemical Company.

Annemarie Vaccaro is Associate Professor and the Graduate Program Director for the College Student Personnel Program at the University of Rhode Island. She earned her PhD in Higher Education Administration from the University of Denver. Her scholarship examines social justice issues in higher education and has been published in a variety of higher education journals. She is also the co-author of two books—*Safe Spaces: Making Schools and Communities Welcoming to LGBT Youth* (Praeger) and *Decisions Matter: Using a Decision Making Framework with Contemporary Student Affairs Case Studies* (NASPA).

Annemieke van Beek is Director and Associate Partner at VanDoorneHuiskes and Partners. Annemieke is a sociologist and Master of Public Management and has many years of experience in research, consultancy, and training regarding diversity issues. She is a leading Dutch expert in gender-related career development issues and mainstreaming gender and diversity issues in organization policy. She has developed several tools for identifying potential career barriers and reinforcing good practices in the development and implementation of inclusive policies, services, and programs in organizations. Her research interests also include the gender-pay gap and how to narrow it. She is chairman of the supervisory board of a group of secondary education institutions.

Daniel Stuart Wilbur is Associate Professor of Communication at Purdue University Northwest. His research examines the intersection of power, gender, and identity issues and includes improving aviation workers' safety behaviors, re-presenting the lived experiences of physicians and healthcare workers, identifying multigenerational differences in the nursing workforce, and feminist organizing.

Patricia Dennis Witherspoon is Professor of Communication at the University of Texas at El Paso (UTEP). She has published books and articles on presidential communication and on communication and organizational leadership. She has also authored or co-authored reports on facilitating diversity in universities and other organizations. She is Dean of the College of Liberal Arts at UTEP.